POETICS OF LIVELINESS

POETICS OF LIVELINESS

MOLECULES, FIBERS, TISSUES, CLOUDS

ADA SMAILBEGOVIĆ

Columbia University Press
New York

Columbia University Press
Publishers Since 1893
New York   Chichester, West Sussex
cup.columbia.edu

Copyright © 2021 Columbia University Press
All rights reserved

Library of Congress Cataloging-in-Publication Data
Names: Smailbegović, Ada, author.
Title: Poetics of liveliness : molecules, fibers, tissues, clouds / Ada Smailbegović.
Description: New York : Columbia University Press, [2021] |
Includes bibliographical references and index.
Identifiers: LCCN 2020046769 (print) | LCCN 2020046770 (ebook) |
ISBN 9780231198264 (hardback) | ISBN 9780231198271 (trade paperback) |
ISBN 9780231552561 (ebook)
Subjects: LCSH: Literature and science. | American poetry—20th century—
History and criticism. | American poetry—21st century—History and criticism. |
Canadian poetry—20th century—History and criticism. | Canadian poetry—
21st century—History and criticism. | Ecology in literature.
Classification: LCC PS310.S33 S63 2021 (print) | LCC PS310.S33 (ebook) |
DDC 811.009/36—dc23
LC record available at https://lccn.loc.gov/2020046769
LC ebook record available at https://lccn.loc.gov/2020046770

Columbia University Press books are printed on permanent
and durable acid-free paper.
Printed in the United States of America

COVER DESIGN: Julia Kushnirsky
COVER IMAGE: Emilie Clark, *Untitled, BBG-1, from My Garden Pets*, 2010.
Watercolor, ink, and graphite on paper, 22" x 15."

*For snake-shark and marmot
and the trees that are
always changing*

bpNichol, "Catching Frogs." Used with permission by the Estate of bpNichol.

CONTENTS

Acknowledgments ix

PART 1: TEXTURES OF CHANGE

INTRODUCTION: POETIC COSMOLOGIES
3

1 SOFT MATTER
30

2 POETRY AND SCIENCE
72

PART 2: POETIC LABORATORIES OF MATTER

3 MOLECULES: FROM CODE TO SHAPE
109

4 FIBERS: EDGE TEXTURES AND NONHUMAN
SCALES OF SENSE
149

5 TISSUES: HISTOLOGICAL LANDSCAPES AND
THE SUBSTANCES OF CHARACTER
189

6 CLOUDS: CLOUD-WRITING AND THE MOVEMENT
OF QUALITIES
227

CODA: TOWARD A HAPTIC POETICS
270

Notes 279
Works Cited 311
Index 323

ACKNOWLEDGMENTS

The first intimations of what was to become this book came as I was doing field research on harbor seal behavior as an undergraduate student in biology at the University of British Columbia under the supervision of Jamie Smith and Lance Barrett-Lennard. While I waited for seals to appear (or not appear) on Saturna Island, I learned what it meant not to exist entirely on human terms and to find myself within the folds of nonhuman temporality. Despite my best efforts to hide myself, the seals noticed me and came to watch the aspiring ethologist, extending their heads curiously out of the water. That became a scene of knowledge-making in which the lines of subject and object were blurred in ways that I would return to again and again, in waves, as I read more deeply in science studies and animal studies, and turned to questions and pursuits of what I may call a poetic ethology.

Much of my thinking about liveliness began when I was introduced to Gertrude Stein's writing by Adam Frank during long conversations about science, *The Making of Americans*, and the textures of feeling-thinking that appear in the space of writing. That early encounter with Stein is still very much at the heart of this book. Laurie Ricou, with his thinking about salal and arbutus trees, taught me about a kind of feeling for the organism that could be found at the intersection of ecology and poetics. I am grateful to Lytle Shaw for opening up the possibility for thinking about natural history alongside contemporary poetry and for setting up the chiasmic relations through which a text, such as Robert Hooke's *Micrographia*, could be read as a poem and contemporary poetry could be read as theory. Some of my early experiments with the poetics of natural history, and in particular Francis Bacon's *The History of Dense and Rare*, came about as a result of a *Triple Canopy* commission where I worked closely with the editors Lucy Ives and Molly Kleiman. During my doctoral studies at New York University I created the first sketches of my thinking about clouds and indulged in considering romanticism and modernism in conjunction with each other in my work with Maureen N. McLane. Una Chaudhuri opened up animal studies as a site where my earlier considerations of ethology could find a new home. I am grateful that in my early attempts to think about biological materiality and feminism I discovered Elizabeth Grosz's *The Nick of Time* at St. Marks Bookshop in New York and was later able to attend her seminars on Deleuze at Rutgers University through the Inter-University Doctoral Consortium.

A version of the cloud chapter (chapter 6) appeared in *Art in the Anthropocene: Encounters Among Aesthetics, Politics, Environments and Epistemologies*. I would like to thank the editors, and in particular Heather Davis, for inviting me to write this piece. Initial writing about Molecules appeared in *differences*, where I would like to thank the editors Ellen Rooney and Denise Davis. The Centre for Expanded Poetics at Concordia University and Nathan Brown hosted several talks that I gave on molecular poetics. Turning points in the project also materialized during an ACLA seminar on "Edge Tempos and Anti-Monuments" (2018) hosted by Anne-Lise François and Chris Malcolm, as well as an MLA session on "Biology and Poetics" (2020) organized by Branka Arsić.

The Departments of English and, more recently, Literary Arts at Brown University have offered a warm and open home for my thinking, allowing me a great deal of creativity in my teaching, with classes such as Zoopoetics, on the intersection of animal studies and poetry, and Tiny Politics, on ecologies of long duration and nonhuman scales of sense, offering a generative space for considering the concepts that appear in this book. Collaborative teaching opportunities afforded by the Cogut

Institute for the Humanities at Brown, with Daniel Kim and Thangam Ravindranathan, have also been invaluable, as has been the lively intellectual energy of many students thinking at the intersection of various knowledge practices and poetry, among them Emily Simon, Cole Adams, Maya Bjornson, Shannon Kingsley, MJ Cunniff, and Claire Grandy. I am grateful for the support from and intellectual exchange with my colleagues, especially Kate Schapira, Tim Bewes, Jacques Khalip, Ravit Reichman, Richard Rambuss, Rolland Murray, John Cayley, Thalia Field, Sawako Nakayasu, Mary-Kim Arnold, Stuart Burrows, Deak Nabers, Kevin Quashie, Stephen Foley, Eleni Sikelianos, Daniel Kim, Tamar Katz, and Cole Swensen. Hannah Freed-Thall and Jerry C. Zee have been important interlocutors in terms of ecology and literature across geographies, as have been the discussions of the Animal Studies Working Group at Brown. I am grateful to Azra Ramadanović for always being such an insightful first reader of my work.

The Organism for Poetic Research and its tentacles and affiliates have been joyful fellow travelers over all these years; I am particularly grateful to Rachael Guynn Wilson for the inventiveness and the reckless creativity that started it all. Poetry land has also been a much more playful place as a result of small-press friends, such as DoubleCross, where MC Hyland, Anna Gurton-Wachter, and Jeff Paterson helped me see that my thinking about the effervescence at the edges of things seeped from poetic projects such as *The Forest/On Waiting* into the thinking about texture in this book. This book carries the traces of many years of reading and walking with Benjamin Phillips, as well as the poetic and visual play and laughter of Tiziana La Melia. The time spent writing this book has also been made much happier by the companionship of Matt Moss, Andrea Actis, Esad Smailbegović, Caitlin Hurst, Matthew Thurber, Leah Pires, Pearl Brilmyer, Daniel Remein, Matt Fehr, Alexander Barrett, Mark Baumer, Kyla Gardiner, David Gorin, Evan Smith, and Little Bear. Finally, a thank you to Philip Leventhal at Columbia University Press and to Emilie Clark for generously providing the illustration for the cover.

POETICS OF LIVELINESS

v

I

TEXTURES OF CHANGE

INTRODUCTION

Poetic Cosmologies

Louis Malle's film *Black Moon* (1975) opens with a scene of a badger sniffing the asphalt of an empty road with audible inhalations and seemingly searching, snorting sounds that place his snout in close tactile proximity to the rough ground. He lingers and then perhaps licks something delectable. It is dusk or perhaps early morning. The badger's plump, bumbling body and a striped, black-and-white head fill up much of the screen. Behind him, visible, are only some shrubs and the faint blue line of the sky making up the horizon, until car headlights come into focus approaching down the hill. In less than a second, the small, orange car cuts off the badger's exploration, striking it.

This moment can be described not only as a collision between a vehicle and a badger, but as a collision between disparate worlds, and yet the encounter, despite the fact that it ends tragically for the badger, seems to open something up, producing a shift in the order of sensory attunement within the film's cosmology. The teenage girl, Lily, played by Cathryn Harrison, steps out of the car disgruntled but is soon forced to keep on fleeing, as the world around her has collapsed into a postapocalyptic landscape of war between men and women.

This moment of the death of an animal can be read as an opening up of a rather strange world, one in which the encounters that Lily has with her environment become increasingly sonorous, as plants and animals begin to vocalize in the woods and fields around her. The film can be read as a kind of postapocalyptic Alice in Wonderland story, but in this rendition there are darker overtones to the world of fantasy that Alice is inhabiting—there is the aforementioned war, and Lily will eventually find herself in the strangely eroticized world of a sprawling house populated by an old woman who keeps on changing size, a talking rat and many other animals, and a brother and sister who are in some sort of an incestuous relationship with each other. But what interests me here is the shift in the sensory order the badger's death seems to produce, one that makes Lily's sensorium attuned to scales of sensation and modes of nonhuman communication to which she previously appeared oblivious. Stumbling through dense brush during the escape from the gendered carnage around her, and incidentally from a herd of slightly menacing sheep that she has come upon, Lily finds herself face to face with the creepy-crawly world of insects and spends a while with her senses literally at ground level as she carefully attends to the movements of a millipede, which begins to take up much of the screen, reorienting the scale at which the film depicts its world to the viewer. In another, similar moment, Lily is running through the woods, when she stumbles and falls on top of some flowers—as this occurs, the flowers begin to emit a sharply pitched cry in response to being trampled. Lily is stunned by the revelation that nonhuman entities are capable of communication, and that the world around her may be full of signs that form complex patterns of nonhuman signifying systems.

Contemporary biological research has been revealing a parallel vision of a world in which organisms in a sense "read" the environment around them for signs of significance. Crows can communicate with one another about human faces, so that even crows who have not been directly exposed to the faces of those humans that their conspecifics have deemed dangerous can later recognize those specific people.[1] Snails can interpret the slime trails left by other snails to navigate, aggregate into groups, or search for mates, and some snails, like the females of *Littorina saxatalis*, can even mask their sex to avoid being followed by unwanted mates.[2] Similarly, in her research on plant communication, the forestry botanist Suzanne Simard has revealed that trees communicate through mycorrhizal fungal networks, transferring nutrients or defense signals from one individual to another.³ Or, as Evelyn Fox Keller and Lee Segel have discovered, even slime molds respond to signs around them, so that a release of a single molecular cue of acrasin can lead thousands of individual amoeba to come together to aggregate into a multicellular entity.⁴ Such studies suggest that there is an unfolding current of conversation in the natural sciences abuzz with a sense that biological materiality possesses a semiotic dimension.

One of the early thinkers about such patterns of nonhuman communication, and consequently one of the founding figures of the study of biosemiotics, is the early twentieth-century ethologist Jakob von Uexküll. At the opening of *A Foray Into the Worlds of Animals and Humans*, Uexküll takes his readers on "a stroll on a sunny day before a flowering meadow in which insects buzz and butterflies flutter."⁵ Each of the organisms situated in this meadow is surrounded by a sheath of sensations that comprises its *Umwelt*, or world. This perceptible "island of the senses," of touch, smell, hearing, and sight, enfolds the animal "like four envelopes of an increasingly sheer garment."⁶ Within this "bubble world," the animal acts as an interpreter of various signs, rather than as an automaton mechanically responding to stimuli, and these modes of "interpretation" are fundamentally subjective in that they take into account the relevance of particular features of the environment for the organism in question. So, for instance, in the case of the tick, the *Umwelt* is composed of three notes, three aspects of sensation that flood its entire perceptual universe and include the smell of butyric acid found in a mammal's sweat, the warmth of blood, and a sensitivity to sunlight, which allows it to climb up a grass stalk and wait for its prey to pass by. One may be tempted to see the tick's world as impoverished in its features and sensations in comparison to the human universe, but Uexküll cautions against this approach, stating that all animals, "from the simplest to the most complex, are inserted into their environments to the same degree of perfection."⁷ The challenge lies in shedding some of our anthropocentric perspectives to realize that what may loom large in our world may not be significant or even perceptible to another organism. Or, as Uexküll suggests poetically, within its world a mosquito may perceive even something as monumental to us as the celestial bodies of the sun, moon, and stars in a different way: "When mosquitoes dance in the sunset, they do not see our big human sun, setting six kilometers away, but small mosquito suns that set about half a meter away. The moon and stars are absent from the sky of the mosquito."[8]

I want to linger for a moment on this scene: a mosquito buzzing and fluttering about under the dome of a "mosquito sky," seeing through its compound eyes many tiny, proximate suns, and to consider how such a view sets out an entire mosquito cosmos to which we as humans may be oblivious. Moreover, I want to note the poetic quality of Uexküll's writing—how unabashedly it offers to the reader a sense of being able to access, even in a fragmentary or an incomplete way, the qualities of this alternate universe. One can already hear the critiques of anthropomorphism coming from the sidelines to pop this miasmic bubble made up of the sheer garments of the mosquito's sensations, cautioning that any such dream of perceiving through nonhuman senses is only just that, a dream of anthropomorphic projection. Perhaps. Although it is tempting to think that the modest ethological experiments that Uexküll performs to determine how rapidly snails sense motion by moving a stick in front of them at different speeds, or his discoveries about how a limpet finds its way home at low tide, do offer some scientific insights about nonhuman perceptions and actions. And yet, even if these experiments are largely imperfect in offering such knowledge, I suggest that they still promise more possibility for getting a sense of the rich field of sensation permeating nonhuman worlds than that offered by a long history of mechanomorphism in Western philosophy. One needs only to remember René Descartes and his statement in *Discourse on Method* that no difference exists between a mechanical monkey and a real monkey to see that this is evidently so.[9]

One of the key questions that this book coalesces around is whether aesthetic objects, including literary texts and artworks, have the capacity to crack open an edge of the *Umwelt* of another organism even just a tiny bit. This is perhaps beginning to happen in the scenes in *Black Moon*, where an entirely different scale of sensation opens up within the human sensorium as Lily finds herself face to face with a millipede crawling with its many delicate legs along the wet ground. In this case, the camera acts as an instrument of amplification, refocalizing nonhuman spatial and temporal scales so that they assume a central position within what had at first appeared as an anthropocentrically driven cosmology. Such a mode of amplification is at play in nearly all the chapters of *Poetics of Liveliness*, grouped together in part 2 of the book under the subheading "Poetic Laboratories of Matter"—each coalescing around a particular materiality of molecules, fibers, tissues, and clouds. The idea behind this grouping is that, in the case of each material configuration, an element of poetic form acts as such an instrument of amplification, rendering perceptible material scales that would otherwise escape the limitations of unaided human sensation. Perhaps the most striking example of such amplification occurs in chapter 4, which addresses the materiality of fibers and explores how the typographic arrangement of the letters on the page in Jen Bervin's book *Silk Poems* evokes for the reader the sequence of the delicate half-moon bites that a silkworm makes into the surface of a mulberry leaf. In reading the poem, one is faced with the way that a silkworm negotiates the movement through the entities that compose its world at scales that would normally appear so minute to the human sensorium that they would be evident only in their overwhelming accretion. Conversely, in the final chapter, on the materiality of clouds, it is the properties of poetic description, influenced by the discourses of natural history, that are able to evoke, in their figurative and rhythmic qualities, the subtle speeds of change and the oscillations in texture that shape meteorological phenomena as they flux in composing the atmosphere.

As such, *Poetics of Liveliness* focuses on the work of twentieth- and twenty-first-century North American poets who have in some way drawn on the methodologies of the natural sciences in their poetic practices. For some of these poets, such as Christian Bök and Jen Bervin, this has meant working in the laboratory with practicing scientists to create their poems. For both Bök and Bervin, this process also entailed a form of interspecies collaboration, in which the material instantiation of their poems has been contingent on the bodies or substances secreted by nonhuman organisms. Bök's *The Xenotext Experiment* involves the insertion of a poem into the DNA of living bacteria in hope that these organisms will, in response, create another poem, in the form of the protein expressed on the basis of the inserted DNA sequence, while Bervin's *Silk Poems* entails generating a poem embedded in liquefied silk that has been fabricated into a thin film to act as a potential biosensor in the human body. Gertrude Stein, on the other hand, studied psychology and medicine and, while a student at Johns Hopkins Medical School, performed research on brain anatomy by using a microscope to carefully map cross-sections of brain tissue—a set of practices that I link in chapter 5 to her subsequent literary descriptions of the textural and reactive qualities of tissuelike substances that underlie character in *The Making of Americans*. Contemporary poet Lisa Robertson has similarly repurposed descriptive techniques derived from the natural sciences in her poetic practice, drawing, for instance, on early meteorological description in the composition of her book *The Weather*. For each of these writers, the use of methods derived from the sciences has allowed them to place emphasis on the apprehension of the sensuous details of the material realms that make up the universe, even as they have also attended to and experimented with the material properties of language.

Structured as a poetic cosmology, akin to Lucretius's long poem *De rerum natura*, which explores how the tiniest of atoms can assemble to form the most complex entities in the universe, *Poetics of Liveliness* moves across a span of scales, from the minuteness of the molecular structure of matter to the vastness of meteorological phenomena such as the movements of vapor that compose the atmosphere. And yet the manner in which it spans across such scales is not linear; rather, the elements of the macrocosm often find themselves embedded within the microcosm, so that a speck of matter may open out to reveal within itself a whole hidden world. Robert Hooke, one of the early microscopists, whose careful observations of the textural qualities of silk fibers opens my analysis of Bervin's *Silk Poems*, notes in his book *Micrographia* the parallel vastness of worlds that would open up to the viewer whether they were making observations through a lens of a microscope or that of a telescope: "By this the Earth it self, which lyes so neer us, under our feet, shews quite a new thing to us, and in every little particle of its matter, we now behold almost as great a variety of Creatures, as we were able before to reckon up in the whole Universe it self."[10] At one point Hooke observes a whole world populated by hundreds of mites living in the craters and crevices that exist at a point of a needle, an instrument that to unaided human senses appears perfectly smooth and sharp. The work of early microscopists was influential for philosophers who have contributed to the genealogy of materialist thought that I am exploring in *Poetics of Liveliness* and the manner in which these philosophers came to conceptualize matter. Gottfried Leibniz, for instance, draws out a famously intricate analogy in which "each portion of matter may be conceived as a garden full of plants, and as a pond full of fish," and then, in turn, each drop of matter within "each branch of a plant, each limb of an animal" in itself unfolding into another such "garden or such a pond."[11] Perhaps it is strange to envision a whole topography within a microscopic droplet of matter, but, as Hooke's observations suggest, this is precisely what the early microscopic studies of matter revealed.

Writing in the introduction to *The Gorgeous Nothings*, a book that reproduces facsimiles of the various paper scraps on which Emily Dickinson composed her poems, preserving their original punctuation and the indexical feeling of the marks made on the surface of the paper, Bervin, who coedited the book with Marta Werner, locates a similar feeling of vast spans of scale in one of Dickinson's poems. In a literal sense, the whole collection of Dickinson's scraps is about smallness, minute surfaces on which a whole poetic cosmology is spun, but in this particular poem Bervin locates a contact, a pressing together, between the cosmological scale of stars and the smallness of atoms. Bervin cites Dickinson's fragment A 636/636a, written "in one corner of the large envelope interior," which states: "Excuse | Emily and | her Atoms | The North | Star is | of small | fabric but it | implies | much | presides | yet."[12] In her commentary on the fragment, Bervin points to an array of materialities operating at variegated scales that find themselves pressed against one another in these lines as atoms appear positioned next to the North Star, which itself figuratively assumes the materiality of fabric, of a scrap of cloth, but also perhaps of fabric as in a sense of a holding together disparate threads to form a structure, an enfolding surface or a ground.[13] Attending to the sheer materiality of the compositional space of the carefully unfolded scraps of envelopes on which Dickinson created her tiny worlds, Bervin similarly brings discordant scales into productive tension with one another: "The writing is small in relation to the compositional space, floating in its firmament." In this instant, it appears that the minute scale of the writing, which exists in a certain proportional relation to the compositional ground of the paper, suddenly fills the whole sky. Or, the scale of this ground for inscription is simultaneously a scrap and also acquires a scale of cosmological proportion, the firmament being the sky or the heavens, or, in terms proposed in Genesis, the division between the waters below the earth and those above the earth—a kind of initial generation of asymmetry that occurs as the world is laid out in a cosmology. In her commentary, Bervin also situates the concept of the atom in relation to the long history of atomic understandings of the particulate composition of matter, starting with ancient Greek philosophy and moving to the recasting of the atom in chemical terms at the outset of the nineteenth century, and finally to the moment that coincided with the year of Dickinson's death, when "Johann Josef Loschmidt first measures the size of a molecule of air." Other possible definitions for the atom abound in the *Oxford English Dictionary*, Bervin points out: "We also find a dust mote, the smallest medieval measurement of time, 'the twinkling of an eye,' and this apt, obsolete meaning too: 'At home.'"

The atomist understanding of matter stemming from the Greek atomist thinkers Leucippus, Democritus, and Epicurus, whose thought was largely preserved and transmitted by the Roman poet Lucretius in *De rerum natura*, forms another important thread within the particular history of materialist thought that I am evoking here. According to the atomist thinkers, all matter can be subdivided into smaller and smaller particles, until this slide into minuteness reaches the smallest and indivisible particle, the atom. The Greek word (*atomos*), in fact, means "indivisible" or "uncuttable." According to atomist philosophers, atoms cannot be created or destroyed. This means that everything arises through the constant movement and the rearrangement of the atoms in the empty space of the void. Or, as Lucretius describes: "Multitudinous atoms, swept along in multitudinous courses through infinite time by mutual clashes and their own weight, have come together in every possible way and tested everything that could be formed by their combinations."[14]

Epicurus and Lucretius offer an important point of divergence from the atomists who preceded them in that they did not perceive the interactions between atoms to be entirely deterministic in nature. Rather, in *De rerum natura*, Lucretius suggests that *"when the atoms are traveling straight down through empty space by their own weight, at quite indeterminate times and places they swerve ever so little from their course."*[15] Without this indeterminate, swerving change in direction "everything would fall downwards like raindrops through the abyss of space," no collisions between atoms would ensue, and "thus nature would never have created anything" (221–25). The swerve, or *clinamen*, disturbs the interlocking effects of cause and effect that would yield a determinate universe; or, in Lucretius's words, the swerve "snap[s] the bonds of fate, the everlasting sequence of cause and effect," and produces the freedom "possessed by living things throughout the earth" (253–57). For Lucretius, such an understanding of causality is illustrative of a fundamentally creative rather than mechanistic nature of matter.

In *Poetics of Liveliness*, I contend that such an understanding of the indeterminacy inherent in the material universe has been significant for poets who have attended to the intricate processes of change within matter in their attempt to create open-ended patterns of meaning in language, which could convey, through the dynamics of their poems, the lively transformations of the material universe. In his essay "Projective Verse," Charles Olson, for instance, provocatively suggests that a poem must be engaged with the "*kinetics* of the thing" so that the poem is in fact "energy transferred from where the poet got it . . . , by way of the poem itself to, all the way over to, the reader."[16] One of the ways through which this transfer of energy is accomplished involves the arrangement of the words, syllables, lines, and the spaces between the words as well as the negative space of the page as a whole, so as to create a parallel set of tensions between the appearance of these entities within the space of the page and the arrangement of the "objects of reality" that compose the world: "Every element in an open poem (the syllable, the line, as well as the image, the sound, the sense) must be taken up as participants in the kinetic of the poem just as solidly as we are accustomed to take what we call the objects of reality; and that these elements are to be seen as creating the tensions of a poem just as totally as do those other objects create what we know as the world" (243). This sense that the different elements of the poem constitute a relational field—a method that Olson specifically refers to as "FIELD COMPOSITION"—offers a way of conceptualizing how the typographical arrangement of the words on the page can register the material arrangements of entities that compose the world. Perhaps the most literal example of this occurs in Olson's *The Maximus Poems* in a poem titled "Letter, May 2, 1959," in which the typography on the page takes the shape of a map of an early settlement on the site of what is now Gloucester, Massachusetts. The typography of the poem marks off key topographical features and structures of human habitation, so that the arrangement of the text on the page corresponds to the arrangement of the actual entities in the landscape, marking off the distances between them and the manner in which a body may habitually move across this lived topography.

In this sense, Olson opens up questions not only about how a poem may represent a material world "out there," but also about how a poem may participate in the creation of such a world, generating an internal cosmology through its formal strategies of *poiesis*, or making. In the "Human Universe," Olson addresses such cosmological properties of poetry, critiquing a philosophical genealogy whose origins he locates in Greek thought, with its tendency to "declare all speculation as enclosed in the 'UNIVERSE of discourse,'" in other words, in the emphasis on practices that render the sensuous and material properties of the universe as locked within the language-based techniques of logic and classification (156). One of the specific sites of Olson's critique is Plato's idealism, with its hylomorphic tendency to extricate form from content: "Plato may be a honey-head, as Melville called him, but he is precisely that—treacherous to all ants," Olson writes, stating that "idealism of any sort, like logic and like classification, intervene at just the moment they become more than the means they are" and become ends in themselves (157). Such discursive and taxonomic modes, in Olson's view, come to ossify the kinetic immediacy of action through which the unfolding of the entities that compose the universe takes place: "It comes out a demonstration, a separating out, an act of classification, and so, a stopping, and all that I know is, it is not there, it has turned false. For any of us, at any instant, are juxtaposed to any experience, even an overwhelming single one, on several more planes than the arbitrary and discursive." Instead, Olson proposes that poetry should be engaged in "direct perception" that acknowledges "that a thing, any thing, impinges on us by a more important fact, its self-existence, without reference to any other thing," in other words not by "the thing's 'class,'" but by its particularity (157–58). Such an approach would loosen the subsuming grip that the "UNIVERSE of discourse" has placed on experience, allowing for a "return . . . to the only two universes which count, the two phenomenal ones," that of the human "as organism, and that of his environment, the earth and planets" (156).

Olson's impulse is clearly a cosmological one, a desire for poetry to return to dimensions of experience that encompass the scales of planetary and interplanetary worlds within which the human would come to be situated not as apart, but as an integral part of the environment, as a biological organism, whose sensuous, proprioceptive, somatic dimensions of experience must navigate the universe and its reenactment within the cosmology of the poem. The human being finds herself here within the celestial realm surrounded by the moon, planets, and stars, much like Uexküll's mosquito with its perceptual envelope consisting of many tiny suns. Yet even amid this cosmological impulse, science, with its desire for classification and description, is often under attack in Olson's essay for what he perceives as the ossifying effects of its methodology. Drawing on moments when science itself points to its own epistemic limitations, such as the Heisenberg uncertainty principle, Olson emphasizes the significance of devising ways of knowing the world that do not deaden the entities one is trying to understand: "The profound error that Heisenberg had the intelligence to admit in his principle that a thing can be measured in its mass only by arbitrarily assuming a stopping of its motion, or in its motion only by neglecting, for the moment of the measuring, its mass.... There is only one thing you can do about kinetic, re-enact it" (162).

It is perhaps contrary to bring up a poet's attack on science in a book about poetry and science, but it is precisely the moments when seemingly disparate epistemic and aesthetic strategies meet to offer an account of material entities without interrupting their kinetics, that constitute what *Poetics of Liveliness* seeks to investigate. Consider for instance, this moment in Gertrude Stein's lecture "Portraits and Repetition" in which she seeks to offer an account of how the movements and actions of a living organism never repeat themselves: "It is very like a frog hopping," she writes, "he cannot ever hop exactly the same distance or the same way of hopping at every hop. A bird's singing is perhaps the nearest thing to repetition but if you listen they too vary their insistence." In this instance, however, Stein is not only talking about frogs or other organisms, or even anything that is typically considered living, she is also writing about a sense of *liveliness* that exists in language: "No matter how often you tell the same story," she suggests, just before bringing up the example of the hopping frog, "if there is anything alive in the telling the emphasis" of the story will be different from any other time that the story has been told. In this way, Stein is concerned with generating a sense of *liveliness* within linguistic phenomena that has the capacity to parallel the dynamic unfolding of living entities, and this problematic leads her to devise a compositional technique in which "each sentence is just the difference in emphasis that inevitably exists in... [each] successive moment."[17] In other words, each time Stein composes a statement about her subject, the living subject is already in the process of change, evoking, as a result, another attempt at composition, or, in Stein's words, "a beginning again." In a sense, returning to Stein's animal examples of the frog and the bird, her compositions must re-create a hop and then follow it with another hop, which will be incrementally different in its distance or in the manner of hopping from the one that preceded it. And then, gradually, through accretion, the varied movement of the continuously becoming, living organism is created in language.

The example of Stein's hopping frog offers one possible solution for how a text can transmit the "kinetics of a thing" through the means of poetic form. Incidentally, the very same problem is at play in the concrete poem "Catching Frogs," which appears as an epigraph for the book. In this poem the Canadian poet bpNichol, who was influenced by Stein, comes up with a very different solution, one in which a variation on the form of a mesostic allows the kinetics of the frog's motion to move through the other lines of the poem, so that the entity of the frog sutures only in this space of motion between the lines. The motion of the frog is itself registered indexically in two curved marks that connect the letters "fr" "o" "g." These occur interspersed within words positioned in different lines, so that a miniature narrative unfolds in the poem with its own spatial and temporal geometry, in which it appears that a "frog" has jumped into the "pond" with a resounding onomatopoeic "glop."[18] Like Olson's anxieties about the deadening effects of the discursive and taxonomic treatments of *lively* material configurations and his desire to, in turn, create poetry that transmits the kinetics of things, these examples point to different solutions for developing aesthetic and epistemic approaches that in some sense possess a comparable dynamism to the changeable nature of the entities that they are attempting to give an account of. The issue here, then, is not one of representation that seeks to convey the likeness of a static object, but rather of what Olson calls "re-enactment"—a re-creation of a particular set of dynamics or movements that compose an entity in its ongoing process of transformation. In other words, a kind of *process mimesis* is at play in the manner in which both Stein's and Nichol's compositional methods seek to convey the modes of unrepeatable movement that a frog makes, so that the differences that arise within the rhythms of the composition re-create the hops themselves, while the coalescing of the frog is merely an aftereffect, a suturing of motion into an entity.[19]

The parallel that these examples posit between linguistic phenomena and living organisms opens up a question that is at the heart of this project's articulation of *poetics of liveliness*: How can language index or somehow register in its syntactic and rhythmic unfolding the temporal flux of materiality that makes and unmakes the rich variability of animal, plant, and mineral worlds? Asking this question involves a kind of triangulation of concerns between language, matter, and time, so that even as one vertex of this triangle attempts to cinch language and matter into a nondualistic relation, the latching of matter and time along the other vertex sets materiality itself on the move, into a kinetic process of transformation or becoming, which must, in turn, be followed by the dynamic qualities of language. In this sense, each of the poets addressed in the book can be understood as creating this triangulation in their work, figuring through this process an array of possible dynamic imbrications of language and materiality that exceed and complicate the contours of their referential relation.

Poetics of Liveliness locates the problematic figured by this triangle within a number of theoretical and disciplinary frames, from poetry and poetics, to the natural sciences, to the conversations occurring at the intersection of science studies, new materialisms, and animal studies, and consequently within the larger conceptual frame in which such conversations have touched on long-standing concerns in feminist and queer thought about anti-essentialist and nondualistic considerations of biological materiality.[20] Such a problematic can be located in the work of the physicist and science studies scholar Karen Barad, who, in *Meeting the Universe Halfway*, insists on an *entanglement* of matter and meaning, as well as on a sense that an agentive liveliness permeates all matter.[21] Drawing on quantum physics and the work of Niels Bohr in particular, Barad develops an onto-epistemological approach called agential realism. Her position involves an even more radical stance than the one that Olson gestures toward via the Heisenberg uncertainty principle. Whereas for Heisenberg the problem of uncertainty is primarily a problem of an epistemic limit, of not being able to know the position and the momentum of a particle at once, for Bohr, who acts as Barad's primary source in relation to quantum physics, the issue is one of complementarity, or the sense that at an ontological level "particles do not *have* determinate values of position and momentum simultaneously."[22] It is this perspective that leads Barad to develop a sense of an experiment as an onto-epistemological apparatus within which agential cuts parse the spatio-temporal fabric of the cosmos into only provisionally discrete entities. As such, according to Barad, there are no "stiff chunks of matter," no discrete entities that preexist an encounter; rather, the world is continuously being made and remade through intra-actions: "In an agential realist account, matter does not refer to a fixed substance; rather, *matter is substance in its intra-active becoming—not a thing but a doing, a congealing of agency. Matter is a stabilizing and destabilizing process of iterative intra-activity.*"[23]

This question of how matter comes to be delineated into discrete entities and the ways in which relations and temporal dynamics of change shape such processes of differentiation and becoming plays a key role in an array of theoretical conversations that have emerged in the first two decades of the twenty-first century. A gradient can be pictured here, with undifferentiated flows of materiality on one end and moments when differently configured processes lead matter to form a variety of entities located somewhere within the middle span of the gradient, transitioning eventually to the world of discrete, autonomous objects on the other end. At this far end, one could place the world of discrete objects theorized by Object-Oriented Ontology (OOO), in itself an approach within a complex field of varying perspectives known as speculative realism, which I am crystalizing here through the figure of Graham Harman.[24] In "On Vicarious Causation," Harman emphasizes that at some fundamental level objects are held apart from one another, never really entering into direct contact and that this "unknown principle of blockage between them" is necessary in order for such objects to remain differentiated one from another. Along these lines, Harman asks, "Why do all the phenomena not instantly fuse together into a single lump?" The answer lies in what he calls "buffered causation," through which the interactions between objects "are partly dammed or stunted."[25] As such, Harman sees a universe that is populated by discrete, individual objects, which always, at some level, withdraw from relation or access to perception, and this withdrawal is necessary not only to ensure their differentiation but also to hold some aspect of them in reserve, beyond all relation, out of which change can ensue. It is particularly this question of relation and change that Harman brings up in his critique of theorists such as Barad (but also Alfred North Whitehead and others), who see entities as arising out of their relational contexts rather than as having autonomous, withheld identities. Harman fears that "by stripping individuals of all cryptic character, by making them nothing more than what they accessibly are here and now, we deprive them of any unexpressed reservoir that might lead to future change."[26]

Harman's emphasis on this sense of withdrawal and autonomy of objects is related to Martin Heidegger's sense that the thingness of the thing remains concealed from perception and representation, so that whereas an object is a thing that has been subjected to these modes of apprehension by the subject, some thingness of the thing always escapes this relation.[27] This inability of the subject to apprehend the thing can be situated within a longer philosophical tradition, reaching all the way back to Immanuel Kant and his sense that "things-in-themselves" are inaccessible to perception and hence unknowable directly. What distinguishes the contemporary moment in thought, with its interest in the nonhuman, is that the split between the human subject and the universe has been decentered, and this has, in turn, opened up the possibility of speaking about the ontology of things that compose the cosmos, as well as a variety of nonhuman epistemologies through which such a universe can be apprehended. While numerous ontological and epistemological possibilities are opened up by this turn to the nonhuman, for Harman and other OOO thinkers, who privilege the existence of discrete entities, this moment has, in a sense, entailed the proliferation of the divide between the subject and the object into the realm of things, so that no object is in direct contact with any other object, in much the same way as no subject has access to things in their entirety. Some version of this withdrawal of entities from apprehension is also present in Jane Bennett's articulation of "thing power" in her book *Vibrant Matter*, in that "things," according to Bennett, are precisely those aspects of an entity that exceed the subject-object relation; and yet, a paradoxical moment arises in her argument, because it is precisely out of this withdrawal that things "issue . . . a call" to the subject or draw the subject's attention to the singularity of their existence. Or, as Bennett suggests, through the words of W. J. T. Mitchell, "'Objects are the way things appear to a subject—that is, with a name, an identity, a gestalt or a stereotypical template. . . . Things, on the other hand, . . . [signal] the moment when the object becomes the Other, when the sardine can looks back.'"[28] In Bennett's argument, it is this moment that signals that things have a kind of agentive power to act in the world. Her position in a way toggles between the emphasis on things that follows from Heidegger's understanding of things, and hence possesses an affinity with OOO, and theories of materiality as a dynamic field of indeterminacy, agency, and change stemming from the philosophical tradition of Lucretius, Spinoza, Bergson, and Deleuze, among others—a tradition that is more closely aligned with a diverse body of thought that has emerged under the heading of "new materialism" in the first decades of the twenty-first century.

As Diana Coole and Samantha Frost point out in the introduction to the edited volume *New Materialisms: Ontology, Agency, and Politics*, this contemporary movement toward materialisms is not really *new* but presents a *renewed* interest in a long-standing materialist philosophical tradition of figures such as Lucretius or Spinoza. This is coupled with a resistance toward mechanistic, and often causally determined, inert and passive understanding of the material world among some of the dualist philosophers, such as Descartes, for whom another nonmaterial realm was necessary in order to ensure the autonomy of the thinking human subject from the mechanistic determinism of matter. Coole and Frost suggest that one of the facets that does make this movement in thought *new* in a contemporary sense is the way it attends closely to how matter has been refigured in the context of the sciences, with quantum physics, for instance, offering a very different view of the fundamental indeterminacies of the material world than that afforded by Newtonian physics.[29] As I will discuss in subsequent chapters, such nonreductive and nonmechanistic views are also emerging in the context of the biological sciences, with processes such as epigenetics and other modulations in gene expression, which result out of the relational interactions of different molecules in the living cell, illustrating that there is far more to how organisms come to assume their forms in a dynamic relational dance with their environments than a model in which genes act as a predetermined map of the organism would suggest.[30]

It is this close proximity between new materialist thinkers and the natural sciences that is of particular interest to me here as I approach the work of poets who have similarly had a close relationship to research in the sciences and have in some way drawn on methodologies such as lab work and experimentation or practices of natural historical description in their poetic process. In charting the large and diverse array of positions in new materialist thought, I situate myself more specifically among the theorists who have been in close dialogue with a tradition of feminist thought in science studies, among them Barad and Keller, but also Elizabeth Grosz, Elizabeth Wilson, Vinciane Despret, Eva Hayward, Isabelle Stengers, Anna Tsing, and Donna Haraway. Many of these theorists have long been attending to the complex onto-epistemological entanglements through which human and nonhuman entities mutually generate lived realities as they undergo situated modes of becoming. In her now famous essay "Situated Knowledges: The Science Question in Feminism and the Privilege of Partial Perspective" (1988), Haraway, for instance, is already setting the ground for how "objects of knowledge" are not really passive objects at all, but "active, meaning-generating" entities that she calls "material-semiotic actor[s]." "Objects are boundary projects," and they are not preexistent; rather they "materialize in social interaction," through complex "mapping practices" of knowledge-making. This conception of the participation of multiple embodied actors, whose existence is engendered through these scenes of knowledge-making (scenes that they also mutually give rise to and shape in embodied, simultaneously material and semiotic ways), is at the heart of Haraway's conception of "situated knowledges." Such forms of knowledge-making resist the disembodied gaze—"the god trick of seeing everything from nowhere"—that has obfuscated its own positionality and has stood for universal knowledge.[31]

What interests me in particular about the work of these science studies thinkers as it intersects with currents in new materialism is the manner in which they have addressed the role of relations in the constitution of material entities, while also attending to the temporal flux of materiality, with its generative modes of ongoing and indeterminate change through which entities differentiate and undergo new becomings. This configuration of dynamic, relationally constituted entities, such as those generated through the agential cuts of Barad's account of intra-action, is at odds with the fully delineated, autonomous objects and things that populate the worlds of speculative realist thinkers such as Harman. In "Speculative *Before* the Turn," Cecilia Åsberg, Kathrin Thiele, and Iris van der Tuin investigate precisely the relationship between feminist materialism and speculative realism, pointing out that "where speculative realists strive for an unmediated, wholly a-subjective real," feminist materialist thinkers have insisted on an immanent ontology in which "differentiated and differentiating ... relations of co-becoming" generate situated, "embodied, [and] perspectival way[s] of knowing and being in the world."[32] Referencing an article by feminist, new materialist theorist Stacy Alaimo, who has written a great deal about how bodies exist in porous, "transcorporeal," coconstitutive relations with their environments, Åsberg, Thiele, and Van der Tuin focus specifically on the distinction of how entities are defined as the crux that distinguishes between speculative realist thought and feminist materialisms: "In her discussion of OOO, Stacy Alaimo claims that OOO is missing the mark with posthumanist and feminist new materialisms. These are, as she points out, movements that do not start from bound, absolute and discrete objects as separated from a human subjecthood. Instead they begin from 'a material feminist sense of the subject as already part of the substances, systems, and becomings of the world.' "[33] The emphasis on such processes of becoming has even led some feminist thinkers to shift the focus away from the category of "new materialism," with its emphasis on matter as a substance that composes discrete, stable entities. While for Barad this is a question of a mutual coconstitution of entities through intra-action, for Grosz the undoing of stable entities is a consequence of the "temporal and durational entwinements" of matter. "Movement does not attach to a stable thing, putting it in motion," Grosz asserts, "rather, movement preexists the thing and [it] is the process of differentiation that distinguishes one object from another." As such, it is not so much the material objects that concern Grosz; rather, she is "interested in the processes that make and unmake objects"—processes that reveal "how change occurs, that is, how difference elaborates itself."[34]

It is this temporal entwinement of materiality, or the sense of matter as an ongoing process of the elaboration of difference, that informs what I come to call *soft matter*. In chapter 1 I theorize the concept of soft matter, situating it within a more in-depth overview of feminist materialisms (which I only begin to unfold here) by pointing out the interconnections between this body of thought and fields such as animal studies, science studies, and affect theory. This opening chapter focuses specifically on the textural properties of matter and their capacities to register the temporal-material entwinements that produce the dynamic qualities and affective resonances of specific materials. *Softness*, in particular, in its textural, conceptual, and affective dimensions, becomes a key coalescing term through which I signal a concern with material transience and the efforts of poetic language to render itself similarly malleable and reactive as a way of responding to this liveliness of matter. *Soft* as a term, then, indexes both a textural quality and a sense of material change. My use of the term stems in part from Lisa Robertson's appropriation of the concept of "soft architecture" from architectural theory, where this phrase indicates both the powdery, liquid, vaporous, plastic, or fleshy qualities of soft materials and a sense that all materials can be rearticulated as variable temporal windows of duration and change.[35] Examples of soft architecture may include inflatables, or tents in a refugee encampment, or, more extravagantly, a building constructed out of water vapor by architects Diller and Scofidio, known as the Blur Building, whose cloudlike shape responds dynamically to the fluctuations in its environment.

As I explore in the final chapter, clouds, in a sense, offer a perfect example of differentiation of *soft matter* into what I come to call *soft entities*, because they are continuously undergoing change at speeds that are readily perceptible to the human sensorium. Consider, for instance, an expanse of blue sky on which a single fluffy cumulus cloud is floating by: one can clearly point it out as a discrete entity, and yet it is made up of a configuration of continuously coalescing and dissipating vapor. Over the course of a few minutes the air currents in the atmosphere bring new configurations of vapor into proximity with this cloud, entirely transfiguring its geometry, and yet, within this continuous process of change, modes of differentiation momentarily unfold as clouds move in and out of different shapes. I will explore the onto-epistemological complexities of what I call a *soft taxonomy* of clouds in chapter 6, but here I would like to consider for a moment the ways in which a cloud as a soft entity sits in relation to the gradient of the configuration of entities I posited a little earlier—a gradient that is populated on one end by the autonomous objects theorized by Object-Oriented Ontology while a sea of undifferentiated matter lies at its other end. Within this span, soft entities exist somewhere in between, continuously undergoing complex modes of change and relational becoming while still retaining some sense of shape that allows them to differentiate both from other entities and iteratively from themselves as they unfold through time.[36]

On one hand, one could think of soft entities as elaborating into such a series of differentiated shapes through processes of becoming that Grosz writes about, and yet, while such theoretical accounts emphasize temporal transfigurations and unfoldings of matter, they rarely attend to the minute details and shifts that make up processes of material transformation. In the course of *Poetics of Liveliness* I open the field of such transformations to poetic forms of attention, which carry with them the capacity of discerning minute details of change: shifts in textural elaboration or granularity, changes in shape or geometry of entities, or the faint flush of color that may appear in an object as it is undergoing change (think of the chromatophores on the surface of an octopus's skin creating a purplish flush so that it can match the changing tone of its surroundings). In the chapter that follows I explore how such minute details of change, which occur particularly on the surfaces of objects as they soften or harden, are stained, altered, or elaborated through encounters with other entities or as their edges crumble into a soft powder with time, come to be registered through modes of description that Stein employs in her nearly taxonomic catalog of objects in *Tender Buttons*.

Texture, in particular, becomes a salient characteristic here because of its way of indexing the encounters that often make up trajectories of temporal transformation, in that, as the queer theorist Eve Kosofsky Sedgwick points out in her book *Touching Feeling*, the perception of texture involves "active narrative hypothesizing, testing and re-understanding of how physical properties act and are acted upon over time."[37] As such, the textural properties of an entity carry with them traces of previous tactile encounters and often play a role in shaping the possibilities for future encounters. It is this temporal entwinement of materiality, or the sense of material entities as sites of action, encounter, elaboration, and differentiation, that brings to mind, once again, Olson's question of how poetry can, through its own materially configured cosmology, transmit the lively kinetics of a thing; in other words, how it can transmit the iterative and yet differentiated movements that Stein's frog makes as it hops along.[38]

In bringing these various disciplinary frames into contact, I argue that poetics can intervene and supplement theoretical discourses of material becomings by generating a particular kind of close attention to the details of the sensuous universe—a kind of attention cultivated by the poets that in my account have used the methodologies of the natural sciences to place themselves in perceptual contact with the entities of the material world. Such poetic modes of attention attempt to render time sensible by shifting the pace of perceptual discernment to emphasize slowness over speed, revealing, through this, minute details of change, so that the dynamics of elaboration and differentiation, which make up the processes of material transformation, become evident. As I have suggested, attending to the cosmology enacted through such material configurations often requires an attempt to discern both material and temporal scales that may be relevant to other entities that populate the universe, even if these scales at times fall beyond the edges of what is perceptible to unaided human sensation. Acknowledging the sensuous worlds occurring beyond the scales perceptible within the human *Umwelt* may be particularly urgent in the present moment, when anthropogenically induced processes, such as climate change or globalization, have accelerated the speed of environmental transformation, affecting the spatial distributions and temporal rhythms of nonhuman organisms in ways that we may only be beginning to understand.[39] Such erosion of spatial and temporal synchronies has in turn led to various forms of disappearance and extinction, but also to transpositions between human and nonhuman worlds that have made humans vulnerable to events such as emergent diseases.[40]

This confluence of concerns about the spatial and temporal topographies through which human and nonhuman worlds come into contact returns me to the question of whether literary texts and artworks, but especially in this case poems, have the capacity to act as instruments of amplification, allowing us to in some way sense spatial and temporal scales that are relevant for other organisms, or the geological or climatic events occurring on the planet, that would otherwise remain sensorially inaccessible to us. As I explore in the remaining chapters, it has often been the "poet-scientists," or poets who have complicated their writing practices by engaging with the methods of the natural sciences, who have configured poetic form and poetic modes of attention into such instruments of amplification, allowing them to remain acutely attuned to the sensuous particulars of the material world in transformation, even as they have coextensively attended to the materiality and kinetics of language.

In chapter 2, "Poetry and Science," I delineate two distinct genealogies of materialist poetics, inflected by the influence of the natural sciences, that have arisen in the twentieth century and have persisted to the contemporary moment. The first of these stems from the reception of Lucretian atomism, and in particular the indeterminacy of the material universe registered by the *clinamen*, or the swerve, as it came to shape 'Pataphysics and consequently Oulipo and various other modes of constraint-based writing, including contemporary conceptualisms and postconceptualisms. In the critical essay "Two Dots Over a Vowel," Bök, for instance, locates the current of conceptualism within contemporary poetry, with its emphasis on "uncreative" practices of appropriation and "antiexpressive" use of "forced rules," within a longer genealogy of Oulipo, as well as the tradition of conceptual art.[41] Existing within realms of both art and poetry, Bervin's work can be understood as a form of often multidisciplinary, collaborative, research practice that is rooted in "poetic and conceptual investigations of material."[42] While conceptualist forms of artistic and poetic practice have often been predicated on a dualist split between the concept or an idea and the often-subordinated aspect of the material execution of this idea, both Bök and Bervin arrive in distinct ways at a kind of materialist conceptualism, in which it is the material properties of nonhuman entities in particular that come to act as constraints on poetic form. In this way, it is the recalcitrance of the material world itself that comes to shape the contours of the poetic experiment, complicating any easy dissociation between concept or idea and its material execution.

The second of the two genealogies of poets who have been influenced by the natural sciences begins with Stein and the manner in which her writing practice has been shaped by the training she received in psychology and medicine. Many critical readings of Stein have attempted to locate a break in her oeuvre between a period subsequent to her training in the sciences, with its emphasis on the exhaustive projects of description and taxonomy, such as *The Making of Americans*, and her later work, which is seen as formally innovative in ways that often unlatch language from its referential function and hence the constraints of the material world outside of language.[43] In contradistinction, my reading of Stein argues for the uninterrupted significance of description in her work, rooted in the descriptive practices of science, as well as the sense that her writing remains attuned to the nondualistically configured entanglements between the materiality of language and the materiality of the world. As I trace this poetic genealogy stemming from Stein, I locate a related focus on description in the work of the language poet Lyn Hejinian, who, in her book of essays *The Language of Inquiry*, herself offers an account of the significance of science for twentieth-century avant-garde poetics. Following its roots all the way back to the work of Francis Bacon, Hejinian argues that "the 'scientific method' has dominated not just the laboratory" but has "also provided a compelling model for writers, who have undertaken a 'poetic method' analogous to it."[44] In considering the relationship between poetry and science, Hejinian places emphasis in particular on how practices of description have navigated between methodologies of natural history and those of poetics—a link that, I argue later, comes to influence contemporary poets such as Robertson. Situating her interest in poetic description in relation to the development of scientific discourses from the Enlightenment and into the nineteenth century, Robertson locates, and amplifies in her poetic writing, moments when "natural history had very minimal and totally erasable boundaries in relation to literary description."[45]

Structured as a poetic cosmology, part 2 of *Poetics of Liveliness* moves from the minute scale of molecules to that of fibers, followed by tissues and finally the atmospheric realm of clouds, with each of these materialities acting as a coalescing ground for addressing poetic texts that have been influenced by the natural sciences. As such, these poetic works can be envisioned as onto-epistemological laboratories within which the methodologies of observation, description, and experimentation allow poetic language to register, through its own material folds and elaborations, the unfolding processes of differentiation and change—the rhythms, scales and durations of material transformation—that make and unmake the rich variability of entities that populate animal, plant, and mineral worlds.

In chapter 3, "Molecules," I develop the concept of *molecular poetics* by examining the material-semiotic enfoldings in Bök's biopoetic project *The Xenotext Experiment*, in which he attempts to encode a poem into the DNA of bacteria, hoping that the bacteria will act as his "posthuman collaborators" to produce a second protein poem based on the expressed sequence of the original DNA poem. *The Xenotext* is firmly situated in the constraint-based practices of 'Pataphysics, Oulipo, and conceptual poetry; however, the challenge of producing a three-dimensional structure of a protein molecule, with its intricate folds, carries these conceptualizations and constraints beyond the arbitrary, textual permutations of linguistic codes, to a careful consideration of the shapes, temporalities, and textures of biological molecules. This, in turn, expands the edges of what may constitute signification, to include the recalcitrant, folded materialities of molecular interaction, suggesting that such molecules act as signs, in a biosemiotic sense, without spiriting away the embodiment of their situated, three-dimensional enfoldings. While the chapter begins with a kind of Lucretian model of a particulate universe in which anything can be created out of different arrangements of discrete atoms, it ends with the intricate problem of folding—of molecular shapes as they flicker in and out of particular conformations, which carry biological, semiotic, and, in the case of *The Xenotext Experiment*, poetic and aesthetic relevance.

A mode of interspecies collaboration is also at play in chapter 4, "Fibers," which addresses Bervin's book *Silk Poems*. Written from a perspective of a tiny silkworm as it traverses its brief but complex lifecycle from egg to caterpillar and eventually moth, *Silk Poems* explores five thousand years of sericulture history, during which humans and silkworms have become interdependent on one another. In one of its versions, created through a collaboration between Bervin and scientists working at the Tufts University Bioengineering Lab, the poem is written on a film made out of silk that had been liquefied and reengineered as a biosensor that could be implanted inside the human body. The chapter investigates how, by engaging the collaborative space between poetry and science, the poem begins to act as a figurative-material microscope to amplify both biological morphologies occurring at the scale of silk DNA and protein structure, as well as the more subjective experiences of the silkworm navigating its environment in close, temporally sensitive ecological association with the mulberry tree.

Similarly, revolving around the microscopic properties of materiality, chapter 5, "Tissues," addresses the relationship between Stein's research in brain histology, performed while she attended medical school, and her subsequent considerations of materiality as constitutive of the "bottom nature" of character in *The Making of Americans*—a project in which she sets out to describe and taxonomize every kind of human being that ever could or would be living. While Stein attempts to describe and classify every kind of human being, she becomes so fascinated with the manner in which characters change over time or as a result of entering into relations with others that the stiff categories of her taxonomy are quickly rendered malleable, and she ultimately comes to construct what I am calling a *soft taxonomy* of relations, rather than discrete types. Stein's training in medicine coincided with a fertile moment in the history of biology, occurring at the threshold of the emergence of genetics. As I argue in the chapter, the still largely hypothetical nature of genetics at this time opened a space for Stein's imaginative speculation about the nature of the material layer whose *expression* would give rise to observable phenotypic qualities. Simultaneously, the research in brain histology that she performed exposed her to the intricate topographies and textures of tissues as she struggled to map their structures. I argue that Stein's attention to the textures of biological tissues, with their specific qualities of translucency, opacity, sheen, smoothness, depth, porosity, luminosity, and roughness, leads her to participate in what I am identifying as a *haptic poetics*, and later comes to inform her interest in the description of changing material qualities in subsequent works such as *Tender Buttons*.

The final chapter, "Clouds," addresses Robertson's poetic text *The Weather*, in which she investigates the work of the nineteenth-century amateur meteorologist Luke Howard, whose *Essay on the Modifications of Clouds* (1803) sought to develop a taxonomic practice for classifying clouds that could remain responsive to their continuous modifications and transformations. Howard, who is responsible for the nomenclature of clouds that we still use today, with names such as *cirrus*, *cumulus*, or *cirro-stratus*, develops what I call a soft taxonomy of clouds in an attempt to model how taxonomic categories may be responsive to the liveliness of the entities that they are delineating. I theorize that clouds can be thought of as *soft entities* in their capacity to act as an exemplary case of how temporality is infused into the material and textural dimension. Such soft entities illustrate how something may operate somewhere between being a discrete object and unformed matter, possessing, at the same time, a capacity for differentiated rhythms of coalescence and change. The chapter in turn explores how formal qualities of natural historical description operate within Robertson's poetics as what I am calling *cloud-writing*, as her text works to re-create, through grammatical variation and descriptive elaboration, the microdynamics of change that characterize clouds.

Finally, in the coda I consider recent developments in theoretical thought that have pushed against the limits of materialism as a way of explaining the semiotic dimension. As a counterpoint, I explore how, for many materialist thinkers, such as Lucretius, the semiotic and even a figurative dimension arises out of an attenuation of matter, which comes to possess the properties of thin films, in texture much like fine sheets of gold leaf. I draw on elements of this Lucretian genealogy as a guiding thread in the book in order to consider how the textural dimensions of both linguistic and nonlinguistic forms of materiality can be used as the basis for configuring a *haptic poetics*.

1

SOFT MATTER

> *The very meaning of softness (for* TEXTURE*), the feeling, is dependent on the dusty approach of a surface toward disintegration, a powdery departure from a plane. As a liminal instance of softness, imagine perhaps stroking either a thousand-year-old feather or a powder puff's residual blush.*
>
> —RENU BORA, "OUTING TEXTURE"

TEXTURES OF ENCOUNTER

"Crenellated corals, curlicued kelps, fluffy-mouthed anemones, the animal undulations of nudibranchs, and trailing chains of siphonophores" all exhibit hyperbolic geometries.[1] In the introduction to the *Crochet Coral Reef*, Margaret and Christine Wertheim explain that such "signature curling contours of these forms enable maximum surface area to be condensed into a small volume," thus allowing these marine filter-feeding organisms to proliferate their capacities for exchanging nutrients with their surroundings: "Whenever there is a need to absorb nutrients from a passing soup, a hyperbolic structure is an effective solution, maximizing surface area and edge-length—which is why nature has discovered these forms time and again" (42). As such, these corals' textured surfaces are a response to a fundamentally geometric problem—the fact that as the volume of an entity increases, its surface area proportionally decreases. Biological organisms, such as corals, are continuously negotiating this geometric constraint as they seek to create relationships of exchange with their environments. And this problematic holds true across the animate and the inanimate divide, so that any crushed material will have more surface area for reaction with its surroundings, as opposed to its whole counterpart. Consider, for instance, how crushing a solid into a fine powder will allow it to dissolve much faster in a glass of water or how a spoonful of sugar will dissolve more quickly in a hot cup of tea than an entire sugar cube.

Within the living world, this geometric constraint has led to a proliferation of possible forms with biological entities undergoing evolutionary transformations in shape and texture, which elaborate their surfaces, creating in the process "brain corals embossed with calligraphic grooves; pulsing pink pom-pom corals; plate corals swooping in arcs of red, yellow and green; pillar corals coated in phosphorescent fur and giant clams, oozing blue flesh in sensuous folds" (17). In a world created by the "Crochet Coral Reef Project," these marine organisms are transformed into "forms so structurally diverse they resembl[e] an assortment of Haeckel's radiolaria," encompassing a shifting array of shapes, textures, and colors that includes "twisting tube worms, branching kelp, cup corals, and a knitted sea cucumber adorned with neon fur" (63). (See figures 1.1 and 1.2.) Such a project entails a very particular kind of mimetic procedure, one that does not just seek to represent the complex geometries of the coral in the form of crotched objects but also seeks to recreate the lively processes that bring coral reefs (both organic and crochet ones) into being: "If crochet reefs evoke the feeling of real reefs, it is not because they rely on techniques of imitation and mimicry, but rather that the *processes* bringing them into being simulate those underlying living reefs" (23). Both, in other words, are produced through collaboration of many participants—the organic corals themselves composing colonies of thousands of coral *polyps*, while

FIGURE 1.1 Christine and Margaret Wertheim and the Institute for Figuring, *Toxic Reef*, detail from the *Crochet Coral Reef* project, installed at the Smithsonian's National Musum of Natural History, 2011. Photo © Institute for Figuring.

the "ever-evolving archipelago of crochet coral reefs" comprises the handiwork of nearly eight thousand participants, making it "one of the world's largest community art endeavors" (18). In this sense the crochet coral reef acts as an evolving entity whose edges are continuously undergoing transformation, and even though it is composed of fibers rather than living tissues, a kind of *liveliness* permeates its multiplicity of shifting shapes and geometric configurations, bringing to mind the question of how poetic and, more generally, aesthetic forms can come to embody the processes of material change.

Crochet is not just an arbitrary choice for this experiment in *process mimesis*, it is one of the only ways for humans to model hyperbolic geometries. In 1997 the Cornell University mathematician Daina Taimina discovered that if one created crochet shapes by adding a number of stiches in a regular pattern, these gradual increases would in turn lead

FIGURE 1.2 Christine and Margaret Wertheim and the Institute for Figuring, *Toxic Reef* (2006–2019), detail from the *Crochet Coral Reef* project, installed at the 58th Venice Biennale exhibition, *May You Live in Interesting Times*. Photo © Institute for Figuring.

to an expansion of surface area, eventually creating a representation of a hyperbolic plane. A similar expansion of surface area is at play "whenever you see an organic ruffle" among living entities, as strange as nudibranchs or sea slugs with their complex "naked gills," located externally on their backs in the shape of a rosette of bronchial plumes, or as commonplace as a lettuce leaf, whose "edge surface area increases and seems to curve away from itself."[2] Even the interior folds of the body, such as the microvilli on the apical surface of the cells lining the small intestine, constitute such elaborations of surface: by forming fingerlike folds of the cellular membrane, the microvilli offer a more expansive surface for reactions to occur, thus aiding in the absorption of nutrients.

"To experience change, we submit ourselves to the affective potential of the surface," writes the poet Lisa Robertson, under the auspices of the Office for Soft Architecture, "this is the *pharmakon*; an indiscrete threshold where our bodies exchange information with the environment."[3] In this chapter I explore this nexus of conceptual and material connections through which the surface becomes a site of relation and change—a site at which different bodies encounter, are affected by, or affect one another—and hence undergo change in relation to what surrounds them, in relation to what happens to them through such encounters. Such a definition of affect is inextricably Spinozan in a sense that a body (and here a body may mean a body of a human or nonhuman animal, but also an inanimate entity) undergoes and instigates affective interactions through which its capacities for future action come to be determined, alternately proliferated, or diminished, as a result of how it is changed by the ways in which it has met what composes its world. When considering the affective potential of the surface, Robertson is theorizing how the properties of this threshold at which a body meets what surrounds it come to shape the nature of the exchanges it is able to have. Texture and the degree of porosity are significant here. The undulating or curlicued surfaces such as those exhibited by marine organisms that make up coral reefs, or modes of ornamentation with their elaborately folded interleaved layerings that Robertson locates among a variety of surfaces, from fabrics and clothing to architectural facades to foliage and the integuments of animals, offer a proliferation of surface area and hence a receptivity and reactivity, while they also, in their many modalities, open up possibilities for differences to arise in the textures and orientations of such encounters. The porous qualities of the surface in turn condition its absorptive qualities, its ability to allow the outside in, to allow a transfer or a crossing of one substance toward and into another.

In writing extensively about the histories of color and in particular the dyes that were derived from plants and animals, Robertson identifies such transferential substances that stain and infuse the surfaces of bodies, as "juice, or pigment," in order to "indicate that aspect of substance that travels across, . . . disrespect[ing] the propriety of borders" between different material entities: "When we say juice, we mean a tinging juice, a juice which marks the surface through co-operation. Such a juice is to be found in the juice of ink, the red juice, things filled with a red juice, a concentrated juice."[4] Historically, the derivation of such "staining juices" often involved the crushing of and extraction of pigments from various plant and animal bodies, with substances such as indigo being derived from the leaves of plants in the genus *Indigofera* and Tyrian purple being derived from a mucous secretion produced by the hypobranchial gland of Murex sea snails—a substance that snails themselves use to sedate prey, to ward off predators, or as an antimicrobial agent covering and protecting their eggs, which humans can acquire either by "milking" this colorful juice from their bodies or by collecting and crushing them in great numbers. (Tyrian purple was used to dye garments in antiquity and was highly valued due to the difficulty of this extraction process.) In *Soft Architecture*, Robertson explores how the processes of using pigments to dye cloth often involve such interspecies trafficking and mixing: "We think that by dyeing our costumes . . . we lend mobility to the plants and deny for a while each species' propriety. The surface of us overlaps with other phyla" (141). As such, the surface acts as a site where mixtures are formed between and within the bodies of different species as specific qualities of bodies are carried across and infused into the surface of another material: consider here for a moment the instant when a ripe blackberry just picked from a thorny bush falls on a white shirt, leaving a purplish-rose stain that persistently indexes this instant of its own making, and whether such a moment entails a dissolution of the discrete qualities of the cloth and/or a ghostly presence of the fruit haunting the surfaces and edges into which the colorful juice has seeped.

SOFT ARCHITECTURE

As Renu Bora writes in "Outing Texture," the surface is often on its way toward its own undoing or disintegration as it rubs, peels, and chips off into a fine dust. Certainly, in how I read it in *Poetics of Liveliness*, it is a site at which change most evidently transpires as entities come into contact with one another. I am reminded here of a moment in Lucretius's

De rerum natura where he writes of "bronze statues by the city gates" whose "right hands [have been] worn thin by the touch of travellers who have greeted them in passing" by grasping them with the touch of their own hands and hence slowly wearing away their surfaces atom by atom with continuous rubbing.[5] When Bora writes about *softness*, he locates it precisely in such moments in which a solid is turning into a delicate dust, the matter itself now dusting the plane of its own surface: "The very meaning of softness (for TEXTURE), the feeling, is dependent on the dusty approach of a surface toward disintegration, a powdery departure from a plane. As a liminal instance of softness, imagine perhaps stroking either a thousand-year-old feather or a powder puff's residual blush."[6] These examples embody a quality of a piece of chalk, which, when held in the hand, leaves a residue of soft dust sitting somewhere between the surface of the chalk and the skin of the worrying fingers. In considering *softness* and *soft matter* as central conceptual terms in *Poetics of Liveliness*, I am investigating precisely this latching between materialities and temporalities of change that affects an entity and is often indexed in the changes of its surface texture or a tint of color that suddenly appears in it as it becomes stained or flushed.

The term *soft* also arrives into the conceptual schema of this book via architectural theory as it filters through poetics and in particular Robertson's appropriation of the concept of "soft architecture" in her derivation of the institutional persona of the "Office for Soft Architecture," from whose perspective *Occasional Work and Seven Walks from the Office for Soft Architecture* is composed. Within architectural theory, "soft architecture" signals both a concern with the malleability of a material and its ability to respond to changing circumstances and needs. In an issue of the architectural magazine *Bracket*, themed "*Bracket* Goes Soft," editors Neeraj Bhatia and Lola Sheppard outline the conceptual history of the term *soft* in architectural discourse, locating its origins in the work of 1960s architects such as Cedric Price, Buckminster Fuller, and the architectural collective Archigram. In one sense, the term signifies the quality of a material that is "yielding . . . to touch or pressure, smooth, pliable, malleable or plastic," while from another perspective it may extend to temporal properties that characterize a particular structure or a system, making it more adaptable to transformations occurring in complex and changing environments.[7] As such, the term *soft architecture* encompasses the idea that an entity may possess a capacity for responsiveness and change, based on both the tactile malleability of the material that constitutes it or as a consequence of operating as a system that is participating in ongoing encounters and feedback relations with what surrounds it in its environment.

An example of a soft architecture project that is resonant with nonhuman materialities and agencies and hence with the work of the majority of the poets that appear in *Poetics of Liveliness*, and in particular Jen Bervin's book *Silk Poems*, is the "Silk Pavilion," a project conceived at MIT's Mediated Matter Group, led by the designer Neri Oxman, and created in collaboration with a swarm of 6,500 silkworms. (See figure 1.3.) The structure of the Silk Pavilion began with the creation of an aluminum scaffold consisting of "26 polygonal panels" over which "a CNC (Computer-Numerically Controlled) machine" strung "a lattice of silk starter threads," generating a set of complex fibrous surfaces onto which the silkworms could tether their own silken fibers.[8] The initial scaffold structure was designed using customized CAD tools, and it allowed for variation in the starter string density and orientation, which in turn guided the silkworms' behavior, producing panels of varying opacity. The activities of the silkworms were further directed by the environmental factors of ambient light and temperature conditions: "A season-specific sun-path diagram mapping solar trajectories in space templated the location, size and density of apertures within the primary templating structure in order to lock in rays of natural light entering the pavilion from the south and east elevations." The silkworms tended to migrate toward darker and denser areas, while a "controlled heat distribution enabled a relatively equal spread of fibers over the surface area of the structure."[9] The silk that makes up the Silk Pavilion is biodegradable, and the initial process of fabrication could be repeated using the moths that emerged from the pupa that were removed from the initial structure, which "produce[ed] 1.5 million eggs with the potential of constructing up to 250 additional pavilions."[10]

FIGURE 1.3 Perspective view of the completed "Silk Pavilion." Courtesy of Neri Oxman and the Mediated Matter Group.

The Silk Pavilion is a relevant example of soft architecture in the context of *Poetics of Liveliness* not only because of its incorporation of textiles and in particular silk fibers into built structures, but also in terms of how it navigates modes of interspecies collaboration, a question that will come up again in relation to Bervin's use of liquefied silk in the creation of *Silk Poems*, as well as in terms of how Christian Bök draws on the genetics of bacteria in the composition of *The Xenotext Experiment*. In "*Rubus Armeniacus*: A Common Architectural Motif in the Temperate Mesophytic Region," a poetic text originally prepared for publication in *Cabinet* and subsequently collected in *Soft Architecture*, Robertson similarly explores an interspecies dimension when she considers the ways in which "the Himalayan blackberry insistently makes new hybrid architectures, weighing the ridgepoles of previously sturdy home garages and sheds into sway-backed grottoes, transforming chain link and barbed wire to undulant green fruiting walls, and sculpting from abandoned cement pilings

Wordsworthian abbeys."[11] With its contingent and leafy morphology, the blackberry plant is figured as a soft architect in the context of Robertson's text, as it transforms the clean lines of architectural surface, in the process often converting the nonmonumental facets of suburban architectural landscape into lively sites of textural elaboration.

In the wider context of Robertson's poetics, the concept of soft architecture comes up as a way of thinking about nonmonumental temporal trajectories and oscillations of architectural form, with a particular focus on the changing properties of surfaces—their textures, their modes of ornamentation, and the transitions in their modes of staining and pigmentation. Writing performatively as the Office for Soft Architecture (OSA), Robertson enacts site-specific work of documenting "the changing urban texture" of the city of Vancouver during a period of accelerated architectural development between "the sale of the Expo '86 site by the provincial government, and the 2003 acquisition by the province of the 2010 Winter Olympics" (n.p.). The manner in which the term *soft* comes to index a kind of latching between temporality and materiality is particularly evident in a figurative parallel that Robertson draws between this recent period of rapid architectural change and the colonial history of the city as a ramshackle collection of rapidly built wooden structures situated on a stump-ridden, deforested landscape:

> Yet our city is persistently soft. We see it like a raw encampment at the edge of the rocks, a camp for a navy vying to return to a place that has disappeared. So the camp is a permanent transience, the buildings or shelters like tents—tents of steel, chipboard, stucco, glass, cement, paper, and various claddings—tents rising and falling in the glittering rhythm which is null rhythm, which is the flux of modern careers. At the center of the tent encampment, the density of the temporary in a tantrum of action. (15)

In an essay titled "Soft Serve Space" in *Bracket*, Geoff Manaugh writes that the most literal instantiation of the soft city is a tent city, which can appear and disappear very rapidly, providing a form of temporary shelter. A tent city not only is soft in terms of its capacity to reconfigure in response to rapidly shifting conditions and needs but is also "soft on the level of tensile materials" that drape and stretch to compose its shifting structures.[12] Robertson's description of the tent city is evocative of temporary forms of shelter that not only formed the first settler-colonial encampments but also, on several subsequent occasions, came to replace much of the city's wooden infrastructure, which was precariously vulnerable to fires. An emblematic image of this is a photograph from the City of Vancouver Archives in which City Hall has come to be housed in a tent, following the Great Vancouver Fire of June 13, 1886, which razed the entire city. In the descriptive passage just quoted, these early tents are haunting the site of the contemporary city in the first decade of the new millennium. Yet in Robertson's description, the expected *soft*, fabric materiality of tents is replaced by types of *hard* materials, producing unexpected tents of steel, glass, and cement. Hence the evident transience of tentlike structures inserts itself surreptitiously and comes to occupy architectural structures seemingly built of more permanent, harder, less-changeable materials. In this transaction, the OSA renders even cement "soft," both by revealing the relationship between economic flux and the instantiation of architectural structures and also, more simply, by shifting the perceptual temporality of flux as it acts within and transforms materials. What becomes evident, as a result, is that even materials that appear static and hard are continuously shifting, although at slower rhythms or rates of change than other more malleable forms of matter. It is through this relationship between texture and change that the term *soft* becomes an indicator of temporal transience within the configurations of material entities.

SOFT MATTER: FOG, BUBBLES, FOAM

The second context that informs my development of the term *soft matter* comes from condensed-matter physics, where the term is used to indicate complex materials such as "polymers, surfactants, liquid crystals," and colloids (substances consisting of suspensions of particles within another substance, such as a liquid or a gas), granular materials such as sand, as well as most materials that constitute biological organisms.[13] Many of these forms of matter appear in everyday life when we encounter substances such as "whipped cream,... rice and sand, soap and toothpaste, inks and paints, milk and airborne particles,... jelly,... proteins, spiders and artificial fabrics, polystyrene and bath foams, concrete,... glass and opals, crude oil,... bacteria, cells and soap bubbles." Even fog is a kind of soft matter: "Fog is not even strictly a liquid (though we get damp enough walking through it), but rather something suspended in air: more than just soft, it is insubstantial matter."[14] What characterizes these materials is that they exhibit properties and behaviors that cannot be fully predicted from the atoms and molecules that make them up; rather, they possess the ability to self-organize at an intermediate (mesoscopic) scale, acquiring an element of form that shapes them even below the scale of the overall macroscopic property of the material. Such self-assembly mechanisms generate ordered structures that are often complex but are created through fairly simple patterns of interaction. Much of the time these substances possess a kind of malleable, soft consistency, but this is not always the case, as cement is in fact a kind of soft matter that hardens in contact with water once the sand and tiny rocks that compose it are suspended in the cement paste and water (a detail about its materiality that seems strangely fitting if one thinks about the section in Robertson's *Soft Architecture* where she compares cement to a soft, fabriclike texture of tents). Glass too is a form of soft matter, because even in the solid state its molecules remain arranged in much the same way as they are in a liquid, and so it is not a true solid even though it feels that way to the touch.[15]

A good example is a surfactant, such as soap. An entity such as a glistening, iridescent soap bubble offers a way to understand some of the qualities of soft matter. What gives soap its properties is that it is built out of molecules that are on one end hydrophilic, or water loving, and on the other end hydrophobic, or water repellant, so that when something is washed with soap, the hydrophobic ends of the molecules surround the dirt particles and allow them to be suspended in water. A soap bubble forms when a very thin sheath of water is trapped between the soap molecules with the hydrophilic ends of the molecules oriented toward it. (A similar mechanism is responsible for the creation of all membranes around living cells: such membranes are phospholipid bilayers consisting of two layers of phospholipid molecules, with the hydrophobic ends of the molecules facing one another in the middle and the hydrophilic layers facing the interior of the cell or the outside of the extracellular environment, thus generating a selectively permeable barrier protecting the cell.) Unlike the examples of organic forms, such as corals, which attempt to proliferate their surface area, a soap bubble is spherical because this geometric form allows it to enclose a certain volume of air most efficiently, using the least amount of soap and hence energy.[16] This property affects how bubbles will aggregate into a foam, so that the bubbles come to touch one another in ways that make their overall surface area as small as possible.

As an example of poetic play with such properties of soft matter, consider, for instance, Francis Ponge's description of soap in *Soap* (*Le Savon*):

> If I rub my hands with it, soap foams, exults . . .
> its rage becomes voluminous, pearly . . .
> The more it forms with air and water
> clusters of scented grapes,
> explosive . . .
> Water, air and soap
> overlap, play
> at leapfrog, form
> combinations less chemical than
> physical, gymnastical, acrobatical
> Rhetorical?[17]

For Ponge, the material expression of soap possesses an affective dimension (what Ponge calls a kind of "rage") as it transforms the landscape around it by taking up water and air into its patterns of formation and arrangement, and as it creates the "clusters of scented grapes" that constitute foam.[18] This section of the poem is followed several pages later by another description of soap, which folds into itself many of the descriptive elements of the above quotation: "It gobbles the air, it gobbles the water" producing "such a voluminous, pearly slobber, consisting of so many clusters of plethoric bubbles. The hollow grapes, the scented grapes of soap. Agglomerations" (14). The words "voluminous" and "pearly" reoccur, as does the image of soap bubbles forming a cluster of scented grapes. As such, Ponge creates a poetic text in which the patterns of repetition behave in much the same way as the materiality of soap, creating, through folds of reoccurrence, a kind of three-dimensional geometry of soap bubbles and replicating the same active rhythms that characterize the patterns of self-assembly that generate foam. In this sense Ponge's text, in modeling the processes through which foam assembles itself, illustrates a *poetics of liveliness* in much the same way that the patterns of repetition and variation in Gertrude Stein's texts model the differences in the movements of a hopping frog.

In "Matter Matters," Manuel DeLanda writes about the various forms that are exhibited by materials that can be grouped under the rubric of soft matter, pointing out that many of them are hybrids of two different states of matter:

> Thus, an aerosol is a mixture of a material in its gas state with extremely small particles of another material in its solid state. Similarly, gels combine materials in their liquid and solid states. These mixtures are referred to as "colloids." But a more interesting coexistence of states, one with a more complex internal architecture and thus with more scope for material design, is that of foams and sponges. A foam can be created in a liquid by a variety of operations that inject gas in it. Some of these operations are physical, such as the beating or stirring that creates whipped cream, others are chemical, like the fermentation used to create such edible foams as beer or bread.

DeLanda is particularly interested in foams, writing about "surfactants, like ordinary soap," as well as soap bubbles, but also about solid foams that he calls sponges, which have an architecture "filled with cavities that enormously increase their surface area": "Like gels and aerosols, they are hybrids of different states of matter. But unlike colloids, they are also hybrids of material architectures of different dimensionality: three dimensional voluminous materials containing a large proportion of two dimensional surfaces." Such hybrid materials, both in terms of the states of matter that they combine and their overall architectures, are heterogeneous, composed out of a kind of coexistence of differences that "opens the doors to endless variability."[19] The question of surface is significant here once again because, with such a proliferation of surface area, these materials have many points at which to touch and interact with what comes in contact with them.

What interests me in particular is how the self-organizing processes of such material configurations of soft matter occur, allowing patterns of arrangement and shaping to develop without a sense of form as superimposition over matter. Such a conception of materiality on its way toward shape but without being fully shaped offers an important antidote to hylomorphic conceptions of form, which have dominated Western thought since Aristotle. This understanding of materiality, which I am developing here through an exploration of soft matter, as this concept arises in the sciences and also as it moves with different meanings and resonances through architecture and poetics, offers a way to locate the creative and expressive properties that give rise to a variety of forms within materiality itself. As such, this project is aligned with different approaches in the critical humanities in the twenty-first century—often referred to as "new materialisms"—which have sought to offer an account of the agentive power of material entities across the span of the animate and the inanimate divide. Many of these approaches have worked to offer alternative ontologies of matter that resist dualist accounts, within which matter is often relegated either to a role of a passive substrate, which must be imbued with form, or according to which matter acts in deterministic or mechanistic ways.[20] Offering an alternate ontology of matter, one in which the generative sense of activity arises out of materiality itself, so that it becomes a site of indeterminate complexity and creative possibility, holds a particular significance for feminist thinkers.[21] The reason for this is that dualistic modes of thought continue to implicitly invoke a sense of matter (gendered feminine) as a kind of passive receptacle for form (gendered masculine), reiterating a split between matter and form that one can locate in Plato's conception of the *chora* in the *Timaeus*.[22] The *chora* or the receptacle (coded as feminine)[23] acts as a "soft substance" without any qualities of its own, upon which ideal forms somehow come to be impressed in order to, however imperfectly, shape the material realm.[24] A related view can be located within Aristotle's gendered conceptions of reproduction in the *Generation of Animals*.[25] Such dualistic, gendered conceptions of matter and form continue to shape modern biology, producing, for instance, the conception of DNA as a form of information that shapes the passive soma or the body of the cell, directing its activities—a view that Evelyn Fox Keller calls "genecentrism" in her feminist refiguring of genetics.[26]

Other theorists working at the intersection of new materialisms and critical race theory have illustrated how such dichotomies between activity and passivity not only structure questions that are of concern to feminist thought, but also underpin systems of power that have been used to justify racist biopolitical regimes. In *Animacies: Biopolitics, Racial Mattering, and Queer Affect*, Mel Y. Chen, for instance, develops the concept of animacy to interrogate "how the fragile division between animate and inanimate—that is, beyond human and animal—is relentlessly produced and policed" and how these processes that structure relations between "animals, humans, and living and dead things . . . [are] shaped by race and sexuality." Drawing on linguistics, Chen takes up the model of "animacy hierarchies" as a way of signaling a continuum of animacy that includes nonliving entities such as rocks but also stretches into the realms of plant, animal, and human life with an awareness that biopolitics has structured these forms of categorization hierarchically and unevenly, "rendering some bodies less animate" based on their race and sexuality.[27] In this regard, Chen's work offers an important examination of the ways in which animation and aliveness are not simply qualities that can be extended to entities that have typically been understood as inanimate, as strands of new materialist discourse have done, but also how such categorizations have already played a constitutive role in objectifying and rendering certain bodies more inert.

A kind of redistribution of activity or agency through which matter in its many varied forms, both organic and inorganic, becomes a site of action, indeterminacy, and change seems to characterize much of the political potential of the "new materialist" archive. In "On Touching: The Inhuman That Therefore I Am," Karen Barad writes, through a queer perspective, about the radical indeterminacy that is at the heart of the view of matter she develops on the basis of quantum physics— "indeterminacy, [that] in its infinite openness, is the condition for the possibility of all structures in their dynamically reconfiguring in/stabilities."[28] The concept of soft matter that I am theorizing is similarly invested in matter as a site of dynamic activity and a mode of shape-shifting, as it spans across a range of animate materialities, and finally the inanimate, atmospheric materiality of clouds. While many philosophical approaches are possible here as a way of grounding such a vision of materiality, this project is perhaps most closely invested in the notion of substance in Spinozan thought. For Spinoza, there is only one substance. It possesses infinite attributes, of which thought and extension are only two that we, as humans, happen to be able to perceive. Such infinite attributes can be understood as "two irreducible 'perspectives,' two forms of emanation or expression of a single substance."[29] The specific entities that we encounter in the world are the modes, in a sense, modifications of such substance into specific bodies, which have a certain proportion of motion and rest that defines them and which can in turn combine to form more complex bodies. As Hasana Sharp explains in *Spinoza and the Politics of Renaturalization*, such modes can consist of "beasts, rocks, and vegetables"—all are subject to the same rules, without either the human, the vegetable, the animal, or the mineral holding a privileged position that would differentiate it in kind from the others.[30]

Perhaps most important for Spinoza, substance is expressive: "Substance first expresses itself in its attributes, each attribute expressing an essence," and then "attributes express themselves in their turn: they express themselves in their subordinate modes, each such mode expressing a modification of the attribute." As Gilles Deleuze explains in *Expressionism in Philosophy*, these two levels of expression account for both the fact that attributes express "the essence of substance" and, in turn, "the very production of particular things."[31] This notion of expression is the basis of the concept of immanence in Spinozan thought, or the sense that the essence of substance (God) inheres in each particular thing, rather than existing in some transcendent relation to it. In other words, there is nothing outside of substance, and yet such substance at the same time comes to express itself in a multiplicity of modes. While thinkers such as Deleuze have further developed these concepts in Spinozan thought, I am interested in turning back to Spinoza in a somewhat unfiltered way, primarily as a way of thinking about how his notion of an expressive, generative substance can inform what I mean by soft matter, and, even more specifically, how his concept of modes allows one to think about a particular existence of human and nonhuman bodies as they enter into textured and various encounters with one another.

SOFT ENTITIES: COALESCENCE, ENCOUNTER, CHANGE

In drawing on notions of *soft architecture* as it percolates into poetics, the understandings of the self-forming qualities of matter in soft-matter physics, and on Spinoza's understanding of substance as itself expressive, I am less interested in questions of vitality and nonhuman agency, which have already been so intricately discussed by many theorists, such as Chen and Bennett, and more interested simply in the problem of ongoing change, and how this problem interfaces with questions of differentiation of discrete entities, as well as the manner in which these entities enter into transformative relations. In some sense, this is a way of asking to what extent one can consider the processes of continuous becoming while also holding in the palm of one's hand a set of discrete particulars—entities differentiated from one another, at least for a moment, through their specific textures and qualities. In *Touching Feeling*, Eve Kosofsky Sedgwick and Adam Frank propose such a thought realm as a way of cultivating nondualistic habits of thought, suggesting that "a number of elements may lie alongside one another, though not an infinity of them,"[32] or that one may be able to consider the conceptual space of *"finitely many (n>2) values"* (where $2 < n < \infty$) as an alternative to binary modes of thought, but one that escapes the trap of an undifferentiated, infinite space for an alternative of a set of discrete particulars with their distinct qualities.[33]

As I explored in the introduction, the problem of how entities are defined has been a bit of an impasse between many of the feminist materialist theorists who have been influenced by the discourses of material becoming, unfolding through a genealogy of thinkers such as Spinoza, Henri Bergson, and Deleuze, and the theorists who have focused on objects or things as discrete entities. Figures such as Graham Harman among the latter group argue that objects are, on some fundamental level, withdrawn from and inaccessible to one another, and that this withdrawal is necessary not only to ensure their differentiation but also to preserve some aspect of them in reserve, a reserve out of which future change can ensue. Harman has been critical of theoretical positions such as that presented by Barad's model of intra-action, which suggests that discrete entities arise only as a result of relations, by arguing that such a model would result in a frozen, static universe because there would be "no hidden volcanic energy" at the heart of things "that could ever lead [them] to turn into something different"; in other words, they would be entirely exhausted by their relations.[34]

In contrast, for philosophers who have addressed the problem of transformation through the question of temporality, such as Bergson, and for the genealogy of philosophers that follows, among them Deleuze and Elizabeth Grosz, entities have no hard edges but are instead conceptualized as processes of temporal unfolding. In *Bergsonism*, Deleuze's book on Bergson's philosophy, he explores this by setting a scene in which a lump of sugar is dissolving in a cup of tea: "Take a lump of sugar: It has a spatial configuration. But if we approach it from that angle, all we will ever grasp are differences in degree between that sugar and any other thing. But it also has a duration, a rhythm of duration, a way of being in time that is at least partially revealed in the process of its dissolving, and that shows how this sugar differs in kind not only from other things, but first and foremost from itself." One dimension of this scene illustrates the difference in duration of the sugar lump and the person waiting for it to dissolve, which "signifies that my own duration, such as I live it in the impatience of waiting, for example, serves to reveal other durations that beat to other rhythms, that differ in kind from mine."[35] The other dimension that appears is the iterative difference of the sugar lump from itself as it is dissolving in time so that it is never selfsame, its edges continuously undoing themselves.

It is this kind of undoing that Grosz addresses in *Becoming Undone* when she writes that "movement does not attach itself to a stable thing putting it in motion; rather, movement preexists the thing and is the process of differentiation that distinguishes one object from another." This leads her to a consideration of "processes that make and unmake objects," or "the conditions under which material and living things overcome themselves and become something other than what they were."[36] I would like to propose a slight coagulation, a slight thickening of the fluidity that matter often assumes within the philosophical discourses of becoming, in order to consider whether it is possible to simultaneously hold on to the notion of provisionally differentiated entities while also considering how such entities are undergoing change as they move through time or as they enter into encounters that shift their textures and geometries, in turn opening up or closing down their capacities for future encounters. I call such differentiated and yet changing configurations of matter *soft entities*.

At the heart of my articulation of soft entities is Spinoza's conception of the body as a particular ratio of speed and slowness, a ratio that may persist in some form even as the body enters into relations, due to its *conative* trajectory, or its desire to persist in its particular proportion of rhythmic geometry.[37] At the same time, Spinoza is also a great philosopher of the encounter and the manner in which bodies transform one another, opening up or closing one another's possibilities for affecting and being affected, and hence, within the Spinozan framework, possibilities for action. As such, Spinoza's philosophy of the body allows for a theorization of continuity and change, as well as relation; in other words, it allows for an articulation of the difference that persists through an encounter, and hence of differentiation between bodies, even as it articulates the manner in which bodies are transformed through such encounters. In drawing on Spinoza, the position that I am developing here is continuous with the theories of material becoming that I have elaborated, but while many of the theorists who have taken up Spinoza in the twentieth century have emphasized speed, elucidating processes through which entities come to be undone or are transformed through "lines of flight" that take them along new paths of becoming, my interest is in considering a more variegated set of rhythms through which entities undergo change, including those that slow down these processes, coagulating such entities into an array of textured modes of differentiation.[38]

Such a thickening or coalescing of matter may not always be a question of shifting the speeds of the entities themselves but may instead be a question of multiplying and shifting the temporal frames through which processes of material "becoming" are registered, perhaps to slow them down and render more discernable the textural nuances and fluctuations through which differentiation occurs as a continuous, unending, indeterminate, and yet often relational process. As I will explore in a sample laboratory of material change at the end of this chapter (designed to preview what will occur in the chapters configured around the particular materialities of molecules, fibers, tissues, and clouds that follow), this is exactly what Stein does in *Tender Buttons* by registering the minute changes occurring on the surfaces of objects in the patterns of color, texture, and shape. Or, as Robertson does, but in the opposite direction of speeding up rather than slowing down, when she figuratively superimposes the fabric, soft materiality of tents onto what are typically considered to be "hard" materials, such as "steel, chipboard, stucco, glass, [and] cement," thus infusing these ostensibly long-lasting, hard materials with a sense of gradual transformation and change.[39] When Robertson writes about steel or cement as composing soft, fabriclike, tent architectures, she is allowing a different scale of perceptual duration to enter these materials, so that a material that, within a human chronology, appears highly stable will also undergo change over a more extended duration, even if the minute processes of such change are not perceptible to the human senses. As such, the term *soft* possesses a double resonance here (as it does within the theories of *soft architecture*) of signifying a specific textural quality, but also of indicating the unfolding process of material change that eventually renders all entities soft in this particular sense.

In developing the concept of a soft entity, I am thinking through the problem of waiting that Bergson posits via Deleuze, or the moment of the discrepancy between rhythms of material duration, as a problem that resembles Robertson's descriptions of a soft, fabriclike quality of cement in her image of a contemporary city. The resemblance arises because both depend on a discrepancy between temporal reference frames, so that what appears as a concrete structure is no less a changing entity if the temporal frame is stretched out far enough. In my thinking about soft entities, I noticed that texture gathers in this gap, in this interstitial space between disparate rhythms of time, but also between incongruous sensoria. In other words, shifts in temporal but also spatial scales can register as texture—something that Robert Hooke makes evident when he writes about how the edge of a razor, which appears sharp and smooth to the human eye, under a microscope opens out into a complex landscape of craters and chasms. Furthermore, texture speaks about histories of encounter, about how an entity has been touched and the traces of that touch that persist as marks on its surface, but it also shapes the possibilities for future encounters, as the expanding surface area of the curlicued and complex undulations of marine organisms such as coral reefs demonstrates.

AN INTERLUDE ON TEXTURES OF SNAIL TIME

As with questions pertaining to scales of spatial perception, *Poetics of Liveliness* is concerned with investigating how poetic and aesthetic objects, including literary texts and artworks, but especially in this case poems, have the capacity to act as instruments of amplification, allowing them to register minute processes of change that are indicated by such textural transformation of surfaces. In this sense the book examines different understandings of nonhuman perception, which have arisen in the context of animal studies, while also attending to processes of transformation that permeate matter. Such processes of change occur at a multiplicity of textural and temporal scales, and varying sensory systems are able to access them to different degrees within very different perceptual reference frames. Jakob von Uexküll writes, for instance, about what constitutes a moment for different species as "the shortest segment of time in which the world exhibits no changes." This differs for different organisms so that "a human moment lasts one-eighteenth of a second," for instance, while "in the snail's environment, a stick that moves back and forth four or more times a second" is perceived by the snail as being at rest. This means that "the perception time of the snail takes place at a speed of between three and four moments a second. This has as a result that all processes of motion take place much more quickly in the snail's environment than they do in our own. Even the snail's own movements do not seem slower to it than ours do to us."[40] One could think of this as a kind of snail animation or snail cinema, in that if one were making a "snail film," one would have to pay attention to how many frames a second to play in order for the stick to appear as a moving object. As such, the very edges of the stick as an object within the snail universe are constituted in relation to time. Following the notion of *softness* as a quality arising at the juncture of materiality and temporality, one way that I wish to theorize texture here is as a recalcitrance or a differential that appears between incongruous rhythms of time and the manner in which they give shape to materials, which are, in turn, encountered by different sensoria with their divergent reference frames for what constitutes change. As such, I understand texture to be an unapologetically onto-epistemological category that occurs in the interstitial space between sensoria, even as it also acts as an indicator of material changes produced through interactions between bodies, which come to touch each other across spatial and temporal scales, with their incommensurable textural qualities. In other words, texture is relational—it requires contact—and yet it allows for the appearance of the edges and surfaces of difference, which shape future encounters: changes in the textural qualities of the surface register material processes of becoming but also carry the traces, the marks of the histories of touch that have shaped them, into the differences that will arise within future instances of haptic contact.

In this understanding of texture, I am inspired in part by the science studies theorist Eva Hayward's encounter with cup corals at the Long Marine Laboratory in Santa Cruz, California. In her essay "Fingeryeyes: Impressions of Cup Corals," she carefully attends to both the possibility of encounter between radically different sensoria and the moments that allow for articulations of difference within such encounters:

> So when a coral's tentacles reached out to eat, and it "tasted" my fingers and retracted, a moment of sensitization, this was a provisional togetherness, a pulse of possession, an instance of fingeryeyes. We did not engulf or overcome each other in this act, but we pressed against the other. . . . Through percepts we improvised and entwined with each other, however temporarily, producing texture, a tissue of incitement that made us with and through the world.

Texture in this context becomes a way of registering such "unmetabolizable" recalcitrance that arises as different sensoria meet and as different geometries of material change encounter one another: "Passing through creates remainders of filterings that result in texture. Boundaries remain refracted interfaces of passage, prepositional orientations. Texture [in this sense becomes] . . . the unmetabolizable more of animate forces moving across bodies and objects." Hayward suggests a new synesthetic amalgamation of the senses at the haptic optic interface that she calls "fingeryeyes" as a way of registering a new sensorium that arises within the "tentacular visuality of cross-species encounters." As such, these in-between spaces of encounter become "thresholds of emergence" through which new geometries of sensation become possible.[41]

Hayward suggests that "attention to texture" in particular "as it is generated through the constitutive supplementarity of vision and touch can offer novel prehensions of the relationships between species." Part of the potential that Hayward locates in texture relies on a kind of complication of theories of material becoming, to suggest that "matter is not only a dynamic becoming" but also "a transmedium mediation" through which surfaces are produced.[42] I am excited by the way that Hayward's thought at this moment complicates Barad's model of intra-action by both retaining the possibilities opened up by relational modes through which bodies are constituted, while simultaneously allowing for the surface to appear as a site that registers unmetabolizable, untranslatable differences through the recalcitrance of textures that arise within the relational processes of becoming, textures that are not entirely subsumed by the contours of the encounter. As such, the sense of texture that I am exploring in relation to the concept of soft entities offers a way of conceptualizing how entities can enter into dynamic relations while still retaining differences that persist even within relational spaces. In other words, such entities neither are autonomous from one another nor arise entirely anew at the instant of relation, as Barad's model of intra-action would suggest. In this way, their textures are repositories of past haptic transformations and processes of change that have shaped their surfaces—surfaces whose qualities will orient their future possibilities for encounter and transformation.

AFFECTIVE GEOMETRIES OF TEXTURE AND TEXXTURE

In framing my discussion of soft entities around the question of texture, I am interested in the sense that texture registers a kind of recalcitrance that arises within the encounter, but also in how changes in texture register modes of material becoming as well as how such resulting textural differences shape the possibilities and orientation of future encounters. As the model of the crochet coral reef with which I opened this chapter demonstrates, the undulations and textural elaborations of the surface give shape to the way that entities can affect or be affected by what surrounds them: as the geometries of the surface fold and proliferate in their curlicued undulations, the expanding surface area multiplies the possibilities for the kinds of relations that can open up between the entity in question and what surrounds it. I would like to suggest that proliferations of the textural qualities of the surface, with their specific reactive geometries, offer a way to model how the nature of the encounter in Spinoza's philosophy is dependent on the activity or the reactivity of the bodies in question, and how the transformation of such bodies through encounters affects their capacities for future relations. Such a model of the textural qualities of the surface as a site that shapes the possibilities for affective transformation is also there in Robertson's understanding of the surface as "an indiscrete threshold where our bodies exchange information with an environment."[43]

In the physical digression in Book 2 of the *Ethics*, Spinoza turns to the question of texture as a way of figuring how transformational contact between bodies is shaped by the textural qualities of their surfaces: "As the parts of an individual, or composite body, lie upon one another over a larger or smaller surface, so they can be forced to change their position with more or less difficulty; and consequently the more or less will be the difficulty of bringing it about that the individual changes its shape." Spinoza goes on to distinguish between textural properties of bodies, identifying those that "lie upon one another over a large surface" as hard, those distributed over a smaller surface as soft, and those that are in motion as fluid.[44] It is in these moments of attending to the textural qualities of bodies as something that conditions their capacities for undergoing change—acting or being affected—when Spinoza's thought lends itself toward an elaboration of how the affective capacities of bodies may be shaped by their textural geometries. Moreover, the contact between bodies, Spinoza proposes, leads to an alteration in their surfaces: "When a fluid part of the human body is determined by an external body so that it frequently thrusts against a soft part [of the body], it changes its surface and, as it were, impresses on [the soft part] certain traces of the external body striking against [the fluid part]."[45] At these moments Spinoza seems to place a particular emphasis on "softness" of the surface and the malleability to contact and impression that it possesses, suggesting that external bodies affect the body by altering its surface, and that the receptivity of the body to being affected in this way is dependent on its textural qualities.

At its basis, Spinoza's conception of a body is fundamentally affective in that each body arises only within a causal sequence in which its particular configuration of movement and rest is a result of the affections produced on it by another body, which, in turn, has been "determined to motion or rest by another body, which has also been determined to motion or rest by another, and that again by another, and so on, to infinity."[46] In other words, Spinoza's understanding of how bodies are constituted relies on an inherent link between affect and action: bodies possess two corresponding and inseparable powers, that of acting and through this affecting other bodies, and that of suffering the actions of other bodies on them, or being affected. According to Spinoza, when the body encounters an external body that does not agree with it, the resulting emotion is that of sadness, accompanied by a diminishment or a blockage of the power for action. In contrast, joyful affects arise from a body's encounter with another body that agrees with it and, in turn, amplifies its capacities for action. It is important to emphasize here, as Spinoza does in Book 4 of the *Ethics*, that this propulsion toward action moves in two directions, so that encounters that are agreeable both render the body responsive to being affected in more ways and, in turn, allow it to affect other bodies in a more differentiated manner. In *Spinoza: Practical Philosophy*, Deleuze emphasizes the ethical implications of Spinoza's theory, suggesting that, for Spinoza, the ethical is inextricably bound up with action: "*Ethics* is necessarily an ethics of joy: only joy is worthwhile, joy remains, bringing us near to action, and to the bliss of action. The sad passions always amount to impotence."[47] Such an approach leads Spinoza to a sense that the ethical arises when bodies affect one another in ways that proliferate their capacities for action and, in turn, create the most differentiated set of possibilities for how they may be affected by other bodies in the future.

The link between affect and action that exists at the heart of Spinozan thought offers a way to theorize how the textural qualities of entities—with their granulated, tacky, or fluffed up properties—can possess affective resonances that arise from the active and reactive qualities of the substances that they are composed of. In emphasizing the question of texture as a site that links affect and action, sensation and change, I am also forging a contact point with currents within affect theory that have not typically been read in relation to Spinoza's thought[48]—in particular Sedgwick's exploration of affect in *Touching Feeling*, where she makes an explicit connection between texture and emotion:

> The title I've chosen for these essays, *Touching Feeling*, records the intuition that a particular intimacy seems to subsist between textures and emotions. But the same double meaning, tactile plus emotional, is already there in the single word "touching"; equally it's internal to the word "feeling." I am also encouraged in this association by the dubious epithet "touchy-feely," with its implication that even to talk about affect virtually amounts to cutaneous contact.[49]

Such an entanglement between texture and *feeling* links the qualities of a particular material—its granularity or tackiness, softness, stickiness, or sliminess—both to its capacities to evoke particular sensations and emotions and to its capacities for indexically carrying the histories of past tactile encounters, which in turn shape how receptive the configurations of the surface will be to future encounters. Or, as Sedgwick writes, the perception of texture involves "active narrative hypothesizing, testing and re-understanding of how physical properties act and are acted upon over time," so that one has not truly perceived texture until one has hypothesized whether the object in question was "sediment, extruded, laminated, granulated, polished, distressed, felted, or fluffed up," or "whether a thing will be easy or hard, safe or dangerous to grasp, to stack, to fold, to shred, to climb on, to stretch, to slide, to soak" (13–14). In other words, textural perception leads one to ask not only what an object is like (a question of description), but also questions about how the object got to be the way it is materially and what possibilities for action are opened up by its textural configurations.

In theorizing how textural properties operate in time, Sedgwick is drawing on Renu Bora's essay "Outing Texture," where he develops two terms for describing the textural quality of materials—"texture" with one *x*, and "texxture" with two *x*'s. Bora is careful to note that both entail a latching of temporality and materiality in that "both beautifully activate narratives of physical transformation via materials, tools, gestures, characters and scenes of full theatrical embodiment." And yet, what distinguishes between them is also their relation to time, which occurs alongside their differential engagement of the senses: "TEXTURE ... suspends time more delicately" (117). It operates along a "partly visual, partly tactile" axis of sensation, and it is this greater reliance on vision that produces, according to Bora, a sense of concealment around its temporal parameters: "Its qualities if touched, brushed, stroked, or mapped, would yield certain properties and sensations that can usually be anticipated by looking" (98). At the most "purely visual" extreme of the aforementioned axis, it may consist simply of phenomena that would not even register via touch, "as in a splotchy color on a petal or a swirl of pink on a book plate" (99). "Texxture," on the other hand, is "violently dependent upon the temporality of touch" (117). It resides in the properties of "crunchiness, chewiness, brittleness, elasticity, bounciness, sponginess, hardness, softness, consistency, striatedness, sogginess, stiffness, or porousness," which Bora locates neither on the surface nor in the depth of material entities, but somewhere at a "medium, inner level ... of the stuffness of material structure" (99). When observing properties of a liquid, for instance, such texxtural considerations would entail thinking about qualities such as viscosity, "density, pressure, ... [and] resilience," what, at another moment, Bora calls "an intimate sponginess," rather than the more surface qualities, such as friction (101). The spatial geometries proposed here attempt to deconstruct the oppositional axis of surface and depth, in much the same way that Robertson's poetics attempts to "reverse the wrongheaded story of structural deepness."[50] In this way Bora offers complex demarcations of regions such as the "intimate sponginess" of the "medium, inner level" of entities as a way of acknowledging that texxture registers a fundamental transformation of form without invoking the notion of structure.[51] Such texxtural transformation, according to Bora, is onto-epistemological in that the object is transformed in the act of encounter and observation: "for touch and physical pressure transform the material one would like to know, assess, love" in that they come to shape the object even in the soft act of caressing it.[52]

When Sedgwick adopts Bora's taxonomic system for theorizing texture, she elaborates on these distinctions by expanding the considerations of time in this model to more extensively include the manner in which texture of an object carries the marks and traces that speak of its narrative history. In Sedgwick's reading of Bora, the term "texxture" comes to be used to designate objects that are "dense with offered information about how, substantively, historically, materially . . . [they] came into being"—"a brick or a metalwork pot that still bears the scars and uneven sheen of its making would exemplify texxture in this sense."[53] "Texture," on the other hand, defiantly obfuscates such information, refusing to reveal the traces of the narrative histories that brought the object into being or have marked its surface. Such a configuration of "texture" is often "smooth" or "glossy" in its form; perhaps in the contemporary moment it would be best exemplified by the slick, glassy, and reflective surface of an iPhone screen, which attempts to nearly dematerialize the medium through which one is looking at information and certainly to erase the histories of the labor through which the object was created; in other words, to erase what Sedgwick calls "the cheap, precious work of many foreign hands in the light of many damaged foreign eyes."[54]

What interests me in particular here, in light of my work of theorizing soft matter as a kind of latching between materiality and its conditions of temporal unfolding, is this extension of texture both into the sphere of the past and the traces of the past histories of touch that it can encode as well as its extension into the realm of the future, in terms of the possibilities for action, reaction, exchange, and mutual encounter that different textures can open up. This way of considering texture is resonant with the "crenellated," "curlicued," and "fluffy" surfaces of the crochet coral reefs as well as the similarly hyperbolic geometries of their oceanic counterparts, showing how varied textures and different geometric configurations of the surface proliferate or diminish the possibilities for interaction between entities and what surrounds them. In other words, reading Sedgwick's and Bora's theories of affect and texture in relation to Spinoza's understanding of the ways in which bodies affect and are affected by one another makes it possible to consider how textural properties shape—and at times even limit, while at other times elaborating—what occurs when entities enter into relation with one another. Similarly, I see in texture, and in particular in the notion of texxtural marks and traces, a possibility of accounting for histories of encounter that entities carry with them, and that, in turn, shape their possibilities for affecting and being affected as they enter new encounters. As such, I would argue that we need models of materiality that can account for such "shaping" histories without giving up on the indeterminacies of shape-shifting and becoming that can ensue as a result of such encounters.

TENDER BUTTONS: A PREVIEW OF A LABORATORY OF MATERIAL CHANGE

In *The Nick of Time*, Grosz suggests that "time is perhaps the most enigmatic, the most paradoxical, elusive, and 'unreal' of any form of material existence." This is in part because "we cannot look at it directly, . . . it disappears the more we try to grasp its characteristics," and so we must examine it "through the temporality of objects, through the temporality of space and matter." It registers itself within materiality as a series of "ruptures, nicks, cuts, [and] . . . instances of dislocation" that in fact take us out of the immersive effects of temporal continuity through the creation of events that "make up the unpredictable emergences of our material universe."[55] In some sense, I hypothesize that the textural qualities of the surfaces of various entities in their shifting configurations are a material site where such "nicks" and "cuts" of time can be attended to as a way of considering the unfolding processes of transformation. The cosmology of various materialities through which this book is structured is designed to create a number of poetic laboratories of material formation and temporal unfolding within which this hypothesis can be tested through observation, description, and various modes of experimentation. While the later chapters allow for this kind of engagement in an extended form, here I am generating a cluster of poetic microcosms designed to act as laboratories, in order to introduce the reader to such poetic modes of paying attention to minute processes of transformation occurring within different material worlds.

Stein's *Tender Buttons* presents an ideal textual laboratory for testing this hypothesis because of her attention to the most minute transformations occurring on the surfaces of often mundane domestic objects, through either shifts in their textural qualities or an infusion of color arising out of a process of exchange with something external to the object, or as a sign of a process occurring within the object itself. The entry titled "A Substance in a Cushion" begins, for instance, with the statement: "The change of color is likely and a difference a very little difference is prepared."[56] This observation indicates how processes of change within material substances are often accompanied by a change in color: think, for instance, of a piece of paper yellowing or the color red appearing on the surface of a ripening apple. Such alterations in an object, Stein reminds us, can be an indication of "a very little difference" occurring within an entity. Attending to such minute modes of difference in the color or tint of an object is not unlike the manner in which she attends to the minute differences that occur each time a frog jumps and noting that in fact there are no exact repetitions, so that each new jump is just a little bit different from any of the jumps that preceded it. A little later in the piece, Stein offers more detail about specific colors: "Light blue and the same red with purple makes a change" (12). Two possible readings appear here: One suggests an experiment in color mixing in which blue and red mix to make purple, so that the process of change that the sentence is referencing is indicative of the new color that is formed as the first two colors encounter one another. The more straightforward nature of such a reading is complicated by the presence of the preposition "with," which suggests that the color purple is on the same temporal plane as the colors blue and red, appearing at the same time to coincidentally produce the change that occurs.

The intensity of the color red and the changes in its tone are often an indication of a process of transformation that is occurring. In the opening sentence of "Roastbeef," Stein attempts to capture the ongoing vibration of such a process: "In the inside there is sleeping, in the outside there is reddening, in the morning there is meaning, in the evening there is feeling" (35). Here the word "reddening" is indicative of something becoming red, along an amplifying trajectory of intensity. Alongside this, the preposition "in" generates a complex spatial arrangement. There is a sense that the configuration of space described by the sentence has an area that is inside and another that is outside, in other words, exterior to this inside space. If one were to literalize the abstraction that is inherent in this spatial description with the help of the times of day that are mentioned in the second half of the sentence, it is possible to read the first part of the sentence as referring to the act of sleeping that is occurring in an interior space, such as a house, while in the outside space—the space of the sky, for instance—dawn is appearing, bringing with it an increasingly red, "reddening" color produced by the rising sun. The spatial complexity arises when the presence of the preposition "in" suggests that this outside space also in itself has an inside, rather than operating just as an externality to the initial inside space of sleeping.

I bring this up, in part, as a way of pointing out the complexity of the relationships between the site of the surface and the sense of the interiority residing within any of these entities. While at times this relation assumes the geometry of surface and underlying depth, where the surface may act as a symptomatic site of the transformations that are occurring in the space within, at other times, as is the case in Robertson's poetic treatment of the surface, such a geometry of hidden depth is occluded in favor of the proliferating elaborations of the surface, with their myriad of possibilities for action, reaction, and transformation. "Burnt, callous, churned, coagulated, crackling, crumbling, woolen; dipped, gilded, glazed, varnished; moist, wet, soaking, sodden; hard or soft; rigid or pliable; shiny or dusty; thin or thick," runs the long and varied list of adjectives that opens Chad Bennett's essay "Scratching the Surface: *Tender Buttons* and the Textures of Modernism," locating in the pleasures of its sheer proliferation a kind of haptic sensibility that leads one to imagine the conditions of objects that these qualities have been ascribed to.[57] Many of these adjectives describe a kind of transitional state, registering the changing qualities of the surface, so that we encounter the object *in medias res*, which, as Sedgwick suggests in her analysis, places the reader in the midst of a temporal history of texture to speculate how the object "got to be that way" and what one may do with it. Or, as Bennett suggests, "Each surface in Stein's domestic mise-en-scene presents a texture to touch, feel, hold, press, gather, handle, dust, mend, polish, shine, cut, grind, hammer, hurt, jerk, pierce, cuddle, squeeze, pet, pinch, or rub." Bennett locates both this extensive list of adjectives and this list of action verbs in *Tender Buttons*, arguing for the significance of touch and texture in Stein's poetics, which had often been missed by critics who have predominantly focused on the primacy of the visual, linking Stein with Cubism and reading her poems in *Tender Buttons* as "a series of verbal still-lifes" written in "an attempt at literary Cubism."[58]

For some critics who have focused on the haptic dimension of Stein's work, this turn to texture has been continuous with a sense that her writing emphasizes the materiality of the signifier over the referential function of language and hence has been read as a "move beyond description" through which language departs from an engagement with the specific features of the material world.[59] In an interview with Robert Bartlett Hass, however, Stein does present her project as one that is not detached from the objects of the world but remains in direct, observational contact with them: "I used to take objects on a table, like a tumbler or any kind of object and try to get the picture of it clear and separate in my mind and create a word relationship between the word and the thing seen."[60] Citing this moment as an example, Harriet Scott Chessman argues, for instance, that even "the most cursory reading of *Tender Buttons* . . . causes us to reconsider Stein's claims about making 'still lives' of actual 'tumblers' and other objects."[61] Chessman's reading on the whole does not entirely preclude a sense that a relationship is being forged between the "words and the world" in Stein's work, but it does emphasize language as the primary site of textural encounter: "Stein thought about language in *Tender Buttons* as a medium closely akin to paint; her method, according to this metaphor, was to apply different textures, amounts, and colors of paint with different strokes onto the canvas of the page" (90). Stein herself avows such a textural relationship to language when, in "Poetry and Grammar," she explains that "poetry is doing nothing but using losing refusing and pleasing and betraying and *caressing* nouns."[62] This moment of haptic encounter with language is resonant with another moment in the interview with Hass when Stein describes handling words and assessing their qualities in the way one would handle the material objects of the world: "I took individual words and thought about them until I got their weight and volume complete and put them next to another word."[63]

I introduce here a provisional laboratory on the processes of material change in *Tender Buttons*—temporal processes that are often registered through transformations in texture—because I feel that Stein's work, with its concomitant effects on multiple poetic genealogies in the twentieth and twenty-first centuries, offers one of the most significant sites for developing a haptic poetics. Moreover, I argue that Stein's work, and in particular the issue of how she negotiates the relationship between words and the world, can stand in as a microcosm that stages how this problematic plays out in the wider circle of experimental poetics in the twentieth and twenty-first centuries. In her reading of *Tender Buttons* and *Lifting Belly*, Rebecca Scherr argues that Stein "invented a 'tactile aesthetic,'" and that "like chairs, pennies, cones, . . . [Stein's] language is a 'thing' that one can grasp." Yet, on some level, such a "tactile aesthetic" remains a discursive prospect for Scherr, so that "textual tactility is never *actual* touch but rather an approximation of it as communicated in words and sounds, lending Stein's tactile aesthetic a melancholic quality."[64] A slight departure from such a discursively inflected perspective is articulated by Belinda Bruner, who argues for a broader reading of sensation in Stein's aesthetics as a form of "somatic intellect" that emerges not in isolation but out of the reciprocity of domestic and erotic relations she was involved in with Alice B. Toklas. My sense is that no choice needs to be made in considering Stein's work between the handling of actual tumblers and the caressing of nouns, and hence no choice has to be made between the material qualities of language and the material properties of the world; both can be held, in a sense, in the palm of a hand at once, without producing the rapid oscillations between the opaque, recalcitrant materiality of language and its referential transparency, options that fail to adequately address the entangled nature of material-semiotic dimensions of the universe, as I will discuss in the following chapter.

In other words, Stein's pieces in *Tender Buttons* can be read as studies in the material properties of language as well as the material patterns of change and exchange that are dependent on the textural properties of the surfaces of various material objects, with the patterns of paratactic indeterminacy with which Stein's words often press against one another acting as a kind of multiplier of surface area through which meaning can arise. Stein's studies of material objects are often concerned with exploring how such exchanges can occur across a surface through a diffusion of various liquids and a reconfiguration of other semiviscous substances such as juices and jellies—substances that are, in fact, exemplary of the scientific definition of *soft matter*. Such material modes of reconfiguration and exchange are evident, for instance, in a piece titled "Cranberries," where Stein states "a remarkable degree of red means that, a remarkable exchange is made."[65] The term *exchange* as it appears here indicates a contact between two discrete things, a contact that leads to a passing of something between them through a process of giving and receiving. The intensity of such a process in this case is paralleled by a matching intensity of the appearance of the color red. An attempt to read the object described in the piece referentially produces the bright red spheres of cranberries filled with their colorful red juice. "Juice" and its coloring properties appear explicitly on other occasions in *Tender Buttons*. In "Breakfast" Stein writes about "ripe juice" and its color, with color in this case being "that strange mixture which makes, which does make which does not make a ripe juice, which does not make a mat" (44). A simultaneous relationship of declared equivalence and difference or nonequivalence unfolds here between the qualities of "a color," which is a "strange mixture," and "ripe juice," and it is not clear if the nonequivalence may have something to do with the tone or the saturation of color arising within a mixture, which may not always be as deep as the color of "ripe juice." This reference to juice brings to mind the moment in *Soft Architecture* when Robertson writes about "the red juice, things filled with a red juice, a concentrated juice," suggesting a little earlier in the passage that such juice is "a tinging juice," which applies a trace, a tint of color to an entity, marking its surface "through co-operation."[66]

Such slight tints, infusions, and stainings of color appear among many of the objects that Stein writes about, which seem to possess a kind of luminosity or a flush or a glow, as is the case, for instance, with this list of qualities and shapes that populates the entry for "A Petticoat": "A light white, a disgrace, an ink spot, a rosy charm."[67] While the intimate nature of the object under examination here, as well as the sense that the garment is somehow defiled or soiled or "disgraced," have clear erotic overtones (a quality many Stein critics have noted),[68] what interests me more is the way that colors appear as slight alterations or variations so that one is led to imagine "a light white," a color that is somehow fainter or more luminous than white itself, or the way that the charm is described as "rosy," as if coming into a kind of flush or a "bloom" of color, but without the intensity of saturation that would be indicated by the adjective "rose," which is itself a diminutive tone in terms of intensity and saturation in comparison to red.

Such quantification of qualities is an important aspect of *Tender Buttons*. It often acts as a demarcation between a moment when something is seen as an alteration of an entity without assuming a dominant relation to its other properties or instigating its complete transformation and a moment when a distinct phase-shift occurs and such a metamorphosis actually takes place. The second of these is evident, for instance, when in "A Waist" Stein writes about a piece of crystal: "A piece of crystal. A change, in a change that is remarkable there is no reason to say that there was a time" (25). The sense here seems to be that if a change is significant enough, what existed prior to it becomes in a sense irretrievable, the metamorphosis is complete, and there is no reason to point to that other time prior to the occurrence of the change. A process of crystallization may operate in this way as a sudden shift in the patterned configuration of molecules. A good example of how a quantity of something makes a difference in its categorical definition, on the other hand, occurs in "A Substance in a Cushion" when Stein states: "It shows that dirt is clean when there is a volume" (11). In other words, this sentence tracks a shift from a definition of dirt as an extraneous substance that does not belong to the object but appears as an accumulation of random matter on its surface to the moment that the volume of dirt increases in quantity until it can no longer be seen as extraneous matter but in a sense becomes an entity in its own right; it can then be considered clean because it is no longer something that does not belong.

A more complicated version of this problem appears in "Cranberries," where Stein, following the sentence in which she sets out the relationship between the matching intensity of the color red and the process of exchange, states that "when there is a solid chance of soiling no more than a dirty thing, coloring all of it in steadying is jelly" (47). Here, more dirt appears to be added to an already dirty thing, until it seems to be suffused not just with a tint of color but with a consistent "steady" color. Read in relation to the title, the word "jelly" that appears at the end of the sentence could indicate the making of cranberry jelly, in other words, the undoing of the discrete, differentiated spheres of the cranberries until they are transformed into a single, "steady," homogenous consistency of the jelly. And yet the textural quality of the aforementioned jelly suggests a kind of rippling surface somewhere between a solid and a thick gelatinous liquid, which itself seems to possess a much more quivering rather than a steadying consistency. Such a jelly, with its ambiguously solid and liquid properties, can be thought of as a quintessential example of soft matter.

At times the surfaces in *Tender Buttons* appear to be covered in a layer of dust in a way that is evocative of the soft, powdery surfaces that Bora writes about in "Outing Texture." In "A Red Stamp," white lilies appear as the cause of such dusty and dirty surfaces: "If lilies are lily white if they exhaust noise and distance and even dust, if they dusty will dirt a surface that has no extreme grace" (15). Here the descriptive emphasis is not so much on a disintegration of a surface into dust but on the lilies themselves as shedding some kind of dust that is falling onto and dirtying a surface. One possible source of such dust could be the pollen grains falling from the lilies and leaving a dusty residue on the surface beneath them. While in this case the dust does not seem to be arising from the disintegration of the surface itself, other moments in *Tender Buttons* reveal instances in which a surface is in some way damaged and deteriorating. This is often the case with Stein's treatment of color. On a number of occasions she makes a reference to "a hurt color," as in this example from "A Carafe, that is a Blind Glass," where she writes: "A kind in glass and a cousin, a spectacle and nothing strange a single hurt color and an arrangement in a system to pointing" (11). It is difficult to know exactly what "a hurt color" is, but one of the ways that this image seems to operate is by figuratively superimposing a sense of a living body that is hurt onto the surface of the object, bringing with it the affective lining and the sensations that would accompany such a scene. The presence of the word "hurt" in this context alongside the word "color" becomes evocative of the presence of blood that would appear if the surface of the body were to be cut or disrupted in some way. At the same time, it is important to note that it is the color itself that is hurt here. In other words, it is color as a quality, rather than the entity itself, that is somehow undergoing damage. Even when Stein negates such a process of damage, as in "A Piece of Coffee," where she writes of "a not torn rosewood color," there is some sense of a disruption or unevenness of color perhaps arising out of the marbling darker patterns of the grain of the wood, accompanied by the streaks of brightness that are typical of the burgundy and at times nearly vermillion color-patterns of rosewood (14). In any case, there is a sense that a "hurt" or a "torn" color is a color that is in some sense disrupted, or activated and changed, by an occurrence, and that this disruption possesses an affective resonance.

In her reading of *Tender Buttons* in relation to the minor aesthetic category of "the cute," Sianne Ngai reads these instances of "hurt" and "tenderness" or surface damage in Stein's text as an effect of aggression that lurks beneath the sense that "a dumb object" is endowed with "expressive capabilities."[69] For Ngai the cute object produces a desire "to fondle and squeeze" it "even to the point of crushing and damaging" it, an effect that she reads in relation to a desire "to 'grasp' the commodity as a product of concrete human labor" (66). Moreover, she imagines a kind of monstrous quality that begins to appear within the object through this dance of damage and the squishy, graspable cuteness that accompanies it, a monstrous quality that transforms the object "into something slightly less easy to consume" (93). What interests me in particular in Ngai's reading of the aesthetic category of cuteness in relation to *Tender Buttons* and the subsequent poetic avant-gardes that emerge out of Stein's work is her sense that the cute object is associated with "softness or pliancy"—qualities that render it vulnerable to haptic desire to grasp, fondle, or squeeze it, but which also elicit a kind of revulsion toward it: "Given how the prototypically cute object evokes the same kind of soft squishy form associated with gelatinous matter, we can see how our desire to cuddle with the commodity might often be shadowed by a tiny feeling of repugnance" (67). While Ngai and I are situated within two distinct theoretical genealogies of materialism, her articulation of the cute object as "gelatinous matter" or "an undifferentiated blob of soft doughy matter" possesses a resemblance to the concept of a soft entity that I am proposing here, offering a shared sense of the significance of such soft, indeterminate, neither entirely liquid nor solid materialities that parse themselves into ephemeral entities in Stein's work.

The moment in *Tender Buttons* that resonates perhaps most directly with the textural properties of soft matter occurs in "A Substance in a Cushion," where Stein explicitly writes about the process that matter undergoes as it is hardening and softening: "Callous is something that hardening leaves behind what will be soft if there is a genuine interest in there being present as many girls as men" (11). Here a callous seems to form out of a process through which soft matter comes to harden, and that process seems to be somehow tied to gender so that the hardening itself may not occur "if there is a genuine interest in there being present as many girls as men." There is clearly a way to read into an essentializing association here between "softness" and the "feminine," but I would like to suggest that there is another way to read the relevance of the concept of soft matter for feminist and also queer understandings of materiality, without simply replicating such an essentializing impasse.

The terms *hard* and *soft* are operative within a modernist poetic sensibility, appearing perhaps most famously in Ezra Pound's essay "The Hard and Soft in French Poetry," where Pound categorizes a number of French poets along a spectrum between "hard" and "soft." At the opening of the essay Pound explicates his conceptual schema by saying that "by 'hardness' I mean a quality which is in poetry nearly always a virtue—I can think of no case where it is not," and "by softness I mean an opposite quality which is not always a fault."[70] While "hardness," compared by Pound to textural phenomena such as "weather-bit granite," is clearly valorized in this schema, "softness" possesses a more ambivalent valence, with some of the poets that Pound taxonomizes in this way being described as beginning "to go 'soft,'" with "just a suggestion of muzziness."[71] In his essay "Hard and Soft Modernism," Peter Nicholls points out how influential Pound's textural schema would be for modernism, with a sense that "hardness"—associated with clarity and definiteness, "precision and economy"—would come to predominate, even though a certain degree of "softness" would still inflect poetic style, a mixture of qualities that Nicholls locates even in Pound's *The Cantos* themselves.[72] Nicholls also points out the "transparently gendered inflections" of these terms, with *hardness* connoting a masculinity and *softness* a kind of decadent, feminine quality. Such a gendered inflection also carries within it a disavowal of emotion, coded as soft and feminine, and a valorization of a "'callous' hardness coded as masculine" and unemotional.[73] Bennett takes up the question of "hard" and "soft" modernism in relation to Stein's *Tender Buttons* to suggest that "Stein does not neatly oppose a burgeoning modernist hardness by reclaiming 'soft,' feminine texture or affect." Instead, Bennett argues, Stein's writing reveals that even "the glint off modernism's hard, smooth edges signals less a lack than a particular kind of texture" in much the same way that Bora's "texture" is still textured, even in its obfuscating smoothness, so that "the 'hardening' of hard modernism . . . implies, almost despite itself, a texture and an emotional stance, too."[74]

In the context of my theorization of soft matter, the term *softness* assumes an entirely different valence in relation to gender as I recode it to subvert the hylomorphic division between matter and form that has underpinned much thinking about gendered notions of material activity and passivity in Western philosophy and history of biology. I draw in part on the meaning of soft matter as it occurs in the context of physics, with its sense that matter possesses an inherent tendency toward form in the particular arrangements and patterns that it can generate, while also considering that, both temporally and texturally, such material forms are often modes of becoming and shape-shifting. In the context of architectural theory, softness similarly offers a way to register a sense of malleability that is tactile but also temporal, often ephemeral and also responsive to the environment that surrounds a particular structure. If one considers softness then to register the processes of change that textured surfaces undergo as they are altered through encounters and the passing of time, the term *soft* in the context of critical theory and poetics that I am developing here begins to encompass a range of textural variations, striking in their differentiated particularity, as many of Stein's descriptions of the textural qualities of matter in *Tender Buttons* demonstrate. In the next chapter I will turn to the question of how such a haptic sensibility informs the materialist poetics of poets whose writing has been influenced by the natural sciences, as they work to develop a continuity between the materiality of the world and the materiality of language through a close attunement to sensation, and touch and texture in particular, in their poetic texts.

2

POETRY AND SCIENCE

> *The fabric of the universe, its structure, to the mind observing it, is like a labyrinth, where on all sides the path is so often uncertain, the resemblance of a thing or a sign is deceptive, and the twists and turns of natures are so oblique and intricate. One must travel always through the forests of experience and particular things, in the uncertain light of the senses, which is sometimes shining and sometimes hidden.*
>
> —FRANCIS BACON, *THE NEW ORGANON*

FINDING MUSHROOMS ON THE FOREST FLOOR OF THE PAGE

Leafing through John Cage's *Mushroom Book*, the reader finds herself wandering across a dense ground of the page, which at times is so opaque that semantic content is scarcely discernible within the multiple layers of superimposed handwritten text. At such moments the language "covers the page" in thick, textural layers of indexical marks, transforming the reading process into much more of a haptic or proprioceptive pursuit of navigating and feeling the crisscrossing marks than one set on discovering referential content.[1] But this is not always so, as the page simultaneously also opens out to other landscapes through the inclusion of line drawings of maps with discernible topographical details, such as roads or lakes, segments of legible handwritten text, as well as occasional drawings that reference in some way the morphology of mushrooms, including a small section of a circular shape showing the foldings of mushroom spores that Cage titles "Sporallitude." And this type of page, consisting of lithographed images of handwritten fragments and sketches, appears in the *Mushroom Book* (1972) interspersed between the strikingly colorful plates of various species of mushrooms by the artist and textile designer Lois Long, as well as notes on the natural history of mushrooms composed by mycologist Alexander H. Smith, both of whom coauthored the book alongside Cage. (See figures 2.1 and 2.2.)

Cage was an avid mushroom collector and enthusiast. In 1962, together with Long, as well as Ralph Ferrara, Esther Dam, and Guy Nearing, he reformed the then defunct New York Mycological Society. The group regularly "went on Sunday mushroom hunting expeditions outside New York City [and] Long assisted Cage in teaching an introductory course in Mushroom Identification at the New School for Social Research" during the 1959–1960 academic year.[2] I begin this chapter on the relationship between poetry and science with the *Mushroom Book* not only because it offers a striking and beautiful example on how poetics can incorporate aspects of natural history to produce a text that in some ways reads as a very unusual field guide to various species of mushrooms, but also because of the way that Cage uses the page as a surface onto which he lays down multiple layers of text and other indexical marks until such deposits begin to function like recalcitrant material, as a ground composed of textural rather than textual layers. In an interview with Joan Retallack, "Cage's Loft, New York City October 21–23, 1991," Cage suggests that these textural arrangements on the surface of the page, which often obscure the semantic detail of the

FIGURE 2.1 Illustration by Lois Long, in John Cage, *Mushroom Book* (1972), with Lois Long and Alexander H. Smith. A set of ten original color lithographs by Long and ten lithographs by Cage in handwriting using superimpositions of five graded lithographic pencils. Botanical statements by Alexander H. Smith printed on sheets of interleaving tissue. © John Cage Trust.

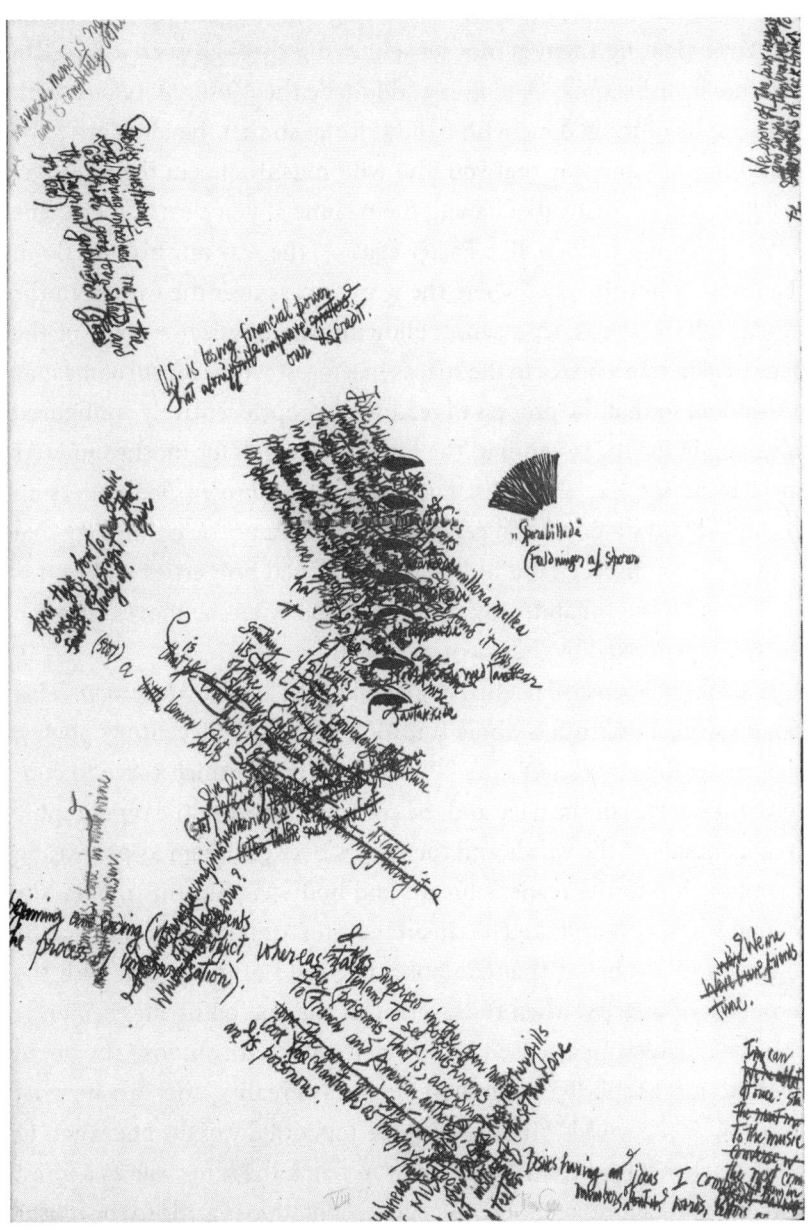

FIGURE 2.2 Lithography by John Cage, in John Cage, *Mushroom Book* (1972), with Lois Long and Alexander H. Smith. A set of ten original color lithographs by Long and ten lithographs by Cage in handwriting using superimpositions of five graded lithographic pencils. Botanical statements by Alexander H. Smith printed on sheets of interleaving tissue. © John Cage Trust.

text, in some way index the spatial configuration of a forest, so that a reader navigating them is in a sense moving through such a forest in search of mushrooms: "And Lois and I made the *Mushroom Book*, with lithographs of mine done with handwriting, so that the ideas are to be found in the same way that you find wild mushrooms in the forest, by just looking. . . . Instead of having them come at you clearly, they come to you as things hidden, like Easter eggs . . . the way mushrooms do in the forest."[3] In this way, "where the words cross over the words" in the lithographs, Cage is, in a sense, allowing the physical surface of the page to generate a proxy to the spaces in a forest where mushrooms may be hidden, so that the process of reading is proprioceptively configured as an analogue to "sweep[ing] the forest" in search for mushrooms. As such, in acting like the forest floor, Cage's *Mushroom Book* offers an example of how a poem can generate a world—a poetic cosmology that is somehow composed out of the poem's formal properties and in this case exists to be inhabited by the reader's body as she moves through the space generated by the poem.

In evoking a sense of reading as an embodied act, the *Mushroom Book* can be situated within a whole tradition of twentieth-century poetry, epitomized by Charles Olson's "Projective Verse," which came to conceive the surface of the page and the contrasts between the typographic arrangements of the words and the spaces between them as possessing a relationship to the reader's breath and body. Within this model, the textual fragments and sketches in all their textural recalcitrance can be understood as objects that compose the world of the poem, with the moments of opacity, when the layering of the text obfuscates semantic valence, possessing a sense that the elements that compose the poem operate "just as solidly" as do those "objects of reality" that "create what we know as the world."[4] In this sense the topography of the poem acts to produce elements of chance encounter in much the same way as a forest floor presents a kind of inherent "chance-operations" game to the mushroom collector.[5] What interests me in particular are these moments of discovery when the page that operates largely as such a textured, opaque surface opens out suddenly to reveal the existence of material worlds beyond itself—in other words, the moments when the workings of language as recalcitrant material suddenly yield to reveal referential content consisting of extralinguistic material entities, such as lakes or mushrooms.

THE VOLUME DIAL OF OPACITY AND TRANSPARENCY

Of course, there is nothing particularly unusual about language pointing to entities outside of itself, but what makes the *Mushroom Book* an interesting specimen for the study of both materialist poetics and the relationship between poetry and science is the way in which the poem slides between these possibilities of reference and material recalcitrance. One way to figuratively sense these oscillating patterns of materialization and dematerialization as they move across the linguistic and nonlinguistic realms would be to imagine a stereo system with a volume dial, which, when turned all the way up, would "thicken" the materiality of language until it assumes more of an opacity of material ground in itself rather than operating in a referential register to the world beyond language. And, perhaps, at the opposite end of the spectrum, with the volume dial turned all the way down, language would operate as more of a transparent pane of glass, which unobtrusively reveals the world beyond itself without drawing attention to its own material configuration. In other words, it is almost as though a dial were being turned up and down in the *Mushroom Book*, creating a sense of language as opaque material, followed by moments of transparency, when such opacity is rendered glassy, revealing through the surface of language the material world beyond it.

In working to characterize the different currents within materialist poetics in the twentieth and twenty-first centuries alongside their critical reception, I have noted a tendency toward reaching for one or the other of the most extreme positions on this dial in isolation, thus privileging either apparently unmediated access to the particulars of the material world "out there" or the arrangements of recalcitrant linguistic matter on the surface of the page. Such a divide between these two extreme settings of the volume dial is encapsulated in an essay published in the October 1979 issue of *L=A=N=G=U=A=G=E*, where the poet Bruce Andrews asks, "How much are we willing to destroy our attentiveness to the way words act and interact in order to gain the advantages of description or of representation?" Within such a representational model words become "transparent tools of reference," acting as "mere windows, substitutes, proper names, haloed or subjugated by the things to which they seem to point."[6] One of the responses of the language poets to this problem of the transparency of language was to turn up the volume on the opacity dial and thicken the signifier in such a way that it assumed material weight in its own right—no longer functioning only as an ephemeral deictic relay system pointing at the thickness of the nonlinguistic world. This produced one possible alignment between language and materiality, in which language itself became the horizon of materiality, thus locating a certain political potential in the disjunctive rearrangement of "linguistic matter" and by proxy, in historical materialist terms, the ideological and material constitution of the world. In an essay titled "Constitution / Writing, Politics, Language, The Body," published in the Canadian journal *Open Letter* in 1981 and subsequently collected in *Paradise and Method*, Andrews, for instance, offers a working account of such a critical methodology: "To oppose the structural underpinnings by an antisystemic detonation—*dizzying... elasticize... by flashes... nonsigns... scrambled*—by a blowing up of all settled relations. *sentence can dislocate. mangled matter*. So that the relational system that seems to underlie the very possibility of signifying would be exploded."[7]

The tendency to read poems as alternately exemplary of either the material opacity of the signifier or, conversely, the erasure of the materiality of language has been exacerbated by the violent swerves in critical thought itself, from the "linguistic turn," which characterized much of structuralist and poststructuralist thought in the humanities in the second half of the twentieth century, to the currently unfolding materialist or "ontological turn." While the "linguistic turn" placed the focus on the material properties of the signifier,[8] often locking modes of analysis within the self-referential properties of language and suggesting that there is no way to get outside of such discursive loops, which mediate our epistemic access to reality, the ontological turn has sought to escape such epistemic confines, often forgoing a consideration of language or mediation entirely in the process.[9] In articulating a materialist poetics here, I am interested in precisely the moments that resist this polarization, locating in the work of poets who have engaged with the natural sciences instants when the materiality of language is evident, but the turning of the volume dial is simultaneously held back from reaching the most extreme position at which language becomes a horizon of materiality and the possibilities for considering other kinds of nonlinguistic matter are occluded. In other words, there is a hope that these possibilities can be held in the palm of one hand without dissolving into a kind of dualist configuration within which language and substance appear to float on entirely separate planes. Perhaps such a position is encapsulated by a moment in *Touching Feeling* when Eve Kosofsky Sedgwick makes the assumption "that the line between words and things or between linguistic and nonlinguistic phenomena is endlessly changing, permeable, and entirely unsusceptible to any definitive articulation."[10] I extend this provocation by suggesting that the work of poets, particularly those who have engaged with the methodologies of the natural sciences and through this with close observation of the material world, can offer an exciting set of specimens through which to examine this permeable relation between words and things or linguistic and nonlinguistic phenomena. This aspect of my argument relies on a sense that works that navigate the intersection of poetry and science, such as the *Mushroom Book*, have maintained an insistence on sensory perspectives that attend to the materialities of nonhuman worlds, which are often in themselves entangled in biosemiotic realities, even as they have simultaneously treated language as a form of material that can act as an experimental substrate for recombination and manipulation.

It is this particular genealogical confluence between poetry and science that is of primary interest to me here among the plethora of possible traditions of materialist poetics that could be traced in the twentieth and twenty-first centuries, from Olson's objectism, to the objectivists, among them Louis Zukofsky and George Oppen, to various traditions of concrete poetry—traditions that I would like to acknowledge as possible alternate routes for constructing a materialist poetics, but which I cannot address within the scope of this book.[11] Other critical studies have similarly focused on investigating the relationship between poetry and knowledge. Key among them is Lytle Shaw's *Fieldworks: From Place to Site in Postwar Poetics*, which situates post-1945 poetry in relation to a number of other epistemic practices, from historiography and architecture to geology and natural history. The crux of Shaw's argument can be located in his reading of a moment in William Carlos Williams's quintessential poem of place *Paterson*, in which Williams lists a "tabular account" of stratified soil samples that were uncovered during a digging of a well in Paterson between September 1879 and November 1880. (See figure 2.3.) The vertical list of various types of soil, rock, and mineral deposits, including layers such as "red sandstone, and a little shale," "red sandstone, fine grained," "soft shale," and "light red sandstone," with accompanying records of the depths from the surface at which the sample was found, can be read as a recreation of the very cross-section of the geological stratification revealed in the dig—in other words, a moment when the arrangement of the text on the page begins to stand in, in a concrete sense, for the material arrangements of the geological particulars specific to Paterson as a place.[12] While acknowledging that in its material specificity such a moment can be read as an accretion of "life-emitting particulars," which constitute "a luminous world of immersive specificity," a reading that would be characteristic of a long tradition of poetics of place in twentieth-century poetry, Shaw is more interested in interpreting the work of poets who were drawing on other epistemic practices, such as Williams, through the rubric of a "discursive site," where the discipline of geology, in this case, could be understood as such a site.[13] The emphasis in *Fieldworks*, then, is less on the poem as offering access to some unmediated sense of the world, of place as an accretion of material particulars that the poem re-creates, and more on the epistemic

SUBSTRATUM

Artesian Well at the Passaic Rolling Mill, Paterson.

The following is the tabular account of the specimens found in this well, with the depths at which they were taken, in feet. The boring began in September, 1879, and was continued until November, 1880.

DEPTH	DESCRIPTION OF MATERIALS
65 feet. . .	Red sandstone, fine
110 feet. . .	Red sandstone, coarse
182 feet. . .	Red sandstone, and a little shale
400 feet. . .	Red sandstone, shaly
404 feet. . .	Shale
430 feet. . .	Red sandstone, fine grained
540 feet. . .	Sandy shale, soft
565 feet. . .	Soft shale
585 feet. . .	Soft shale
600 feet. . .	Hard sandstone
605 feet. . .	Soft shale
609 feet. . .	Soft shale
1,170 feet. . .	Selenite, 2 x 1 x 1/16 in.
1,180 feet. . .	Fine quicksand, reddish
1,180 feet. . .	Pyrites
1,370 feet. . .	Sandy rock, under quicksand
1,400 feet. . .	Dark red sandstone
1,400 feet. . .	Light red sandstone
1,415 feet. . .	Dark red sandstone
1,415 feet. . .	Light red sandstone
1,415 feet. . .	Fragments of red sandstone
1,540 feet. . .	Red sandstone, and a pebble of kaolin
1,700 feet. . .	Light red sandstone
1,830 feet. . .	Light red sandstone
1,830 feet. . .	Light red sandstone
1,830 feet. . .	Light red stone
2,000 feet. . .	Red shale
2,020 feet. . .	Light red sandstone
2,050 feet. . .	
2,100 feet. . .	Shaly sandstone

At this depth the attempt to bore through the red sandstone was abandoned, the water being altogether unfit for ordinary use. . . . The fact that the rock salt of England, and of some of the other salt mines of Europe, is found in rocks of the same age as this, raises the question whether it may not also be found here.

FIGURE 2.3 List of soil sample specimens compiled by William Carlos Williams, from *Paterson*, copyright © 1951 by William Carlos Williams. Reprinted by permission of New Directions Publishing Corp.

dimension of discursive practices, which in themselves begin to act as a site of investigation for these poets.

Rather than focusing on the discursive dimension of epistemic practices, in *The Limits of Fabrication* Nathan Brown evokes the concept of "fabrication," as a way of linking a sense of poetry as "making" or *"poiēsis"* and the techno-scientific practices of "material construction."[14] In this sense, poetry comes to be configured as "a branch of materials research and fabrication," continuous, for instance, with practices of nanotechnology, which have sought to arrange individual particles of matter into specific configurations, at times even reaching toward modes of tiny forms of inscription or "micrographia."[15] As such, Brown is interested in the material limits of scale at which poetic forms of fabrication can occur, with the sense that language itself is a kind of particulate matter that can assume different configurations through the process of micropoiesis: "To situate [materials science and materialist poetics] at the *limits* of fabrication is to open a space between 'there' and 'here' in which we are approached by bodies and words, in which the poetic image gives way onto invisible structures, wherein text passes over into texture."[16] *Limits of Fabrication* contends with the relationship between linguistic and nonlinguistic forms of materiality by eliding the sense that language is representing the material world "out there," in favor of a model in which forms of *"poiēsis"* are generating or fabricating such a world, often at tiny, microscopic scales. Such a critical move can be understood as taking Olson's dictum that "every element" of the poem must be thought of "just as solidly as we are accustomed to take what we call the objects of reality," except in this case such objects are operating at scales well below those that are perceptible to unaided human senses and may entail a manipulation of matter at microscopic scales as itself a form of inscription.[17] Brown is careful to stress, however, that such an approach to configuring a materialist poetics is not simply a way of operating "under the banner of 'the materiality of the signifier,' . . . which address[es] the materiality *of* the language system" but "can occlude attention to the manner in which the materiality of language is predicated upon the transformation of 'non-language material.'"[18] It is in particular this aspect of articulating a materialist poetics not solely through the emphasis on the materiality of the signifier that *Limits of Fabrication* and *Poetics of Liveliness* share, even as the two texts are working with quite divergent philosophical archives, with Heidegger acting as a pivotal figure for Brown, who argues against forms of biocentrism that privilege "life" as a governing rubric for understanding materiality in contemporary theory, while I focus on questions of "liveliness" of soft entities and the transformational encounters they undergo through the philosophical lens of figures such as Spinoza. In other words, what the two books share in their articulations of a materialist poetics is a desire to maintain a coincident, and perhaps even continuous, relation between linguistic and nonlinguistic materials that is forged in many ways in the laboratory where poetry comes in contact with science.

A different, more figurative way of suturing the gap between poetry and science is at play in two other books on materialist poetics—Daniel Tiffany's *Toy Medium: Materialism and Modern Lyric* and Amanda Jo Goldstein's *Sweet Science: Romantic Materialism and the New Logics of Life*. Once again, the question of scale emerges as the most significant aspect of such a suturing in Tiffany's *Toy Medium*, where he contends that poetic modes of figuration have played an important epistemic function in helping to create a sense of the invisible worlds of atoms or primary corpuscles. Tiffany's argument is predicated on a sense that the most fundamental aspects of materialist philosophy are not in fact sensible and thus cannot be empirically verified. Poetry intervenes here through its modes of figuration to help create an image of the invisible reality that is posited by science, producing a sense that material substances have a lyric dimension, a quality that Tiffany refers to as "lyric substance." In this sense the poetic mode allows analogies to be forged between the miniscule worlds of atoms and the phenomena that can actually be sensed, with one such sensible realm being that of "meteoric bodies," consisting of "*any* atmospheric phenomenon (clouds, dew, winds, lightning, rainbows, comets, and so on)."[19] Like atoms, such meteoric bodies can be thought of as so "ephemeral" that they are "almost nothing," and yet they are not nothing, and can hence be used to understand something about the miniscule, invisible, and similarly ephemeral realm of atoms. What *Toy Medium* and *Poetics of Liveliness* share (aside from a fascination with atmospheric entities, such as clouds) is an interest in the investigation of phenomena across scales of perception and a sense that the poetic modality or the aesthetic, more broadly, may be used to expand capacities for sensation. While *Toy Medium* enacts this primarily through poetry's propensity for the figurative, I am more focused on the manner in which observational or experimental procedures structure forms of perceptual attention in both poetry and science.

For Tiffany, the relationship between atomist philosophy and the desire to articulate something about the most attenuated forms of matter, operating nearly at the limits of materialism, is rooted in Epicurus's and subsequently Lucretius's sense of thin films (*eidola*) that continuously fly off the surfaces of objects and lead to perceptual experiences as they come in contact with the senses. These thin films also play an important role in Goldstein's book *Sweet Science*, where she explores the manner in which the reception of Lucretius shaped the relationship between poetry and science within the romantic period. In her argument, Goldstein emphasizes how Lucretius's thoroughgoing materialism posits a continuity between the particulate materiality of atoms, which in their plentiful recombinations compose everything in the universe, and processes such as thought, language, and even figuration, which for Lucretius are equally material and arise as thin films "touch" the senses and in turn combine with the fine substance of the mind. *De rerum natura* is not only a striking example of a text that combines poetry and science, or, in Goldstein's words, "a monumental and gorgeous case for poetry's role in the perception and communication of empirical realities," but it also acts as a foil for a number of romantic poets, among them Goethe and Shelley. In Goldstein's argument, this aspect of Lucretius's thought, which "grant[s] substance to tropes and tropic activity to nonverbal things," allows poetry to assume a role as a mode of empirical investigation within the romantic period, even as "disciplinary consolidation" in the early nineteenth century was generating a separation between the literary and the scientific: "To think with Lucretian materialism was to accept figuration as an indispensable object, medium, and means of empirical investigation, without invalidating any of these phases as 'mere' metaphor, anthropomorphism, or linguistic construction."[20] Many of the poetic figures that I address, including Christian Bök and Lisa Robertson, explicitly reference Lucretius in their work, and as such, *Poetics of Liveliness* can be considered a further exploration of the continuation of a Lucretian reception in the poetry of the twentieth and twenty-first centuries. I will return to Lucretius's manner of exploring even the figurative dimension of language as inherently material in the coda at the end of this book as a way of reaching toward an articulation of a haptic poetics in the contemporary moment.

Focusing on two distinct genealogies of poets who have been influenced by the natural sciences, one of which draws on a particulate, atomistic conception of matter and a sense that language also acts as a kind of recombinatory particulate substance, and the other that draws on the histories of description in natural history as a way of examining material phenomena, I argue that these poet-scientists have a unique position from which to engage with questions of materiality. It is my sense that these poets who were attuned to the procedural methods of science remained consistently concerned with the problem of the sensory encounter with the particulars of the material world and that this remained true even at the height of the "linguistic turn," when predominant emphasis in theoretical thought was placed on the materiality of the signifier.

THE QUESTION OF SENSATION IN SCIENCE AND POETRY

In *The Geographical History of America*, Stein tells an anecdote about a perceptual experience of words she had while getting a haircut: "I found that any kind of a book if you read with glasses and somebody is cutting your hair and so you cannot keep the glasses on and you use your glasses as a magnifying glass and so read word by word reading word by word makes the writing that is not anything be something."[21] This moment of perceptual metamorphosis, when language suddenly becomes granular and Stein finds herself considering the discrete qualities of individual words, is reminiscent not only of the moment when she is writing about evaluating "the weight and volume" of words but also of the extensive time she spent observing the microscopic qualities of tissues during her stint as a brain researcher at Johns Hopkins Medical School. I explore Stein's study of brain tissues and how it led to her understanding of the materiality of character in *The Making of Americans* at length in chapter 5, but here I would like to linger briefly on this image of Stein bent over a microscope to consider how this moment places her in a long continuity of figures in the history of science who have in much the same way labored over their instruments in the hopes of intensifying their modes of sensation and hence achieving an accuracy of perceptual contact between their senses and the material objects of the world. (See figure 2.4.) In *Micrographia*, Robert Hooke, for instance, bares his anxieties about the questionable accuracy of perception as a way of acquiring knowledge about the world, anxieties that he locates, at least in part, in the disproportionate relationship between the object under observation and the sensory organ, resulting from the fact that "*an infinite number of things* [that compose the detail of the universe] *can never enter into*" such limited organs of sensation.[22] In the face of these disjunctures between the scales of objects and the perceptual resolution of sensation (a problem I will return to through the work of Ernst Heinrich Weber in chapter 4), Hooke hopes that a "reparation" of the senses may be made with the aid of instruments such as telescopes and microscopes.

Hooke at one point speculates about the possibility of amplifying other senses, such as smell and even touch—predicting that soon instruments will exist that will have such a capacity, a prediction that, at least in terms of touch, has not been realized more than three hundred years later. In pointing to this discrepancy between the histories of amplification through the use of instruments, I am less interested in reiterating the well-known story about vision as a privileged mode of sensation in the history of Enlightenment science and more interested in ways in which texture complicates an alignment with any particular sense as its point of registration.[23] Or, as Sedgwick points out in *Touching Feeling*,

FIGURE 2.4 *Gertrude Stein Looking Through a Microscope*, 1892, photograph, reprinted by permission of the Gertrude Stein Estate. Beinecke Rare Book and Manuscript Library, Yale University.

texture "is not coextensive with any single sense," involving "other senses beyond the visual and haptic . . . as when we *hear* the brush-brush of corduroy trousers or the crunch of extra-crispy chicken."[24] Registering texture, in other words, need not coincide with touch, or, as Gilles Deleuze and Félix Guattari explain in their account of smooth and striated space, the haptic "may be as much visual or auditory as tactile," and yet they do distinguish its modality from optical perception with its concomitant sense of distance: " 'Haptic' is a better word than 'tactile' since it does not establish an opposition between two sense organs but rather invites the assumption that the eye itself may fulfill this nonoptical function."[25]

In following this distinction between sensory absorption and distance, I would like to suggest that there is a kind of haptic dimension to the immersive moment of looking that transpires when Stein takes off her glasses to look at words one by one in that even though vision remains a sensory modality here, a sense of optical distance is collapsed. Moreover, what interests me about this moment is the manner in which it creates a parallel between how one may engage words through the senses and the way that one may engage other objects of experience, as Stein does in closely observing the properties of objects in *Tender Buttons*. This parallel is a kind of crux in my articulation of the relationship between poetry and science in this chapter and in the book as a whole, leading me to a view that the poets who were in some way influenced by the methodologies of the sciences attempted to engage both the material qualities of language and the materiality of nonlinguistic entities without losing "sight" or "feel" for either of these two material dimensions. For such poet-scientists, the aesthetic process (which in their case often borrowed methods such as direct observation, description, or experimentation from the sciences) offered the means of sensory intensification in much the same way that natural philosophers such as Hooke used instruments of amplification to aid the accuracy of their own sensations and immerse themselves more closely in the material world at scales that often exceeded the capacities of the human senses.

In beginning this chapter with an epigraph from Francis Bacon, I am drawn not only to how he himself worried about the proper practices for sensory observation in the sciences, but also to how the notion of the experimental method he developed sets the conditions for poetic experimentation. In describing the relevance of "the scientific method" for contemporary poetry, Lyn Hejinian links Bacon's work to the writers who adopted "an 'experimental method'" parallel to it, among them Stein, for whom the practices of "patient attention, demanding long and close observation" became "bound to an infinite project" of acquiring knowledge about the world.[26] As such, Hejinian places the emphasis on forms of poetic knowledge that, like scientific knowledge, focus on careful observations of the particulars that make up the universe. She locates an ongoing inquiry into the problem of ordering such dynamic particulars in Bacon's work—a project that, I would argue, could just as easily describe what Stein is up to with her monumental taxonomy of human character in *The Making of Americans*, or what Robertson discovers in the complex, dynamic taxonomy of clouds in Luke Howard's early meteorology. "Bacon goes on to speak of the 'great number of particulars,'" Hejinian writes, "'an army of them you might say,' lying 'so scattered and diffuse as to distract and confuse the understanding'" (153). In *The New Organon*, from which Hejinian draws this quotation, Bacon states that deriving knowledge from such an overwhelming disarray of particulars requires that they be arranged into "well-organized and living (so to speak) tables of discovery," which can provide the ground for further analysis.[27] The sense of "living" tables of discovery is curious, especially in the light of my interest in liveliness here, and is suggestive of an ongoing project of knowledge-making, in which new observations are added to sit beside the ones that have already been recorded without supplanting them, shifting, instead, in their accumulation, the meaning of the overall pattern that emerges. This means that both the epistemic process and the entities that emerge into discernment through it are rendered lively and dynamic. Such a process of constructing "living tables of discovery" is evident, for instance, in the modes of cloud-writing or cloud annotation, which allow Howard to record the rapid transformations of clouds from one type to another in an effort to preserve an ontological sense of them as active, changing entities even within the epistemic moment of their classification, leading him to construct what I call, in the final chapter of this book, a *soft taxonomy* of clouds.

In the quote from *The New Organon* that serves as the epigraph for this chapter, Bacon generates a kind of miniature cosmology and contends with the question of whether the senses will consistently be able to register accurate perceptions of the particulars that make up the universe: "The fabric of the universe, its structure, to the mind observing it, is like a labyrinth, where on all sides the path is so often uncertain, the resemblance of a thing or a sign is deceptive, and the twists and turns of natures are so oblique and intricate. One must travel always through the forests of experience and particular things, in the uncertain light of the senses, which is sometimes shining and sometimes hidden."[28] While the focus of my discussion is the influence of science on poetry, one cannot help but be struck by the poetic qualities of this passage, in which the figurative properties of metaphor generate multiple layers of meaning, with the universe forming a kind of "cosmological fabric," through which the mind moves proprioceptively as through a labyrinth, lit by the "uncertain light" of the senses. Perhaps the most intricate and striking part of the figurative structure comes from the phrase "forests of experience," which gestures toward both the setting of a forest as a site where the specimens for natural historical exploration may be found, a site continuous with the other figurative landscapes through which the seeker of knowledge moves, and also to a forest as an entity composed as an aggregate of numerous particulars, dense with trees (or mushrooms), and hence with the particulars of experience. While the senses may offer "uncertain light" in not always being able to perceive accurately, Bacon is unambiguous in stressing the importance of persisting with the quest of apprehending such sensuous particulars.

One way that Bacon devises for rendering the senses more reliable is through the method of inductive reasoning, where it is the careful examination of particulars that leads one to more general conclusions: "For the nature of things we use induction throughout, and as much for the minor propositions as for the major ones[,] [f]or we regard induction as the form of demonstration which respects the senses, stays close to nature, fosters results and is almost involved in them itself." While other forms of reasoning, such as "proof by syllogism," let "nature slip out of our hands," the inductive method, however imperfect, allows the senses to return to the material particulars of the outside world.[29] Another way that Bacon devises for rendering the senses more reliable is through the epistemic structure of the experiment, which allows for an insight into "how nature would behave under previously unobserved circumstances."[30] "The subtlety of the experiments is far greater than that of the senses," Bacon suggests, because it creates a kind of remove or distance between the possible errors in perception caused by the senses and the thing under observation: "We do not rely very much on the immediate and proper perception of the senses, but we bring the matter to the point that the senses judge only of the experiment, the experiment judges of the thing" (18). In this sense, the experiment acts as a kind of mediator, structuring sensation, but also altering the normal course through which "nature" unfolds: "We are making a history not only of nature free and unconstrained (when nature goes its own way and does its own work), such as a history of the bodies of heaven and the sky, of land and sea, of minerals, plants and animals; but much more of nature confined and harassed, when it is forced from its own condition by art and human agency, and pressured and moulded" (20–21). In some sense, then, the contours of the experiment place a kind of restraint both on the process of sensation and on the select aspects of the material world that are revealed, isolated, and perhaps transformed through the manipulations of the experimental procedure. Or, as Bacon states, the premises of the scientific method seek to "preserve sensation by putting a kind of restraint on it" (28).

Aspects of Bacon's articulation of the scientific method are clearly relevant for poets who have directly engaged with science as a practice in their work, as well as for those who have modeled their own poetic procedures on those of the natural sciences. The contours of this sense of relevance can be located, for instance, in the *Routledge Companion to Experimental Literature*, which situates the intersection between scientific and literary understandings of the term *experiment* in the literary innovations of Émile Zola, stating that "the model of scientific experiment would not become fully available for describing literary innovation until . . . Zola applied it to the naturalist novel at the end of the nineteenth century."[31] Hejinian traces this same genealogy when she locates Zola's interest in the notion of the "experimental" in his reading of Claude Bernard's *Introduction à l'étude de la médecine expérimentale* (Introduction to the Scientific Study of Medicine), pointing out Zola's desire to expand the scientific method to the naturalist novel.[32]

The notion of the "experiment" when translated into the context of poetics opens up a sense of poetry itself as an epistemic practice that is capable of innovation and discovery. Following the history of the "experiment" further back to Bacon's delineation of the scientific method emphasizes the significance of the senses as modes of engaging with the particulars of the material world, with the experiment itself acting as a mediating site that attunes and, in a manner, "restrains the senses," but only for the purposes of intensifying their acuity. One of the parallels between poetry and science that becomes salient in this context is the relationship between the restraint on the senses produced by the experiment and the use of constraint in poetics. One could ask, then, if they both seek a similar intensification of perception—perhaps something akin to the call of the Russian Formalist Viktor Shklovsky "to make the stone stony" through the act of aesthetic defamiliarization or "*ostranenie.*"[33] It can be said that an experimental constraint designed to produce such an intensification of sensations is operative, for instance, in a piece such as John Cage's 4'33," in which the performer is instructed to not play any of the instruments for the duration of the piece, which consists of four minutes and thirty-three seconds. While on one hand the piece can be thought of as four minutes and thirty-three seconds of silence, the instructions provided actually delineate the edges of what I would call a block of intensified sensation, which includes the audience's heightened attunement to all the sounds occurring in the environment around them. In a different sense, elements of this kind of intensified attunement to ambient detail are also present in the work of the second-generation New York School poet Bernadette Mayer, who often restricted durational frames in her own life and attempted to record the dilation of detail that ensued as a result of this intensified mode of attention, with a book such as *Midwinter Day* recording all the occurrences of daily life in its inner and outer dimensions of sensation that unfolded over the span of a single day, December 22, 1978.[34] In the contemporary moment in poetics, such a desire for an attunement of the senses through a set of constraints and procedures is also evident, for instance, in the (Soma)tic Poetry Rituals of CA Conrad, which consist of instructions that often instigate a direct encounter between the body and various minerals, such as crystals, as well as plants and animals, including human animals.

MATERIALIST CONCEPTUALISMS: EXPERIMENTS IN REARRANGEMENTS OF PARTICULATE MATTER

While certain kinds of experimental constraint in twentieth-century poetics focus on restraining and intensifying the sensation of lived experience of the material world, others focus on restraining the scope of linguistic permutations, so that language itself becomes, for them, a primary ground of experimentation, while access to extralinguistic materiality is occluded. At times, such use of constraint acts to reproduce a kind of dualism between the materiality of language and the materiality of the world, which I have been working to subvert in this chapter. One genealogy of poet-scientists who have focused on the particulate, recombinatory possibilities of language as a primary site for experimentation in their work can be traced to Lucretius's atomist physics. These poets who belong to the tradition of 'Pataphysics and Oulipo primarily use language-based constraints, such as lipograms, palindromes, or simply various forms of replacement or recombination, such as N+7, in which every noun in a text is replaced with the seventh noun following it in a dictionary, with varying dictionaries producing varying results.

'Pataphysics was invented by the French writer Alfred Jarry at the turn of the twentieth century and can be thought of as one of the complex branches of the reception of Lucretius in twentieth-century poetics, one in which Lucretius acts as a model for how poetry and science can come to intersect. A Lucretian conception of a cosmology is influential for the development of 'Pataphysics in two key ways: One is the particulate conception of language evident in Lucretius's miniaturization of language into nearly atomic, single-letter particles, which, according to an analogy in *De rerum natura*, in their many recombinations alternately compose everything that exists in the universe: "For the same elements compose sky, sea and lands, rivers and sun, crops, trees and animals, but they are moving differently and in different combinations."[35] Language, similarly, within the Lucretian model, operates as a permutation of a finite set of letters that compose the alphabet: "The letters which denote sky, sea, earth and rivers also denote crops, trees and animals" as they repeat to a great extent in all these words, differing primarily in their position and combination.[36] The other link between 'Pataphysics and a Lucretian cosmology is the swerve, or *clinamen*, and the interest in 'Pataphysics in the question of how to study the singularity, the unrepeatable quality of any occurrence. This is something that the scientific method has a difficult time accounting for because of its insistence on replicability and on a kind of flattening out of differences, which is produced by averaging out specific instances, with the effect that the particularity of each one comes to be lost.

The Lucretian origins of this impulse toward the singular chance occurrence can be traced to Jarry's novel *Exploits & Opinions of Dr. Faustroll, Pataphysician*, in which Jarry draws on the concept of the Lucretian *clinamen* in order to describe a painting machine spewing paint onto a series of empty canvases: "The Painting Machine . . . dashed itself against the pillars, swayed and veered in infinitely varied directions, and followed its own whim in blowing onto the walls' canvas the succession of primary colors ranged according to the tubes of its stomach . . . this modern deluge of the universal Seine, the unforeseen beast *Clinamen* ejaculated onto the walls of its universe:."[37] Jarry's Painting Machine inhabits a seemingly postapocalyptic landscape devoid of human beings or any other form of life, and yet it possesses its own autonomous activity capable of spewing paint in indeterminate patterns. The indeterminacy that Jarry locates in the machine is evident even formally in the syntax of this passage, with the final sentence (like many of the sentences in *Exploits & Opinions of Dr. Faustroll*) ending with an open colon, suggesting the open-ended, unforeseeable nature of the pattern created by the painting machine and thus departing from a sense of a cosmology that is driven by a mechanistic conception of matter.

Bök situates himself within a genealogy stretching from Jarry, the Italian futurists, the French Oulipians,[38] and finally extending toward a group of Canadian poets who call themselves the Canadian "Pataphysicians." One of the things that interests me in Bök's work, in relation to my argument that poets who are invested in the methodologies of the natural sciences remain attuned to a sensuous apprehension of nonlinguistic forms of materiality, is the manner in which his projects oscillate between a more idealist realm, within which the rearrangements of letters through constraint procedures such as palindromes and lipograms resemble Oulipian "language games," and other moments when such rearrangements of letters remain in close relation to the molecular shapes and structures that compose matter. In Bök's book of poetry *Eunoia*, for instance, each of the five different sections of the book contains only the words that use just one of the vowels in the English language, operating largely in this text in terms of the notion of constraint as a set of permutations within language. In the preceding book, *Crystallography*, described by Bök as "a pataphysical encyclopedia that misreads the language of poetics through the conceits of geology,"[39] the compositions of the letters on the page behave much more like Lucretian atoms, forming arrangements that correspond to the molecular forms of various crystals. In his latest project, *The Xenotext Experiment*, which I discuss at length in chapter 3, Bök extends this engagement with *molecular poetics* by entangling his poetic practice even further with the natural sciences, this time by working with scientists at a biotechnology lab at the Institute for Biocomplexity and Informatics (IBI) at the University of Calgary to insert a poem into the DNA of a bacterium in the hope that this microorganism will express a second protein poem based on the DNA poem that had been inserted into its genome. At some point in the creation of *The Xenotext Experiment*, the concerns of a molecular poetics come to no longer be operating within the space of analogy between the letters of the alphabet and the molecules that make up DNA nucleotides; rather it is the three-dimensional, textured quality of biological materiality itself that begins to set the parameters of the constraints imposed on the form of the poetic text that Bök and the bacterium are composing in their interspecies collaboration.

Bök is not the only poet whose work I address who is heading to the lab in order to compose his poems. In creating *Silk Poems*, the poet and artist Jen Bervin worked with scientists at a lab at the Tufts University Department of Biomedical Engineering to construct a poem out of liquefied silk that had been turned into a thin film to act as a biosensor within the human body. As I discuss in chapter 4, Bervin's poem acts as an amplification device, akin to a scientific instrument, such as a microscope, to magnify, through poetic form, different scales of biological materiality, generating, in the process, morphological analogues within the formal properties of the poem that correspond to the biological structure of silk. Constraint as method plays an important role in Bervin's poem, but, as is the case with *The Xenotext Experiment*, this form of constraint remains resolutely embodied within the configurations of biological materiality, so that the line length of the poem embedded within the silk film, for instance, consists of six letters corresponding in this way with the six-nucleotide repeat sequence within the DNA that codes for the protein that composes silk. While Bervin does not directly situate herself as a 'Pataphysician, her work can be understood as a form of research poetics driven by collaboration among multiple disciplines. Such extensive research process offers the conceptual ground for investigating material form, which in turn comes to act as a constraint guiding poetic form.

In their emphasis on the relationship between poetic form and biological materiality, Bök and Bervin complicate the process of dissociation between the materiality of the signifier and nonlinguistic forms of materiality that I have figured in this chapter through the image of the sharply oscillating volume dial as an analogue for such dualist tendencies within twentieth-century and contemporary poetics. This opens up a space for what I would call a "materialist conceptualism," in which the constraints of the poetic experiment are not set by an abstracted space in which the permutations of language are dissociated from modes of nonlinguistic materiality, but where the aspects of the material world in their variegated but also specific and delimited folds and textures impose a constraint on such linguistic permutations, and hence on poetic form. Conceptualism within contemporary poetry shares its origins with the genealogy of Oulipo, as well as the tradition of conceptual art:

Works of conceptual literature have primarily responded to the historical precedents set by two disparate movements in the avant-garde: first, the systematic writing of Oulipian pataphysicians (like Raymond Queneau, Jacques Roubaud, among others); second, the procedural artwork of American conceptualists (like Joseph Kosuth, Douglas Huebler, among others)—precedents that, in both cases, reduce creativity to a tautological array of preconceived rules, whose logic culminates not in the mandatory creation of a concrete object but in the potential argument for some abstract schema.[40]

In this sense, conceptualism can be understood as primarily concerned with the intervention that an idea makes in the course of the history of art, rather than with the creation of a specific material object, a view that can neatly be summarized by Douglas Huebler's statement in 1969: "The world is full of objects, more or less interesting; I do not wish to add any more."[41] Such a disavowal of the creation of objects as a primary activity of art was likewise theorized in Lucy R. Lippard and John Chandler's essay "The Dematerialization of Art" (1968), in which they argue, following Joseph Schillinger's book *The Mathematical Basis of the Arts*, that art history has moved through a set of progressive stages, which are culminating in the 1960s in the development of "an ultra-conceptual art that emphasizes the thinking process almost exclusively" and within which the art object itself becomes dematerialized, becoming nearly or even entirely obsolete in the face of the idea.[42]

In *Fieldworks* Shaw complicates how Lippard and Chandler's argument plays out in the context of poetry, pointing out that the move toward the dematerialization of the art object was accompanied by a concomitant move toward the materialization of language so that "at the same moment [that] dematerialization becomes a value in art," materialization, in turn, "becomes a goal in poetry."[43] Perhaps a quintessential joint of this inversion can be located in the artwork titled *A Heap of Language* (1966) by the Earthworks artist Robert Smithson, whose simultaneous investment in site-specificity of artworks such as the *Spiral Jetty* and the creation of elaborate written texts engaging a number of epistemic practices, from astronomy to paleontology, plays a pivotal role in Shaw's argument about the transition from place to site as a concern in postwar poetics. In *A Heap of Language*, Smithson creates a heap of words, written out in cursive, in pencil, on a sheet of graph paper, generating a sculptural-form of a triangular pile, testifying to his sense of language as material: "My sense of language is that it is matter and not ideas—i.e., 'printed matter.'"[44] Returning to my figure of the volume dial of materiality, one could locate *A Heap of Language* somewhere in the vicinity of the extreme position on the dial where the opacity of the linguistic space is turned all the way up, thickening the signifier until it no longer points to or reveals the notion of the signified beyond itself. In the case of *A Heap of Language*, this is enacted by the heap itself being composed of synonyms for language, including words such as "speech," "Mother tongue," and "Babel," so that in some sense it can be read self-referentially, as pointing at language itself. While at first glance such a materializing of language seems to shift sharply away from the idealizing dematerialization associated with conceptualism's privileging of the idea over the creation of the "object," as Shaw points out in *Fieldworks*, they are in fact closely tied together, forming two sides of the same coin. I want to suggest that what registers as an uncanny proximity between these seemingly opposite moves of materialization and dematerialization is a rustle of a hidden dualism that lurks within either of these extreme positions of the dial, no matter how much they profess to materialize either the space of language or the things of the world, because as these approaches generate that thickening or opacity, they simultaneously create an invisible, intangible, idealized realm beyond it, which is either perceptually inaccessible or concomitantly evacuated of materiality. In positing the term *materialist conceptualism* in *Poetics of Liveliness*, I am interested in resisting this slide into dualistic modes of thinking by focusing on the work of poets who do not neatly inhabit either of these two extreme positions, in which it is either the materiality of language that becomes the limit of the perceptible, or where language is rendered so insubstantial that it seems to offer an entirely unmediated access to the particulars of the world.

"ANIMALS ARE DESCRIPTION SPARKLING"

This question of whether a poetic text can hold both the materiality of language and the materiality of the nonlinguistic world in hand at once is also present as a guiding thread in my examination of the second of the two genealogies of poets who have been influenced by the sciences that I am exploring in *Poetics of Liveliness*. This one traces its path beginning with Stein's training in psychology and medicine, weaves its way alongside Hejinian's reading of Stein through the lens of natural historical description, and eventually meanders up the West Coast of the North American continent across the Canadian-U.S. border to influence Robertson. In other words, there is a direct line of transmission between the significance that Hejinian places on the "scientific method" and the sensible realities that it reveals, and, in particular, on the manner in which description traffics from the discourses of natural history to those of poetics, and the work of Robertson, who herself takes up description as both a poetic method and a conceptual tool.[45] Such transmissions are historically unsurprising considering the connections between the West Coast poetic communities that often crossed and transcended the national boundary between the United States and Canada, with Hejinian, for instance, initially composing the essay "Strangeness" as a "talk sponsored by the Kootenay School of Writing in Vancouver, B.C., in October 1988"—the Kootenay School being a writer's collective of which Robertson was an active member.[46]

The contours of the difficulty of attending to multiple materialities of both language and the world, which I have been tracing throughout, is evident in much of Stein's critical reception both in the scholarly communities that have addressed her work and among the post-1945 poets whom she has come to influence. While within both of these intellectual communities Stein's writing has often been lauded for its nonrepresentational qualities, and a sense that it does not operate in a deictic relation to the entities of the world, it has been my view that no choice has to be made here between the representational and the nonrepresentational capacities of language, and that often the most delightful moments in Stein's texts illustrate copresence and complexity of this double relation.

A great example of how this double movement operates can be found in *Disjunctive Poetics*, where Peter Quartermain, at first, positions Stein's writing as moving along a different axis from one of deictic representation: "Stein's writing perpetually destabilizes itself (no easy accomplishment) by foregrounding linguistic (as opposed to referential or representational) concerns." As an example, Quartermain points out a sentence from "Sentences" that states, "A lake is an article followed by a noun a lake is an article followed by a noun a lake which is there," where Stein is "being descriptive not of a feature of the physical landscape (lake) but, through its illustrative nature, of parts of speech and thus of a sentence." While Stein's sentence does undoubtedly point to the grammatical features of the language itself, Quartermain also notes that it possesses a double deictic movement, which simultaneously points "to a feature of the physical landscape"—"indeed, this sequence of transformations, this double movement in the sentence, has been encouraged by the introduction of *lake* into the paragraph in the first place." In pointing to a lake in the physical landscape alongside a lake in language, Quartermain suggests, Stein's writing evokes a sensuous entity, one that she descriptively elaborates by adding that "'a lake is really very nearly never frozen over'" and that "'it is very pretty.'"[47]

The December 1978 issue of *L=A=N=G=U=A=G=E*, in which several writers, including Bob Perelman, Michael Davidson, Robert Grenier, and Steve McCaffery, respond to a selection from Stein's *Tender Buttons*, can act as a litmus test of how this problematic in her writing plays out in the context of her post-1945 reception among a group poets as well as several literary critics. A number of responses in the issue substantially complicate the sense that Stein's writing is propelled directly toward the elision of the referential function of language in lieu of the recalcitrance of linguistic materiality. Grenier, for instance, writes that Stein's texts "show her thinking language not as object-in-itself, but as composition functioning in the composition of the world," so that her writing is directed "equally/simultaneously, [toward] sentience, world & language as relation."[48] Similarly, Davidson writes that "Stein's prose is firmly tied to the world—but it is a world constantly under construction, a world in which the equation of word and thing can no longer be taken for granted."[49]

It is Hejinian, however, who offers the most textured, extensive, and influential engagement with Stein's work among the language poets, and who places significance specifically on the integral role of description in Stein's work, making a clear connection between such uses of description and the practices and methods emerging out of science and natural history, tracing these all the way back to Bacon and the invention of the scientific method in the seventeenth century. I argue that it is this emphasis on the scientific method, and description in particular, that allows Hejinian's work to remain engaged with the sensuous particulars of the world at a moment when the "linguistic turn" in critical thought and poetics is leading many other poets, particularly language poets such as Andrews, to focus on language as a primary material site. As I have pointed out earlier, Andrews, for instance, attacks description for its representational qualities, which transform words into "transparent tools of reference."[50]

In some sense, description suffered a parallel fate as an abnegated and yet persistent technique of observation in the world of twentieth-century science (as it did in the world of twentieth-century poetics), where it was often associated with observational techniques of natural history rather than with the experimental tradition, which developed into modern science. This hierarchical dichotomy between *description* and *experimentation* has in many ways persisted in how the two terms have been taken up in twentieth-century literature. The experimental mode has often been associated with a detachment of language from nonlinguistic forms of materiality and its closure into a self-referential loop, while description has been seen in the opposite way, as actually not foregrounding its linguistic opacity adequately and offering instead an unfounded promise of an unmediated access to the material particulars of the world. In the intellectual ecology of *Poetics of Liveliness*, I am working to cultivate a more complex relationship between the two, one that is rooted in a coextensive sense of the materiality of language and the world, rather than the alternate shuttling between the two, and hence one that is much closer to what science studies scholars such as Donna Haraway and Karen Barad would respectively call the *material-semiotic* or the *material-discursive*, terms that have signaled the commitment of such thinkers toward nondualist modes of meaning making and epistemology.[51] Or, as Barad suggests in *Meeting the Universe Halfway*, matter and meaning "are inextricably fused together, and no event, no matter how energetic, can tear them asunder.... Mattering is simultaneously a matter of substance and significance."[52]

In considering such nondualist alignment between matter and language, I am interested in how experimentation and description have coexisted and intertwined in natural history and science from their incarnation in the work of figures such as Bacon or Hooke, who often worried as much about how to "correctly" write or annotate the phenomena they were studying as they did about setting the correct conditions for observation through the attunement of the senses, constraint, and distance created by the experiment. While the relationship between description and experimentation in the history of science since the Enlightenment is a complex topic, which I cannot fully encompass in this study of poetics, it is clear from the literature on the history of science that the two do not possess a simply sequential relationship, where one just supplants the other, and that experimental and observational procedures possess an intertwined relationship in the history of science itself.[53] In her essay "On Scientific Observation," the historian of science Lorraine Daston points out that "eighteenth century scientific observers would have been mightily puzzled by [the]... stark oppositions... between 'active' experiment and 'passive' observation" that were subsequently reinforced by nineteenth-century scientists: "For earlier practitioners and philosophers of observation, it was self-evident that observation uninformed by theory was not only impossible but senseless and that observation and experiment were inextricably intertwined."[54] It may be difficult to recapture this space of intertwinement between the two in the epistemic ordering of the present, but as I will explore in relation to my reading of Stein's morphological studies of the brain, even in the twentieth century observation and description persisted alongside practices of experimentation, and in the current moment in the humanities there has been a resurgence of interest in description as a methodology for literary and cultural study.[55]

More specifically, in the context of poetics, Hejinian argues that "the ontological and epistemological problem of our knowledge of experience is . . . inseparable from the problem of description," as she points to the significance of what she calls "essentially literary activity" of describing the sensuous particulars of the world, which ended up being key for the development of scientific inquiry: "It is not knowledge per se that is to be learned, but rather the world, and the method for achieving this learning is a descriptive method, one in which the observing senses are fundamentally aided by language."[56] In parallel with this consideration of the significance of language, and description in particular, for the development of the scientific method, Hejinian likewise resolutely complicates the relationship between description and experimentation in avant-garde poetics: citing Zola's provocation from *The Experimental Novel* (*Le Roman expérimental*) that "an experiment is . . . only a provoked observation," she shifts the emphasis away from experimentation as a primary scientific technique that literature can draw on, in favor of the experiment as simply a formulation of specific constraints that create an occasion for observation and hence description.[57]

The emphasis on description and its relationship to scientific practices became significant for poets who were influenced by Hejinian and her sense of poetic language as a *language of inquiry*, and who were also hoping to explore the sense of poetry as an epistemic practice. In an interview in the fall 2011 issue of the *Capilano Review*, Robertson situates her interest in poetic description in relation to the historic moment when scientific and literary modes of description still converged with one another: "It was a discourse that was happening before science and literature were differentiated, strictly speaking, and so it was like the last gasps of a more integrated practice of description, where natural history had very minimal and totally erasable boundaries in relation to literary description."[58] In her book *The Weather*, Robertson turns to Howard's work on clouds as a way of exploring how descriptive and taxonomic practices can index the temporal flux of materiality. In chapter 6 I explore how formal qualities of description in Robertson's writing recreate the microdynamics of change through grammatical variation—a question that is resonant with Olson's concern with kinetic qualities of objects or Stein's desire to re-create the movements of a hopping frog inside one of her portraits; in other words, the question of *poetics of liveliness*.

In conjunction with her concern about the kinetics of atmospheric entities such as clouds, Robertson's writing simultaneously allows description to exceed its representational capacity in order to offer a distinct sense of description as a mode of elaboration or ornamentation: "We think of the design and construction of weather description as important decorative work. What shall our new ornaments be? How should we adorn mortality now?"[59] These sentences, which open the introduction to *The Weather*, latch together description and decoration, suggesting that description operates as a mode of ornamentation, which elaborates the surfaces of phenomena, in this way inverting the model in which descriptive language is just a clear pane of glass through which the sensuous particulars are accessed, and suggesting instead that description in some sense augments or adds a layer to materiality.

The significance of texture as a facet of linguistic phenomena becomes increasingly evident as Robertson further complicates the relationship between matter and language by considering linguistic structures themselves as "material specimens."[60] Referring to herself as "a gentleman collector of sentences," she evokes with this characterization an explicit resemblance between her writing practice and the collecting and taxonomizing practices of the natural historians. Her writing in one sense, then, becomes a display cabinet in which such carefully collected syntactic specimens can be exhibited, and where convoluted baroque grammars find themselves next to specimens with "grand neo-classical symmetries." In particular, Robertson is explicit about her interest in the differentiated textures of syllables and the way that they suture themselves into syntactic structures: "About syllables—I mean that nubby material edging up of consonants against airy vowelness in a line. How for me a line has to have a presence in this way. . . . It has to, for me, have this sort of full knobbly quality, or a torsion or a jaggedness or a swoony kind of movement from syllable to syllable, although now I seem to be exploring flatness as a sound quality. Are there kinds of flatness?" By thinking of syllables as possessing specific textural qualities, Robertson begins to think of sentences as built surfaces, composed of texturally differentiated and affectively resonant materials.

The irresolvable quality of attachment between description and materiality in Robertson's work, which cannot be easily parsed into either a representational dissolution of the opacity of the linguistic signifier or a foreclosure of a possibility of contact between language and nonlinguistic materiality, testifies to a kind of lively entanglement between matter and meaning in which my overall project is invested. In "Residence at C__," one of the shorter lineated poems in *The Weather*, Robertson directly addresses the work of description, presenting it in a sense as the primary task of the poem:

> Everything I'm writing about
> begins as the robin as the song
> sparrow begins is description
> animals are description sparkling
> scrapping in loose shrieks teenagers also
> utopia is memory the broken
> bits running motors leaves remarkably
> simple and heart shaped and practical
> as leaves the gentlest flavor of them is
> description and islands of written
> stuff love operas and suicides vast
> itineraries of error, memory
> grey silk sky with pigeons circling
> description because memory can't
> love as the orange lights of description[61]

In this poem Robertson constructs declarative statements that assert what description is; thus the definition of description becomes a series of entities or qualities. Some quality of the robin and the song sparrow beginning is description, and this quality of beginning is attached to writing. In setting up this series of adverbial qualities regarding a manner in which something begins, description is operating within the plane of writing, but also within the irreducibility of nonhuman articulation of some form of beginning. Robertson's poetics of description in these lines places a direct emphasis on the relationship between description and the lives of nonhuman animals, in this case birds—robins, sparrows, and pigeons—which circle, through the enjambment of the lines, in and all the way around the irresolvable loop between materiality and description. These animals seem to alternately flicker as figures within the tissues of language and as figures that lift off the surface of language, circling it as a ground, so that Robertson moves in this poem from a line such as "animals are description sparkling" to a moment, a few lines down, where she writes of the "grey silk sky with pigeons circling/description."[62] Language, in these lines, as they curve through enjambment around one another, becomes an environment, a landscape, a textured field, a site that can for an instant hold a sparkle of an ephemeral configuration of animate, material forms, even as it also creates an additional descriptive layer of material signification over the surfaces of the world.

II

POETIC LABORATORIES OF MATTER

3

MOLECULES

From Code to Shape

THE COSMOS AND THE MOLECULE

In "Death of the Literary 'I'; Matter and Molecular Life," published in *Lacerba* in 1913 as a section of the futurist manifesto "Destruction of Syntax—Untrammeled Imagination—Words-in-Freedom," the Italian futurist poet Filippo Tommaso Marinetti offers a manifesto calling for a materialist poetics that would avoid the pitfalls of anthropomorphism and would reverberate instead with an interest in vital, molecular materialities: "To get rid of . . . [the] obsessive 'I,' we must abandon the habit of humanizing nature by attributing human passions and concerns to animals, plants, water, stone, and clouds. Instead, we have to express the infinitesimally small things that surround us, the imperceptible, the invisible, the whiz of atoms, Brownian motion, all the enthusiastic hypothesis and all the domains explored by the dark field microscope." In this statement Marinetti proposes a shift away from an anthropomorphic perspective toward the worlds of animals and plants, and even the materiality of stone or the atmospheric phenomena of clouds. He then goes one step further by suggesting what implications this may have for literary, and, specifically, poetic language, by proclaiming: "I want to introduce the infinite life of molecules into poetry, not really as scientific document but as an intuitive element that must be merged, in the work of art, with the spectacle into drama of the infinitely huge, for it is this fusion that represents the total synthesis of life itself."[1] This passage serves as a departure point for my chapter on *molecular poetics* by posing a question of what it may mean to introduce "the infinite life of molecules into poetry." This desire may constitute a provocation to consider language not only as a human phenomenon, thus opening up the possibility that language is imbued within nonhuman materiality and that a kind of poetics may exist within the biosemiotic modes of communication among nonhuman organisms or even perhaps the textural configurations of how elements of matter interact at molecular or atomic scales.

Marinetti's provocation that poets must find a way "to introduce the infinite life of molecules into poetry" relies on a scalar understanding of the movement toward the molecular as the movement toward the minute, the particulate, or the microscopic. From this perspective, Marinetti's provocation can be said to push poetry toward expressing the "infinitesimally small" or the imperceptible realm that belongs to the Brownian "whiz of atoms" and molecules.[2] This movement toward the miniaturization of language or the shift away from syntax of the line or a sentence and toward the word as a semantic unit, and, eventually, the particulate element of the letter as a unit of composition, is formally evident in Marinetti's manifestoes and poetic texts. In the "Technical Manifesto of Futurist Literature," for instance, he writes that "only the poet who is detached from syntax and is in command of Words-in-Freedom will know how to penetrate the essence of matter." Marinetti views syntax as "a sort of interpreter or boring tour guide," which acts as a go-between or an "abstract codebook that allow[s] poets to inform the masses about the color, the musicality, the plasticity, and the architecture of the universe." The breakdown of syntax then becomes a condition that allows poetry to enter directly "into the cosmos and become . . . one with it."[3] In this context, the arc toward the miniaturization of language or the sense of language becoming molecular becomes synonymous with the assertion of a material continuity between language and other material phenomena that make up the universe.

Marinetti's interest in the relationship between language and matter carries a distinctively proto-posthumanist resonance,[4] as he asserts and reasserts his desire to get away from any attempt to humanize matter: "Instead of *humanizing* the animal, the vegetal, and the mineral (an outmoded system) we shall be able to *animalize, vegetalize, mineralize, electrify or liquefy style*, causing it to live something of the same life as matter itself."[5] Within the style of Words-in-Freedom, language and matter relate in a way that bypasses the axis of "the psychology of man" and "catches unawares the breathing, the sensibilities, and the instincts of metals, of stones, of wood," in other words, not the qualities of human feeling, but the different determining impulses of matter, "its compressive and its expansive forces, what binds it, what breaks it down, its mass of swarming molecules or its swirling electrons" (111). There is a parallel here between the dynamics of movement and the durations of relative persistence or instability that occur as words latch and unlatch along new configurations, freed from the constraints of syntax, and the manner in which molecular configurations of matter enter into swarming and swirling relations with one another. This indicates not only that language may be able to convey these dynamics of matter through its own grammatical rhythms or lexical textures, but that matter itself may possess a kind of poetics that plays out in its own parameters of force, relation, and textural particularity.

Whether the relationship between matter and language is approached from the perspective of how language conveys the dynamics of matter by becoming *animalized, vegetalized, mineralized, or liquefied*, or whether molecules themselves become a site of poetic intervention, there is a draw or a tendency in each case toward miniaturization of poetic substrates. At the same time, this draw toward miniaturization is somehow also revelatory or resonant with what Marinetti calls the "drama of the infinitely huge" (126). The span of scales, including the collapse of distance between the tiny scale of atoms and molecules and the vastness of the universe, occurs here, evoking a relation between cosmic phenomena and what appears when one parses the material world into smaller and smaller fragments. This pattern of the macrocosm folding into the microcosm or the microcosm ultimately opening out into the macrocosm appears on several occasions in *Poetics of Liveliness*. I locate it in reading Jen Bervin's interpretation of Emily Dickinson's Fragment A 636/636a in the introduction, and it certainly returns once again in Bervin's own work in *Silk Poems*, as well as in parallel conceptual inflections that come from the work of early microscopists, such as Robert Hooke, who discover a similar cosmological vastness in the tiny specks of matter they observed through the microscope, as they do in their observations of stars, planets, and moons through the lens of the telescope. One way to view the overall cosmological arc of *Poetics of Liveliness* is as a circular collapse of scales, which moves from the tiny worlds of molecules all the way to the vastness of atmospheric phenomena, even as such phenomena are ultimately just percolations of those same molecules, while the molecular worlds themselves, upon amplification, present whole complex topographies of shapes and surfaces of the cosmos.

The term *molecular poetics* appears in the work of the Canadian critic and poet Fred Wah, who, in his book of essays *Faking It*, suggests that Stein develops a molecular poetics by multiplying the productive possibilities of language. In reference to Stein's sentence in *Tender Buttons* "Roast potatoes for.," Wah writes that "Stein inserts the preposition 'for' into a syntactic and poetic site that suddenly multiplies its productive possibilities in at least five ways."[6] This moment is evocative of the anecdote Stein tells about reading while getting a haircut and using her glasses as a magnifying lens, so that she is reading for the *molecular* properties of words, passing across a defamiliarized landscape of language where words appear one by one as they slip and morph under this instrument of amplification. In response to Stein's attention to particulate qualities of individual words, Wah suggests that a molecular poetics is "a set of tools in writing that amplify the minute and particular, the discernment of cells in composition" (238).

As Wah's essay illustrates, this concern with the miniaturization of language or its molecular qualities passes from the work of modernist antecedents, such as Gertrude Stein and Marinetti, to be channeled into certain currents in the post-1945 poetic landscape. Canadian "Pataphysicians, for instance, cite both Stein and the Italian futurists as their influences, alongside Alfred Jarry.[7] The Canadian "Pataphysics movement is an offshoot of the resurgence of 'Pataphysics among midcentury French writers, including Raymond Queneau and Georges Perec, who were interested in using scientific procedures and methodologies in their artistic practices, inflecting them in the process with absurdity and playfulness. Christian Bök, whose poem *The Xenotext Experiment* forms the primary concern of this chapter, can be thought of as a second-generation Canadian "Pataphysician, as well as a literary critic and a theorist of 'Pataphysics. In his critical book *'Pataphysics: The Poetics of an Imaginary Science*, Bök constructs a genealogy that extends from Jarry's work to the Italian futurists, the French Oulipians, and the Canadian "Pataphysicians, explaining that 'Pataphysics is a science interested in the deviation from a deterministic course of events, as its focus is the singular or the particular.[8] Or, as Steve McCaffery, another Canadian poet, critic and "Pataphysician, who belongs to the initial, founding generation of the movement along with bp Nichol and Christopher Dewdney, writes in his essay "Zarathrustran 'Pataphysics," 'Pataphysics is not interested in generalization that would flatten all exceptions, but in the particularity or singularity that constitutes these exceptions. Pushing against the epistemological tendency of science to subsume the exceptional or simply locate it outside of the purvey of its methodologies of iterability, Bök sees 'Pataphysics as operating at the possible intersection between poetry and science as he argues that 'Pataphysics has had an extensive, if underresearched, influence on radical poetics, and that it "sets the parameters for the contemporary relationship between science and poetry."[9]

Bök's own experimentations with poetry and the epistemologies, instruments, and objects of science in his books *Crystallography* and *The Xenotext Experiment* clearly incorporate a 'Pataphysical dimension, which often manifests on a formal level as a result of his attention to how individual letters combine to form molecular structures, composed of several different varieties of atoms. As such, Bök's work is significant for an articulation of molecular poetics because it brings together, even in the early work of *Crystallography* and especially in *The Xenotext Experiment*, both trajectories that I am associating with molecular poetics—the increasing miniaturization of language and the actual exploration of molecular structures of matter as a site of poiesis. Considering once again the question of cosmic and molecular scales, it is significant to note that McCaffery has theorized the movement toward the miniaturization of language by linking Jarry's invention of 'Pataphysics, which is itself dependent on the atomism of Lucretius, with a kind of particulate logic in which atoms and letters become discrete and interchangeable units. In *Prior to Meaning: The Protosemantic and Poetics*, McCaffery develops the term *protosemantic* to conceptualize these movements toward miniaturization of language by engaging the semantic drift of language bellow the unit of the word: "In our age of incipient miniaturization, it might be apt to return to the rumble beneath the word. . . . Conceived as atoms, letters intrude themselves as protosemantic events strictly defined by their dynamics. Being perpetually and unpredictably volatile, they introduce deviance as the basic rule of all grammata." He draws on *De rerum natura* in order to formulate a parallel between the atomic constitution of matter and the sense that language functions as a permutation of letters constituted as a set of finite but differentiated elements:

> Atoms are to bodies what letters are to words: commonly heterogeneous, deviant, and combinatory particles. The implications of this analogy should not be underestimated. . . . Via Lucretius's analogy we can articulate the dynamics of physics onto the incalculable errancy of the graphic and thereby revision writing as a complex particle interaction organized in grammatical and syntactic flows by which the declination manifests as verbal or lettristic deviation.[10]

By following the implications of Lucretius's analogy between atoms and letters, McCaffery opens up the possibility of using physical properties of atomic interaction as a frame through which to examine the dynamic interactions of linguistic particles and flows. A parallel concern plays out here in the realm of both language and nonlinguistic materiality: How do the finite particulate elements that compose words, letters, or the particulate elements that compose matter, atoms and molecules, create the multifarious array that is the composition of the universe?

MATERIALIST POETICS

Such complex and long-standing traditions in materialist poetics are resonant with more recent and emerging conversations in the sciences and the theoretical humanities, which seek to uncover how semiotic processes may permeate even nonhuman material worlds. In this context, poetics, with its attunement to the material textures and qualities of language, can expand our understanding of what may constitute processes of signification. Starting with its emergence in the poetic genealogy that I have outlined above, I develop the formulation of *molecular poetics* in order to address how a materialist approach to poetics can theorize processes of signification that occur within and among the recalcitrant materialities of biological molecules, which act as signs through the minute and nuanced enfoldings of their three-dimensional forms as well as the nonmonumental temporalities of their interactions. In the wider theoretical context, a molecular poetics can be situated along a vertex of reorientation away from the sole consideration of language as a material site of signification, associated with the "linguistic turn," and toward a more complicated view in which linguistic and nonlinguistic forms of materiality mutually constrain one another in the enactment of the poem.

The contemporary refiguring of matter, including biological materiality, as itself possessing the possibilities for indeterminate, unforeseeable unfoldings, carries a special significance for feminist theory because it subverts a long-standing gendered alignment between the inert, essentialist qualities of matter and the feminine. As I mentioned previously in the chapter "Soft Matter," this gendered conception of matter can be traced all the way back to Plato's cosmological account in the *Timaeus*, where the chora or the receptacle acts as a site, coded as feminine, where shapeless and passive materiality is imbued with the contours of form, which carries a masculine valence. Aristotle and his explanation of embryological development in the *Generation of Animals* follows the same dualist pattern, one in which the motive force that gives form to the embryo is ascribed to the male, while the female contribution is seen as a passive material substrate into which form can be imbued. As Evelyn Fox Keller points out, this hylomorphic understanding of reproduction has been partially transposed onto the contemporary understandings of the gene, where the DNA is often transformed into an agentive, dematerialized, and transposable form of information, which shapes the surrounding soma of the cell. This hylomorphic position has been a subject of a long-standing feminist critique by philosophers including Karen Nielsen, Lynda Lange, and Charlotte Witt.[11] In one of the recent commentaries, *Feminine Symptom: Aleatory Matter in the Aristotelian Cosmos*, Emanuela Bianchi notes that even in Aristotle this relationship between form and materiality operates in a manner that complicates these gendered alignments between passivity and agency. Materiality, within the Aristotelian cosmology, for instance, possesses an aleatory quality, associated with the feminine, which often subverts the determinism inherent in conceptions of form as a process of teleological unfolding.

Many of these accounts of matter as a site of open-ended transformation, rather than passivity, fixity, and predetermined patterning, have provided a powerful antiessentialist intervention within feminist discourses, allowing questions of embodiment and biological materiality to be foregrounded in ways that were less accessible to the discursively grounded modes of critique that characterized the "linguistic turn." I would like to suggest that at times this much-needed intervention has come at a cost of failing to seriously consider that materiality and signification are complexly and perhaps irresolvably imbricated. As such, materialist accounts that have completely turned away from the linguistic in favor of the material risk reproducing a hidden dualism, one that reasserts the division of matter and meaning even as it claims to undo it. In *The Incorporeal: Ontology, Ethics, and the Limits of Materialism*, Elizabeth Grosz offers a critique of such "reductive materialisms" as limited in their ability to explain how matter may unfold along as yet undetermined trajectories or how thought may arise within the material, proposing instead not an ontological, and hence dualist, separation between the mind and the body, but an "intimate entwinement of the orders of materiality and ideality." In the midst of what Grosz diagnoses as emergence of various "so-called new materialism[s]," she calls for "a *new* new materialism," one in which ideality and materiality are mutually immanent and implicated in each other, and where what she calls the incorporeal "frame[s], orient[s], and direct[s] material things and processes," allowing them to open up to a "horizon of future possibilities" and to possess "possible meanings and directions that exceed their corporeality." Other thinkers within feminist science studies have similarly insisted on an indissoluble bind through which meaning and materiality inhere in one another, with Donna Haraway and Karen Barad developing terms such as *material-semiotic* and *material-discursive* as a way of working toward nondualist, situated understandings of material meaning-making and epistemology.

The feminist and often queer thinkers I discuss here have made a powerful intervention in how the relationship between materiality and ideality, and hence signification and matter, may be reconfigured in nondualist terms. In their insistence on semiosis, or what Grosz in broader terms calls the "fringe or force of the ideal inevitably surrounding and infiltrating, or even composing, matter,"[12] these theorists also offer a refinement in the current conversations about "new materialisms"— one that seeks to formulate a less reductive understanding of matter by acknowledging that materiality and language may be complexly and perhaps indissolubly entangled. The approach of molecular poetics that I develop here seeks to offer one possible further refinement in this conversation by elucidating how the powerful but as yet perhaps cloudy categories such as the incorporeal, material-discursive, or material-semiotic may operate within the specific example of living systems. In formulating a molecular poetics around the specificity of the three-dimensional shapes of biological molecules, including DNA and proteins as constitutive of the signifying processes that occur within the cell, my argument in this chapter attempts to walk along the same nondualist tightrope. Such emphasis on the shapes of molecules around which I formulate molecular poetics stems in part from resonances with contemporary research in molecular biology, which has emphasized not only the complex, nearly sculptural intricacies of protein-folding but also the three-dimensional genome architecture of the DNA as key for understanding how living processes unfold in situated, embodied ways that resist a hylomorphic sense of biological molecules as merely a form of storage for disembodied forms of information. At the same time, attending to such intricacies of molecular shapes is not only a matter of contemporary discoveries in the natural sciences. In this sense, as a concept, molecular poetics reaches also toward philosophical figures such as Lucretius, who writes about the variegated shapes and textures of atoms as constitutive of their capacity for interactions that produce different properties of matter.

Taking into account these understandings of the significance of the three-dimensional shapes of atoms and molecules, this chapter investigates how poetics, with its attunement to the linguistic dimension, can attend to liveliness of materiality in ways that do not compromise the capacity of poetry to consider the aesthetic dimensions of the textured sounds and shapes that language makes. As such, the current influx of theoretical considerations of nonhuman materialities in the humanities has found a fertile ground for considering the materiality of semiotic processes in the study of poetry and the emerging critical conversation that is unfolding within the subfield of materialist poetics. Within this critical landscape, this chapter develops the formulation of molecular poetics as a way of working toward an expanded sense of signification, one that includes the recalcitrant, folded materialities of molecules, whose shapes are responsive to the subtle changes in the shapes and electrical force fields of other molecules around them. Proteins, for instance, can be understood as such microsculptural shapes that carry signifying capacities in the intricacy and specificity of their folds, which often change just slightly in conformation as a protein molecule comes into contact with the electrical force field produced by the equally intricate folds of another molecule. Within the material-semiotic frame of molecular poetics, such molecules can be understood as signs that possess a nonarbitrary relation to the specific and dynamic materialities that constitute them. As such, they operate not through a kind of Saussurean logic of conventional alignment between the signifier and the signified or sign and matter, but rather through an inseparable and precise relation within which signification is imminent within materiality.

Located at the contact zone between the language of poetics and considerations of the biosemiotic dimension of biological materiality, *The Xenotext* provides an ideal case study for considering how material-semiotic enfoldings may complicate the sense that signs are latched to materiality only through an arbitrary set of relations. In creating *The Xenotext*, Bök encrypts a poem in a sequence of nucleotides that compose the DNA of a bacterium and then gets this microscopic organism to become a kind of "posthuman collaborator" in his project by producing a second poem in the molecular structure of a protein that is expressed on the basis of the inserted DNA sequence. The aesthetic qualities of Bök's "genetic text" are reliant on the sense that the molecular dynamics of a living organism are simultaneously a site of a lively form of biological materiality and an active site of signification. In other words, as Bök engages what he comes to describe as a "literary dimension" of biological molecular substrates, his poetic writing becomes molecular in its form. As a poet using the techniques of biotechnology to insert a "genetic text" into the DNA of bacteria, Bök is shifting the material possibilities of poetry by directly engaging the micropoetics of matter in a way that hybridizes poetry and bioart practices. He suggests that this kind of extension of poiesis to DNA will create a sense that the genome can now become a "vector" for heretofore unimagined modes of artistic innovation and cultural expression. As a result, in the future, genetics might lend a possible literary dimension to biology, granting "geneticists the power to become poets in the medium of life."[13]

Bök's work on *The Xenotext* has now been ongoing for over fifteen years (with the project receiving substantial funding from the Social Sciences and Humanities Research Council of Canada [SSHRC] in 2009), and over this span of time it has been documented in a number of ways, from various interviews, to an article in a top-tier scientific journal, *Nature*, to an art exhibition at the Bury Art Gallery in Manchester.[14] In 2015 the Canadian press Coach House Books published *The*

Xenotext: Book 1, to be followed by volume 2, which promises to document the unfolding of the laboratory work on the poem in greater detail, once it is complete. The poem that was inserted into bacterial DNA at the University of Calgary's Institute for Biocomplexity and Informatics (IBI) does not appear directly in the volume that has been printed so far, but many of the poems that do make up the book can be thought of as paratextual documents that record the process of the composition of the genetic poem in the lab.[15] In the concluding section of the book, Bök briefly describes the details of the experimental protocol he has developed to generate the poetic text of *The Xenotext*, suggesting that the reader can think of the printed text as both a "genetic primer," whose role is to reacquaint "the reader with some basic idea of genetics," and an "infernal grimoire," a kind of book of magic spells or invocations, which introduces "the concepts for this experiment."[16]

As a "primer on genetics," *The Xenotext: Book 1* elucidates the procedures undertaken in the lab to bring the book to fruition, while simultaneously performing alternate textual experiments that explore various constraint-based compositional methods. As such, *The Xenotext* is firmly situated in the constraint-based practices of 'Pataphysics, Oulipo, and, most recently, conceptual poetry, and, initially, in an informational understanding of DNA as a code, which can be abstracted and transposed from one biological context to another without paying much attention to the specificity and three-dimensionality of biological molecular substrates. As I discuss in chapter 2, the use of constraint in Bök's poetic practice is nothing new. His book of poetry *Eunoia* is divided into five discrete sections, each of which uses only words that contain only one of the vowels available in the English language. In *Crystallography*, these problematics of constraint are coupled with a consideration of the molecular structure of various crystals. For instance, in the poem "Opal," Bök recreates the atomic structure of opal in the form of an acrostic. (See figure 3.1.) The chemical composition of opal consists of a silicon atom, two oxygen atoms, and a molecule of water, which itself contains an oxygen and two hydrogen atoms. Its chemical formula, then, is $SiO_2 \cdot nH_2O$. The poem "Opal" thus re-creates the chemical composition of opal by naming the atomic elements that compose this crystal and arranging

OPAL

```
        H
S       Y
I   H Y D R O G E N
L       R
I   O   O X Y G E N
C   X   G
O X Y G E N
N   G   N
        E
        N
```

FIGURE 3.1 Christian Bök, "Opal," from *Crystallography* (Toronto: Coach House, 1994).

them in an acrostic structure. While Bök's engagement with actual configurations of living matter in the course of composing *The Xenotext Experiment* appears as a radical departure from his previous textually based compositional process, I would like to suggest that these diverse poetic practices share many continuities with one another, because they are both concerned with developing a poetics that is reliant on the relationship between code and shape, or, in broader terms, the relationship between materiality and semiosis.[17] I would argue, however, that Bök's understanding of constraint-based poetic practices transforms and expands in the course of working on *The Xenotext*, in order to encompass not only the arbitrary constraints, imposed by the understandings of DNA as a sequential code of nucleotides or the sense of protein as a linear string of amino acids, but also the nonarbitrary constraints, imposed by the biomaterial properties of proteins as three-dimensional molecular shapes, which can fold in a limited number of ways. My argument traces how this hylomorphic trajectory of the project changes as Bök's lab experiment progresses, and he encounters the challenge of producing the intricate structures of protein molecules, with their complex and specific folding topographies, which operate not through arbitrary constraints of transposable, disembodied codes, but through a specifically constrained recalcitrance of material configurations. As such, as the arc of *The Xenotext* develops from the insertion of an enciphered poem into the DNA of bacteria to the expression of the protein molecule by the organism, the very notion of constraint is transformed from a relatively arbitrary set of rules governing the relationship between the letters of the alphabet and the sequence of nucleotides that compose DNA to a sense of constraint governed by the specific folding topographies of protein molecules.

FROM CODE TO SHAPE

Initially Bök's poem is reliant for its method of encryption on the conceptualization of DNA as a code made up of four letters that are assigned to the four different nucleic acids that make up each of the strands of the double helix of the DNA molecule. The four letters stand for adenine (A), thymine (T), cytosine (C), and guanine (G). Each three-letter combination made up of three nucleotide bases is called a DNA codon, and it corresponds to one amino acid molecule—so, for instance, the codon TTC corresponds to phenylalanine. As Bök assigns a codon of DNA to each letter of the alphabet, the complementary amino acid gets assigned to a letter of the alphabet in the second protein poem. But there is an intermediate step. For a DNA sequence to be translated into a sequence of amino acids in the living cell, it first has to be transcribed into an mRNA transcript. The mRNA is a kind of complementary base-pair copy of the DNA sequence, composed of the same nucleotide sequences of letters except for the substitution of uracil for thymine. Figuratively, the mRNA can be conceptualized as a reverse-mirror image "photocopy" that is made from a select "book" or gene in the "library of the DNA" that the cell is currently using. Complementary base pairing is the cell's way of making such mirror-image reverse copies, and it involves the pairing of adenine with thymine or uracil, and the pairing of guanine with cytosine. In figure 3.2, the mRNA sequence is represented as the black letter sequence in the bottom part of the image—the AGG codon of DNA, for instance, produces the UCC sequence in the mRNA. In turn, this mRNA sequence is responsible for selecting the corresponding amino acid—and in this case, within Bök's cipher, the amino acid must be arginine—which he has assigned to the letter T. Thus A and T always correspond to each other, as do S and F. The coding process in question is called encipherment because it involves pairing off each letter of the alphabet with another so that they are mutually correlated with each other—as in S correlates with F, F correlates with S, and so on. Bök then uses one of these ciphers to write the first poem, and as each letter is replaced with a complementary letter from the cipher, it has to produce the corresponding amino acid poem.

The text of the first poem, dubbed "Orpheus," consists of the line "ANY STYLE OF LIFE IS PRIM" and is encoded by Bök into the nucleotide sequence of the DNA, while the complementary protein poem "Eurydice" is composed of a sequence of amino acids and states: "THE FAERY IS ROSY OF GLOW." The content of this second poem actually refers to the fluorescent tag that Bök has added to his gene construct, which will get converted into a protein that fluoresces when the poem is expressed, thus indicating that the experiment has worked. This is a technique commonly used by molecular biologists, and one can think of it as a kind of genetic Post-it Note, in which the fluorescence of the

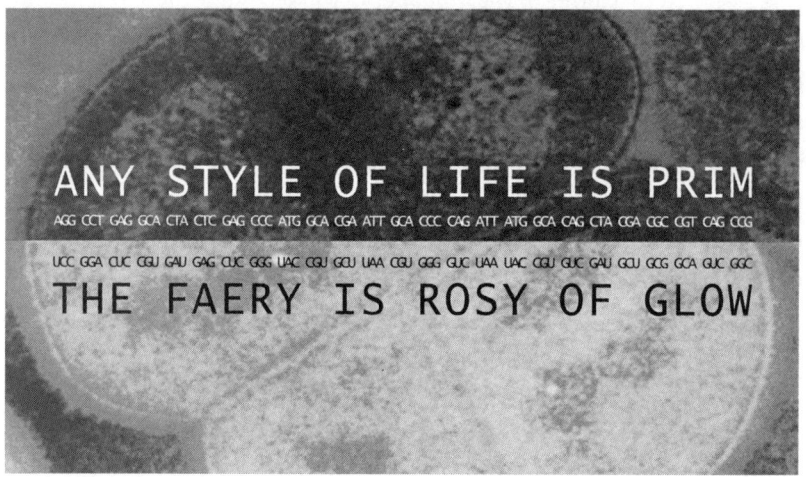

FIGURE 3.2 Christian Bök, "Orpheus" and "Eurydice," from *The Xenotext Experiment*. The Triple Helix Online: A Global Forum for Science in Society, January 8, 2014. Credit: Alexander B. Kim.

protein acts as an indexical sign to indicate that the gene construct has been correctly inserted.

In an interview in the online magazine *CultureLab*, Bök describes the DNA poem as "a very masculine assertion about the aesthetic creation of life." In contrast, Bök describes the tone of the second poem as "melancholy, feminine—almost surreal."[18] His rather surprising use of gender in the descriptions of these two poems aligns with the gendering effects in the history of biology, which have rendered the cytoplasm of the cell, where the majority of the proteins are found and where the proteins are synthetized, as the "feminine sphere" of the cell, while the nucleus, where the genes are housed, at least in eukaryotic cells, assumes the qualities of the "masculine arena." In spatializing gender within the cell in this way, *The Xenotext* can be read in relation to the long-intertwined histories of heredity and biological development, out of which the science of modern genetics emerged. In *A Cultural History of Heredity*, Staffan Müller-Wille and Hans-Jörg Rheinberger point out that "development and inheritance were not seen as two distinct, autonomous processes" until the rise of modern biology in the nineteenth century, or even "as late as the beginning of the twentieth century, when genetics established itself as a discipline." This meant that understandings of how heritable qualities could be passed on from parents to offspring were irresolvably entangled with "the series of circumstances that accompanied copulation, conception, pregnancy, birth, and even weaning in mammals," and, as a result, the various, oscillating histories of how gender was seen to play a role in these processes influenced the understandings of gender in the context of heredity.[19]

Writing precisely about the understandings of maternal and paternal contributions to reproduction in the history of biology, Keller addresses the work of the geneticist Ruth Sager, who studied the effects of maternal or cytoplasmic inheritance in the single-celled protist *Chlamydomonas*. Keller notes that even though Sager tried to relabel the term *maternal inheritance* with the term *uni-parental inheritance*, her colleagues "derisively referred to her work as 'Ruth's defense of the egg.'" Keller situates this particular remark in a wider history, which has typically attributed the locus of activity to the nucleus and aligned it with paternal contributions, while relegating the cytoplasm to the role of a passive environment, in which the activity of the nucleus plays out:

> Thus many debates about the relative importance of nucleus and cytoplasm in inheritance inevitably reflect older debates about the relative importance (or activity) of maternal and paternal contributions to reproduction, where the overwhelming historical tendency has been to attribute activity and motive force to the male contribution while relegating the female contribution to the role of passive, facilitating environment. In Platonic terms, the egg represented the body and the nucleus the activating soul.[20]

While contemporary understandings of reproduction, where both the sperm and the egg contribute genetic material, have displaced these historical understandings of what happens during fertilization, the dualist tendency itself has been erroneously transposed onto the relationship between the DNA and cytoplasm to produce what Keller critically calls the "gene-centric" perspective, where genes are understood to be the central controlling agents programming and informing the functioning of the other cellular components. As such, this "gene-centric" tendency within contemporary biology shares a historical genealogy with the hylomorphic logic through which materiality and semiosis are seen as distinct in gendered terms.

In his explorations of the aesthetic potential of genetics in *The Xenotext Experiment*, Bök at first uncritically imports these dualist assumptions, which distinguish the genes as disembodied carriers of information from the materiality of the cytoplasm, which acts as a site of their "expression." The conceptualization of DNA as textual information has been a subject of a long-standing critique among researchers in science and technology studies. In her book *The Poetics of DNA*, Judith Roof takes up the question of the relationship between language and DNA by examining "various analogies, metaphors, and other figurations" that have configured DNA as a language that is at the core of "all life." She suggests that as the metaphors such as those of "the code, the book, the alphabet, sentences, words, . . . blueprint, the text, the map, the homunculus, software, and others" are used to describe DNA, a certain sense of it as a materially situated biological molecule is elided.[21] Roof's critique is particularly significant in that it points to a risk of a hylomorphic split between information and materiality, one in which codes can easily become detached from the material substrates that bind them to specific circumstances of embodiment. Müller-Wille and Rheinberger point out that the understanding of heredity as a form of information, figured through a number of concomitant textual metaphors, arose specifically in the context of the twentieth century with the rise of molecular biology and the discernment of DNA as the material substrate of heredity: "The textual metaphors that accompanied the rise of molecular biology now came to be materialized in these technologies: reading as DNA analysis; writing as DNA synthesis; copying as the polymerase chain reaction; and editing as procedures for mutating genes." As such, heredity came to be conceived not "as the transmission of bodily characters, but as an information system, as a semiotic universe in its own right."[22]

THE VAGARIES OF INTERSPECIES COLLABORATION, OR "THE BACTERIA ATE MY POEM"

The majority of bioart projects that Bök references as an art-historical context for the creation of *The Xenotext* rely precisely on this kind of conceptualization of DNA as information,[23] thus risking the same hylomorphic logic in which information is dualistically split from materiality that Müller-Wille, Rheinberger, Roof, and Keller identify in their critique. One project that Bök cites as the inspiration for *The Xenotext* is the encoding of a line from Book 2 of Virgil's *Georgics* into the genome of a plant known as thale cress or *Arabidopsis thaliana*, so that the DNA of the plant now contains the encoded Latin line "*Nec vero terræ ferre omnes omnia possunt* ('Nor can the earth bring forth all fruit alike . . .')."[24] To deal with the possible deterioration of the message due to mutation, the scientists working on this experiment proposed making duplicate copies of this line at multiple locations within the genome. Bök is explicit about the influence of such earlier projects for his own genetic poem, thus situating *The Xenotext* within a longer history of research in genetics that has attempted to configure living organisms as infinitely reproducible bioarchival repositories: "Many scientists have already encoded textual information into genetic nucleotides, thereby creating 'messages' made from DNA," Bök writes. Such DNA messages could theoretically persist as "data," encoded inside of the genes, "undamaged and unaltered, through myriad cycles of mitosis, all the while saved for recovery and decoding" (150).

However, actually getting a living organism to replicate over many generations without the incremental changes caused by processes such as mutation has proven challenging to execute in practice, because living organisms are dynamic, lively entities, which are continuously undergoing change and transformation, even if these processes are occurring very gradually at rhythms that are not always perceptible to humans. Bök's selection of his ultimate target host organism for *The Xenotext*, the bacterium *Deinococcus radiodurans*, has been an attempt to address this problem of gradual change that seems to undermine the possibility of using living organisms to permanently archive information. According to Bök, *Deinococcus radiodurans* is particularly suitable for thinking about the longevity of such archival inscription procedures because it is "an extremophile, capable of surviving, without mutation, in even the most hostile milieus, including the vacuum of outer space."[25] As an extremophile bacterium, *D. radiodurans* is quite resilient to radiation and desiccation, maintaining relative genetic stability even under these conditions. Bök's desire to use *D. radiodurans* as the ultimate host for *The Xenotext* is also inspired in part by the fact that scientists have already attempted to use the genome of this organism to store information. In 2003 scientists inserted the song "It's a Small World" as a 150-base pair long DNA segment into the genome of this bacterium and were able to retrieve it and decode it one hundred generations later without alteration. One snag in this bio-archival experiment has been the fact that only a limited amount of information can be stored in each bacterium, so that several distinct species of *D. radiodurans* had to be created, and, as the experiment unfolded, some of these were more likely to emerge as dominant, while others would go extinct, taking the portion of the message they contained with them into the oblivion.

A significant difference between these experiments and *The Xenotext* consists in the fact that the scientists working on inserting a line of the *Georgics* into the genome of *Arabidopsis thaliana* or those attempting to "archive" the lyrics of a song in the genome of *D. radiodurans* are explicit about the fact that the encoded line of text they are inserting into the DNA sequence "does not contain information expressed by the organism."[26] In other words, for them, the genome of this plant is simply a repository or a form of storage for the information, while Bök's insistence on producing two poetic sites in *The Xenotext*, one based on the inserted DNA sequence and the other on the protein produced as this sequence is expressed, enters into a much more complex relation with the dynamics enacted by the somatic unfolding of the organism in question. It is this aspect of Bök's poem, where the organism itself is supposed to express the DNA sequence into a shape of a protein that will persist for some time in the cell without getting digested, that has proven to be the most difficult to realize. As such, the difficulties that Bök encounters in the execution of *The Xenotext* inadvertently reveal that the hylomorphic conception of biological molecules as simply repositories for information that many bioart projects rely on does not correspond to the much more intricately configured material-semiotic operations of living systems. While the creation of the protein poem has been successfully executed in another bacterium, *Escherichia coli*, which is commonly used as a model organism in molecular biology but lacks the tendency toward immutability that Bök is seeking, after fifteen years of effort Bök has not yet been able to execute this aspect of the project in his intended experimental organism, the extremophile bacterium *D. radiodurans*. To succeed, he would have to "design a genetic sequence so that the resulting protein can fold viably and then persist detectably within the cell," but because of the complexities inherent in protein folding, each time the protein poem is created, the bacterium simply recognizes it as a molecule that does not belong and eats it.[27]

The framing narrative of the myth of Orpheus and Eurydice that Bök draws on through his translation of Virgil's *Georgics* in the textual version of the poem, *The Xenotext: Book 1*, can be read as a form of commentary on the vagaries of attempting to get the protein poem to express correctly in the laboratory. The naming of the protein poem "Eurydice" is evocative of the sense of loss that is brought about by the repeated disappearance of the protein poem, which echoes the iterative sense of loss that cuts through the narrative of Orpheus and Eurydice. The double loss of Eurydice is caused in the first case by the attempted rape by Aristeaus, which leaves her vulnerable to a snakebite and leads to her death, and in its second iteration it is a result of Orpheus's famous attempt to rescue her from the underworld, which is blighted by his impatient and forbidden look back, dooming her once again. Entwined with the double loss of Eurydice is the disappearance of Aristaeus's bees, which occurs in the *Georgics* as a punishment for his attempted rape.

The disappearance of the bees redoubles as an echo of loss once again, because of the contemporary conditions of environmental degradation, which have brought about a decline in bee populations known as Colony Collapse Disorder—which serves as a kind of portent of the telos of environmental catastrophe in Bök's poem.[28] Naming the protein poem "Eurydice" is suggestive of the sense that the execution of this poem has nearly come within Bök's grasp but has so far eluded him by repeatedly disappearing, thwarting his conceptual goals for the creation of a poem that will last forever, "outliv[ing] every civilization, persisting on the planet until the very last dawn, when our star finally explodes."[29] This "loss" or dissolution of the poem is obliquely thematized in the concluding poem of "The Colony Collapse Disorder" sequence, which also includes Bök's translation of Book 4 of the *Georgics*:

> The Poet forsakes every word in trade
> for such favor—but like pollen fallen
> upon a pale rose, forlorn in the shade,
> his cantos bring scant life to her garden.
>
> She listens, but the lament that he sings
> dissolves in the cells of all living things.[30]

In a sense, these lines serve as a double lament, implicitly recalling the irrecoverable loss of Eurydice and also the repeated loss of the protein poem, with its pale rose glow, produced by the fluorescent molecular tag attached to it, which has dissolved over and over again inside of the bacterial cells where it has been expressed.

While the framing narrative of the myth of Orpheus and Eurydice has allowed Bök to comment on the implicit failure of getting the protein poem to persist as a correctly folded shape in the bacterial cell at least at this stage in the project, in several interviews he has expressed a deep sense of dissatisfaction with this aspect of the project's execution, avowing to endure in his efforts and refusing to recuperate this sense of failure within the conceptual parameters of the project: "The failure of the ski-jumper who crashes, after flying off the ski-jump is far more interesting to an audience than it ever might be to the skier," Bök writes in an interview in the online magazine *Divedapper*. "I am doing my best not to fail. To me, failure is not very interesting."[31] In contrast, as my reading of *The Xenotext* through the framework of *molecular poetics* suggests, this moment of failure makes a significant conceptual contribution to Bök's poetic project because it brings to the forefront the sense that code is not free floating and disembodied, but that living organisms are material-semiotic folds. In other words, the snag or the difficulty that Bök encounters in the execution of *The Xenotext* plays an important role in the interpretation of the project, shifting the impetus from the smooth figuration of the DNA as information, and hence as an unproblematic archival repository of textual data, to the problematics of molecules as folded shapes that carry biosemiotic significance through their interactions. Such interactions often involve shifts in conformation or shape, which can be understood as tiny alterations in their folds, and which, in turn, take place within the variegated rhythms of somatic and genetic, and hence lived, temporalities. By creating a differentiated set of less essentializing biological rhythms, such lively, nonmonumental temporalities offer an oppositional pull in relation to Bök's desire to create an eternal artwork that would survive ecological catastrophe.[32] Moreover, such nonhuman temporal rhythms open up the space for considering the biosemiotic relevance of specific molecules from the perspective of another organism, in this case the bacterium *D. radiodurans*. This transforms the parameters of constraint in the project from permutations of codes assigned in an arbitrary fashion to particular molecules by human signification systems to a sense of the folded topographies of the molecules—as themselves carriers of significance for the bacterium—which selects the ones that signify within its cell, while digesting others that it perceives as misfolded. Furthermore, the temporalities that this organism operates within have a microgranularity that may not clearly correspond to a human sense of time, and certainly not to the teleological sense of immutable time that Bök is anthropocentrically projecting onto the future of the planet, when he imagines *The Xenotext* as an archival project that could survive environmental apocalypse.

Bök's project is most vulnerable to the critique of hylomorphism when he engages in arbitrarily assigning letters of the alphabet to certain molecular structures. In the poem "The Genetic Code," which appears as part of a longer sequence of *The Xenotext* titled "The March of the Nucleotides," Bök describes his reliance on the conceptualization of the genetic code as "a limited lexicon, consisting of sixty-four 'words' called *codons*, created by permuting all possible trigrams (4^3) from a set of nucleobases in RNA (A, C, G, and U)" (96). Bök explicitly follows up on this textual or linguistic understanding of the codon as word in "The Central Dogma," where he explains that "a set of three consecutive bases in a strand makes a *codon*—a 'word' that can instruct a cell to create one of the twenty amino acids found in all proteins" (78). Each of these codons, in Bök's words, "signifies" a specific amino acid, although the code contains redundancy in that an amino acid can have multiple codons that refer to it, so that, for example, there exist six "'synonyms' for arginine: AGA, AGG, CGA, CGC, CGG, and CGU—but each one refers only to this molecule" (96). Bök explains that this "code is virtually universal" and that "no word used to create anything alive needs to be longer than three letters" (154). In composing the suite of poems titled "The Nucleobases," Bök relies on such arbitrary or conventional assignment of particular letters of the alphabet to particular molecules to create a series of "modular acrostic[s], in which the structure of a molecule defines the arrangement of a restricted vocabulary—only words of nine letters, beginning with one of the following: C (for carbon), H (for hydrogen), N (for nitrogen), or O (for oxygen)" (154). The resulting poems are formally continuous with many of the poems that appear in *Crystallography*, in that both draw on the atomic composition of molecules to restrict their possible lexicons. In the poem "Cytosine," for instance, Bök takes the molecular formula of the nucleotide cytosine ($C_4H_5N_3O$), which is comprised of four carbon atoms, five hydrogen atoms, three nitrogen atoms, and one oxygen atom, and composes an acrostic, which uses all these elements in its composition the appropriate number of times so that the resulting poem textually replicates the same numbers of specific atoms that also occur in the molecule itself. (See figure 3.3.) On the facing page Bök presents a schematic image of cytosine's molecular structure as it would be annotated in organic chemistry, with a characteristic shape of an aromatic carbon ring and an amine group composed of nitrogen and hydrogen, as well as a keto group consisting of a doubly bonded oxygen atom. Below this image Bök composes a short poem that is constrained in such a way that each of the words begins with the same letter as one of the atoms that composes the cytosine molecule, so that there are four words that begin with the letter *c* (cultivate, chrysalid, cloisters, culturing), five that begin with the letter *h* (heedfully, husbanded, hereafter, helotries), three words that begin with the letter *n* (nymphlike, nunneries, necropoli), and one word that begins with the letter *o* (orgiastic). The thematic material for the poem references back to the earlier "Colony Collapse Disorder" sequence and in particular the bees, which appear (and disappear) in Book 4 of Virgil's *Georgics,* so that the poem reads in sequential order as "nymphlike, honeybees[33] / cultivate orgiastic / nunneries, / chrysalid necropoli, heedfully husbanded— / cloisters, hereafter / culturing helotries."[34]

Even though, in composing "The Nucleobases," Bök is at times clearly quite attentive to the three-dimensional shapes of biological molecules, drawing on the various resources of concrete and visual poetry in order to represent them, the formal patterning of the poem is still reliant primarily on a constraint-based practice, which draws its limitations from the letters that begin the names of the elements that compose the molecular structures of specific nucleotides. As such, there is a kind of arbitrary or primarily conventional alignment here between language and materiality. In other words, signs operate through a kind of Saussurean logic, which does not produce any inherent link between names and the molecules that they designate, so that the poetic constraint-based procedural play that Bök is engendering here operates primarily within the register of language, rather than the actual molecular structures of the nucleotides. One way that the form of the poem does entangle itself more deeply with the structure of the nucleotides occurs through the patterning and repetition of sounds in that the repetition of words that

Cytosine

```
                    H
              H Y D R O G E N
                    D
              C A R B O N
              A   O
          H Y D R O G E N
          Y       B   E   I
          D       O   N I T R O G E N
      C A R B O N         R
      A   O                O
  H Y D R O G E N   O X Y G E N
      B   E                E
      O   N I T R O G E N
      N
```

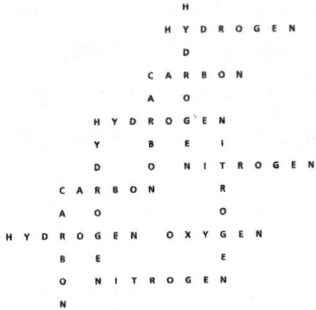

---

nymphlike, honeybees
cultivate orgiastic
nunneries,
chrysalid necropoli, heedfully husbanded –
cloisters, hereafter
culturing helotries

Cytosine ($C_4H_5N_3O$)

FIGURE 3.3 Christian Bök, "Cytosine," from *The Xenotext: Book 1* (Toronto: Coach House, 2015).

begin with the letter *n*—nymphlike, nunneries, necropoli—in the case of the "Cytosine" poem is indicative of the number of times that an atom of nitrogen appears in the molecular structure of cytosine. Similarly, in composing the poem "Adenine," Bök uses five words that begin with the letter *n*—nurturant, nursemaid, nectarous, narcotics, numbingly—because the nucleotide adenine has five nitrogen atoms. As such, the formal properties of poetic structure generated through alliteration register the patterning of molecular structure. Bök employs this formal patterning to an even more interesting effect when it comes to the poem "The Virelay of the Amino Acids," in which, as he explains in "Vita Explicata," "the arrangement of words in a line corresponds to a specified structure in each molecule, and wherever this structure recurs among the molecules, so also does the line of poetry recur among the acrostics" (156). For instance, all the amino acids share a common backbone, composed of "a complex of amine (-NH_2) and carboxylic acid (-COOH)," and as a result, Bök explains, "every poem in the suite ends with the same refrain: (*no hummingbirds have / copied our opulent hymns*)" (156). Other lines repeat as well, so that the line "nursemaids, held hostage," appears in the poems for both Asparagine and Arginine because both of these molecules share the H_2N amino group. As such, the patterns of repetition and variation that shape the poem register the molecular repetitions and variations that structure the amino acids as building blocks of proteins, and as a result, the poetic form is indicative of molecular structure.[35]

LUCRETIAN TEXTURES: 3D RECOMBINATIONS OF LETTERS AND ATOMS

Much of *The Xenotext* is structured through an analogy between the letters of the alphabet and specific atoms, so that the molecular permutations the poem depicts play out in a parallel, formally constrained poetic space, where choices in diction, as well as sound patterns, such as alliteration, allow Bök to register elements of molecular structure and interaction. The parallel that Bök posits between the discrete and recombinable properties of the letters of the alphabet and the conceptualization of atoms as similarly discrete and recombinable particles is evocative of the aforementioned analogy between atoms and letters that is described by Lucretius and that comes to inform McCaffery's notion of the protosemantic and, more broadly, the whole larger tradition of materialist poetics I am delineating in this chapter: "It makes a great difference in what combinations and positions the same elements occur and what motions they mutually pass on and take over, so that with a little reshuffling the same ones may produce forests and fires? This is just how the words themselves are formed, by a little reshuffling of the letters, when we pronounce 'forests' and 'fires' as two distinct utterances."[36] Through this comparison between "forests" and "fires," Lucretius posits an overlap between linguistic and material registers, indicating that a different arrangement of atoms constitutes, for instance, a forest and a forest fire, while a slight rearrangement and addition or subtraction of letters produces the words "forests" and "fires."[37] In other words, for Lucretius the composition, whether of the material world or of language, is a matter of such particulate recombinations, so that in both cases a finite number of variable shapes can recombine to form everything that constitutes the cosmos. Thus language and matter operate in a parallel manner, creating change and differentiation of forms through shifts in "combination, motion, order, position or shapes of the component" elements, whether they be letters or atoms.[38]

It is not surprising that Bök models his compositional practice in part on the analogy between letters and atoms that is offered in *De rerum natura*, considering that Lucretius is a key source for the 'Pataphysical literary tradition. As I have illustrated, many of the poems that Bök constructs in *The Xenotext: Book 1* rely on such 'Pataphysical strategies of realignment of discrete, particulate elements, where the recombinations of the letters on the page can be used to model the patterns and movements of matter. This logic of creating analogous relations between letters and atoms carries the same arbitrary quality that I have been identifying as inadequately concerned with the imbricated alignment of signification and materiality. The same arbitrary logic governs many of the strategies that Bök employs in the lab in enciphering the poem into the structure of the DNA—in that, as I have elaborated earlier, he simply assigns a letter of the alphabet to a particular DNA codon and then, through encipherment, assigns another letter of the alphabet to the corresponding amino acid. The difficulty here lies primarily in this double layer of code and the challenge this double constraint poses for producing two cogent lines of poetic text. The approach, in this iteration, still retains an arbitrary nature in that the letters of the alphabet hold a kind of random, albeit constrained, position in how they are assigned to the DNA codons or the amino acids. But this logic begins to shift once Bök starts to consider the structure of the protein molecule that is formed on the basis of the DNA sequence. In other words, in this transition the poem becomes involved with the problematic of shape or the question of how a protein can fold into a viable three-dimensional molecule, rather than remaining solely concerned with the sequence information of how the nucleotides or the corresponding amino acids are strung together into a linear code.

A parallel shift occurs in Lucretius's thinking when he considers textures and shapes of atoms and how these three-dimensional aspects of their structure condition the interactions and sensations they are able to produce. At these moments, Lucretius moves outside the framework of dualist configurations of an analogous relationship between letters and atoms to a comprehensively materialist framework within which even figurative structures, such as analogy and metaphor, are continuous with movements and unfoldings of matter. Within this materialist framework, it is both the textures and shapes of the particulate elements of matter, as well as the sense of how dense or rare, attenuated or flimsy a particular form of materiality is, that condition its possibilities for interaction. Lucretius suggests that the surfaces of the atoms are covered with minute hooks or latches, which intertangle with one another in different ways, forming degrees of different strengths of attachment. In the Latin original, the word for this property of atoms, which describes them as possessing hooks or latches, is *hamatis*, which means barbed. It is the degree to which the atoms are barbed, as well as their shape and texture, that lead them to form substances of different densities or viscosities. The atoms of hard substances, for instance, diamond or iron, are formed of "deeply indented and hooked atoms" that are held firmly by their intertangled branches, which latch them to one another.[39] These textural properties of atoms are linked to the kinds of sensations they can produce, because, according to Lucretius, the process of sensation, regardless of its specific modality, is inherently tactile and involves an interaction between varying atomic textures, so that honey and milk, which generate sweet sensations, are composed of "smooth round atoms," for instance, and the harsh, bitter taste of wormwood and centaury are a result of the rough "tightly compacted . . . hooked particles."[40] This model of sensation expands beyond the very textures of atoms to include Lucretius's broader theory that sensations are evoked as very thin films fly off the surfaces of objects and strike the senses, so that, for instance, vision arises as such films come in contact with the eye, conveying the shapes of objects just in very attenuated form.

An emphasis on the significance of molecular shapes and textures has also been a part of a prominent shift in thinking that is taking place in contemporary research in molecular biology, where understandings of biosemiotic frameworks of molecular signaling and interaction are stretching away from sole considerations of codes as disembodied forms of biological information. The studies that have assessed the impact of the mapping of the sequence of the human genome since its completion nearly two decades ago have emphasized the importance of the three-dimensional structure of the DNA and its sculptural molecular form for understanding the way that DNA interacts with other molecules. In an article titled "Genomics: Genomes in Three Dimensions," published in *Nature* in February 2011, Monya Baker offers a review of the recent research into the significance of the three-dimensional genome architecture for the regulation of gene activity. One of the researchers Baker cites, Wouter de Laat, a genome biologist at the Hubrecht Institute in Utrecht in the Netherlands, suggests that understanding gene regulation involves understanding the structure of the complex assemblage of DNA and proteins that make up the chromosomes: "There are many more sites with regulatory potential than we have genes, and the only way to know which site is acting on which gene is to get three-dimensional."[41] This emerging trend in biological research indicates that the way DNA operates in living cells must include the poetics of interaction between different three-dimensional shapes and not only the textual poetics of codes. Bök's decision to include a second poetic site in *The Xenotext* in the form of the protein molecule reflects this shift away from the dogma of "gene-centrism" in molecular biology, with its insistence that the DNA acts as a primary site of agency programming the operations of the rest of the cell, to a sense that the three-dimensional shapes of a variety of molecules are at play in signaling pathways and cellular processes. As such, in his struggle to realize *The Xenotext* project, Bök actually creates a poetic experiment that powerfully embodies the dynamics of this paradigm shift in biological research itself.

Proteins are folded shapes, often made up of a number of complex subunits, and their bioactivity is contingent on the shifting shape of these subunits in relation to one another and in response to the shapes and electrical force fields of the molecules that interact with and bind to them. I am interested specifically in how Bök's project explores the three-dimensional nature of these interactions in the extension of the practices of micropoetics to the surfaces, shapes, and textures that affect the active interplay of matter even at this minute molecular scale. In the opening section of "The March of the Nucleotides," the poem "The Central Dogma," Bök describes in detail the process of protein folding that occurs once the amino acids have been strung together by the ribosome:

> The ribosome builds a string of such amino acids, until encountering a codon that signifies the punctuation of a full stop—and because each acid has its own unique charge, parts of the created protein become either hydrophilic or hydrophobic when exposed to the solvent in the cytoplasm of the cell. The forces of both mutual attraction and mutual repellency, distributed among the acids in the chain, cause the strand to fold and bend, torqueing the protein into a conformation that requires the lowest amount of energy to sustain. The surface contour of such a folded strand determines the biochemical interaction that the protein can finally perform with other enzymes in the cell.[42]

It is in considering the properties of protein folding that Bök's analysis departs from the conceptualization of a linear sequence of amino acids, which figuratively appear as beads strung together into a strand of a necklace, and opens out to a consideration of a three-dimensional topography of the protein surface, which forms as the charges enveloping the molecule cause it to torque, bend, and fold until it settles into a particular shape.[43]

In the concluding sections of "The March of the Nucleotides," Bök draws on protein modeling software that he used in the lab to model the proteins that would arise from a particular sequence of DNA in order to create protein "translations" of specific lines of text.[44] In "Death Sets a Thing Significant," for instance, Bök takes the title from a poem by Emily Dickinson and uses it as a lipogram on the basis of which a computer generates an image of a protein shape that would arise if the letters were fed to it as though they were the letters that designate specific amino acids. As there are only twenty amino acids with their corresponding letter designations, this means that the constraint for the lipogram would be to use only the following subset of the alphabet—(A, C, D, E, F, G, H, I, K, L, M, N, P, Q, R, S, T, V, W, Y)—with "each letter indicat[ing] a specific molecule: D (for aspartic acid), E (for glutamic acid), A (for alanine), T (for threonine), H (for histidine)," and so on (155). One could describe this process as a kind of translation in which a text is converted into the molecular structure of a protein. In other words, language is translated into the materiality of molecular form. In his description of the method through which the poem is created, Bök suggests that the poem is engaged in a translation that parallels the process of translation from DNA into protein that occurs inside of the living cell: "A supercomputer has simulated atomic models for the structure of this protein after a few femtoseconds of coiling and bending. The images depict not only the folded sequence and its atomic backbone, but also the entire molecule and its charge envelope. The poems thus replicate the translation of nucleotides into a polypeptide" (98). (See figure 3.4.) In this conceptual account of the poem, Bök emphasizes how the computer tests out or experiments with the ways that the protein molecules torque, bend, and coil to eventually assume the most

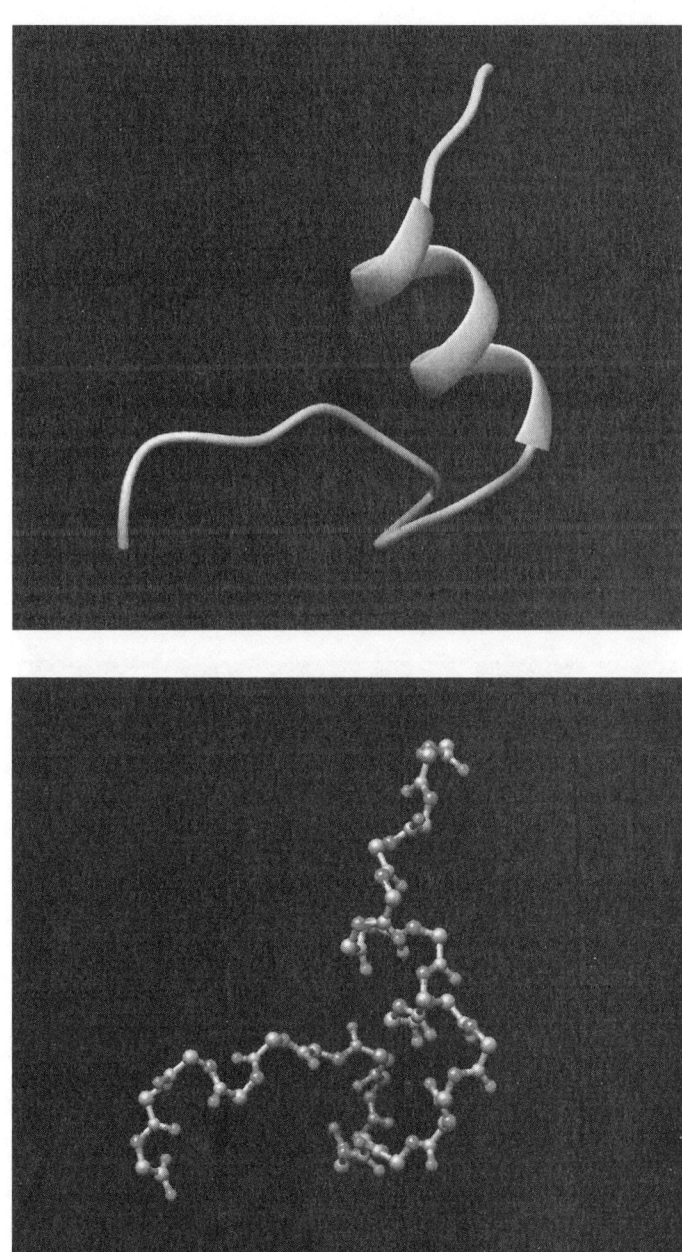

FIGURE 3.4 Christian Bök, "Death Sets a Thing Significant," from *The Xenotext: Book 1* (Toronto: Coach House, 2015).

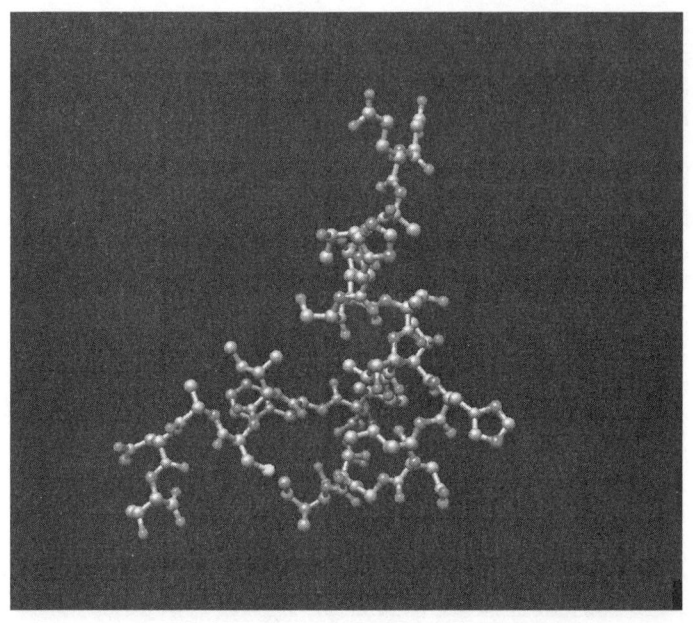

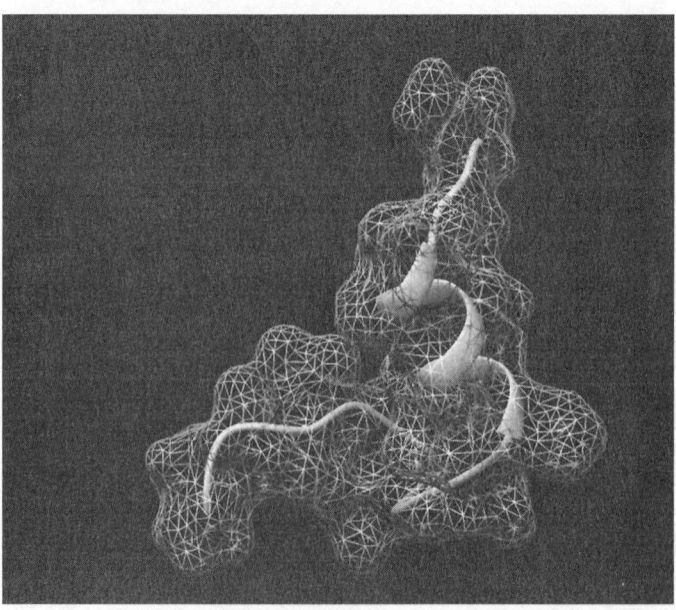

FIGURE 3.4. Continued.

likely shape. Similarly, he extends the sense of topography or shape of the protein molecule to include its charge envelope, which, in the modeled image, appears represented as a fine mesh of geometric surfaces, or a web composed of tiny triangles made of white threads. While it does not represent an actual molecular structure, this electrochemical topography of the molecule extends the concept of shape as I am using it here to include the clouds of electrical potentials for attraction and repulsion that will govern the molecular interactions between this molecule and others, and so it, in a sense, represents the "effective shape" of this protein by showing "a nimbus of electrical polarities (+,—, 0)," which will, in turn, form the "contours for a biochemical interaction" (104). In these ways, *The Xenotext* begins to take into account not only the arbitrary constraints based on the permutations of one code into another, but also the constraints created by the shape of the protein or the material behavior of molecular structures.

Bök's attempts to create a second poetic site in the execution of *The Xenotext* in the lab extend the use of constraint-based procedures in the project much further toward the explorations of the materiality of molecular shapes, permitting the poem to act as a site of experimentation through which one can ask questions both about the relationship between constraint and poetic form but also broader, more interdisciplinary questions about the relationship between semiotic processes and situated and lively forms of unfolding biological materiality. As such, the constraint parameters set by the properties of the string of amino acids, which allow it to fold into a subset of some but not all possible shapes, produce specific limitations for the formal composition of the poem. Such limitations in this case operate not through an arbitrary or analogous alignment between letter and molecule, which Bök largely relied on to set up the procedures for the encipherment of various codes in the poem, but through the literal limitations imposed by molecular structure as it assumes a particular folded shape. In other words, the primary constraint for the project comes to be located in the capacity of the amino acid string to fold into a viable protein molecule, and all other constraint-based compositional procedures radiate outward from this problematic. As such, the molecular structure itself, or the three-dimensional shape of the molecule, comes to bear a direct and constraining relation on poetic form and linguistic meaning.

BIOSEMIOTICS AND POETRY

Within the conceptual framework of molecular poetics I develop here, such folded topographies of molecular shapes, which operate within both semiotic and material registers without completely resolving into either, complicate the contemporary discussions of materiality that have been loosely grouped within the theoretical current of "new materialisms." In other words, molecular poetics offers a way to remain attuned to the semiotic and the linguistic dimensions that are immanent within the indeterminacies of material unfolding. Inasmuch as this is a materialist poetics, then, it is also an attempt to extend our understandings of signification into the intricate realms of biological materiality and beyond the edge of human signification systems, and a concomitant refusal to allow such realms to dissociate hylomorphicly into a dualist topography of matter and meaning. As such, my articulation of molecular poetics resonates with theoretical frameworks I discuss in the previous chapters as helping to constitute and delimit my conceptualization of *soft matter*, such as Barad's "material-discursive" or Haraway's "material-semiotic," which have worked to elaborate accounts of materialism to allow for the inclusion of semiotic registers within materiality without replicating a hidden dualism through their metaphysics.

As I have argued in this chapter, in attending to the complex entwinement of code and shape, *The Xenotext Experiment* similarly offers an exploration of the material dimension of biosemiotic processes, enacting a poetic experiment that, in facing the many challenges to the execution of its original conceptualization, actually testifies to the irresolvable complexity of material-semiotic entanglements. As the protein poem repeatedly fails to fold into a shape that can persist in the cell of *D. radiodurans*, Bök is forced to confront the fact that interspecies collaboration, which he hopes to enact, entails a refiguring of what may constitute processes of signification. As such, the molecular poetics that I trace through the changing aesthetics of Bök's poetic experiment involves an expansion of what may constitute processes of signification, to include the folded topographies of molecules, which, through the minute shifts in their conformations or shapes, operate as relevant signs within the material-semiotic world of *D. radiodurans*.

Such a view that linguistic and material processes are inextricably entwined has been emerging within various approaches to nonhuman semiotics or, more broadly, biosemiotics, within posthumanism and animal studies, where expanded understanding of what may constitute language has allowed for the inclusion of a widening range of interactions within the purview of signification. In *How Forests Think: Toward an Anthropology Beyond the Human*, anthropologist Eduardo Kohn, for instance, writes that "along with finitude, what we share with jaguars and other living selves—whether bacterial, floral, fungal, or animal—is the fact that how we represent the world around us is in some way or another constitutive of our being."[45] In other words, by drawing on the semiotics of the American pragmatist philosopher Charles Sanders Peirce, and in particular his notion that indexical signs possess material relations with the objects they represent, Kohn investigates how linguistic signs move across human and nonhuman worlds in nonarbitrary ways. In this sense, the indexical relation between smoke and a fire would constitute such a nonarbitrary sign within Peirce's semiotics, while within the context of the molecular poetics I am elaborating here, it may include the complex, folded, three-dimensional shape of a protein, which, with the specific configuration of its electrostatic envelope, touches another protein molecule, subtly changing its conformation and thus initiating a signaling cascade within the cell.

Approaching Bök's project through the lens of molecular poetics brings to the forefront a sense that code is not free floating and disembodied, but that living organisms are material-semiotic folds; moreover, the molecules that they are composed of are specifically folded shapes, which generate the processes of life only through their materially and temporally situated interactions. The shape of biological molecules acts, for instance, as one of the defining patterns in the "Alpha Helix" sequence of *The Xenotext*, where Bök draws on the three-dimensional shape of the alpha helix, with its right-hand-coiled or spiral conformation, in which hydrogen bonding links the amine (N-H) and the carbonyl (C=O) groups of the different amino acids to create a set of analogies between different biological and material systems. The alpha helix is one of the most common molecular shapes that underlies the secondary level of structure in protein folding, and in this poem Bök takes advantage of its prevalence to create a series of analogous relationships by following its shape: "It links the flinching of jellyfishes to the twinkling of dragonflies. It binds us all together via ligatures of carboxyl and amidogen" (141). In this instance, Bök is referring to luciferase, a protein responsible for emitting light in fireflies and jellyfish and other organisms with bioluminescent properties. Luciferase is an enzyme that oxidizes another protein, luciferin, and the protein structure of both consists in part of several alpha helices combined with other protein folding shapes. As such, the same molecular shape of the alpha helix reoccurs in different organisms, producing a parallel effect. The powerful litany Bök produces in "Alpha Helix" relies precisely on this continuity of shape to string or tether a variety of contexts, ranging from the animate to the inanimate. The alpha helix conjures forth "the jigsaw puzzle of a rose, whose perfect pieces lie in scattered fragments on the steps of spiral stairs, ... ivy that, like a verdant feather boa, curls around the barberpole ... [or] a Slinky, which must somersault forever down the ascending escalator" (143). In this way, molecular shape becomes a structuring principle for the poem, allowing it to coalesce a variety of images into "a delirious catalogue ... of helical imagery in the world, testifying to the ubiquity of living poetic forms by imbuing everything with the proteomic structure of life itself" (156).

And yet, despite this prevalence of the formal constraints of shape in the poem, Bök also returns again and again to the purely informational conceptualization of the genome, often insisting on the figurative language of textuality to describe living processes:

> Whatever lives must also write. It must strive to leave its gorgeous mark upon the eclogues and the georgics already written for us by some

ancestral wordsmith. It must realign each ribbon of atoms into a string of words, typing out each random letter in a stock quote, spooling by us on a banner at the bourse. It is alive because it can rebuild itself from any line of text. It must twist and twine upon itself, just as the grapevine does upon the trellis. (140)

This passage effectively points to another aspect of this problematic, one that is not so easily and productively subjected to the critiques against the figuration of DNA as a text, because it suggests that at some more fundamental level there is a continuity between language and the biological processes that underlie the existence of language. In other words, a space is opened up within which it is possible to consider the various processes of life unfolding within the cell of an organism as on some level semiotic processes. And in this passage, these semiotic dimensions come intertwined with the language of shape, so that the kind of biological "writing" that Bök is referring to also "twists" and "twines," "spools" and forms ribbons as it alludes to the three-dimensionality of its semiotic forms. In a footnote in "Alpha Helix," Bök explicitly cites one of the leading figures in the field of biosemiotics Jesper Hoffmeyer, stating that "the basic unit of life is the sign, not the molecule" (140). I would argue, however, that what is at stake here is not a dematerialization of the molecule into information but a refiguring of what may constitute a sign in more material terms, to include the examples of biosemiotic processes among nonhuman organisms.

In *Signs of Meaning in the Universe*, Hoffmeyer writes specifically about proteins as participants in semiotic processes, attending to the role their structure plays in the case of the receptor proteins on the surface of the cell, which interpret and respond to the signals around them: "The receptor's spatial surface is covered with hollows and projections which form a sort of cast of the corresponding spatial surfaces on the signal molecule. The bonding process also receives a helping hand from the electrical charge on the molecule surfaces. In short, the receptor is, both spatially and electrostatically, an analogic code of the signal molecule."[46] This way of thinking about the semiotic possibilities of the protein molecule in relation to its three-dimensional surface and its charge envelope corresponds closely to the images generated by Bök as he models the protein shapes in "Death Sets a Thing Significant," but while the poem, on one hand, points to an analogical relationship with language figured through transpositions of code, reading it, on the other hand, through the lens of biosemiotics, opens up the possibility of sensing the semiotic dimension of the multitude of folds and foldings of biological materiality it conveys. Thus, viewing *The Xenotext Experiment* not through the analogous relation between code and molecule but through the poetics of surface and three-dimensional latching and unlatching of atomic and molecular particles offers a way to place emphasis on the textural, rather than the textual, dimensions of exploration in this genetic poem. The framework of molecular poetics developed in this chapter reveals the three-dimensional nature of these interactions, extending the practices of "micro-poetics" beyond the recombinations of code to the surfaces, shapes, and textures that affect the active interactions of matter at these minute molecular scales, thus formulating, through these experiments with the textural dimension of matter, a current within the tradition of haptic poetics that I am exploring in *Poetics of Liveliness*. From this perspective, *The Xenotext Experiment* can be seen as a springboard for developing a poetics of other molecular interactions, including signaling and regulatory pathways in which complex bioactive molecules change in shape or conformation, giving rise to many of the processes we associate with life.

4

FIBERS

Edge Textures and Nonhuman Scales of Sense

*Inconspicuous perceptions constitute the obscure
dust of the world.*
—GILLES DELEUZE, *THE FOLD*

*On this strip I sit cross-legged
Weaving the fabric as a caterpillar spins its cocoon
Using threads of experience and imagination in
undreamed design.*
—BOB BROWN, "WRITING" FROM *WORDS*

POEM AS MICROSCOPE

Describing the texture of lawn or fine linen cloth in *Micrographia*, seventeenth-century natural philosopher Robert Hooke observes that it is "so curious that the threads were scarce discernable by the naked eye, and yet through an ordinary *Microscope* you may perceive what a goodly piece of *coarse Matting* it is." As with the point of a sharp needle and the edge of a razor, objects created through artifice that appear to the naked human eye to be smooth and finely formed on a closer look, through a lens of a microscope, begin to reveal an unsettling realm of uneven surfaces, rugged chasms, micro-abysses—a whole geography of "hills, and dales, and pores"—that appears "big enough," Hooke suggests, "to have afforded a hundred armed Mites room enough to be rang'd by each other without endangering the breaking one anothers necks, by being thrust off on either side." Not only does this image reveal a whole hypothetical world populated by creatures that would not even register at unamplified scales of human perception, but tiny creatures and their parts, such as various kinds of gnats, a flea, and a snail's tooth, abound in Hooke's text, their *"hairs,... bristles,* and *claws...* many thousand times sharper" than any human-made object. At one point Hooke compares the lawn he is describing to silk, noting that while the flax threads that compose it appear "exceedingly small, as to equalize, if not to be much smaller then the clew of the Silk-worm," the manner in which they are twisted causes them to appear "plain and base" and lacking in sheen. While the filaments of silk "are *small, round, hard, transparent,* and ... *stiff,"* so that each filament "preserves its proper *Figure,* and consequently its vivid *reflection . . .* those of Flax are *flat, limber, softer,* and *less transparent,"* so that as they twist and lie compressed together, they "lose their own, and destroy each others particular reflections." (See figure 4.1.) As a remedy for this problem, Hooke imagines making artificial fibers that would be able to absorb "a great variety of very vivid colours" and would to the naked eye look very much like the substance of silk: "And I have often thought, that probably there might be a way found out, to make an artificial glutinous composition, much resembling, if not full as good, nay better, then that Excrement, or whatever other substance it be out of which, the Silk-worm wire-draws his clew."[1]

Hooke's pronouncement can be read as one of the moments when the prophetic imaginary of science fiction makes an incursion into the mode of natural historical description in *Micrographia*. And this moment is not isolated: in the preface to the book, Hooke, for instance, predicts that along with the instruments for amplifying visual phenomena, either to rescue them from the obscurity of distance with the use of telescopes or, as the silk example demonstrates, to open up the

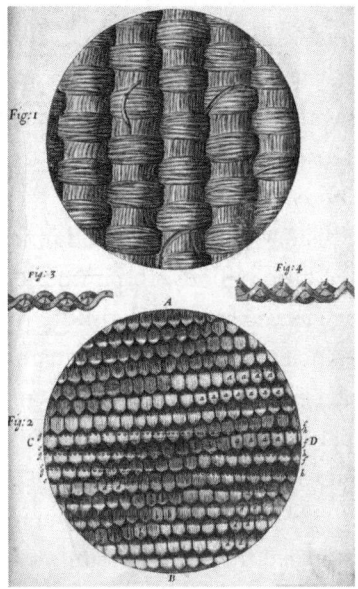

FIGURE 4.1 Robert Hooke, "Of fine waled Silk, or Taffety" (fig. 1) and "Of watered Silks, or Stuffs," (fig. 2) in *Micrographia*, 1665. Courtesy of the Linda Hall Library of Science, Engineering & Technology.

minute crevices of matter with the help of microscopes, human beings will soon be able to expand their sensoria to be able to touch, smell, hear, and taste things that have hitherto been imperceptible to them. As time has shown, some of Hooke's predictions have proven more discerning of the future than others, with our capacity to amplify touch remaining fairly rudimentary, as I will explore later in the chapter, while the possibilities for amplifying sound and transmitting it across distances abound. Likewise, Hooke's sense that someday we will be able "to make an artificial glutinous composition, much resembling" the liquid secretions that the silkworm draws out into the silk fiber in the process of making its cocoon, has come to pass in the invention of nylon fibers in the 1930s. The contemporary moment, however, casts Hooke's prediction in an even stranger light. In the first decades of the twenty-first century, scientists, including David Kaplan and Fiorenzo

Omenetto, working at the Tufts University Department of Biomedical Engineering, have reverse-engineered silk fibers, turning them back into a liquid from which they were initially formed in order to transform this liquefied matter once again, this time not into fine fibers but into a thin film that can act as a biosensor, detecting the minute fluctuations of certain molecules in the body.

Silk has had a long history of use in biomedicine because it is largely biocompatible with the human body, the immune system accepting it on surfaces as sensitive as the human brain. In an article titled "New Opportunities for an Ancient Material," Kaplan and Omenetto explain that "silk sutures have been used for thousands of years" due to their strength and biocompatibility and are still used in medicine today.[2] But silk has also been used to create a variety of replacement tissues, from blood vessels to heart valves. Most recent technological developments have completely transformed the set of possibilities for how silk may be used in biomedical procedures by allowing scientists to turn the silk fibers spun by *Bombyx mori* into a liquid, which can then be fabricated into a variety of shapes with diverse textural, optical, and biodegradable properties. When the poet and artist Jen Bervin first encountered the research on reverse-engineered liquefied silk happening at the Tufts Bioengineering Lab in 2010, she was struck by the written content she discovered when silk films were used as surfaces of inscription by recording information at the nanoscale of the molecular arrangements of proteins that make up silk: "This type of film, due to its optical nature, can be read as a projection with fiber optic light. When I projected the test film in Fio's office, the clip art on the prototype I saw there gave me pause—the content gap really surprised me. I thought, if it is possible to write in that context—inside the body, on silk, at that scale, I wanted to think further about what else might be inscribed there."[3] Attuned to the vulnerability of the biomedical context in which the body of the patient with a silk sensor implanted under her skin is negotiating a precarious relation to mortality and health, Bervin responded by researching the long and complex cross-cultural history of how written inscription on garments or wrappings around a body has been used to render protection to the wearer. Among her sources, she specifically references the use of inscription on cloth for such protective purposes in the Islamic tradition "between the eighth and the twelfth century" in which "single, horizon-like inscriptions were written on tiraz, (from *tarz*, Persian for embroidery), in Arabic letters embroidered in silk on a linen or cotton ground" and intended to bless and protect "the recipient of the cloth" (158–59). Bervin's project *Silk Poems* can be understood as continuous with these longer histories in which the inscribed cloth object acts as a kind of talisman, protecting someone from harm.

In one of its several material iterations, the project assumed a form of a long poem inscribed into the same kind of silk film that is used to create the biosensor. In 2016 at the Tufts University lab, Omenetto and Bradley Napier "used a mask to etch the poem in gold spatter on a wafer and poured liquid silk over it," so that "when the silk dried, the letters were suspended in the film."[4] Formally, the shape of the poem embodies the morphology of silk occurring at two different scales. Each of the lines of the poem consists of six letters, echoing the six-letter repeat sequence of nucleotides that occurs within the DNA that codes for silk protein. There are no spaces between the words, and some words are interrupted through enjambment, with their concluding syllables moving onto the next line to meet the six-letter constraint imposed by the morphological analogue of molecular form, in a way that is evocative of Christian Bök's use of the morphological features of molecular shape as a form of poetic constraint. Seen from a different perspective, the letters neatly stacked in rows on top of one another compose a shape of a long strand whose winding pattern, formed of a number of loose, crisscrossing loops, registers the shape of a silk strand as it is laid out by the silkworm in the process of making its cocoon as it "moves its head 150,000 times from side to side" over the course of two to three days.[5] (See figure 4.2.) This version of the poem was exhibited at Mass MoCA from May 28, 2016, to March 19, 2017, as part of a group exhibition called "Explode Every Day: An Inquiry Into the Phenomena of Wonder." The reader had to view the poem through a microscope, discerning the glistening golden letters forming the winding strand. (See figure 4.3.) While an as yet unpublished version of the poem accompanied the microscopic iteration of the text (which subsequently appeared in its published form in fall 2017 as a book by

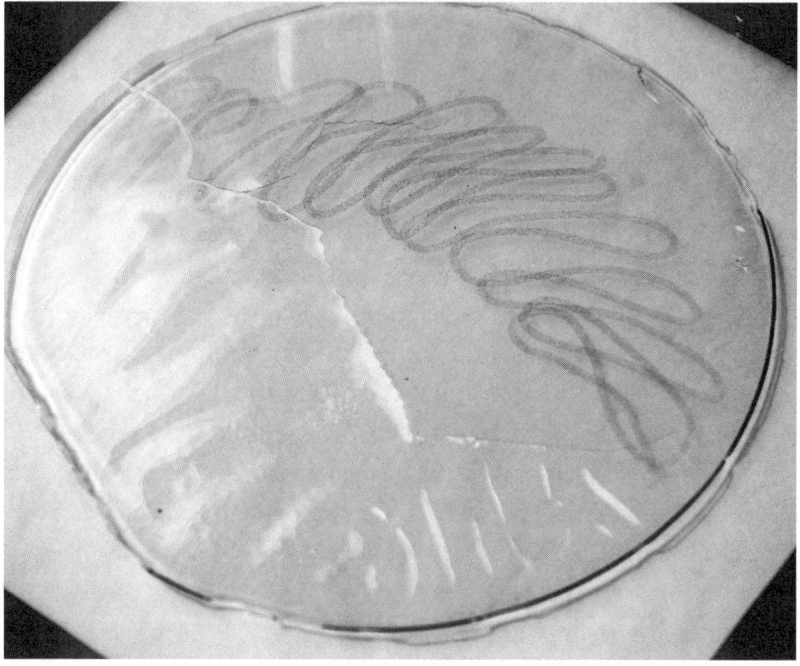

FIGURE 4.2 Jen Bervin, *Silk Poems*, microscopic view (2010–2017).

Nightboat Books), allowing the reader to reencounter the text in a different material iteration and engage in the reading process at a more familiar scale, the microscopic version rendered out of silk film and gold spatter provocatively posed the question of what it would mean to read at a scale that is relevant to the silkworm as it secretes its fine strands of silk. The meticulous perfection of the gold letters, all there, composed the same words and phrases as in the printed iteration of the poem, so that the task that they presented to the reader, while technically possible, would require a profound sense of defamiliarization—a kind of shedding of the scales at which the human sensorium operates comfortably and a willingness to open up, even for a short while, to the *nonhuman scales of sense* at which the silkworm discerns the elements of its world.

The use of a microscope as a way of performing an *interspecies translation* that can carry even a small aspect of the sensorium, or what Jakob von Uexküll would consider the *Umwelt*, of one species into that of

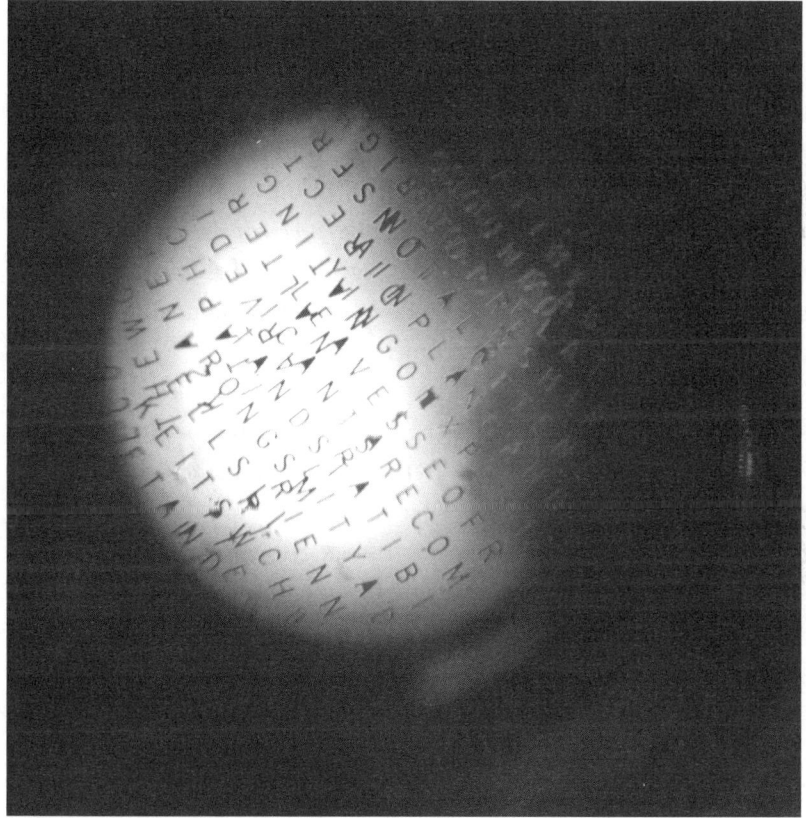

FIGURE 4.3 Jen Bervin, *Silk Poems*, microscopic view (2010–2017).

another, is evocative of the hope that Hooke vests in the power of instruments, even as he is dismayed by a sense that "productions of art are such rude mis-shapen things, that when view'd with a *Microscope*, there is little else observable, but their deformity."[6] As *Micrographia* is an early scientific text that seeks to establish a set of reliable epistemological practices of observation, Hooke is preoccupied by this inadequacy of the human senses to perceive the world in the immense detail in which it exists. Rather than positing some kind of anthropocentric hierarchy that would still evaluate the human sensorium as possessing the superior powers of perception in comparison to other animals, Hooke is humbly aware that many nonhuman animals often possess more intense and precise ways of sensing and vests all his hope in the remedial power of instruments, which can be affixed to the senses to repair their inadequacies: "*As for the actions of our Senses, we cannot but observe them to be in many particulars much outdone by those of other Creatures.*"[7] Such inadequacies may arise "*either from the* disproportion of the Object to the Organ, *whereby an infinite number of things can never enter into them*," or the many things that come within the reach of perception may not be "*received* [by the senses] *in a right manner*." To remedy this, Hooke suggests that the infirmities of the senses can be addressed by the addition "*of* artificial Organs *to the* natural" ones, through the use of instruments.

In this chapter I consider whether a poem, or another aesthetic object, such as an artwork, can act as such an instrument that could attune the human sensorium to scales of sensation that are not otherwise available to it. Consider, for instance, how Bervin's poem not only has to be viewed through such an instrument—a microscope—to become discernible to a reader, but itself acts as a kind of amplification device, allowing dimensions of scale within the material constitution of silk (that would otherwise be out of range) to become perceptible to human sensation. Read through the figurative lens of such an amplification instrument, it is evident that a poem amplifies invisible dimensions of matter through its formal qualities. What coalesces in the form of the tiny looping strand is a much more minute dimension of the molecular structure of DNA, aspects of its morphology carried in the six-letter width of the strand that echoes the six-letter repeat sequence of nucleotides occurring within the DNA that codes for silk protein. These morphological analogues do not end there. The shape of the poem itself, with its looping strand, registers two additional morphologies that occur at two different scales, that of the β sheet, which is the shape assumed by the silk protein fibroin, and that of the weft looping pattern of yarn that is crisscrossed by the warp yarn to constitute the weave structure of woven fabric. (See figure 4.4.)

While these modes of amplification are concerned with rendering access to scales of matter that are otherwise too minute to be perceptible to humans, the poem also works to aesthetically amplify scales of sensation that are relevant within the sensorium of a nonhuman

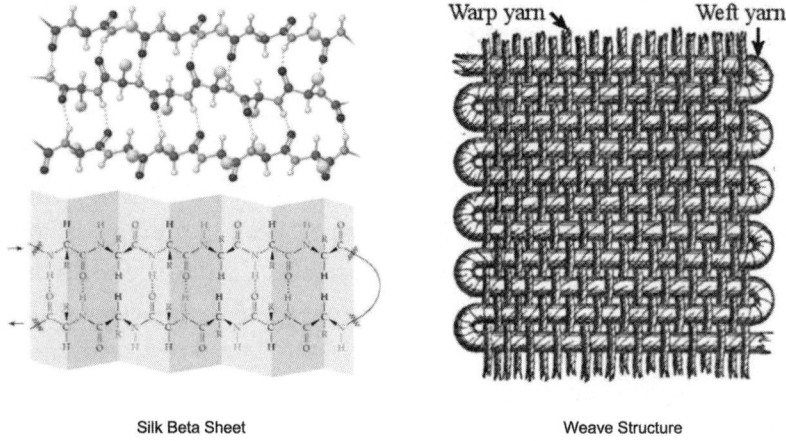

FIGURE 4.4 Jen Bervin, *Silk Poems*, research image of silk beta sheet and weft thread (2010–2017).

organism, in this case a silkworm. Another dimension of scale present in the poem is simply that of the silk fiber as it emerges from the mouth of the silkworm, so that the winding shape of the poem translates the proprioceptive motion of the silkworm's head, moving from side to side. As such, the poem, in its form, carries across the species divide traces of embodied sensation. One may be reminded here of Charles Olson's dictum from his essay "Projective Verse" that the layout of the poem on the page registers in some sense the "*kinetics* of the thing," transferring the energy "from where the poet got it, . . . by way of the poem itself . . . all the way over to, the reader."[8] The shape of the poem in this case not on the page but embedded within the materiality of the silk film registers the nature of the proprioceptive movement of the body. This body, however, in the case of *Silk Poems*, is not human. The silkworm and its sensuous universe are what gives the poem not only its form but also its perspective and voice, as Bervin imagines the poem as a "love poem" written "from the perspective of a silkworm" and addressed to the patient with the biosensor under her skin. Here the poem is an amplification device through which the voice of the silkworm renders the sensuous detail of its perceptual and embodied experience, including the precise descriptions of its intricate and yet minute anatomical parts. While Bervin's poetics is largely research based, with the composition of *Silk Poems* leading her to consult over "thirty international textile archives, medical libraries, nanotechnology and biomedical labs, and sericulture sites in North America, Europe, the Middle East, and Asia," it is this emphasis on including sensuous detail with its embodied registers of texture, affect, and temporal rhythm that distinguishes her research poetics from primarily conceptual, discursive, or appropriative practices.[9] As a result, she can be placed within the genealogy of haptic poetics, inflected by the observational, descriptive, and experimental practices of the natural sciences that I am delineating in *Poetics of Liveliness*. And, in Bervin's case, considering that the site of sensuous perception and subjectivity is not a human body but a body of a silkworm, the poem performs a series of what I am calling *interspecies translations* that work to open up aspects of the sensuous universe of the silkworm to the reader.

INTERSPECIES TRANSLATION AND NONHUMAN SCALES OF SENSE

In my discussion of poetic cosmologies at the beginning of this book, I introduced the work of Jakob von Uexküll and his observation that each organism is enfolded within a sheath of sensations that composes its *Umwelt* or world, with this perceptible "island of the senses"—of touch, smell, hearing, and sight—enfolding the animal "like four envelopes of an increasingly sheer garment."[10] While my focus in the "Molecules" chapter was on early conceptions of biosemiotics in Uexküll's work, here I turn to his understanding of the differing scales of sense that make up the worlds of different organisms. Consider, for instance, this scene in which he describes how an object, in this case a flower stem, is transformed almost entirely as it passes from the perceptual world of one organism into that of another: "A flower stem that in our Umwelt is a support for the flower, becomes a pipe full of liquid for the meadow spittlebug (*Philaenus spumarius*) who sucks out the liquid to build its foamy nest. The same flower stem becomes an upward path for the ant, connecting its nest with its hunting ground in the flower. For the grazing cow the flower stem becomes part of a tasty morsel of food for her to chew in her big mouth."[11] As this example illustrates, scales of sensation produce worlds of difference for various biological organisms, even as these organisms navigate the same environments populated by the same entities. These refocalizations of perspective midway through a descriptive account offer a kind of wondrous malleability to the objects that are being described, as they shrink and expand in size, change in texture from being a source of a liquid that can be transfigured into a foamy architecture to becoming a structural element of the landscape itself, a kind of bridge that can support a body of an animal as it navigates a precipice within its environment. One of the central factors that changes the appearance of an object—in this case the stem of a flower—as it moves from one *Umwelt* to another, is scale. Scale, in other words, has the capacity to transform a stem from being a morsel of food to becoming an entire structure that connects different parts of a landscape.

According to Uexküll, scale possesses a subjective aspect, which allows things to be ordered by the significance and the attention they require in an organism's life. This renders the things that are near and have an immediate impact on life visible in full size, while other, much vaster things may appear imperceptible: "Among the animals, with their smaller Umwelt horizons, the celestial bodies are essentially different," Uexküll writes. "When mosquitoes dance in the sunset, they do not see our big human sun, setting six kilometers away, but small mosquito suns that set about half a meter away. The moon and stars are absent from the sky of the mosquito."[12] As I explore in the introduction, where the celestial dimension of the mosquito's *Umwelt* first arises, scale, in this sense, is a factor not only of relative size but also of attention and significance. And it is, in fact, Uexküll's insertion of a kind of poetic or imagistic dimension of description—in this case the image of mosquitos dancing in the sunset—that unsettles the anthropocentric perspective of the celestial dimensions of the mosquito's *Umwelt*. In other words, it is not only that the sun shrinks and multiplies, and the stars and the moon disappear, but that the moving body of the mosquito enlarges in a sense, taking up the central position of significance in this scene of the sunset, in a way that profoundly unsettles how any human would perceive it.

Silk Poems opens with an epigraph from the minimalist painter Agnes Martin's text "The Untroubled Mind": "The wiggle of a worm as important / as the assassination of a president." This epigraph signals the sense that within the cosmology of the poem, nonhuman scales of relevance do not exist in a hierarchical relation to scales that are anthropocentrically relevant to human beings. Just as Uexküll's writing draws on what I have been calling *interspecies translation* to convey that a sunset of a mosquito consists of a multiplicity of tiny, proximate suns, or that the sensuous plenitude of a tick's universe is filled with a diffused sense of scent, temperature and light, Bervin opens up a world of sensuous details in *Silk Poems* that to a human being may appear tiny, or even indiscernible, and amplifies them until they flood the poem to its brim with sensations that a silkworm experiences as it touches and tastes and "wiggles" through the complex geometries of its environment or as it senses the transformations occurring within its body. And some of these transformations are so nearly all-encompassing that by any human standards of development they seem radically unimaginable, as when a silkworm's body almost entirely liquefies and turns into "goo," only to assume form again as a winged creature.

Consider, for instance, the silkworm's relationship to the mulberry leaf. Bervin reminds us of its specificity:

WEARE

OLIGOPHAGUS

MULBERRY

MONOGAMOUS

LEAF

POLYAMOROUS[13]

To say that an organism is oligophagus is to indicate that it eats only very specific foods, and while it does not have to indicate a one-to-one relationship between a particular species and its food source, in the case of the silkworm (*Bombyx mori*), as its name indicates, "the silkworm of the mulberry tree," the preference is for the leaves of the white mulberry (*Morus alba*), although it is not absolutely monophagous and may eat other species of mulberry and even Osage orange, which also belongs to the mulberry family (*Moraceae*). In *The Story of Silk*, John Feltwell writes that the "close coevolution between" *Bombyx* silkworms and the mulberry tree "has to be admired for its intricacy and uniqueness."[14] And in this poem, Bervin uses the language of love and specific geometries of attachment to articulate a kind of opening out that occurs as a result of narrowing down, so that in being chosen by the silkworm as its primary (if not only) food source, each leaf of the mulberry opens out to a field of tiny differences, delicate and sumptuous textures, or, as Bervin points out, "MULBERRY / LEAVESNO // TWOALIKE" (72). The tightknit relationship between the silkworm and the mulberry leaf is a thematic motif that Bervin returns to again and again in *Silk Poems* in order to emphasize its relevance to the survival but also to the aesthetic dimensions of the sensuous universe of the silkworm. This poem depicts in rich perceptual detail the first instant when the newly emerged silkworm tastes the plant that will form its sole nutritional source for the entirety of its lifespan:

SOMETHING

DELICIOUS

HITSMYMOUTH

INSTINCTIVELYIOPEN

MULBERRYLEAF

NECTARFLOODSIT[15]

One of the interesting aspects of how description operates in this moment is its anterior relationship to the silkworm's subjectivity. In other words, this poem depicts the as yet unfamiliar world, as the silkworm encounters for the first time an object that will become perhaps the most important entity within the repertoire of entities that compose its universe. As the stanza of the poem unfolds, the unnamed "delicious" sensation becomes the named and bounded entity of the mulberry leaf even as the leaf itself liquefies and leaks nectar.

As the poem progresses, other moments of sumptuous mulberry consumption arise, each offering more insight into the sensations that a silkworm experiences as it encounters the mulberry leaf:

MULBERRYMULBERRY
MULBERRY

IMOVESLOWLY
STARTFROMTHEINSIDE

THEFINEHAIRS
AREASHIVER[16]

Here the reader's attention is drawn to the way that the silkworm proprioceptively navigates the spatial dimension of eating a mulberry leaf, its slow pace as it begins the process, starting from the inside of the leaf, and the textures it encounters. As it brushes past the fine hairs of the leaf, it finds itself immersed in a whole-body sensation of a shiver. An echo also forms between the lines "THEFINEHAIRS/AREASHIVER," in which the silkworm describes the sensation of encountering the texture of the mulberry leaves, and the way that the act of reading is described in a citation by Vladimir Nabokov that Bervin includes in the "Research Sampler" at the end of *Silk Poems*: "Vladimir Nabokov, in his novel *Transparent*: 'the spine is the true reader's main organ.' In a private letter to Archibald MacLeish, he writes: 'there is that movement of light in one of your most famous poems that invariably sends a shiver of delight up and down my spine whenever I think of it'" (160–61). This quotation evokes a sense of reading as an embodied process through which the aesthetic qualities of texts are capable of producing sensuous effects on the body of the reader, quickly disavowing any dualistic sense of reading as the transmission of semantic content to the mind rather than the body. Earlier in the poem, this sense that one reads with *the body* comes up alongside a direct interspecies parallel of how a silkworm experiences breathing:

NABOKOVWRITES

YOUREADWITHYOURSPINE

IREADWITHMYBREATHING

ATRANSPARENTCHAINOFTUBES[17]

In referring here to a network of tiny tubes called tracheae that line the insect abdomen, allowing the air to enter the body through small openings, Bervin creates a direct interspecies parallel that attempts to translate one set of embodied sensations into those that can be perceptible to another species.

Such an account of reading fits the contours of my argument about interspecies translation in that a poem may act as a kind of amplifier of sensations, which may bring perceptions that make up the essential elements of a universe of a nonhuman organism across the species line. This could account for the way that *Silk Poems* brings into the perceptual and specifically haptic purview the presence of "THEFINEHAIRS" on the inside of the mulberry leaf and the ways that they produce a shivering sensation in the silkworm, a parallel that is echoed by a shivering sensation that can arise as a consequence of the sensuous and fully embodied effects of aesthetic stimulation during the process of reading. Reading as an embodied process is clearly at play here, as Bervin confirms when she asserts, following Nabokov, "YOUREADWITHYOURSPINE," signaling a kind of investment in a sensuous research poetics, which is characteristic of both her artistic and poetic work (118). But what does it mean to suggest that a silkworm reads with her breathing, and how can this assertion be understood as anything other than an analogy that places undue anthropomorphic burden on the silkworm's actions?

While this is a complex set of questions that I turn to again and again, I would like to propose in this iteration that there is a strategic anthropomorphism at play here, one that suggests that the ways in which other organisms crawl or "wiggle" through the world may possess proprioceptive and sensuous parallels to the more familiar activities of human organisms. In her "Note on Anthropomorphism" in *Vibrant Matter,* Jane Bennett defends the theoretical possibilities opened up by anthropomorphism, focusing specifically on Charles Darwin's work with worms as predicated on an anthropomorphic perspective, which permitted him to see "in them an intelligence and willfulness that he recognized as related to his own," while also prompting him "to pay close attention to the mundane activities of worms," thus allowing him to recognize "their own, distinctive, material complexity." As Bennett points out, "a touch of anthropomorphism . . . can catalyze a sensibility that finds a world filled not with ontologically distinct categories of beings . . . but with variously composed materialities that form confederations," in turn revealing "isomorphisms" across what had previously seemed to be "categorical divides."[18] While a sense that a silkworm "reads" with its tracheal tubes can be interpreted as an analogy that allows Bervin to perform a kind of interspecies translation across worlds of sensation opened up by very different forms of embodiment, her attempt to compose a poem from a perspective of a silkworm has far deeper formal implications for the text that ensues. As a way of examining how a sensuous universe of a silkworm can be conveyed formally in the shape of the poem, let us return once again to the silkworm's relationship with the mulberry leaf and the way that Bervin registers the ecstatic nature of this encounter between insect and plant through the repetition of the word mulberry: "MULBERRYMULBERRY/MULBERRY" (107). On one hand, the repetition of the word "mulberry" here signals once again the prevalence of this plant, which makes up much of the silkworm's encounter with the external entities of its world, but at another, more subtle proprioceptive level, it signals the continuity of the silkworm chewing through a mulberry leaf. These lines, along with the others I have quoted so far, transposed here as they appear in the printed version of the poem, reveal the unusual spacing, or rather no spacing, between the words that occupy the same line. Here, the form of the poem begins to act as a biomimetic analogue for the manner in which the silkworm chews on a mulberry leaf, taking bites out of the leaf one after another to form a continuous pattern without interruptions, as Bervin explained during her talk for the launch of the book at the Rhode Island School of Design on October 3, 2017. Whereas the action of the individual silkworm's chewing is minute and nearly unnoticeable from a human perspective, the formal dimension of the poem generates an analogue that scales up the manner in which the silkworm moves along and marks the substrate of the leaf. I "CHEW / SIDEWAYS," the silkworm informs the reader, "INTHOUSANDS / OFARCS // INDIZZYING / DETAIL"[19]—a process that, when it involves many silkworm caterpillars, produces a striking sound, "like that of torrential rain falling on leaves" that "can be heard up to several meters away."[20] The poetic attention in these examples moves from the tiny detail of each individual silkworm marking a leaf with a specific arc of a single bite to the accretive effects of thousands of such markings and their concomitant sound.

Such ways of marking a substrate through the actions of nonhuman organisms resemble the way that human writing is likewise a form of mark-making that leaves a trace on a material ground such as fabric or paper or, in the case of the first materials that were used for writing, even shell or bone—a history in which silk as a ground and as a material of inscription plays an instrumental role.[21] This question appears in Jacques Derrida's *The Animal That Therefore I Am*, where he points out that "no one has ever denied the animal this capacity to track itself, to trace itself or retrace a path of itself," but that for much of the history of Western philosophy "it has been refused the power to transform those traces into verbal language, to call to itself by means of discursive questions and responses, denied the power to efface its traces."[22] In developing the concept of molecular poetics in chapter 3, I have already addressed the ways in which molecules participate in systems of signification within the body of a living organism, both as forms of code and through the configurations of their three-dimensional shapes as they interact with one another. When it comes to *Silk Poems*, all these aspects of molecular poetics are still at play in how Bervin draws on the molecular structure and patterning of the DNA and proteins that constitute silk as she shapes the form of the poem at different scales. Bervin's primary way of engaging with these molecular forms is through the modes of amplification that the poem enacts as it represents these different molecular shapes and sign systems at an alternate material scale, where they become perceptible or nearly perceptible to the human sensorium with the aid of instruments, such as microscopes. What this strategy allows is for the poem embedded within the nanoscale structure of silk film to reveal even more of micro patterning of silk as material at the molecular scales of DNA and protein, while using the materiality of the silk itself as a site of composition of the poem.

At the same time, as the poem scales up to reveal a connection between the pattern through which the silkworm chews a mulberry leaf and the typographical arrangement of the poem on the page through which the human reader parses different lexical elements, a sense of subjectivity floods these material relations, evoking once again the question of whether an aesthetic object can, through its material modalities, offer some partial glimpse into the embodied experience of another species. In a sense, the formal dimension of the poem performs an interspecies translation, which carries across a textural or sensuous dimension of how the silkworm experiences its contact with the mulberry leaf to the experience that a human reader has of the poem. At the same time, the uninterrupted flow of words gives the poem a kind of recalcitrant or intransigent quality, especially at first, transforming the semantic valences of words into an unfamiliar field of relations and forcing the reader to insert the required cuts or interruptions in order to parse the words into meaningful units. Considering that the poem is written from a nonhuman perspective, this formal feature contributes to a sense that the reader finds herself in an unfamiliar landscape, not only in relation to the sensations that arise as the silkworm interacts with its environment but also in relation to a defamiliarized sense of human language, which acquires a kind of opacity or material weight that one must move through with difficulty before the words parse into discrete units of meaning.

In theorizing the concept of interspecies translation, I am asking how a poem or another aesthetic object may carry sensation across a species barrier, however imperfectly, even as it also carries across various modes of anthropomorphic projection. It may be helpful to draw on examples here external to *Silk Poems* to explore how other artists and writers have attempted to perform acts of interspecies translation within the aesthetic objects they have constructed.²³ The artist Natalie Jeremijenko, along with collaborators Chris Woebken, Lee von Kraus, and Leigha Dennis, has created a device for interspecies translation that entails active, even if technologically mediated, interaction between a nonhuman and a human animal. Their project "Beetle Wrestler," showcased as part of Museum of Modern Art's online curatorial experiment "Design and Violence," aimed to create an interspecies translation machine that would allow a human to wrestle a rhinoceros beetle: "Beetle Wrestler pits a Hercules Beetle (*Dynastus Hercules*)—the largest in the rhino beetle family—against a human, who clips her head into a helmet device scaled to allow her to imitate the range of movements and strength of her insect opponent."²⁴ In a scientific article, "Inexpensive Load Carrying by Rhinoceros Beetles," Rodger Kram suggests that rhinoceros beetles "appear to be the world's strongest animals," citing anecdotal evidence that "some species are able to support 850 times their own body mass," as well as his own experimental findings that the beetles could sustain a steady speed for a long time "with loads of more than 30 times their body mass." Kram postulates that this ability to carry a great deal of weight at a low metabolic cost may have evolved as a result of the fact that the beetles "exert high forces during battles for mates."²⁵ In the notes that accompany "Beetle Wrestler" on the museum's website, Hugh Raffles explores the potentials and also the limitations of the "Beetle Wrestler's" capacity to convey to the human something of the beetle's sensorium and perceptual experience: "Try to imagine that you are the beetle. It's not possible. You can try to imagine it, but you can't get close. You're physically too different. Your sensoria don't correspond. You occupy an entirely different world, not only in temporal or spatial scale and experience but in texture and chemistry. The signals you receive are not the same; the signals you send don't translate."²⁶ This analysis of the "Beetle Wrestler" opens up the questions of what the value may be of performing this imaginative but also embodied exercise even with all its inadequacies and limitations—in other words, what the value may be in attempting to translate sensation across interspecies differences even if what is primarily sensed is the opacity of that difference itself.

This desire to translate the movements and sensations of one species into the movements of another can be read as a form of interspecies translation as I have been theorizing it here within the context of animal studies, but this impulse for carrying sensation across bodies may likewise be situated within the history of poetics, and in particular the way that Olson engages with the layout of the page as a register and a site of transmission of bodily movements and perceptual energies from the poet to the reader. One of the ways through which this transfer of energy is accomplished involves the positioning of the words, syllables, lines, and the spaces between the words, as well as the negative space of the page as a whole, so that the arrangement of these elements on the page can generate a set of proprioceptive tensions in a way that material objects do as they compose the universe. This sense that the different elements of the poem constitute a relational field—a method that Olson specifically refers to as "FIELD COMPOSITION"—offers a way of conceptualizing how the typographical arrangement of the words on the pages of *Silk Poems*, uninterrupted by spaces between them, is able to register the material configuration of the movement of the silkworm as it chews the mulberry leaf with continuous bites.

In another essay on poetics, "Proprioception," Olson theorizes even further how a poem may register the "kinetics of the thing" as he explores the ways that the body's felt sense of its own movement through space can enter the space of composition:

> Today: movement, at any cost. Kinesthesia: beat(nik)
>   the sense whose end organs lie in the muscles,
>   tendons, joints, and are stimulated by bodily
>   tensions (—or relaxations of same). Violence:
>   knives/anything, to get the body in.

To which
PROPRIOCEPTION: the data of depth sensibility/the 'body' of us as
object which spontaneously or of its own order
produces experience of, 'depth' Viz
SENSIBILITY WITHIN THE ORGANISM
BY MOVEMENT OF ITS OWN TISSUES[27]

In considering proprioception, or the body's ability to sense the positioning of its own tissues and the way that the parts of the body are moving in space, Olson is opening up a way of thinking about how a poem may generate a universe of sensations that arise out of a process of autostimulation, of a body sensing itself. And when this deliberation of proprioception is brought in contact with his broader discussion of kinetics in "Projective Verse," it is clear that the shape of the poem on the page registers a sense of the kinetic movement of the body and transmits it to the reader by guiding her body in some analogous way across the page in the process of reading.

It is clear from the significance of the precision of the typographic arrangement and the overall shape of the poem that results that the different iterations of *Silk Poems* can be situated within this longer poetic genealogy in which the movements of the body are transmitted to the page. In the case of the gold spatter poem embedded in silk film, which takes the shape of the looping strand of silk that is re-creating the back-and-forth movement of the silkworm's head, a hypothetical reader reading the poem with the aid of a microscope will find herself moving across the surface of the poem along the same loops that are suggestive of the movement of the silkworm's head. A similar mechanism of interspecies translation is at play in the case of the densely packed typography in the printed version of the text, in which spacing between the words is omitted so that the reader, in moving across the recalcitrant surface of the text, finds herself experiencing a sense of a continuous texture and rhythm of the tiny bites that a silkworm takes out of a mulberry leaf. One of the things that interests me specifically here is the way that these formal poetic techniques perform an interspecies translation at a specifically somatic level, acting as amplifiers of the tiny movements of the silkworm's own body as it transforms the texture of the boundary at which the inside of the body meets its external environment by either oozing strands of silk into it or chewing elements of it away. As such, a poem becomes an unusual kind of amplification instrument, one that still has not been invented in the scientific context, even though it has been anticipated since the seventeenth century, one that is able, like the "Beetle Wrestler," to amplify the somatic sensations of the body's movement through the world and the haptic sensations of texture as different aspects of this world are encountered by an organism.

MICROHAPTICS AND NONHUMAN TEXTURES OF FEELING

One of the instruments in *Micrographia* that Hooke hopes will soon be available to science is an instrument that could amplify the sensation of touch, so as to render textures that are too minute to be discernible as differentiated to the human sensorium perceptible in all their haptic intricacy. As I point out on several occasions in discussing the relationship between poetry and science, the visual amplification enabled by the microscope offers a kind of tantalizing, even if also frightening, prelude to the world that would open up in the crevices and craters that rupture what to the human eye is a glistening, sharp point of a needle or an edge of a razor, not to mention the hidden openings and forms of roughness and unevenness that appear in fabrics that are manufactured through human artifice. In light of my reading of the silkworm's negotiation of its somatic universe, the question now becomes what the silkworm itself is sensing as it touches and moves over the surface of the mulberry leaf, and whether poetic form deployed by Bervin can open up avenues for translating these imperceptible sensations to the reader. In the introduction to *Touching Feeling*, Eve Kosofsky Sedgwick points out that "the sense of physical touch itself, at least so far, has been remarkably unsusceptible to being amplified by technology." She brings up the example of touch-enhancement techniques that are taught to women as a way of performing breast self-exams in a medical context, involving "a film of liquid soap, a square of satiny cloth," or alternatively "a pad of thin plastic filled with a layer of water," which are intended to amplify the contours and the textural feel of the underlying tissue. And yet these are clearly minimal enhancements in comparison to the way that the visual sense, with its concomitant association of Enlightenment epistemic lucidity, has been enhanced and mediated since the seventeenth century.[28]

In considering the experiential scale of the silkworm and the problem of amplifying tiny forms of haptic sensation, it may be helpful to ask whether there is a kind of minimum of repetition that must occur in a pattern for it to act as texture. Sedgwick anticipates this question at least when it comes to human perception of texture: "Whatever the scale, one bump on a surface, or even three, won't constitute texture. A repeated pattern like polka dots might, but it depends on how big they are or how close you are: from across the room you might see them as a flat sheet of gray; at a few feet, the dots make a visible texture; through a magnifying glass you'll see an underlying texture of paper or fabric unrelated to the two or three rounded shapes that make a big design" (16). As such, the constitution of texture is once again dependent on the perceptual vantage point and the acuteness of one's sensorium so that the texture of paper or fabric may not even be a discernible property unless one's fingers or face were proximate to them. One is reminded here of the mites populating the point of a needle in *Micrographia*—to the unaided human eye and touch an example of smooth sharpness, but to the mites a textural wonderland of uneven surfaces, rugged chasms, micro-abysses—a whole geography really of "hills, and dales, and pores."[29]

It could be said that texture telescopes as one slides across scales reconstituting the edges that demarcate the relevant entities within a particular sensorium: one may recall here Uexküll's account of how a flower stem can be transformed from a delicate texture of a morsel of food to the structural sturdiness of a bridge traversing a landscape. It is helpful also to evoke here Sedgwick's example where she considers how texture as it slides across scales may in one moment encompass "a whole acre of trees" while at another it becomes a question of "the cross-grained fibers of the wood" as they are attacked by "the sleek bite of the axe."[30] Returning to *Silk Poems*, I would argue that the ability of texture to move perceptually across scales offers a way of bringing into relation different iterations of the poem while also opening up ways for thinking about the microhaptics and the manner in which the form of the poem can embody and amplify textural scales in ways that span and translate across interspecies lines. The gold spatter poem embedded in silk film creates a set of textural fields across multiple scales in much the same way as Sedgwick's example of the forest focalizes across several dimensions. The poem appears at one scale as the looping scrawl of the silk strand being deposited by the figure-eight movement of the silkworm's head from side to side, while at another, more microscopic scale, it appears as a translucent field shimmering with angular shards of gold letters, which at times overlap one another at the points where the different parts of the strand overlay and cross, emphasizing the recalcitrant materiality of the gold composing the letters. In other words, the poem acts as a kind of amplifier, permitting a form of interspecies translation that renders aspects of a textural experience that occur at the scale of one sensorium to be transfigured into that of another.

As I have suggested, such a process is at play in the way that the spacing, or rather its absence, between individual words in the poem creates a textural analogue for the way that the silkworm experiences chewing into and through a mulberry leaf in a continuity of sumptuous bites with no interruptions or breaks, so that her textural, rhythmic experience of this encounter with the leaf is, as Bervin describes it, a continuous semantic and textural string. Some textural element is carried here from the tiny bites in the surface of the mulberry leaf to the way that the reader encounters the text on the page. One of the aspects of this interspecies translation is that the poem does not operate in a mode that could be simply parsed into text or texture; rather, the semantic and the material registers work hand in hand, so that finding the semantic register by parsing the words one from another becomes possible only if one relinquishes some level of control and moves through the text as texture, where patterns of continuity and discontinuity may not correspond to ones that are usually relevant to human beings. In a sense, the poem in this case acts as an apparatus for interspecies translation precisely because it shifts the boundaries of such patterns of continuity and discontinuity or shifts the grain of their resolution. Such patterns of resolution, which demarcate differentiated "droplets" of sensation as distinct from one another, differ between organisms but also within the different areas within a sensorium of a single organism, contributing to differences in how edges of experience both spatially and temporally come to frame certain entities as distinct objects or certain frames of time as distinct moments in the flow of experience. The term "edge texture" as it appears in the title of this chapter offers a way of conceptualizing such temporal and spatial edges and ways that their geometries may shift upon encountering the different scales of sense that are operative within different sensoria.[31]

This problem of differences in the microhaptic perception of the world between different organisms can be illustrated vividly through the work of the artist Nina Katchadourian and her series "Uninvited Collaborations with Nature," in which she attempts to enter into collaborative relations with the tiniest of organisms, from mushrooms to barnacles and spiders. Katchadourian's project "The Mended Spiderweb Series" consists of her searching and repairing spiderwebs over a six-week period in a forest near the house where she was living. (See figure 4.5.) She used red sewing thread to meticulously and very slowly repair the spiderwebs, inserting segments of the thread directly into the web, using the stickiness of the spiderweb itself as adhesive, and sometimes using white glue. In the morning after the first repair, she discovered a pile of red threads lying on the ground below the web: "At first I assumed the wind had blown them out; on closer inspection it became clear that the spider had repaired the web to perfect condition using its own methods, throwing the threads out in the process. My repairs were always rejected by the spider and discarded, usually during the course of the night, even in webs which looked abandoned."[32] A pile of red threads was usually left discarded on the ground next to the web. This example of a failed collaboration across species lines is reminiscent of the difficulties of

FIGURE 4.5 Nina Katchadourian, *Mended Spiderweb #14 (Spoon Patch)*, 1998, Cibachrome 30 × 20 inches. Courtesy of the artist, Catharine Clark Gallery, and Pace Gallery.

collaborating with nonhuman organisms that Bök likewise experienced in the course of working on *The Xenotext Experiment*. And yet, lit through the lens of Hooke's microscopic observations of silk next to the kinds of cloth produced through "human artifice," it becomes evident that Katchadourian's failure to repair the web in a way that is convincing to the spider arises at least in part from incommensurate scales of sense, so that what to her eye and fumbling fingertips may appear seamless and smooth and adequately taut to receive the vibrations of squirming prey is immediately discernible to the spider as crude and inferior in its construction as he feels out with his spindly legs the chunky, rough seams between his own silken fibers and the red threads bound to them.

One way to conceptualize what emerges as texture in the context of this scene would be to focus precisely on this discrepancy or difference that points to what remains resistant to any form of interspecies translation—a sense of texture as this differential recalcitrance that cannot be refigured or remediated entirely. In the case of Katchadourian's artwork, such a formulation would entail the residual roughness of what to human eyes and fingers seem like perfectly fine red threads, yet threads that still fail to convince a spider of an appropriately delicate texture that could match its own silken fibers. This is resonant both with Hooke's shock at the rough edges of fibers seen through a microscope and with Eva Hayward's conceptualization of texture as an "unmetabolizable" recalcitrance that arises as different forms of interspecies matter encounter one another. For Hayward, such "filterings that result in texture" operate through an amalgamation of different sensoria across species lines to produce novel possibilities for sensing, such as that indicated by her term "fingeryeyes." This term emerges directly at the haptic-optic interface: as Hayward reached her fingers toward the coral, its "tentacles reached out to eat, and it 'tasted' . . . [her] fingers and retracted," creating a moment of "provisional togetherness, . . . an instance of fingeryeyes."[33] Hayward is careful to note that such moments of overlap between sensoria are imprecise or are never about static mappings of one sense onto another in ways that subsume or metabolize difference:

> I know that they don't have "eyes" or "fingers," even if I must know them through my own fingeryeyes. Their sensory capacities are decidedly their own, with chemoreceptors (which transduce a chemical signal into potential action) and mechanoreceptors (which react to mechanical pressure or distortion) measuring the flow of water and the presence of prey or potential predators around them. It is tempting to translate their senses through my own—a "tasting touch" or a (c)orality—but what is at work in the intersections of species and senses might more approximate a synesthetic multispecies reach, exchange, thrill, a transmission among sensing bodies. (591)

Rather than sensory correspondence or overlap, what is at stake here are moments of incomplete translation between sensoria that may be very unlike one another, such as those of cup corals and human beings, or, in the case of *Silk Poems*, silkworms and human beings.

Hayward's conceptualization of such interspecies encounters is a part of a whole mosaic of theoretical frameworks that I am working with in *Poetics of Liveliness* (many of which have emerged out of feminist and queer currents in animal studies and science studies) that have sought to explore the nonautonomy of the entities that participate in an encounter. Such frameworks focus rather on the space of the encounter as an intra-action, in Karen Barad's terms, or an attempt to imagine an emergent temporality in which the entities that enter an encounter are also constituted by it through a continuous process of relational change or becoming. What Hayward likewise powerfully points to is that such moments of encounter may not be, and likely are not, totalizing; rather, they leave *untranslatable* residues or modes of recalcitrance that emerge as *texture*. Moreover, the sensoria in question here are not fixed or static meeting points but rather act as emergent sites that are transformed through such encounters. Thus Hayward's concept of "fingeryeyes" offers a resilient heuristic for including the complications of the unmet or the untranslatable within interspecies contact without either foreclosing the possibility of such contact or resorting to simplistic forms of anthropomorphism, which often collapse forms of difference: "I invoke fingeryeyes to articulate the in-between of encounter, a space of movement, of potential: this haptic-optic defines the overlay of sensoriums and the inter-and interchange of sensations. Fingeryeyes, in this instance, is the transfer of intensity, of expressivity in the simultaneity of touching and feeling" (581).

If texture for Hayward is a kind of residue that appears at the edges of incompletely overlapping sensoria, the concept of the edge as I am delineating it here also opens the question of how the scale resolution of a particular sensorium allows it to delineate a specific object as such, differentiating its edges from what surrounds it. In other words, I keep returning to the question of what demarcates the boundaries of discrete, salient experiences within a particular sensorium and how the resolution of such bright particulars or the luminous edges of them participate in constituting texture. An attempt to theorize how the granularity of perception is constituted and how different organisms come to perceive the edges that designate certain droplets of sensory experience as discrete appears in Uexküll, who turns to the work of one of the first experimental psychologists, Ernst Heinrich Weber, as a way of considering patterns of sensory resolution. One aspect of Weber's research that is particularly significant for my theorization of how scales of sensation may be translated between different organisms through the formal properties of aesthetic objects is the concept of "just-noticeable difference," which suggests that in perceiving, one is able to sense the relative difference, rather than the absolute difference between particular items or entities. For instance, if one were to pick up two wooden cubes from a surface of a table on which they are resting, a red one weighing 100 grams and a blue one weighing 108 grams, it would be possible to discern the heavier cube from the lighter one. This would, however, not be true if the cubes were much heavier, weighing 1 kilogram and 8 grams and 1 kilogram, respectively. As such, the concept of "just-noticeable difference" in this case depends on a kind of proportional relation, rather than an absolute difference between these weights. When it comes to haptics and sensory resolution, Weber performed a famous experiment in which an experimenter places "the points of a compass" in contact with different areas of an experimental subject's body. While the distance between the compass points remains the same, the resolution of sensation changes, so that when the compass points are pressed "more than one centimeter apart on the nape of an experimental subject's neck, the subject can clearly distinguish between the two points," while when these move down the back, "they get closer and closer in the tactile space of the experimental subject until they seem to be at the same place."[34] In his book *De Tactu* (Concerning Touch), Weber calls this the "two-point threshold," which is really equivalent to the smallest distance between the two points where a person determines that it is two points and not one. Such a threshold is a matter of precisely the problem of sensory resolution that I have been working to define, so that, according to Weber, "two objects touching the skin simultaneously seem to be separated by a smaller distance the less sensitive the touch-sense is in various parts of the skin."[35] Uexküll expands Weber's ideas within his own system of sensation to reach a conclusion that the resolution of the haptic sense "confer[s] a fine mosaic of place" on the surface of everything that is touched. Such a "mosaic of place of the objects of the places of an animal is a gift from the subject to the things in its environment in visual as well as in tactile space, one which is not at all available in its surroundings."[36] What Uexküll means to convey through such a concept of a "gift" is precisely what I mean here by a sense of "resolution," in that the grain of sensitivity that allows the subject to parse the world into distinct entities or distinct droplets of sensation is a matter of the size and granularity of such mosaic pieces, so that the world can be only as detailed within a certain subject's sensory universe as their resolution allows.

This concept becomes clearer if one considers visual sensation. As with touch, Uexküll turns to the sense that "the eye that glances about spreads a fine mosaic of place over all the things in its environment," and the fineness of this mosaic depends on the number of visual elements that are located on the surface of the eye or its retina, depending on whether the eye is a compound eye of an insect or a complex eye of a vertebrate.[37] Since different animals possess very different numbers of such visual elements, the visual mosaics they confer on the world vary widely in terms of their resolution. As a way of illustration, Uexküll takes an image of a street scene, reduces it in size, and then rephotographs it against a grid whose resolution corresponds to the resolution of such a mosaic of perception. Once the photograph is enlarged again, it "change[s] itself into an ever more coarse mosaic" (63). Through this method and a more impressionistic use of watercolor, Uexküll reproduces the street scene as he thinks it would look like seen through the eyes of a human, a fly, and a mollusk, with the final image of the street scene from a perspective of a mollusk "contain[ing] nothing but a number of dark and light surfaces" (63). While Uexküll's pictures are imaginative and impressionistic and risk teeter tottering at the edge of anthropomorphism, his sense, following Weber, that there is an alignment between how fine-grained the sensory receptors of a particular sense are and the resolution of detail that an organism is able to perceive in the world offers a way to begin to theorize the interspecies differences in microhaptic perception of texture. In other words, turning back to the example of Hooke's descriptions of cloth woven from fibers manufactured through artifice or the edge of a razor, it becomes clear how the perceptual resolution of the human sensory system may not be delicate enough to discern the rough unevenness of such objects. On the other hand, the silkworm's textural sense of smooth fineness of a silk fiber as it leaves its spinnerets far surpasses the fine granularity of haptic detail that can be perceived visually by a human being only with the aid of a microscope, although it may be evident at a more macroscopic scale in the fine luster of silk as it refracts light rays in a particular pattern or its general sheen or smoothness.

Another figure who addresses this problem of the resolution of perception and the limitations of sensoria in discerning particular objects, and who was coincidently influenced by the discoveries of the early microscopists, is the seventeenth-century philosopher Gottfried Leibniz. While Weber describes the concept of "just-noticeable difference," Leibniz turns to the concept of "little perceptions" to describe those perceptions that are just below the threshold of becoming present to consciousness, such as the noise of the sea, which is made up of the summation of the sounds of individual waves even though those are "too similar to each other for us to be able to ... pick out the sound of one specific wave."[38] As such, Leibniz is concerned with sensations that occur at the edges of what is perceptible and even with how what is imperceptible conditions what can be perceived. Writing as one of the twentieth-century commentators on Leibniz in *The Fold: Leibniz and the Baroque*, Gilles Deleuze points out that for Leibniz, "every conscious perception implies ... [an] infinity of minute perceptions."[39] Such "tiny perceptions" constitute "as much the passage from one perception to another" as they make up the "components of each perception," and as such they contribute to the transitional affective states, such as anxiety or disquiet or apprehension, which may not be disclosed at the level of conscious perception.[40] For a particular perception to arise as a conscious perception, a nescient sense of differentiation and heterogeneity must emerge among the microperceptions that surround it: "For example, the sound of the sea: at least two waves must be minutely perceived as nascent and heterogeneous enough to become part of a relation that can allow the perception of a third, one that 'excels' over the others and comes to consciousness (implying that we are near the shoreline)."[41]

The resolution of perception is an important concern in Leibniz's thought in a way that addresses the relationship between scales of sensation at which a particular sensorium operates and the manner in which this coincides with the edges of particular, discrete entities that are being perceived. If a perception is composed of units that are not individually discernible by a particular sensorium, the distinct edges between such perceptions become blurred, leading to what Leibniz calls a confused perception. The way that the sea is composed of an infinite multiplicity of waves is one example, but others that appear are almost equally poetic. Leibniz writes about seeing a fish pond from a distance "in which we see a confused motion and swarming of the pond's fish without making out the fish themselves."[42] And in his commentary on Leibniz's *Monadology*, Lloyd Strickland used the example of how, in a large crowd, one can perceive "the faces of the individuals turned toward us," but the distinct qualities of those faces remain confused.[43] Such blurring or confusion of edges speaks to the problem of scales of sensation I am discussing here, where the different scales of resolution at which different sensoria operate lead to a constitution of different textural edges at which objects come to be delimited as such.[44]

TINY COSMOLOGIES OR, STARS INSIDE OF A SPECK OF DIRT

The image of a pond in which individual fish are at the edge of discernment, or the sense of the sea where a distinct wave appears even as a multiplicity of others surround it indistinctly, offers an analogue for performing a haptic or textural reading of Bervin's poetic work even beyond *Silk Poems*. Bervin's work is influenced by textile artists such as Anni Albers. "River," a piece in which Bervin sews silver sequins by hand into a scale model of the Mississippi River over the course of twelve years, clearly fits within the realm of textile art itself. But even a purely textual piece such as the book *Nets*, in which Bervin uses Shakespeare's sonnets as a ground or a palimpsest by selecting specific words of the text while fading others into the background, is informed by haptics and the creation of textiles. In *On Weaving*, Albers writes about nets as one of the earliest forms of fabric as they "require hardly any tools [in order to be constructed] except, perhaps, a stick as a bobbin to carry the ... yarn" and could have been made at first out of "short ends of soft, pliable longitudinal materials" even before yarn was spun through a process of attaching "short bits of ... [material] to each other to form a flat expanse."[45] The result of this process would "be an open, netlike fabric."[46] Bervin's book *Nets* can be placed within a longer genealogy of erasure poetry, alongside such works as Ronald Johnson's *RADI OS*, which is based on a selective erasure of the first four books of *Paradise Lost*. Likewise, Bervin's conceptualization of *Nets* is informed by the textile construction of nets as an "open fabric," with such sense of a gap or an opening acting as a form of erasure. In the conceptual notes to *Nets*, Bervin writes: "I stripped Shakespeare's sonnets bare to the 'nets' to make the space of the poem open, porous, possible—a divergent elsewhere. When we write poems, the history of poetry is with us, preinscribed in the white of the page; when we read or write poems, we do it with or against this palimpsest."[47] What the material-figurative model of nets allows for in this case is a sense that rather than erasure, the process at play here is one of generation, so that the words that remain encircle what become the openings in the text, those openings themselves retaining a sense of inherent possibility of alternate arrangements.

Each of the pages of *Nets* presents to the reader a space akin to the chasm of Leibniz's sea: much of the text of the sonnet appears in a faded, barely perceptible gray and only a few words are isolated in clearly visible black ink. (See figure 4.6.) It is as if the remainder of the sonnet becomes the ground, the fabric on which the new poem is inscribed. In the case of "Sonnet 14," for instance, the words that Bervin selects, when strung together, say: "Pointing to each / constant / from / this / date."[48] Beneath them shimmers a landscape of "stars," "astronomy," "fortune," "thunder, rain, and wind," which gets focalized in a much more intimate universe of a pair of eyes.[49] In a sense, Bervin's poem repeats the arc that the sonnet itself follows as it traverses from the changeable elements of fortune figuratively registered within the cosmic and earthly elements of the stars and the weather to a discovery of constancy somewhere more proximate. However, the teleologies of the temporal arcs that they open differ. The original sonnet subverts the temporality of prognosticating future time through omens deposited in the cosmic elements, such as stars, by finding "constant stars" in what already exists and foreseeing the loss of virtues of "truth" and "beauty," which will inevitably accompany the disappearance of the figure being addressed to whom these qualities are being ascribed, unless these qualities are somehow reproduced and converted for the future. The version of the poem that Bervin presents in *Nets* makes a mark in time instead, sets a date as such a demarcation, and then points to the constants that unfold from it. Both temporal arcs deal with the problem of thinking the simultaneous recalcitrance and vulnerability of entities or qualities deposited in the unfolding of time with its perishing effects, but while the temporal arc of the sonnet likely folds in on itself toward a future disappearance, the

> Not from the stars do I my judgment pluck,
> And yet methinks I have astronomy;
> But not to tell of good or evil luck,
> 4 Of plagues, of dearths, or seasons' quality;
> Nor can I fortune to brief minutes tell,
> **Pointing to each** his thunder, rain, and wind,
> Or say with princes if it shall go well
> 8 By oft predict that I in heaven find.
> But from thine eyes my knowledge I derive,
> And, **constant** stars, in them I read such art
> As truth and beauty shall together thrive
> 12 If **from** thyself to store thou wouldst convert;
> Or else of thee **this** I prognosticate,
> Thy end is truth's and beauty's doom and **date**.

FIGURE 4.6 Jen Bervin, "Sonnet 14" from *Nets* (Brooklyn: Ugly Duckling Presse, 2004).

version of the poem in *Nets* unrolls a series of "constants" that move in an ongoing way toward the open of future time.

I tease out the configurations of some of these temporal arcs in part to point to how "erasure" as a poetic method in this case is proliferative rather than subtractive. Read through the figurative lens offered by Leibniz's image of the sea in movement, with a multitude of waves, or a crowd in which individual faces remain indistinct to perception, the grayed-out words on the page remain a site of possibility, a site of glimpsed microperceptions that act as the differential ground against which the selected words come into discernment. The proliferative effects arise out of the sense that a different grid of resolution can produce a different pattern, and that such a layering of patterns can exponentially proliferate the possibilities for meaning generation in the poem.[50]

In reading *Nets*, one can already foresee elements that will come to inform *Silk Poems*. While the reader of *Silk Poems* is at work navigating the recalcitrant texture of continuous language, attempting to parse the edges of words so as to insert cuts or discontinuities, the text acts as a kind of fertile ground that is continuously casting other lexical patterns or possibilities. Some of these are "actually" there, and some appear as momentary acoustic patterns or "microperceptions." Consider, for instance, this poem that appears early in the book, as the yet unborn silkworm, from whose perspective the poem is ostensibly written, describes a time antecedent to its existence when her mother, having emerged from her cocoon, seeks a mate:

SOAWING

ISATHING

THATGETSYOU

THERE[51]

Perhaps it takes an attentive glance, but these lines resolve fairly easily after one first encounters them into "so a wing / is a thing // that gets you / there"—referring perhaps to the fluttering of the silkworm's wings during coitus—a scene that is complexly inflected with silk moths' flightlessness, as they have lost their ability to fly through their coevolutionary interdependence with humans and rely on their human caretakers to place them in proximity to their potential mates.[52] But beneath or within the line "so a wing," other words begin to flutter in a momentary, almost unconscious way within the reader's eyesight: in an alternation of vowel sounds, "sawing" appears as does "sewing," both of these ostensibly present within the text as a kind of excess of its palimpsest. And then the invisible vowel appears through a kind of suggestion produced by the emphasis on fabrics and textile production in *Silk Poems*, and one sees "sewing" for an instant only to realize its absence, but the word lingers for long enough for the poem to utter "sewing is a thing that gets you there," a reading that echoes the text's overall concern with textile and textual practices alike. What interests me in part here is this ephemeral flutter of meaning that appears in the mind and then disappears, in that it denaturalizes the temporality of the reading process to open up a nearly preconscious dimension of minute "microperceptions," which in their accretion generate the rippled surface of the text within which an excess of meaning is possible.

At one point in *Silk Poems*, the silkworm utters the statement "IMAGINETHELANGUAGE / WRITTENINME" (105). This line provocatively points in multiple directions as it opens up the possibilities for what may constitute language in this context. This opening up is in part contingent on the pivotal preposition "in," which suggests a biosemiotic interiority residing within the body of the silkworm at the material microscales of protein structure and DNA patterning. In this sense, the intricately folded materiality of DNA or the shapes of protein molecules can be understood as a sea of biosemiotic signs that constitute the body of the silkworm. At the same time, another possible reading opens up here, one that Bervin repeatedly gestures toward as she points out how the radical for silk appears again and again within hundreds of Chinese characters. The radical within the Chinese character is usually a semantic indicator pointing to the meaning of the character while also allowing the taxonomic grouping of related words in texts such as dictionaries, even though over vast spans of time such semantic relationships may have shifted, obscuring the initial connections in meaning between words. Nevertheless, what Bervin is pointing to here in listing some of the words that contain the radical for "silk," including "paper," "textile," "warp," "weft," "latitude," "longitude," "parallel," "route," "compose," "edit," "weave," and "write," among others, is a set of semantic connections between contexts as diverse as textile weaving, mapping, and writing. All these are linked through the materiality of silk and the five-thousand-year-long history of silk cultivation, trade, and textile production, as well as its use as a medium of written inscription.

In this sense, the exclamation "IMAGINETHELANGUAGE / WRITTENINME" that is uttered by the silkworm can be reversed to indicate not just the sense that the silk secreted by the silkworm or the microcosm of its body are the material substrates within which biosemiotic signs reside, but also that the materiality of silk itself is constitutive of an array of meanings that ripple across different words and discursive contexts. This double movement is one way in which Bervin's poem disrupts the hylomorphic logic through which the semiotic and the material have often been split. In other words, *Silk Poems* points to how material practices associated with sericulture shape the language that arises around them, even as silk itself acts as a material of written inscription. Within this complex material-discursive landscape, systems of written signs, such as Chinese characters but also Arabic script, in which a single character contains other character elements nested inside it, offer another morphological analogue for the nested modes of materiality that traverse across scales in *Silk Poems*.

At the same time, the preposition "in" points to a sense of silk as a medium of inscription, so that the meaning of the line torques to encompass the sense of all the human language that has found its substrate of inscription in the materiality of silk. Bervin draws on a long history of silk being used as such a medium of inscription, stretching from its uses in mortuary rituals, or as a way of inscribing cloth for protection of the one wearing a specific garment, a tradition that she complicates by fabricating her biosensor, which bridges this exteriorized sense of using silk as a means of inscription with the signaling, biosemiotic pathways of molecules that flux within the interior geometries of the body. As such, Bervin's work gestures toward complexly nested material configurations through which silk can act as a medium and a mark of written inscription both inside and outside the body, evoking different geometries of embodiment, secretion, envelopment, and interiorization.

The complex, nested material scales of Bervin's poem, in which the form of the DNA is re-created within a morphological analogue of the six-letter line that composes the poem strand and the β-sheet structure of silk protein is echoed, in turn, by both the warp and weft structure of weaving and the figure-eight looping through which the silkworm deposits the silk strand, illustrate a conception of matter in which nearly infinitely complex material forms find themselves embedded within one another. Moreover, in the printed version of the poem, Bervin includes the macrocosm of the partial, unfolding shape of the gold spatter, silk strand poem as a miniature animation that appears in the corner of each page. This tiny, convoluted shape is meticulously executed, so that the gradually lengthening line matches the exact position in the progression of the text, corresponding to the same moment occurring in the unfolding poem strand that is inscribed on silk film. The miniature animation of the silk strand in the printed text lends the poem an animate, dynamic quality when the pages are flipped rapidly, replicating the movement of the silkworm as it deposits the silk fiber and placing the reader herself, as she moves through the text of the poem, within the durational and proprioceptive analogue of the silkworm's movement. Within the conceit posed by Bervin in which it is the silkworm that is composing the poem, the unfolding animation of the silk fiber in the corner of the text literalizes the sense that the poem is both a material and a semiotic construction that is written by the silkworm as it secretes the fibers of its cocoon. Furthermore, the unfolding strand of the poem in the corner of the page creates a sense that the macrocosm of the gold spatter poem is present within the microcosm of the individual lines of the poem.

Bervin's inspiration for the insertion of the miniature poem strand is Bob Brown's book *Words* (1931). "[It] was the first place I saw something like this," Bervin writes in the "Project Note" at the end of *Silk Poems*, "and I still marvel at how his poems disappear in plain sight, even when you're looking for them" (172). In this case Bervin is referring to Brown's use of microscopic font in *Words* to create a miniature set of poems that sit in tandem on the page with another poem printed in regular-sized font: "One set of poems was printed in 16-point Caslon Old Face, a classic font style used in all Hours Press publications. The other was relief-printed from engraved plates at less than 3-point size (perhaps, according to Cunard, less than 1-point)." As is the case with Bervin's gold spatter poem printed on silk film, "the microscopic text ... [was] 'too small to be read without a magnifying glass' or without using a variant of Brown's proposed reading machine."[53] Brown imagined (but never actually built) such a machine as a way of revitalizing "the Optical Art of Writing" that would allow the reader to read the indiscernible aspects of his texts.[54] As such, both Brown's and Bervin's poems rely on the modalities of amplification generated through the use of instruments, in order to enhance the human senses so that they may be able to discern scales of sensation that are otherwise imperceptible. Likewise, they are both concerned with forms of microscopic writing or micrographia, a writing practice that is also resonant with various instances of the uses of the genome as an archival repository of information that Bök is drawing on in conceptualizing *The Xenotext Experiment*. In *Micrographia* (which means "tiny writing"), Hooke actually discusses the use of miniature writing as a way of "convey[ing] *secret Intelligence*," referencing "certain pieces of exceeding curious writing" he has seen, "one of which in the bredth of a *two-pence* compris'd *the Lords prayer, the Apostles Creed, the ten Commandments, and about half a dozen verses besides of the Bible,* whose *lines* were *so small* and *near together,* that [he] was unable to *number* them with [his] *naked eye.*"[55] In *Silk Poems*, not only does Bervin deploy "micrographia" as a poetic technique, generating in the process a poetic text that can be read only with the help of a microscope, but her poem in a sense acts as a microscope, amplifying through the aesthetic means of poetic form the textural and semiotic dimensions of biological materiality and nonhuman sensation that would otherwise escape the bounds of human capacities for sensation.

5

TISSUES

Histological Landscapes and the Substances of Character

BUTTERFLY AND BEETLE COLLECTION

At one point in *The Making of Americans* the narrator tells a story about making an insect collection. The anecdote tells of a young boy who informs his father that he wishes "to make a collection of butterflies and beetles." The father agrees but simultaneously poses a disguised question about the ethics of such a project, saying to his son, "You are certain this is not a cruel thing that you are wanting to be doing, killing things to make collections of them?" The ensuing conversation convinces the son that the idea of making an insect collection is indeed "a cruel thing," and he agrees not to pursue this project and is in turn commended by his father, who says that "the little boy was a noble boy to give up pleasure when it was a cruel one." The narrative turn occurs in the early morning when the father wakes and sees "a wonderfully beautiful moth in the room," catches and kills it, and, after pinning it in the boy's insect collection, wakes his son, shows him the moth, and says, "'See what a good father I am to have caught and killed this one.'" In response, "the boy [is] all mixed up inside him" but decides that he will "go on with his collecting."[1]

This anecdote about the butterfly and beetle collection can be seen as a kind of microcosm for Gertrude Stein's own anxieties about how her projects of literary taxonomy and description, such as the one she pursues in *The Making of Americans*, where she sets out to describe and classify "every kind of human being," risk turning into a collection of dead rather than living specimens. On a most literal level, the contours of this anxiety play out in terms that resonate with William Wordsworth's famous dictum from the *Lyrical Ballads*—"we murder to dissect"—in that making a collection of natural historical specimens involves collecting, killing, and preserving living organisms so that they can be described and classified.[2] Yet, even if read more figuratively, the line from Wordsworth's poem is suggestive of how epistemological practices, in their attempt to identify and order the world, may impose a sense of fixity on the fluid and changing shapes of entities, which may slip, slide, and ooze through the rigid geometry of the identity rubrics created to classify them.

Stein was no stranger to the problematic of gathering the requisite specimens for observation and description in order to meet the epistemic demands of various disciplinary perspectives. In a photograph from the summer of 1897 taken at the Marine Biological Laboratory (MBL) at Woods Hole, Massachusetts, she is depicted in the center of the image, looking on as her brother Leo Stein holds up a collecting jar into which he has just captured a ctenophore, an invertebrate organism consisting of a jellylike body and cilia for locomotion.[3] (See figure 5.1.) The photograph was taken during a specimen collecting trip that was a part of an embryology course Stein was enrolled in that summer at the Marine Biological Laboratory, a moment sandwiched between her completion of training in psychology with William James and Hugo Münsterberg at the Harvard Psychological Laboratory and her enrollment in medical school at Johns Hopkins between 1897 and 1901.

While the impact of Stein's training in psychology has been well documented in the critical literature, only a few studies have directly addressed how her training in medicine and biology shaped her subsequent literary career.[4] In one of the notable studies on the topic, *Irresistible Dictation: Gertrude Stein and the Correlations of Writing and Science*, Steven Meyer situates Stein's mode of composition in relation to the organicist discourses that were circulating in the biological sciences, as

FIGURE 5.1 *Invertebrate Course Collecting Trip at the Woods Hole Marine Biological Laboratory in 1897.* Leo Stein is holding up a specimen jar, while Gertrude Stein looks on. MBL Archives, Marine Biological Laboratory, Woods Hole, Mass.

well as philosophy, at the beginning of the twentieth century, and in particular the conceptual frameworks, such as Alfred North Whitehead's "philosophy of the organism," that drew on understandings of living organisms in order to redefine "entities" in terms of "process" and hence as a function of differential relations.[5] While Meyer's approach to the biological inflections in Stein's literary work is attentive to the open-ended processes through which organisms are constituted, many of the other critics who have addressed this aspect of her work have understood the biological dimension as a site of essentialist fixity. In "Gertrude Stein's Brain Work," Maria Farland suggests that Stein's research into the anatomy of the brain during her studies at Johns Hopkins acted as a source of biological essentialism that appeared in aspects of her work, arguing that Stein had to break away from the biological anatomy of the body as well as forms of taxonomic practice associated with the sciences in order to achieve her breakthrough as a modernist writer.[6] In another essay on Stein and the biological sciences, "The Mechanistic Conception of Life: Loeb the Teacher, Stein the Student at the MBL," Gerald Weissmann directly addresses Stein's experiences as a student in an embryology course led by Franklin Pierce Mall during the summer of 1897 at the Marine Biological Laboratory, arguing that "Stein was an old fashioned Woods Hole mechanist" and that her subsequent compositional tendencies as a writer were shaped by these mechanistic and reductive accounts of biological life.[7]

This chapter offers a sense of the continued significance of the biological sciences for Stein's subsequent practice as an avant-garde writer, situating her work, and specifically her early novel *The Making of Americans*, not in relation to a notion of biological materiality as a site of essentialist fixity but instead in relation to how the biological sciences have understood material change at the turn of the twentieth century. This moment involved a complex interrelationship between different methodologies in the life sciences, one that has often been characterized as a shift away from practices of natural history, with their emphasis on observation, description, and taxonomic classification of various specimens gathered during field expeditions, to the more experimentally driven methodologies that would characterize much of the research in biology during the twentieth century. While this shift had been underway since the beginning of the nineteenth century, when biology emerged as a discipline, particularly through the development of the experimentally driven practices of physiology, as Paul Farber points out in "The Transformation of Natural History in the Nineteenth Century," natural history did not simply wane with the emergence of biology; rather, the vast influx of natural historical specimens was by this time becoming organized into "large, serious, working collections," housed in "public natural history museums," which formed the basis for the emergence of more specialized natural historical disciplines, such as "ornithology and entomology."[8] At the same time, the observations made on the basis of vast numbers of natural historical specimens, along with the studies of how they varied across their geographic distributions, led to synthetic theoretical developments, such as the emergence of the theory of evolution, which moved across and "united all the many disciplines of the life sciences."[9] The practices of observation, description, and taxonomy, associated with natural history, similarly remained an undercurrent within twentieth-century biology. As I point out in chapter 2, such natural historical practices also became a site of methodological appropriation by literary and artistic practitioners, for whom they came to formulate another paradigm for how the natural sciences could shape aesthetic practices in addition to the one offered by the model of experimentation.

The problem of transformation of biological organisms over time that had come into focus in the nineteenth century through the work of various evolutionary thinkers, most prominent among them Darwin, created a sense that biological materiality was malleable, continuously undergoing gradual processes of change.[10] This ultimately lead to a whole revolution in thought about the plasticity of the living world, with thinkers such as Elizabeth Grosz suggesting that such anti-essentialist, temporal dynamics of matter are still transforming conceptual frameworks within the humanities. It is ultimately this movement in critical thought that has inspired the conceptual formulation of *soft matter* in this project.

The theory of evolution by natural selection produced an open question about an underlying mechanism through which characteristics could be transmitted from generation to generation, around which the nascent science of genetics was coming into form. *Gemmules, germplasm*, and *pangenes* were some of the many early terms for the kinds of tissues that could be transmitted from generation to generation and that could in their qualities somehow give rise to observable, macroscopic effects. While I will explore these in greater detail later, what is key for all these theories is that they required imagining and attempting to observe a mysterious doubling of tissues, with one microscopic layer giving rise to the macroscopic, the observable, or what we would now call the phenotypic features of the organism. This is a similar problem of nested scales of biological materiality that Jen Bervin's *Silk Poems* attempts to depict through the creation of morphological analogues that amplify and reveal the underlying layers of matter hidden within the scales of materiality that are observable to the human senses. I suggest that Stein's desire to elucidate the material bases for character traits in her attempt to classify "every kind of human being" in *The Making of Americans* involved a similar tendency toward amplification and a desire to think and make observations across scales. She attended, in particular, to how the textural or the haptic properties of specific, microscopic tissues could produce the forms of activity and reactivity that could give rise to the character effects she was observing in her taxonomic project. And it was the volatile nature of such biological substances, with their unpredictable reactivities and effects, that ultimately led her to loosen up the taxonomic categories of her classification system to create a more dynamic classificatory geometry, or what I come to call a *soft taxonomy*, in other words, a taxonomy that would remain responsive to the processes of change occurring among the *soft entities* it is classifying, even as it simultaneously attends to their differentiation.

The fundamental premise of the taxonomic system that Stein develops in *The Making of Americans* is the division of people into two basic types, "attacking" and "resisting." This division is based on the idea that human beings have a "bottom nature," which is of either the attacking or the resisting kind. While bottom nature represents one's "natural way of winning, loving, fighting, working, thinking, writing," many variations exist in how a particular type of character approaches these aspects of living.[11] This means that, at times, people who appear to possess observable traits of the attacking character type may, in fact, belong to the resisting type. While Stein acknowledges that her system for classifying kinds of people "is often very confusing," she insists that the basic division that undergirds her taxonomic project is illustrative of a meaningful distinction between two fundamental types of character, which is rooted in the relation between manifested traits and the underlying material substrates out of which these qualities of character arise.

One of the problems that Stein faces in completing her monumental taxonomic project is how to remain attentive to the particular variations or differences that each specimen brings into the picture without losing sight of the grid of taxonomic categories she had originally set up to classify her specimens. This becomes a particularly complex task when she encounters "specimens" that share many qualities of one type of character and yet, according to the classification criteria, still firmly belong to the other characterological grouping. For instance, while resisting types most of the time have compositions that are "earthy" or "wooden" and hence not as sensitive to stimulation as the attacking types, which possess a distinct quickness of reaction and sensation, sometimes the narrator of *The Making of Americans* comes across specimens of the resisting type that are composed of substances that are much more reactive than is typical of the resisting kind of being, making them as reactive as some of the examples of the attacking type. As this example illustrates, at a fundamental level Stein's project is troubled by a problematic that troubles any project of taxonomic classification: how to organize an array of singular particulars into a grid of typological relations without subsuming and instrumentalizing the relevant details of each individual specimen in this pursuit of taxonomic order.

Constructing a taxonomy, by definition, requires typological categories to be more general than the individual instances that populate them. Otherwise, each new specimen that appears with its own particular variabilities would open up a new taxonomic category, and these would in turn produce an infinitely proliferating series. Something like this happens in Michel Foucault's preface to *The Order of Things*, when he writes about reading Borges's appropriation of a passage from a certain Chinese encyclopedia, which offers a classification of animals into "(a) belonging to the Emperor, (b) embalmed, (c) tame, (d) sucking pigs, (e) sirens, (f) fabulous, (g) stray dogs, (h) included in the present classification, (i) frenzied, (j) innumerable, (k) drawn with a very fine camel brush, (l) *et cetera*, (m) having just broken the water pitcher, (n) that from a long way off look like flies."[12] Foucault suggests that encountering such a taxonomy is disturbing, not because of the unexpected juxtapositions it produces between living animals and those that belong to the world of myth, but because it makes it difficult to discern whether the enumeration of animals above rests on any underlying epistemic ground that would guarantee this particular delineation of classificatory categories. As a taxonomic project, *The Making of Americans* oscillates between Stein's desire to make "generalizations as complicated as the facts,"[13] in other words, to allow the particular variability of each new specimen to open out its own categorical space in the grid of classification, and other moments of confidence about the fundamental premises of the project, when the classificatory grid she had set out, with its primary division of people into attacking and resisting types, seems to offer a set of generalizations that can encompass all the variation she is encountering. At moments when the former impulse is pervasive, the project hovers at the edge of a disorder, in which, in Foucault's words, "fragments of a large number of possible orders glitter separately in the dimension, without law or geometry."[14] And then Stein cinches her observations of "facts" into the taxonomic grid she has set up, and the project lurches forward, at times with an altered set of categories that had been deformed by an encounter with some unexpected alignment of particulars. This constant negotiation between "generalizations" and "facts" acts as a motor that drives the lively dynamism of Stein's project, in which the multiplicity of, at times, discordant observations is allowed to deform the initial classification criteria in order to engender a set of generalizations that is complex enough to encompass the ongoing influx of observational particulars. In this way, a dynamic tension arises between the systematizing set of categories required for the monumental task of classifying "every kind there is of men and women" and the fact that, in the course of observation, Stein comes to a fuller understanding of the complex ways different substances or elements of character change, intermix, and, through these interactions, seem to produce, at least in terms of observable effects, forms of character that subvert the categories of the original classification system.

These oscillations between generalizations and particulars that propel *The Making of Americans* as a project are themselves mirrored in the epistemic history of taxonomy and its struggles to discern an order among various specimens it encounters. In this way, the project of taxonomy that Stein embarks on in the course of composing *The Making of Americans* can be situated within a wider history of taxonomic classification that arose in the context of Enlightenment practices of natural history: "Since the seventeenth century the description and classification of minerals, plants and animals had prospered and progressed," as early empiricist thinkers about nature sought to create elaborate collections of natural historical specimens, which were often accompanied by descriptive accounts, outlining their morphology, development, and characteristics that placed them in relation with other organisms.[15] In *Objectivity*, historians of science Lorraine Daston and Peter Galison trace the epistemological shifts in taxonomic practices between the eighteenth and nineteenth centuries, observing a transformation from the eighteenth-century search for ideal types—an episteme they refer to as "truth-to-nature"—to the nineteenth-century impulse to document every variant among the specimens, which they refer to as "mechanical objectivity." The practitioners working under the epistemic framework of "truth-to-nature" sought to discern ideal types that were hidden by the variability of particulars: "To see like a naturalist required more than just sharp senses: a capacious memory, the ability to analyze and synthetize impressions, as well as the patience and talent to extract the typical from the storehouse of natural particulars, were all key qualifications."[16] As an illustration of how the "truth-to-nature" episteme could offer a set of "epistemic virtues" to a practitioner of natural history, Daston and Galison evoke the example of the Swedish naturalist Carolus Linnaeus, who developed the binomial system of taxonomic nomenclature for classifying living organisms.[17] In works such as *Hortus Cliffortianus*, Linnaeus attempts to tame "the untamed variability, even monstrosity of nature" through disciplined modes of observation that would allow him to discern the significant features that brought specimens into taxonomic relation, while allowing what he perceived as insignificant variations to blur into the sea of irrelevant details.[18] This method would allow the discerning naturalist "to distinguish genuine species from mere varieties."[19] In contrast, "mechanical objectivity," which arose in the mid-nineteenth century, brought with it an epistemic impetus to collect and describe a wide array of variants that an observer of nature would encounter. As a result of this new mode of articulating epistemic virtue, all kinds of natural objects and phenomena, from snowflakes, to blood crystals, to the splatter patterns of drops as they fall onto a surface of a liquid, were revealed to lack the perfect symmetry that they had hitherto been imagined to have. The epistemic pursuits of the naturalists shifted toward diligent recording and describing of every variant that they encountered, rather than seeking to smooth out the variations in order to reveal the hidden, idealized types underneath. Extending these notions of "mechanical objectivity," botanists in the late nineteenth and early twentieth centuries developed a new understanding of type—known as holotype—"in order to stabilize nomenclature."[20] A holotype referred to an individual specimen, usually the first one that was discovered, collected, and preserved, and to which the name of the species would be affixed for all future reference. As the precepts stemming out of the epistemic virtues of "mechanical objectivity" would suggest, a holotype does not need to be a "typical" specimen characteristic of the species; rather, it is the variations inherent to its singularity that authenticate it as a specimen.

While Daston and Galison posit that the shift toward "mechanical objectivity" was a consequence of cultivating a particular version of a scientific-self, I would like to emphasize that the desire to enumerate and document as many variations among natural historical specimens as one encounters was also inflected by the underlying problematic of the relationship between taxonomy and the variegated temporalities of change within the materiality of natural worlds that were coming into view with various stirrings of evolutionary and geological thought in the course of the nineteenth century. It is not my goal here to speculate about the directionality of the causal relationship between the emerging interest in enumerating variations among natural historical specimens and the conceptual transformation that allowed natural historians to discern that the natural world was not a repository of static types but a dynamic site of gradual transformation. I would like to suggest, however, that variation and change appear to be linked on both an ontological and an epistemological level. The epistemic framework of "truth-to-nature" relies on the sense of underlying idealized archetypes that seek to stabilize the variability of the natural world, in a manner that is evocative of a long tradition in Western thought, stretching all the way back to Plato, of counterpoising the unchanging realm of perfect, idealized types to the messy, unstable materiality of nature. The episteme of "mechanical objectivity," in contrast, brings into view a vast array of specimens, permitting natural historians, who were becoming interested in processes of transformation, to discern the significance of variability as a motor of change. Darwin's discovery of natural selection as the mechanism of evolution, for instance, relied on attentive observation of the particulars of the world, and it was only through the enumeration of the specific differences among the specimens that he collected that the overall picture of evolutionary change began to emerge.

Darwin's ability to conceptualize natural selection as the mechanism of evolutionary change depended on his observations of variation among many specimens he collected during his five-year voyage as a naturalist on board the HMS *Beagle* between December 1831 and October 1836.[21] During the voyage Darwin collected and made careful observations and descriptions of insects, plants, birds, along with other living things, while also making note of geological and meteorological phenomena that he encountered.[22] A famous example of how these specimen collections later affected his thinking about evolution involves several closely related species of finches that he observed on the Galapagos Islands: "The remaining land-birds form a most singular group of finches, related to each other in the structure of their beaks, short tails, form of body and plumage: there are thirteen species, which Mr. Gould has divided into four sub-groups. . . . The most curious fact is the perfect gradation in the size of the beaks in different species of Geospize, from one as large as that of a hawfinch to that of a chaffinch."[23] While in this case Darwin is noting variations among distinct species of finches, he will later draw on this example in *On the Origin of Species* to explain modification of species through the process of natural selection. Darwin's evolutionary argument in regard to the finches relies on the fact that they constitute twenty-five distinct but closely related species, all of which resemble species that inhabit the mainland of South America but are at the same time different from them. In this way the Galapagos Islands became a kind of naturally created laboratory for the study of evolution, because they allowed Darwin to observe how the finches from the mainland became isolated on the islands, diverging into different species by adapting to

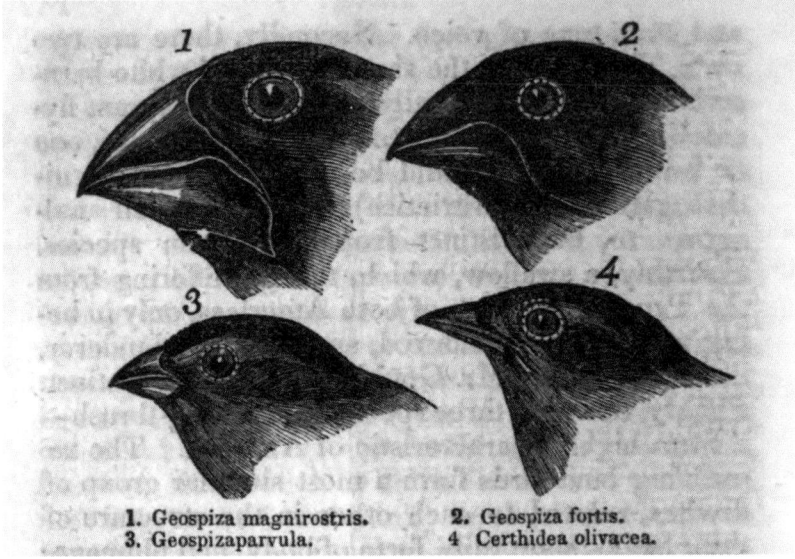

FIGURE 5.2 Charles Darwin, Darwin's finches. Journal of researches into the natural history and geology of the countries visited during the voyage of H.M.S. *Beagle* round the world: under the command of Capt. Fitz Roy R.N., 1846. Courtesy of Hathi Trust.

different food sources and aspects of their new environment. (See figure 5.2.) However, while geographical isolation of populations is an important factor in this example of speciation, the underlying engine of change is the inherent variability between individuals, which offers a reservoir of potentiality on which natural selection acts in hewing the shape of a particular population. This variability is not only evident between species but, at a more basic level, punctures the taxonomic designation of species itself, rendering evident the singularity of each individual and the manner in which this irreducible particularity in its collectivity acts as a substrate of change. As such, both variability and change, and especially the lively relationship between them, pose a problem for the potentially ossifying project of "truth-to-nature," with its promise of bringing taxonomic order to the objects of the natural world by uncovering the underlying ideal types beneath the particularities of variation.

In an article published in a special issue of *Twentieth-Century Literature* on the topic of Darwin and literary studies, Omri Moses writes that Stein and Darwin both shared a "fascination with the dynamic relation between repetitive processes and innovation," concentrating their "attention on microevents that reveal emergent changes." As Moses notes, in *Everybody's Autobiography* Stein proclaims that "evolution was still exciting very exciting."[24] And in one of the last texts that she composed, *Wars I Have Seen*, Stein expresses her interest in nineteenth-century practices of natural history, making specific reference to Darwin's attempts to discern patterns of evolutionary change in the lush variability of the natural world: "There was nothing more interesting in the nineteenth century than little by little realising the detail of natural selection in insects flowers and birds and butterflies," Stein writes, "and comparing things and animals and noticing protective coloring nothing more interesting."[25] Such desire to enumerate minute differences and similarities stemming from the practices of natural history came to shape several of Stein's exhaustive taxonomic projects. In these she sought to describe and classify entities that belong to a particular category, be they human beings, as in *The Making of Americans*, or various objects that appear in *Tender Buttons*. In expressing an interest in "the detail of natural selection" as it occurs in the observable variations between different species of insects, plants, birds, and other organisms, Stein is pointing to a mode of attending to the material world that parallels her attempt to describe and bring into view an array of variations among her specimens, in order to explore the dynamic forms of mixing, interchange, and simply the mercurial qualities of what I am calling *soft matter*.

If the butterfly and beetle collection is a kind of micro-analogue for Stein's taxonomic project in *The Making of Americans*, then Stein shares in the anxieties of collecting experienced by the little boy. These anxieties are fueled by the association that taxonomy shares with fixity or *deathly* stasis, which could easily turn the project into a collection of dead rather than living specimens. With stirrings of evolutionary thought and a sense that the natural world is continuously undergoing gradual change, these instabilities began to permeate varied projects of taxonomic classification in the nineteenth century as they sought to develop a way of ordering the transforming entities of the natural world without ossifying their lively dynamism. In other words, such underlying processes of material change shook the ground or *the table* upon which, in Foucault's terms, the grid of taxonomic relations finds its stability. An example from *The Order of Things* vividly illustrates what happens when the ground that guarantees a particular taxonomic order is shaken, creating radical uncertainty in how to select the salient features that are supposed to bring particular specimens into relation. Foucault sets the conceptual scene in which this problem plays out by drawing on an example in which the condition of aphasia affects one's capacity to isolate consistent and relevant qualities that would permit a set of items to be ordered into a taxonomic grid. Given the task of arranging "various differently coloured skeins of wool . . . the aphasiac will create a multiplicity of tiny, fragmented regions in which nameless resemblances agglutinate things into unconnected islets; in one corner, they will place the lightest-colored skeins, in another the red ones, somewhere else those that are softest in texture, in yet another place the longest, or those that have a tinge of purple or those that have been wound up into a ball." None of these patterns of categorization will produce semantic stability, and the tiny islets of arrangement will quickly "dissolve again, for the field of identity that sustains them, however limited it may be, is still too wide not to be unstable."[26] This example can act as a kind of allegory for the moments when proliferating levels of detail lift off their anchoring categories, disrupting their coherence by generating not a nested set of qualities that can be ascribed to specific taxonomic groupings but an ever-expanding set of possible modes of categorization in which no detail is insignificant enough to be subsumed by its governing rubric. Such moments of taxonomic instability seem symptomatic of transitional moments between one epistemic framework and another. And, in the context of the relationship I am positing here between variation and change, they may also be indicative of a deeper ontological instability, one in which differences between specimens are no longer modifications of an underlying archetype, but where each new variant offers, in a Darwinian sense, a new vector of possible transformation, generating the changeable material entities that constitute the living world.

TISSUES: HISTOLOGICAL LANDSCAPES AND POETICS OF DESCRIPTION

Stein composed *The Making of Americans* in the first decade of the twentieth century—a time when dominant historical narratives of the flourishing of modern biology would suggest that the techniques of collection of natural historical specimens and their organization into various taxonomic grids, guided by parallel practices of observation and description, were on the wane, as these methodologies came to be pushed to the background in favor of experimentation. Even though the specific historical moment at which Stein is composing *The Making of Americans* coincides with the epistemic turn toward experimentation as a dominant mode in scientific pursuits, with this propulsion toward experimentation clearly spilling over into critical understandings of literary modernisms, I would like to complicate that account by suggesting that Stein remains preoccupied with the methodologies that more properly belong to the observational purview of natural history, such as taxonomic classification and description of specimens. I argue that these preoccupations continue to play a significant role for subsequent generations of twentieth-century and contemporary writers that I will turn to in the next chapter. The work of this genealogy of poet-naturalists, among them Lyn Hejinian and Lisa Robertson, is often grouped under the rubric of experimental poetics, but I suggest that a subset of figures within this lineage could more accurately be critically understood to formulate a descriptive poetics, informed by the role that description and classification play in the context of natural historical investigation.

This is evident in the way that Hejinian links the pursuit of description in avant-garde poetics to the methods of scientific description that emerged in the context of natural historical practices, positing "descriptive language and, in a broader sense, poetic language as a language of inquiry, with analogies to the scientific method." In citing Émile Zola's provocation that "'an experiment is basically only a provoked observation,'" Hejinian, in a sense, shifts the emphasis away from experimentation as a primary scientific technique that literature can draw on, in favor of the experiment as simply a formulation of specific constraints that create an occasion for observation and description. In several of the essays in *The Language of Inquiry*, Hejinian specifically takes up Stein's work, suggesting that it presents a kind of culmination of "various [literary] 'realisms' that emerged from the mid-nineteenth century on," and that sought to model "artistic researches" on the methods of science.[27] Hejinian's insight opens up the possibility of linking the poetics based on the descriptive techniques of natural history that arise in the second half of the twentieth century to a longer history of literary traditions, such as realism and naturalism, which have been influenced by the observational and descriptive procedures of the sciences.

Other critics, however, have pointed to a discontinuity in whether description remained relevant as a literary technique for Stein throughout her career, with many critics arguing that there was a stylistic break in Stein's writing between her early texts, which were influenced by the modalities of scientific description, and her subsequent work. In *Irresistible Dictation*, Steven Meyer, for instance, argues that in the course of writing *The Making of Americans*, Stein came to reject the project of description as mechanistic and deterministic: "It was this dependence of all projects of 'complete description' on an atomistic and ultimately materialistic and deterministic model that Stein, in the course of writing *The Making of Americans*, came to distrust." As such, Meyer comes to associate Stein's initial impulse toward description with a mechanistic quality of her writing:

> Certainly, Stein's understanding of science was initially mechanistic; thus in *The Making of Americans*, written between 1902–1911, she attempted to describe the precise mechanisms of human personality in greater detail, with the ultimate aim of describing every possible kind

of human being. . . . Careful attention to repetition, with its capacity for "minutest variation," supplied Stein at this stage of her career with a methodology appropriate in equal measure to her research and her writing. Yet with *Tender Buttons*, composed the year after she completed her monumental novel, she embraced a vigorously nonmechanistic outlook. In this collection of prose poetry, and in hundreds of pieces, large and small, written over the next twenty years, she endeavored to portray consciousness in terms of the experience of writing, as she moved to a more fully "organic" sense of composition.[28]

While there is a clear shift in Stein's compositional style between *The Making of Americans* and *Tender Buttons*, Meyer's account of *The Making of Americans* as mechanistic and *Tender Buttons*, as well as Stein's subsequent writing, as "vigorously nonmechanistic" posits, in my view, too stark of a dichotomy between these two moments in her oeuvre. Rather than viewing Stein's technique of "repetition, with its capacity for 'minutest variation,'" as mechanistic and deterministic, I see it as integral to the capacity of Stein's writing to convey the liveliness of biological organisms as they continuously undergo change. This, in turn, closes the conceptual loop between the practice of description, as it operates in the context of natural history, with its capacity to register the most minute transitions and variations between specimens, and a parallel role that a focus on description plays in Stein's writing.

Meyer's critical interpretation of Stein's early literary output as primarily focused on a descriptive, mechanistic modality is not an isolated occurrence in the critical literature. Gerald Weissmann posits a parallel analysis of the relationship between mechanism and Stein's literary style. Referring back to the summer that Stein spent at the MBL studying embryology with one of the prominent proponents of mechanistic biology Jacques Loeb, Weissmann suggests that the exposure to this context led Stein to subsequently develop mechanistic tendencies in her writing:

> My hunch is that Gertrude Stein was an old fashioned Woods Hole mechanist, a reductionist of the school of Jacques Loeb. Her revolution

of words owed as much to *The Mechanistic Conception of Life* of Loeb (1965 reprint) as to her study of "Normal Motor Autonomism" (Solomon and Stein, 1896), which she had written for William James, or to the "Demoiselles d'Avignon" of her Picasso years (the first version of which showed a medical student as spectator).[29]

Weissmann in many ways offers a parallel account to Meyer's assertion that Stein's early literary work is imbricated in the mechanistic outlook, stemming from the specific context of her training in the sciences. A little later in his essay he comes to associate the practice of description, in particular, with scientific methodology, drawing on a citation from one of Stein later works, *How to Write*, written in 1931: "But words, sounds, *things* were not descriptions: 'A daffodil is different from a description, a jonquil is different from a description. A narrative is different from a description.' . . . Neither modern writing nor modern art were going to *describe* things, that was the job of science" (16).

Rather than locating a clear break with description in Stein's work, my reading suggests that description, with its roots in the natural sciences, remains a modality in her writing well beyond the early years of her writing practice, generating productive continuities between works such as *The Making of Americans* and later works, such as "An Acquaintance with Description," published in 1929. In the introductory comments to the latter in *A Stein Reader*, Ulla Dydo writes that Stein remained interested in description beyond the early stage of her writing that followed immediately on her training in science: "Even before 1926, in works like *A Third*, *Natural Phenomena*, and *A Novel of Thank You*, begun the preceding year, description had preoccupied Stein." Dydo points out that in her lecture "What Is English Literature," Stein returns to the question of description and states that "the thing that has made the glory of English literature is description, simple concentrated description."[30] It is evident in reading "An Acquaintance with Description" that Stein, in this text, is taking on the project of theorizing description as a method: "Description having succeeded deciding, studying description so that there is describing until it has been adjoined and is in a description. Studies description until in attracting which is a building has been described as an in case of planting. And so studying in description not only but also is not finishing but understood as describing." These sentences present an inquiry into a sense of description as a method and yet this meta understanding of description continuously fades into becoming the description itself. This is perhaps most explicit in the first sentence, where Stein writes "studying description so that there is describing until it has been adjoined and is in a description."[31] There is something autopoietic about this sequence in that autopoietic systems are capable of generating themselves or their components as they operate, and here, for Stein, it is the consideration of description as a method that produces describing.[32] Similarly, in the second sentence the word "attracting" produces a sense of gradual accretion that unfolds in the course of studying description, as though an array of magnetic particles or even dust were being drawn together until they come to be built up. And it is this process that produces a description, which has a grounding quality registered by Stein through the term "planting," even as she also reminds the reader in the culminating sentence that "studying in description" is "not finishing" and can be understood as a continuous process of describing. What is clear from these examples is that description remains a preoccupation for Stein well into her writing career. In other words, going back to the passage Weissmann cites from *How to Write*, the question of description itself is as much of a concrete object of inquiry in Stein's writing as any daffodil or jonquil.

Stein's interest in description can be situated within the overall arc of my argument about how her training in the sciences came to influence her literary practice. In her lecture "The Gradual Making of *The Making of Americans*," Stein explicitly links her interest in a project of descriptive taxonomy that she pursued in *The Making of Americans* to her exposure to scientific methodologies during her studies of psychology with William James:

> Then as I say I became more interested in psychology, and one of the things I did was testing reactions of the average college student in a state of normal activity and in the state of fatigue induced by their examinations. I was supposed to be interested in their reactions but soon

I found that I was not but instead that I was enormously interested in the types of their characters that is what I even then thought of as the bottom nature of them, and when in May 1898 I wrote my half of the report of these experiments I expressed these results as follows: In these descriptions it will be readily observed that habits of attention are reflexes of the complete character of the individual.[33]

One of the things that seems striking about the account that Stein offers here is that her sense of scientific practice is illustrative of the historical tension between experimentation and description that was unfolding at the end of the nineteenth century. In transforming the project of psychological experimentation she was conducting into the project of literary taxonomy in *The Making of Americans,* Stein comes to transform an experimental project of testing the reactions of her fellow students into a descriptive project that attempts to taxonomically delineate every possible type of personality that exists among men and women.

Following her studies of psychology at the Harvard Psychological Laboratory, Stein attended Johns Hopkins Medical School, leaving to pursue her literary career in Paris, without taking her degree, in 1901. In between, as I elaborate at the opening of the chapter, she spent the summer of 1897 enrolled in an embryology course at Woods Hole Marine Biological Laboratory, where she took part in field outings during which she learned the practices of collection and classification of marine invertebrate specimens. As such, Stein was exposed firsthand to three of the leading institutions that played a dominant role in the development of biological research in the United States and her training at this historical juncture would have certainly offered her exposure to a range of research practices, including morphological description, conceptual speculation about heredity, and various experimental protocols in embryology, psychology, and so on.

The intellectual atmosphere at these institutions favored an approach to education in which students engaged in original scientific research. The Marine Biological Laboratory, for instance, established in 1888 to provide a research station where scientists and their students could gather, particularly during the summer months, to collect and study marine specimens, was a good example of this kind of mixing of education and research that Stein was exposed to during her studies. In his account of Stein's experiences as a student in an embryology course led by Franklin Pierce Mall during the summer of 1897 at the MBL, Weissmann includes photographs that show Stein engaged in field outings, during which the students and teachers collected natural historical specimens. Weissmann describes the photo that appears at the beginning of this chapter (figure 5.1) as "a stunning icon of natural science," in which the collecting jar, with its captive specimen, appears as a focal point of the composition, an "apex of a visual pyramid at which life has been caught in a jug."[34] This scene in which, in Weissmann's words, a "creature from the ocean has been plonked into a glass pot to become a specimen for science" is evocative of the incident of the butterfly collection that occurs in *The Making of Americans* and carries with it the same drama of what it means to capture something living and transform it into a frozen instance in a scientific collection of specimens.

The establishment of the MBL was preceded by another educational research station, the Anderson School of Natural History on Penikese Island, started by the Harvard morphologist Louis Agassiz. The method of teaching that Agassiz introduced emphasized "collecting, observing life histories of organisms, and tracing embryonic stages of development." The school's existence was unfortunately short-lived due to Agassiz's death in 1873. With his death "and the opening of [Johns] Hopkins [in 1876] the dominant morphological tradition in America passed from Harvard to [Hopkins]," where the morphologist William Keith Brooks was training a new generation of American morphologists.[35] This spirit of closely combining education and research fit with the spirit under which Johns Hopkins was established as an institution: it came into being through an endowment of "a wealthy Baltimore businessman and a Quaker, Johns Hopkins," who had a vision of developing "a modern hospital" in Baltimore, side by side with "an associated medical school and research university."[36] As a result, when Stein enrolled in medical school there in 1897, she found herself in an environment where more practical sides of her medical education were closely accompanied by original scientific research that she was conducting by observing the developmental morphology of brain tissues under Franklin Mall and his assistant Lewellys Barker.

In *Transforming Traditions in American Biology, 1880–1915*, the historian of biology Jane Maienschein explores the significant role that the intellectual climate at Johns Hopkins played in shaping developments in American biology in the twentieth century. Her detailed study follows the careers of four pioneering American biologists—Edmund Beecher Wilson, Edwin Grant Conklin, Thomas Hunt Morgan, and Ross Granville Harrison—all of whom received their postgraduate education at Johns Hopkins. Each of these figures was at least a partial participant in what Maienschein delineates as the *morphological tradition* in American biology, even while they each also, to varying degrees, assumed the responsibilities of conducting research programs in experimental biology. In this way, Maienschein's study offers a clear account of the continuing role of morphological observation and description in the shaping of biological research at the beginning of the twentieth century.[37] By the second half of the nineteenth century the morphological tradition, like other related biological disciplines, was under pressure to account for how processes of evolutionary change transformed the materiality of tissues into the dynamics of temporal unfolding: "By 1880, the morphological tradition was concerned with problems of form and patterns of change in form, and it relied on a mixture of descriptive, observational, and comparative methods."[38] As such, at the close of the nineteenth century the morphological tradition was concerned with conjoining the problem of description of form with that of change, in order to produce a more dynamic sense of shape and texture of tissues and organs that would link the concerns of phylogeny, or the relationships produced between organisms through evolutionary change, with those of ontogeny, or development.[39]

Maienschein illustrates the complex epistemic relationship between experimental biology and the natural historical practices of specimen collection, classification, and description that informed the intellectual climate at Johns Hopkins at a time that coincided with Stein's study of medicine there. Stein famously "failed at medicine" when she did not get a passing grade in obstetrics from Professor John Whitridge

Williams. She was given a second chance to obtain her degree by Mall, who thought that her scientific research showed promise, and who set her to work on a model of an embryo human brain. Stein botched the model by bending the spinal cord under the head of the embryo and as a result failed to graduate. She did submit a manuscript of her brain research (not the ill-fated brain model but her earlier attempts to elucidate the morphology of the nucleus of Darkschewitsch) for publication to the *American Journal of Anatomy*. This ghost manuscript received mixed reviews from Mall, Barker, and Stein's illustrious peer at Hopkins Florence R. Sabin, was never published and has subsequently been lost from the archive.[40] While this manuscript would prove an invaluable comparative study in description to Stein's later literary descriptions, it is sadly missing; however, a version of Stein's attempt at the description of brain tissues has been preserved in Lewellys Barker's book *The Nervous System and Its Constituent Neurons*, in which he draws on Stein's work to describe the nucleus of Darkschewitsch:

> Miss Gertrude Stein, who is now studying a series of sagittal sections through this region from the brain of a babe a few weeks old, describes the nucleus of Darkschewitsch as follows: "The nucleus is more or less conical in shape. It lies dorso-medial from the red nucleus, being about as thick in a dorso-ventrical direction as is the dorsal capsule of the red nucleus in which it lies. At this period of medullation the commissura posterior cerebri, considered simply topographically (that is, as a medullated fibre-mass without particular reference to the course of the fibres), appears as a dorso-ventral bundle, solid in the middle, subdivided dorsally into an anterior (proximal) portion and a posterior (distal) portion, while ventrally it expands in the form of a hollow pyramid, which rests directly upon the nucleus of Darkschewitsch." As to the bundle of fibres described above as being situated ventral to the nucleus, and passing forward and ventralward, Miss Stein in the brain she is studying can follow the fibres only as far as the fasciculus retroflexus. The fibres most ventrally situated are very complex in arrangement, forming a whirl in the substance of the nucleus ruber.[41]

This passage inside of Barker's text offers a brief glimpse of a mode of description that Stein was engaging in during her morphological studies of brain tissues. Rather than being strictly experimental, Stein's work on the brain was primarily descriptive in nature, attempting to construct a three-dimensional model of a brain region by observing microscopic sections of its tissues and reconstructing its tracts and nuclei. The interpretation of Stein's writing I am developing here involves a sense that the formal qualities of her style are informed in part by her exposure to the biological study of living organisms. In this context, I argue that these attempts at detailed morphological description of specific tissues, in which Stein explored the capacities of descriptive language to amplify and delineate the intricate details of biological materiality, came to inform the techniques of description that she later employed to convey how character arises out of detailed, texturally differentiated qualities of material substances in *The Making of Americans*.

Stein formulates an explicit link between her concept of "bottom nature" and the material qualities of substance: "This then is then one way I have been seeing kinds in men and women, the way I see the bottom natures and other natures in them. Always I see them as kinds, always as kinds of substance and ways of that substance being in them as bottom nature."[42] As such, the taxonomic sorting of manifested character types that Stein is developing in *The Making of Americans* depends on an underlying sense of a differentiated "bioactive" materiality out of which these personality traits arise. This preoccupation with the underlying materiality of character plays out predominantly over the course of thirty or so pages in the first third of *The Making of Americans*:

> There must now then be more description of the way each one is made of a substance common to their kind of them, thicker, thinner, harder, softer, all of one consistency, all of one lump, or little lumps stuck together to make a whole one cemented together sometimes by the same kind of being sometimes by other kind of being in them, some with a lump hard at the centre liquid at the surface, some with a lump vegetablish or wooden or metallic in them. Always then the kind of substance,

the kind of way when it is a medium fluid solid fructifying reacting substance, the way it acts then makes one kind of them the resisting kind of them, the way another substance acts makes another kind of them the attacking kind of them.[43]

The description of substances in this passage moves from their thickness to their texture and shape, and then it transitions to their active "fructifying [and] reacting" properties. There is a sense that a substance consisting of one lump would offer less reactive edge than a substance composed of multiple "little lumps stuck together." An intermediary or interstitial substance "cements" the smaller pieces together and mediates between them. Sometimes there is an emphasis on textural contrast, with a lump that is hard at the center and liquid at the surface. The description of the arrangement of substances in relation to each other unfolds a spatial dimension, with a central area, surfaces, and interstices.

In the textural dimensions of surfaces and the reactive qualities they evoke, such moments of tissue description in Stein's text can be read through the instances in Book 2 of Spinoza's *Ethics* that I isolated in my theorization of soft matter in chapter 1. At these moments Spinoza delineates the manner in which bodies come to affect one another through textural relations that occur as their surfaces touch, with "soft part[s] [of the body]" being more easily impressed and hence changeable in relation to the contact with the surfaces of a harder external body.[44] Placing these moments of textural description from the *Ethics* next to those from *The Making of Americans* opens up questions about how the potentiality for action or reaction (in Spinoza's terms, affecting and being affected) arises out of the geometric and textured qualities of materials that compose different bodies.

While Stein's accounts of the underlying substances of character are quite abstract, these descriptions of textured shapes, arranged in three-dimensional space, are at the same time evocative of the interior of a cell or the arrangement of cells in a tissue, conveying a sense of physical structures that seem microscopic in their textured qualities. As such, they can be conceived as histological landscapes, depicting the morphology of the brain that Stein was investigating during her studies at Johns Hopkins.[45] In Stein's description of the nucleus of Darkschewitsch, fortuitously preserved inside the prose of *The Nervous System and Its Constituent Neurones*, she similarly works carefully through descriptive language to create an account of three-dimensional geometries of tissues. The language that Stein employs to describe the nucleus of Darkschewitsch involves delineating precise and contained geometric shapes as landmarks within a less distinct mass of tissues. In this way the conical shape of the nucleus of Darkschewitsch becomes one geometric form. It is nested, in turn, within a dorsal capsule of the red nucleus. Another element in this three-dimensional landscape of geometric shapes is the "hollow pyramid" of the "commissura posterior cerebri," which comes to rest ventrally on the nucleus of Darkschewitsch. In between, and among these more distinct geometric layers of tissues, Stein notes a plethora of neuronal fibers, which she traces along the three-dimensional axes of the body, dorsally, ventrally, and toward the body's anterior and posterior ends. It is in these less distinct sections of tissue, where Stein's sense of description has to accommodate itself to the unknown and often confusing set of histological topographies, that the relationship between language and materiality comes paradoxically into the most meticulous form of realist representation, having to attend indiscriminately to every detail, without knowing which of them is anatomically significant, while also producing a heightened sense of abstraction, in which the concreteness of these material tissues dissolves into geometric shapes, whose exact form and proportion can often only be ascertained comparatively. As such, description in these sections has to be able to carry a quality from one material region and superimpose it onto another, so as to position topographically the regions that are completely unknown in relation to the geometric fragments of tissues that have already been discerned into anatomical visibility and tactility. This sense of description that must articulate all features of this unknown neuronal topography comes to reflect the "epistemic virtues" of "mechanical objectivity" described by Daston and Galison, as it plunges into the morphological thickness of tissues without having a clear grid of significance through which to discipline the vision of the observer. Stein's descriptions of substances in the literary prose of *The Making of Americans* possess a similar desire to amplify and differentiate particular morphological forms. In this way she comes to compose a detailed "morphology of lumps," some of which are "hard at the centre" but become more liquid at their surface, and many of which are composed of very different materials with distinct textural properties, ranging from "vegetablish," to "metallic," to "wooden." One can make a comparison here to the "lump" of the "commissura posterior cerebri" in Stein's morphological description, which she describes as "solid in the middle" but expanding ventrally to form "a hollow pyramid."

It is important to note here that histological practice involves a careful piecing together of three-dimensional shapes from two-dimensional sections that the observer has to navigate in sequential order, so as to be able to note where in the three-dimensional morphology of the organism particular structures and organs make their appearance. This means that Stein's work at Johns Hopkins, where she labored over descriptions of two-dimensional sections of brain tissues in order to construct a three-dimensional model of a particular region of the brain, would have involved looking at one thinly sliced microscopic section at a time and then moving through them in sequence while remaining highly attuned to the slight differences between each slide. This way of piecing together a three-dimensional form out of a sequence of slightly varying sections of tissue resembles Stein's compositional method in *The Making of Americans*, in which two-dimensional planes of each syntactic iteration suddenly accrue to generate a three-dimensional shape, as is evident here where she is giving an account of her epistemology: "Always then when I come to know the whole meaning of any one, that one is then there inside me. I am more or less filled up then with that one, sometimes I am filled up so full with that one that I must tell it then to every one, sometimes I am filled up so full with that one that I must then certainly tell it to that one" (325). In this regard, Stein's descriptive method in *The Making of Americans* is almost sculptural, evoking a spatial quality similar to the sense of volume present in her descriptions of the morphology of neuronal tissues. This aspect of Stein's writing has most often been read in relation to the emergence of cubism at this historical moment and its particular manner of approaching three-dimensionality of objects by breaking them up into a series of flat two-dimensional planes.[46] I would like to suggest here that it was perhaps Stein's exposure to the new techniques for sectioning the body that were emerging in histology and the morphological study of tissues that first alerted her to this problematic of transforming a three-dimensional shape into a series of two-dimensional planes.

Stein's literary project of *The Making of Americans* creates a space for a kind of amalgamation of a typological project that she fantasizes about during her studies of habits of attention and motor automatism at the Harvard Psychological Laboratory and her subsequent studies of brain morphology at Johns Hopkins. In the literary space of description produced in *The Making of Americans*, Stein creates a bridge between the two by beginning to hypothesize how qualities that she associates with character arise out of the relations between bioactive—"solid fructifying reacting"—substances, which, in their interaction, compose anyone's personality. The textures and qualities of specific differentiated materials that compose character come to index within Stein's taxonomy the active and reactive properties of particular kinds of character: "In some it is as I was saying solid and sensitive all through it to stimulation, in some almost wooden, in some muddy and engulfing, in some thin almost like gruel, in some solid in some parts and in other parts all liquid, in some with holes like air-holes in it, in some a thin layer of it, in some hardened and cracked all through it, in some double layers of it with no connections between the layers of it" (348–49). There is a correspondence between the harder materials and the more inert qualities of the resisting type of people. This correspondence makes sense in terms of the textural qualities of these materials, because sensation, according to Stein's theory of emotions, must pass through the "slow resisting" substance making up this type of person before it can emerge into emotion: "Generally speaking then resisting being is a kind of being where, taking bottom nature to be a substance like earth to some one's feeling, this needs time for penetrating to get reaction" (347). In contrast, attacking being arises out of substances that seem either more malleable or more reactive: "I am thinking of attacking being not as an earthy kind of substance . . . it can be slimy, gelatinous, gluey, white opaquy kind of thing and it can be white and vibrant, and clear and heated" (349). Stein's insistence on using descriptions of substances that compose a particular type of character brings with it several significant qualities. These descriptions convey a spatial arrangement, a volume composed of heterogeneous areas, which together form a bounded whole. In her descriptions of these substances, Stein is usually particularly attentive to the textural qualities and the ensuing reactive properties of the enclosing surface material, which determine how a particular character type interacts with the environment. In a sense, in *The Making of Americans* Stein is at work on devising a theory of affect that relies on the textural qualities of substances, as she develops a model of the relationship between sensation and emotion, which is attentive to the material dimension of how the emotional disposition of a particular body is an effect of the reactivity of the bioactive substances that make it up.

LIVING SPECIMENS: HEREDITY AND TYPOLOGIES OF RELATION

To conclude, I will turn briefly to the discussions of heredity that were coalescing at the beginning of the twentieth century around the emerging science of genetics. The context of heredity offers a way to explore the relationship between textured, seemingly microscopic, forms of tissues that give rise to the macrocosm of observable affective dispositions of character in *The Making of Americans* and the as yet indefinite material substrates that were posited as modes of transmission of specific traits by Darwin's elucidation of evolutionary theory. In an initial, manuscript version of *The Making of Americans*, written in 1903 and held at the Beinecke Rare Book and Manuscript Library, Stein explores how the emergence of the science of heredity in the second half of the nineteenth century inflected the shifting historical understanding of the relationship between physical features and character:

> In the eighteenth century that age of manners and of formal morals it was believed that the temper of a woman was determined by the turn of her features; later, in the beginning nineteenth, the period of inner spiritual illumination it was accepted that the features were molded by the temper of the soul within; still later in the nineteenth century when the science of heredity had decided that everything proves something different, it was discovered that generalizations must be as complicated as the facts and the problem of interrelation was not to be so simply solved. You reader may subscribe to whichever doctrine pleases you best while I picture for you the opposition in resemblance in the Dehning sisters.[47]

In this passage, which never made it into the much longer, final version of *The Making of Americans*, Stein offers a brief history of the relationship between physical features and temper. When it comes to the later part of the nineteenth century, the historical moment when her own training in science took place and which immediately precedes the writing of *The Making of Americans*, Stein explicitly refers to the science of heredity as the context for theorizing this relationship.

Questions of heredity are a clear concern for Stein in *The Making of Americans*, considering that at least on one level she is writing a "history of a family's progress," a focus that she makes direct reference to in this passage when she refers to the question of the opposition in resemblance of the Dehning sisters. Stein's account of nineteenth-century discourses of heredity offers a complex and often contradictory landscape in which "the science of heredity had decided that everything proves something different." This leads to a kind of collapse in the hierarchy between more general categories and the underlying facts upon which they are founded, resulting in a sense "that generalizations must be as complicated as the facts," which, as I have pointed out, often brings Stein's taxonomic practice nearly to a point of collapse.[48] The problematic that Stein explores in *The Making of Americans* of how underlying material substrates produce particular observable character traits closely parallels the difficult task set before nineteenth-century natural historians who turned toward the study of heredity. Their task was to ask how the varied traits they observed among living organisms could be a consequence of invisible and as yet mysterious material elements that could transmit these traits unchanged from generation to generation, but could also act simultaneously as a generator of variability and transformation.

These material elements go by several names, from Charles Darwin's *gemmules*, to August Weismann's *germ-plasm*, to Hugo de Vries's *pangenes*, and yet, despite of the distinctions between these hereditary models, their hypothetical existence poses the same conceptual problematic of the doubling of material layers that constitute an organism, so that whatever traits are manifested possess a relationship to an underlying material substrate of hereditary factors. Without an understanding of material mechanisms of inheritance that would allow characteristics to persist over time through multiple generations, while simultaneously permitting variability and novelty to arise, Darwin's take on evolutionary change would have been untenable. This problem fueled Darwin's desire to explain the mechanism of inheritance, and in 1868 he published *The Variation of Animals and Plants Under Domestication*, in which he outlined his theory of inheritance, known as pangenesis, which proposed the existence of microscopic hereditary particles called gemmules. The theory proposed that gemmules were continuously shed by all the cells of the body and traveled through the blood to the reproductive organs where they could form germ cells. The theory of pangenesis was in a way strangely Lamarckian, because it suggested that as the bodily cells underwent changes during the life of the organism, they could pass these "acquired characteristics" on to the next generation. For Darwin, the key significance of the theory lay in its ability to provide an explanation for the continuous source of variation on which natural selection could then act, a problem he also attempted to address through theories of sexual selection. In other words, while the theory of natural selection explains how "less fit" organisms may be eliminated from a population, it does little to explain how variation itself arises. Without this account of how the organic world comes to be populated with a vast array of organisms, each slightly distinct from the others, the eliminative processes of natural selection would have very little to work with. Darwin himself had been plagued by this question and spent a great deal of time, following the publication of *On the Origin of Species* in 1859, trying to figure out how variation arises in the organic world and how such appearance of variation is linked to change. This difficulty of grasping the relationship between variation and change was compounded by the equally puzzling mystery of how any trait could be transmitted through inheritance from one generation to the next. As far as pangenesis was concerned, after many lengthy experiments conducted with the help of Francis Galton, involving blood transfusions between rabbits with differently colored fur to test for the presence of gemmules in their blood that could transmit the heritable traits for color between individuals, no strangely colored rabbits appeared, indicating that pangenesis was a dud.

It is important to pause here to note the difficulty of solving the mystery that heredity posed to these nineteenth-century biologists, not only because it forced them to surmise how something that could be a mechanism of fixed transmission through time could simultaneously be a mechanism of change, but also because they had to account for a double material layer out of which particular traits arose, one that was observable and the other, underlying one, that somehow governed the manifestations of these traits but was invisible and intangible. Stein's theorization of character in *The Making of Americans* is based on a parallel negotiation between manifested characteristics she observes and the underlying material substrates that give rise to these characteristics. At times, Stein identifies contradictions within her classificatory system, based on the lack of correspondence between the underlying material layers and the outward traits they give rise to: "In some of such of them they seem to be winning by acting by attacking they live so very successfully in living but nevertheless they are of the kind of them that have resisting winning as their real way of fighting although never in their living does this act in them."[49] This quotation illustrates the paradoxical tension between the modes of activity that can arise from a particular substance and the properties of that substance. As such, Stein's classificatory system leaves a kind of gap for indeterminacy, within which the substances that make up a particular character do not simply mechanically give rise to determinate properties. In this case, for instance, a personality that in every active way has an attacking nature is classified as inherently resisting. In another example, in which an attacking type is "so slow in action one almost could think of it as [a] resisting [type]," Stein makes two conflicting observations about the substance this particular type is composed of. The substance is "so thick, so gluey," and so slow in acting that it resembles the resisting type, and yet it is not the resisting type, "it ... [is] a different substance in its way of acting, reacting, of being penetrated, of feeling, of thinking than any slow resisting dependent independent being" (349). The substance that composes "the bottom nature" in someone, even if it induces a character type that is atypical, is at its basis not transformed by this process—it remains either a resisting or an attacking substance. This means that Stein, while interested in observing the complex transformative processes that constitute different character types, seeks to impede the unraveling of her classification system by evoking the comparatively static properties of "bottom nature," which, in her system, hold these types to their designated categories.

Stein's insistence in her typology that "the important thing ... [for classifying types of character] is knowing the bottom nature in any one" carries with it elements of hereditary fixity, because it privileges the concept of an inherent nature over the "mixing" that arises as elements of the bottom nature intermix with other natures that are present (299). This perspective ignores the "problem of interrelation," which ensues as "this [other] nature or natures in them mixes up well with the bottom nature of them to make a whole of them as when things are cooked to make a whole dish that is together then" (152). Descriptions of the mixing process, on the other hand, emphasize the relationships between different parts that make up a particular character, and, as such, they present personality as emerging out of the reciprocal patterns of interaction and change. Complexity arises because the "bottom nature" in many kinds of people is intermixed in various ways with the other natures present in them:

> As I was saying some men have it in them to be made altogether of the bottom nature that makes their kind of men. Some have it in them to have other nature or natures in them, natures that are the bottom nature

to make other kinds of men, and this nature or natures in them mixes up well with the bottom nature of them to make a whole of them as when things are cooked to make a whole dish that is together then.... Some have other nature or natures in them that never mix with the bottom nature in them and in such ones the impulse in them comes from the bottom nature or from the other natures separate from each other and from the bottom nature in them, in some of them there is in them so little of the bottom nature in them that mostly everything that comes out from inside them comes out from the other nature or natures in them not from the bottom nature in them. (152)

These complex patterns of intermixing explain Stein's observations that sometimes people who, while their bottom nature is of one kind, resisting or attacking, have a personality characteristic of the other kind. But these patterns of intermixing and interchange do not remain contained within each individual; rather, they cross the boundaries of an individual and place her in relation with the environment that surrounds her.

Stein explores the qualities of such interchanges between the characters and their surroundings by describing the delicate gradations of feeling that accompany the exchanges between inside and outside, which are necessary for anything to be living:

> How anything coming into that one comes out of that one, how some things coming into that one hardly are coming out of that one, how much the things coming out of that one are different from the things going into that one, how quickly and how slowly, how completely, how gradually, how intermittently, how noisily, how silently, how happily, how drearily, how difficulty, how gaily, how complicatedly, how simply, how joyously, how boisterously, how despondingly, how fragmentarily, how delicately, how roughly, how excitedly, how energetically, how persistently, how repeatedly, how repeatingly, how dryly, how startlingly, how funnily, how certainly, how hesitatingly, anything is coming out of that one, what is being in each one and how anything comes into that one and comes out of that one makes of each one one meaning something and feeling, telling, thinking, being certain and being living. (783)

The array of qualities ascribed to how "anything is coming out of that one" brings out the complexity with which this process is unfolding. Some of the qualities demonstrate the temporality of this process in a direct way, by making reference to speed: "how quickly and how slowly, . . . how intermittently" it is taking place. In fact, most of the adverbs used to describe how "anything is coming out of that one" on this list convey an affective resonance. Placing the question "how" in front of an adverb opens it up from a single quality into a more gradated space, generating a sense that each specific manner in which something is occurring is varied in itself. Thus the complexity of the manner in which "anything is coming out of that one" arises out of both the variety offered by the twenty-nine different adverbs and the fact that embedded in each one of them is a range of possible degrees at which this quality of action can be manifested. In "Poetry and Grammar," Stein states that adverbs, along with verbs, articles, conjunctions, and prepositions "are lively because they all do something and as long as anything does something it keeps alive."[50] The liveliness in this passage arises out of the tension between the adverbs, which are numerous, varied, gradated, and at the same time delicately specific, and the fact that the dominant actions in the passage, conveyed by the verb "to come," are unspecific, except in assuming an inward or an outward direction of movement. The lack of specificity and the continuous repetition of actions, as well as the syntactic repetition, such as the coupling of the action of coming in and coming out in the first three phrases of the passage or the numerous repetitions of the question how, create a background against which the multiplicity of very specific adverbs can generate delineated areas of variation. This example conveys the complex and varied ways in which the exchange between inside and outside must take place in order to sustain something living.

In emphasizing the relational nature between character and the surrounding environment, Stein unsettles a sense of essentialist fixity that could accompany her conceptualization of "bottom nature." In *The Making of Americans*, she describes that people often derive a feeling of themselves inside them not from their "natural way of being," but from being "cut off" from their natural way of living and exposed to a different environment (135). The wealthy Hersland family, despite of their wealth, inhabit a part of Gossols where no other rich people are living. This dislocation from "right rich living," which is, as Stein suggests, "the natural way of being" for them, affects members of the family, particularly Mrs. Hersland: "In her living with the servants and governesses and seamstress in her daily living she had a feeling of herself to herself inside her, this was more of an individual being in her than ever had been in her when she was leading with her own kind of people around her the right rich living which was the natural way of being to her" (159). Her feeling of herself inside her arises largely through her contact "with the governesses and seamstresses and servants who lived in the house with her, and with the, for her, poor queer kind of people who lived in the small houses near her" (115). In *The Making of Americans*, Stein specifically addresses the circumstances that give a character a feeling of themselves inside of them. The occurrence of this feeling is rare, with most of the characters never experiencing it in relation to anything around them. It is significant, then, that for Mrs. Hersland, this feeling is induced specifically in relation to a change in her external circumstances, which dislocates her from her "natural" surroundings, unsettling her into a feeling of herself. This environmentally induced change in Mrs. Hersland can be theorized in terms of Stein's willingness to perturb the fixed strictures of her typology and pay attention to the way changing circumstances cause transformations in the characters she is describing.

This problematic of change not only affects the entities that Stein is working to describe but also comes to encompass the descriptive and classificatory project of *The Making of Americans* as it undergoes its own epistemological shifts over the long course of nearly a decade of its composition. In other words, the living beings that Stein attempts to re-create compositionally are not the only entities that are continuously undergoing change; the practices of coming to know someone or something also possess their own lively histories: "Of course all the time things were happening that is in respect to my hearing and seeing and feeling. I found that as often as I thought and had every reason to be certain that I had included everything in my knowledge of any one something else would turn up that had to be included."[51] It is difficult to ascertain from Stein's reflection on the process of composing *The Making of Americans* whether the new information that is continuously arising is a result of changes in the subjects of her observation, or whether the sense of new developments within their characters is a parallax effect produced by the changes in the gradually developing knowledge of the observer. This points to a more fundamental problematic of how changes in the epistemological premises of any system of knowledge enter into relation with the ongoing processes of change that constitute the objects of that knowledge.

In fact, the question that the little boy with a butterfly and beetle collection faces of whether to "go on with his collecting" is one that Stein herself will face at the juncture between *The Making of Americans* and her composition of *A Long Gay Book*. Stein sees *The Making of Americans* as a totalizing project of "describing everything" and subsequently, in *A Long Gay Book*, reaches the culminating point at which she comes to a conviction that as "a description of everything is possible it was inevitable that I gradually stopped describing everything."[52] Rather than accepting Stein's claim that her movement from *The Making of Americans* and on to the writing of *A Long Gay Book* was a result of her certainty that the project of describing "every kind there is of men and women" could be accomplished, and, as such, was no longer of interest to her, I am proposing that it was the contradictions arising out of the emphasis on the role of relations in the constitution of personality that led her away from the typology of individual characters in *The Making of Americans* and toward the description of "every possible kind of pairs of human beings and every possible threes and fours and fives of human beings and every possible kind of crowds of human beings" in *A Long Gay Book* and later on in her descriptions of groups in her plays.[53] As such, Stein's literary practice, both in her early projects, such as *The Making of Americans*, and in her subsequent work, such as *A Long Gay Book* and "An Acquaintance with Description," and stretching all the way to the end of her literary career—as is evident from her reference to "the details of natural selection" in *Wars I Have Seen* (1945)—remains invested in a taxonomic delineation of specimens, even if these specimens are not isolate but are instead imbricated in a complex web of relations with their environment. In this way Stein's descriptive practices, while continuously changing in response to the lively dynamism of the entities she is describing and their arrays of relation, retain an affinity to Stein's training in the biological sciences. While critics have often thought of Stein's writing as experimental, seeking to locate a demarcating point in the chronology of her work at which she turns away from practices of description, my chapter suggests that such experimental tendencies in her writing can exist hand-in-hand with other methodologies that have emerged from the scientific tradition. As such, Stein's writing can be situated at the inflection point when observational, descriptive, and classificatory practices associated with techniques of natural history came to intermingle with the developing science of experimental biology. In her persistent interest in the literary adoption and transformation of such scientific techniques as a way of studying the lively configurations of materiality, Stein can be located among what Daston and Galison have called the current of "many anatomists, crystallographers, botanists, and microscopists, . . . [who] had set out to capture the world in its types and regularities," or, as I would argue, its dynamics, particulars, relations, and irregularities.[54]

6

CLOUDS

Cloud-Writing and the Movement of Qualities

> *Cloudiness what is cloudiness, is it a lining,*
> *is it a roll, is it melting.*
> —GERTRUDE STEIN, "ROASTBEEF," *TENDER BUTTONS*

BLUR BUILDING: THE ISTHMUS BETWEEN CLOUDS AND ARCHITECTURE

At this instant the sky is bright blue. In the foreground, halfway up the frame, a low-lying cumulus cloud is forming above the surface of the lake. A white volume begins to change and spread outward. At its middle the mass of the cloud is wide and vibrant so that it appears to form a bright solid. Moving and unmoving blocks of sky become visible. A steel structure appears as an orbit of vertical columns and a tensile spun canopy resting on the surface of an elevated saucer. The vapor begins rising again from the left corner of the frame, filling and filling the space until no discernment is possible between the shape of the cloud and the sky.

At this instant the sky is bright blue. In the foreground, halfway up the frame, a low-lying cumulus cloud is forming above the surface of the lake. A white volume begins to change and spread outward. At its middle the mass of the cloud is wide and vibrant so that it appears to form a bright solid. The woolpack begins unraveling at the edges, the wind rending it into fine wisps that involute in the way that smoke strands bend, thicken for an instant, and then move outward until they are morselled to nothing and consumed. Moving and unmoving blocks of sky become visible. A steel structure appears as an orbit of vertical columns and a tensile spun canopy resting on the surface of an elevated saucer. The vapor begins rising again from the left corner of the frame, filling and filling the space until no discernment is possible between the shape of the cloud and the sky. Darker clouds appear, overhung by straggling clouds that sail over them passing quickly driven by the lower winds. Then the sky is spread over with one continuous cloud, streaked by silver lines of water running between the ridges of the vapor.

At this instant the sky is bright blue. In the foreground, halfway up the frame, a low-lying cumulus cloud is forming above the surface of the lake. A white volume begins to change and spread outward. At its middle the mass of the cloud is wide and vibrant so that it appears to form a bright solid: solid but not crisp, white like the white of egg, and bloated-looking. The woolpack begins unraveling at the edges, the wind rending it into fine wisps that involute in the way that smoke strands bend, thicken for an instant, and then move outward until they are morselled to nothing and consumed. A shallow valley forms in the middle with widening slopes, which begin to form a shape of the letter v. Moving and unmoving blocks of sky become visible. At once the clouds seem to cleave asunder. A steel structure appears as an orbit of vertical columns and a tensile spun canopy resting on the surface of an elevated saucer. The sky is flat, unmarked by distances, a white thin cloud, chalky and milk-colored, with a remarkable oyster-shell molding. The vapor begins rising again from the left corner of the frame, filling and filling the space until no discernment is possible between the shape of the cloud and the sky. Darker clouds appear, overhung by straggling clouds that sail over them, passing quickly driven by the lower winds. Then the sky is spread over with one continuous cloud, streaked by silver lines of water running between the ridges of the vapor.

I open this chapter with an experiment in description, composed in an attempt to depict the vaporous dynamics of the architecture of a cloud that constitutes the Blur Building. Created by Elizabeth Diller and Ricardo Scofidio as a temporary installation for the Swiss National Expo held in Yverdon-les-Bains, Switzerland, in 2002, the Blur Building appears as a dynamic shape of a cloud floating above a metal platform. As primary construction material, the architects used water and air, drawing up the lake water available at the site and atomizing it into a fine mist by passing it through "a dense array of high-pressure water nozzles."[1] The result is a cloud building, composed of innumerable tiny droplets of vapor suspended above a steel pavilion elevated over the surface of Neuchâtel Lake. (See figure 6.1.) The steel structure of the Blur Building is minimal, acting primarily as a "soft pneumatic skin" that houses the water nozzles, a viewing platform, which elevates the visitors above the cloud, "an angel bar," which serves many different kinds of bottled water, and a media installation.

In a monograph that documents the conceptual development and the construction of the project, Diller and Scofidio state that their design "weave[s] together architecture and electronic technologies" in a way that "exchange[s] the properties of each for the other" so that elements of architectural structure become dematerialized, while the "normally ephemeral" electronic media "become palpable in space."[2] While the design of the Blur Building entails a departure from the monumentality of structure as imagined stasis, this move can alternately be described as a thickening of the diachronic axis rather than as the process of dematerialization: the vaporous bodies that compose the building are no less material than steel, but they possess a different grade of malleability or responsiveness, allowing them to rapidly undergo change in relation to other bodies that surround them, which operate at slower rhythms of transformation. As a consequence of this proclivity for rapid change, the Blur Building acts as an indicator of temporal flux within materials. The manner in which the speed of movement is registered in the vaporous composition of the building produces a softening at the edges of structure, resulting in its signature blurring effect or the difficulty of discernment of the discreteness of its edges as they come in contact with

FIGURE 6.1 *Blur Building*. Courtesy of Diller Scofidio + Renfro.

the vaporous bodies that surround it. In part, this dynamism of contact between the Blur Building and its surrounding environment is facilitated by electronic technologies, which act as an interface that places the shape of the building itself in dynamic, vicissitudinous relation with the surrounding meteorological phenomena: "A built-in weather station reads the changing weather conditions and electronically adjusts water pressure in response to shifting temperature, humidity, wind direction, and wind speed. The resulting fog mass is thus a dynamic form that combines natural and artificial weather forces."[3] The intermixing of the artificial cloud and the weather dynamics of the surrounding environment acts to dissolve distinctions between nature and artifice, *blurring* the boundaries between the Blur Building and the other vaporous bodies, clouds and mists and air currents, surrounding it.

As such, the Blur Building acts as an architectural construction that emphasizes temporal transience, operating within a nonmonumental temporality that is responsive to the vagaries of the weather, rather than the more monumental temporality of structure. In this way it models the relationship between dynamics of temporality and the shapeliness of structure, even if this shapeliness is vaporous, infused with activity, and soft at its edges, or rather only provisionally bounded into the discreetness of an entity. In this way, the Blur Building acts as a conceptual isthmus for this chapter, situating my developing discussion of how taxonomic and descriptive procedures respond to the problem of material change in relation to both the *soft taxonomies* of clouds and the architectural concept of "soft architecture"—or architecture that is plastic and adaptable to change, which I discussed extensively in the opening chapter on the concept of soft matter.

DESCRIPTIONS OF CHANGE

As a temporary construction, the Blur Building was dismantled following the Expo, and so the descriptions with which I opened this chapter were not created through direct observation but instead come from viewing the vapor dynamics that constituted the building in a video recording on display as part of the Museum of Modern Art's *Applied Design* exhibition (March 2, 2013–January 20, 2014).[4] The procedural imperative for creating these descriptions comes from "The Perfume Recordist," a project by Lisa Robertson and Stacy Doris.[5] Writing collaboratively through the persona of the Perfume Recordist, the two poets theorized a procedure for documenting the luminous and changing detail of the present: "If, as Wavists, we believe that change is not determinate, and if we can record the present in enough detail within a series of temporal frames, then varieties of change will emerge from the detail of sensing."[6] This passage elaborates a methodology according to which description can act as a technology of amplification, flooding the delineated frame of the present with luminous grain of detail, and, in turn, rendering perceptible a more variegated sense of the kinds of change that are dynamically constituting the present, thereby opening the unfurling edge of this present toward the future in indeterminate ways. In other words, through this amplification in the "detail of sensing," differentiated rhythms of change become evident, as "varieties of change" sift themselves into minute and heterogeneous temporalities of changing shapes and qualities.

It could be said that description in this sense is acting as an instrument of amplification so that its formal features, such as the minute patterns of repetition and variation that come to compose its textural topography, allow nearly imperceptible intervals of time that structure qualities of change within material phenomena to enter into sensory awareness. This can be compared, for instance, to how the formal typographical features of *Silk Poems* enact the scales of sensation that are operative for the silkworm as it interacts with the mulberry leaf, even though much of the textural detail of such interaction would normally escape the parameters of what is notable or even perceptible to the human senses. The case of description, then, extends the inquiry pursued in *Poetics of Liveliness* of examining how the formal properties of aesthetic and particularly textual objects, existing within the purview of poetics, can reveal and attend to what occurs at scales that may otherwise be imperceptible.

Upon first attempts at observation, the shape of the Blur Building seemed uniform, white, and "bloblike," once the initial wisps of vapor had thickened into a cloudlike volume. But what at first seemed like an exercise in mesmerizing pulses of repetition opened itself out to an increasing resolution of detail: the variance in the brightness of the nearly solid vapor mass, the differentiated shapes of the fraying edges of the vapor unfurling into the blue of the sky—were they like curling wisps of smoke or like tearing cloth? Other vocabularies seemed necessary to articulate this detail. To facilitate this, my process of repeated observation and description opened out to a longer history of weather description, drawing on the modalities of description employed by two literary figures of the late eighteenth and early nineteenth centuries, Dorothy Wordsworth, who wrote extensively in the form of journal entries that kept a careful and often ecstatic daily record of the weather, and the Victorian poet Gerard Manley Hopkins, who likewise kept a weather journal filled with luminous detail. With the help of these atmospheric vocabularies, the vapor of the Blur Building and the surrounding clouds acquired the sheen of egg white, the texture of wool, the inner marbling of an oyster shell.

This process of layering several finite and idiosyncratically dispersed historical frames parallels Robertson's own methodological impulse to draw on descriptive practices of natural history, and in particular early meteorological description, tracking their passage through eighteenth-century and romantic poetry. Or, as Laurel Peacock suggests in "Lisa Robertson's Feminist Poetic Landscapes," Robertson uses "scraps of antique discourses, [to] fashion a new garment," and through this "construct[s] more livable poetic habitats." In this way, Robertson's work offers an "inventive *ecopoiesis*," which "reads the earth's climate as a diary," always seeking "to engage it as a temporal phenomenon, . . . a soft, viable architecture lining the movement of days and weeks and years."[7] Robertson's book *The Weather* operates as such a chiasmic site of description, forging connections among natural history, feminist thought, and experimental poetics, to develop a way of diachronically indexing change through the differentiated grammar of its sentences.

The Weather was composed as part of a site-specific six-month research residency at Cambridge, during which Robertson "embarked on an intense yet eccentric research in the rhetorical structure of English meteorological description."[8] This interest led Robertson to research, among else, BBC shipping forecasts, William Wordsworth's *The Prelude*, John Constable's cloud sketches, Thomas Ignatius Forster's meteorological treatise *Researches About Atmospheric Phaenomena*, Alexander Cozens's painting manual *A New Method of Assisting the Invention in Drawing Original Compositions of Landscape*, as well as the work of the nineteenth-century British amateur meteorologist Luke Howard, who, in his *Essay on the Modification of Clouds*, devised a system for taxonomic nomenclature of clouds by carefully observing how clouds in the sky were diachronically changing from one form to another.

Speaking about the composition process she used in writing *The Weather*, in an interview in the *Capilano Review* (Fall 2011), Robertson situates her interest in mixing these descriptive practices in relation to the moment when scientific and literary modes of description still converged with one another: "It was a discourse that was happening before science and literature were differentiated, strictly speaking, and so it was like the last gasps of a more integrated practice of description, where natural history had very minimal and totally erasable boundaries in relation to literary description."⁹ In seeking a historical connection between the descriptive practices of poetics and natural history, Robertson situates herself in a longer tradition of twentieth- and twenty-first-century avant-garde poetics, whose practitioners, including Gertrude Stein and Lyn Hejinian, have forged intersections between literary and natural historical practices of description. Within this genealogy Robertson's work in particular has offered one of the most insightful examples in contemporary poetry for thinking about the traditions of description emerging out of natural history as a way of considering how materiality and temporality triangulate in relation to language—in other words, for investigating a *poetics of liveliness* as I have been conceptualizing it here.

In many ways Robertson's poetics is an investigation of how to construct epistemic and aesthetic practices that are responsive to ongoing processes of material change. In composing *The Weather*, Robertson became particularly interested in how different practices of description depicted meteorological phenomena, which are continuously undergoing transformation: "Clouds [in particular] presented a specific formal difficulty to description and nomenclature . . . since [their] appearance as a thing was so ephemeral."¹⁰ As such, the changing countenance of the sky, in which clouds are continuously transforming from one form to another, offered Robertson an ideal perceptual and conceptual site for investigating the relationship between description and change. The work of the amateur meteorologist Luke Howard, who, in his *Essay on the Modifications of Clouds* (1803), devised a system for taxonomic nomenclature of clouds that we still use—with names such as cirrus, cumulus, and stratus—offers a particularly fruitful context for thinking about the problem that I first addressed in regard to Stein's lively taxonomy: how taxonomic practices can remain responsive to processes of transformation in the phenomena they are attempting to order and classify. Howard's project of cloud classification, like Stein's in *The Making of Americans*, is plagued by anxieties. He worries that his attempt at taxonomic classification is at risk of replacing lively entities with dead taxonomic categories, or, conversely, that the phenomena he is classifying are so infinitely variable and disordered that any effort at classification is doomed to failure.

CLOUD-WRITING: LUKE HOWARD'S SOFT TAXONOMY

Howard was concerned that the transience and mutability of clouds made their all too soft edges incongruous with the scientific project of taxonomic classification. The secret of Howard's taxonomy lay in its capacity to avoid the typically ossifying, atemporal effects of classification and attend instead to the mutability of clouds. Thus in addition to the three primary cloud types, cirrus, cumulus, and stratus, Howard develops the taxonomic categories of cirro-cumulus, cirro-stratus, cumulo-stratus, and cumulo-cirro-stratus or nimbus. These transitional categories offer a way of attending to the qualities of clouds as activities that possess some patterned modes of behavior, causing them to transition from one of these forms to another with some regularity. In other words, Howard devises what I am calling a *soft taxonomy* of clouds, which attempts to order their vaporous modifications into discrete types without freezing the active dynamics that cause these types to continuously transform into one another. Figure 6.2 depicts an engraving from the 1865 edition of the *Essay on the Modifications of Clouds*, based on the watercolor by Edward Kennion, in which Howard makes note, for instance, of how cumulus clouds in conjunction with cirro-stratus clouds have a tendency to become cumulo-stratus clouds.

Howard's focus on the temporal dynamics of cloud taxonomy allows him to remain attentive to the continuously shifting boundaries of clouds: their movement between existing as discrete entities and the sense that cloud edges always remain pliable and soft, casting them toward other clouds and the infinite possibilities of mixing and dissolution. While Howard is careful to devise a form of taxonomy that is "soft" enough to respond to the plastic and transient qualities of clouds, he is also insistent that there are regularities in the behavior of clouds and that the whole project of devising a taxonomy of various atmospheric vapors is not a futile one. "If Clouds were the mere result of the condensation of Vapour in the masses of atmosphere . . . [and] if their variations were produced by the movements of the atmosphere alone," Howard

FIGURE 6.2 Plate from Luke Howard's *Essay on the Modifications of Clouds* depicting the formation of cumulo-stratus clouds (London: John Churchill & Sons, 1865).

conjectures, then the study of them would "be deemed an useless pursuit of shadows," as their forms, in this case, would be merely "the sport of winds" and would hence be ever varying and indefinable.[11] Still, Howard argues that the various modifications of clouds are a result of specific causes that govern the movement of the atmosphere, and that, through a careful observation of "the countenance of the sky, and of its connexion with the present and ensuing phenomena," one can come to understand how these causes will operate and how the different varieties of clouds will transition from one form to another (1). Howard bemoans that the experience produced through the labors of "frequent observation" is "usually consigned only to the memory of the possessor, in a confused mass of simple aphorisms," and that, as these single observations lose "connexion with the rest of the Chain" of weather events that accompany them synchronously in space or sequentially in time, they often serve only to mislead the meteorologist who is trying to discern regularities in cloud phenomena (2).

As a result, Howard believes that the secrets of effective meteorological observation come to reside "only in the mind before which their relations have passed, though perhaps imperceptibly, in review" (2). It is his desire in devising a methodological nomenclature of clouds to expose and make available to others the transient flow of relations that constitutes the changes in weather phenomena. For this purpose he also devises a form of cloud-writing, suggesting the use of concrete, nearly hieroglyphic marks as indicators of specific cloud types, which would help convey the sequence of transitions and relations between weather phenomena. Howard suggests that such marks be inserted into "a column headed *Clouds*" in meteorological registers and that "modifications which appear together be placed side by side, and those which succeed to each other" in the sequential order within the column (14). Such a mode of cloud-writing would create a diachronic and synchronic field of relations, which would allow the reader of the meteorological register to gage the coincidence of cloud types and to envision the temporal flux through which different cloud types would metamorphose from one modification to another. Figure 6.3 shows Howard's proposed cloud typography as it appears in the 1865 edition of the *Essay on the Modifications of Clouds*, while the accompanying figure 6.4 is a page from one of Robertson's research notebooks (archived at the Contemporary Literature Collection at Simon Fraser University). On this page of the notebook, Robertson has copied out Howard's typographic system for annotating clouds while she was conducting archival research for *The Weather* at Cambridge.

❚ Cirrus: ◠ Cumulus: — Stratus: ❚◠ Cirro-cumulus: ❚— Cirro-stratus: ◠— Cumulo-stratus: ❚◠— Cirro-cumulo-stratus, or Nimbus.

FIGURE 6.3 Cloud-writing typographic marks from Luke Howard's *Essay on the Modifications of Clouds* (London: John Churchill & Sons, 1865).

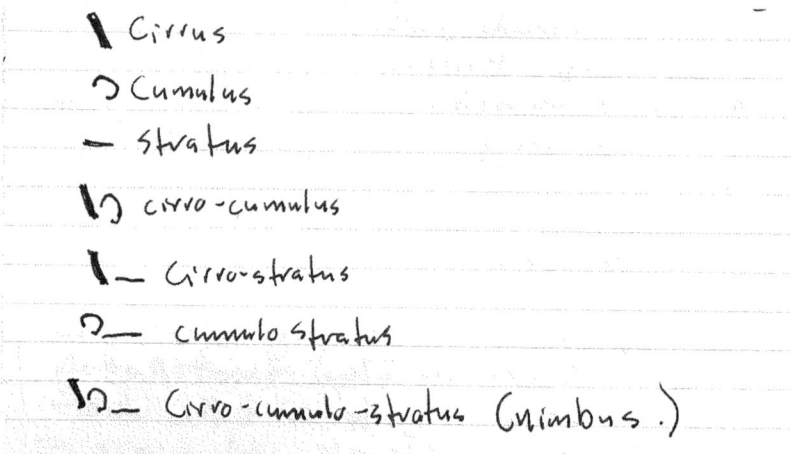

FIGURE 6.4 Lisa Robertson, transcription of Luke Howard's cloud annotation symbols in a research notebook for the composition of *The Weather*. Lisa Robertson Fonds, MsC38, Simon Fraser University Library.

SPEED OF DESCRIPTION AND THE SKETCHES OF THE SKY

I propose that Robertson's book *The Weather* can be read as a form of "cloud-writing" that similarly sets up fields of synchronic and diachronic relations, in order to produce descriptions of change that attempt to convey the activity of the changing sky in another medium, in this case poetic language, with its own distinct capacities for lively dynamism. Robertson divides *The Weather* into seven discrete prose pieces, each titled for an eponymous day of the week and interleaved with short pieces in verse titled "Residence at C_," finally ending with a longer verse section titled "Porchverse." This serves to draw conceptually on the daily patterns of weather description, which tune perceptual attention to the minute variations of the changing skies. While Roberson's text is not based on direct observation of meteorological phenomena, each of the discrete daily sections formally relays the microdynamics of change through grammatical variation. As a result, varying rhythms of activity are produced in each section of the book through the diachronic dimension of the syntax and its capacity to convey differentiated rhythms and causal relations. In a sense, then, the act of reading *The Weather* is akin to asking about the particularities of the weather on a given day and taxonomizing the differences that arise at the level of the syntax to produce varying rhythms and modalities of instability.

This difficulty of recording a continuously changing sky is addressed by Robertson in such a way that the patterns of repetition and change within descriptive passages of the poem relay the effects of flux:

> The tint twice over. Days heap upon us. Where is Kathleen. The tint twice. The clouds darker than the plain part and darker at the top than the bottom. The clouds lighter than the plain part and darker at the top than the bottom. The lights of the clouds lighter. The others smaller. The same as the last. The same as the last. The tint twice in the openings and once in the clouds. Days heap upon us. The tint twice over. Days heap upon us. With others smaller. With others smaller.[12]

This is a concluding section of the poem "Tuesday," and it repeats many of the syntactical patterns that have already occurred earlier in the poem. The most explicitly descriptive sentence, "the clouds darker than the plain part and darker at the top than the bottom," directly precedes a nearly identical syntactic iteration of itself with the substitution of the adjective "lighter" in lieu of the initial "darker" in the first part of the sentence. Both of these sentences have occurred earlier on in the poem, with the sentence beginning with the "darker clouds" repeating in succession, followed by the three iterations of the sentence beginning with the "lighter clouds." These minute diferences and repetitions re-create the states of temporary suspension that Howard describes in his natural historical accounts of the sky. Along with the subtle changes in the patterns of light and dark, these repetitions and alternations infuse the clouds with changing variegations of color and brightness. Even the instances of complete syntactic repetition interject temporality into this description of the landscape of the sky. Robertson enters almost into an ironic play with this impossibility of repetition when she writes two identical sentences in the passage just quoted, each of which states "the same as the last," so that in its second iteration the sentence points at the preceding sentence, ironically producing the opposite effect of consistency, in a way that parallels Stein's insistence in "Portraits and Repetition" that there is no such thing as repetition—only variations in emphasis or insistence. The sense of an ongoing temporality in the poem is punctuated by the reoccurring statement "days heap upon us," which suggests that the iterative meteorological shifts that occur in between may cover a narrative span of days. Strangely, the verb "heap" at the same time transforms this movement of time into matter that can heap into a pile, in a way that seems to almost exert physical pressure, as though time were a little pile of sand pressing down onto a sense of the collective experience of the weather that Robertson instills through her use of a collective pronoun "us."[13]

The depiction of clouds simultaneously points to the difficulties of description, particularly when the object of that description is something as spatially amorphous as vapor, which is devoid of clean lines of topographic demarcation and varies primarily in its "tint" and the way that these appearances of color or brightness or density are produced through the interactions between light and water molecules that are dispersed in the air. The lines in this section of *The Weather* originally come from Alexander Cozens's text *A New Method of Assisting the Invention in Drawing Original Compositions of Landscape* (1785), in which Cozens offers various instructions about landscape painting. Some of the plates in this painting manual are the images of clouds in the sky depicted in figure 6.5. For instance, in one panel (not depicted here), Cozens includes these textual descriptions of the sky: "All cloudy except one large opening, with others smaller, the clouds darker than the plain part, or darker at the top than the bottom. The tint twice over." Or in another panel he writes: "The same as the last, but darker at the bottom than the top."[14] A page from one of Robertson's notebooks has versions of these cloud images copied in pencil, along with some of the annotations. And then in the margin she has scribbled: "These are verbatim copies from Cozens." (See figure 6.6.) On one of the pages in the

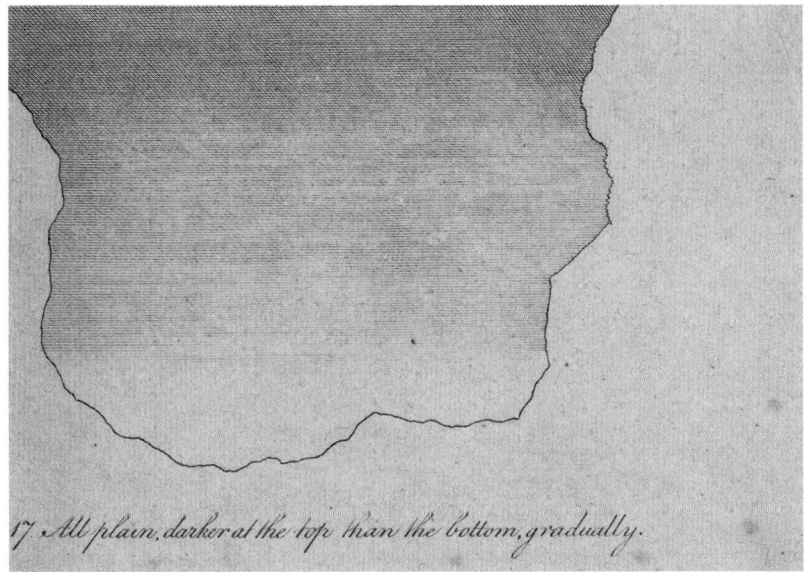

FIGURE 6.5A–6.5D Plates from Alexander Cozens's *A New Method of Assisting the Invention in Drawing Original Compositions of Landscape*, 1785. Lift-ground aquatint and engraving on paper. DAC accession numbers: 1960.25.1.24, 1960.25.1.27, 1960.25.1.28, 1960.25.1.29. Open Access Image from the Davison Art Center, Wesleyan University.

21) The same as the last, but darker at the bottom than the top.

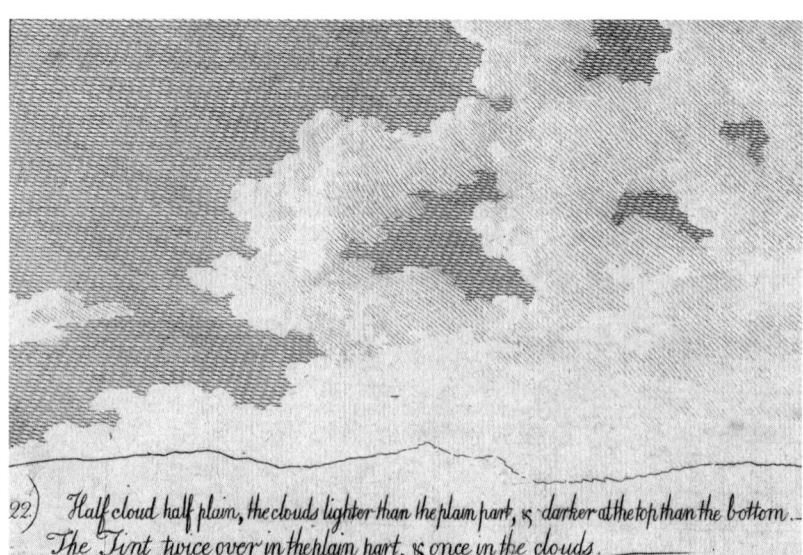

22) Half cloud half plain, the clouds lighter than the plain part, & darker at the top than the bottom. The Tint twice over in the plain part, & once in the clouds.

FIGURE 6.5A–6.5D Continued.

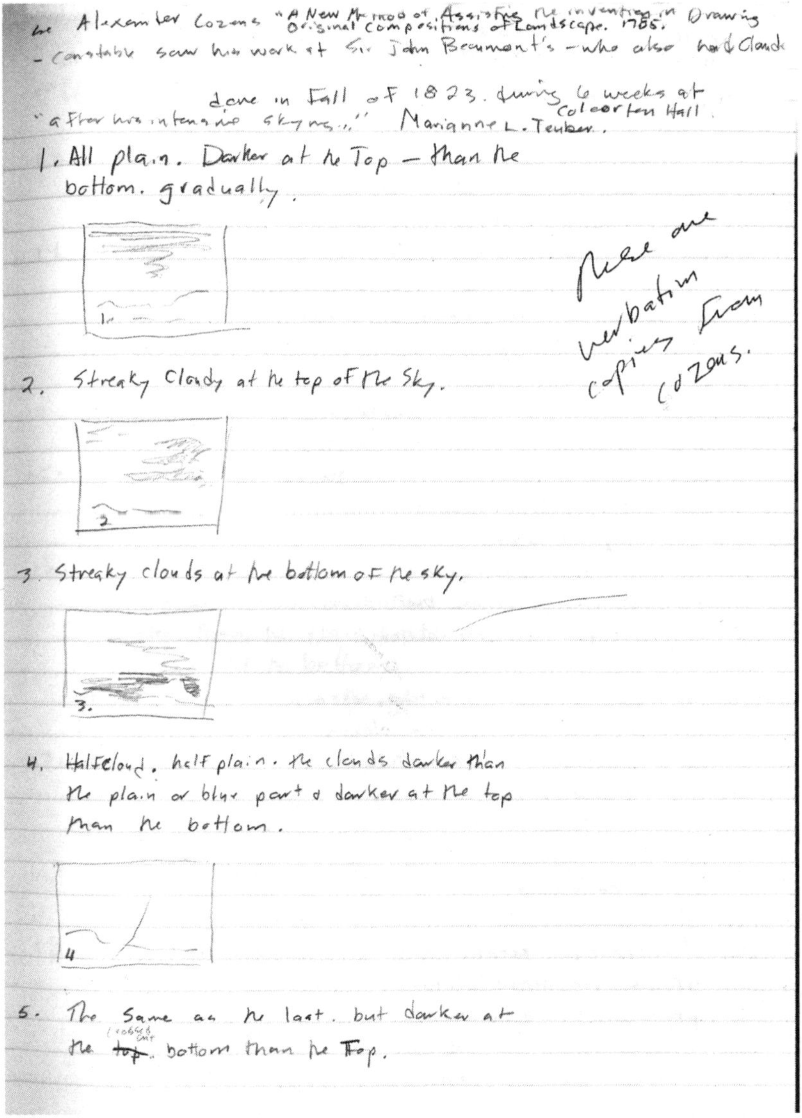

Alexander Cozens "A New Method of Assisting the invention in Drawing Original Compositions of Landscape. 1785." — Constable saw his work at Sir John Beaumont's — who also had Cozens done in Fall of 1823. during 6 weeks at Coleorton Hall. "after his intensive skying." Marianne L. Teuber.

1. All plain. Darker at the Top — than the bottom. gradually.

[sketch 1]

These are verbatim copies from Cozens.

2. Streaky Clouds at the top of the Sky.

[sketch 2]

3. Streaky clouds at the bottom of the sky.

[sketch 3]

4. Halfcloud. half plain. the clouds darker than the plain or blue part & darker at the top than the bottom.

[sketch 4]

5. The Same as the last, but darker at the ~~top~~ bottom than the Top.

FIGURE 6.6 Lisa Robertson, transcription from Alexander Cozens's *A New Method of Assisting the Invention in Drawing Original Compositions of Landscape* in a research notebook for the composition of *The Weather*. Lisa Robertson Fonds, MsC38, Simon Fraser University Library.

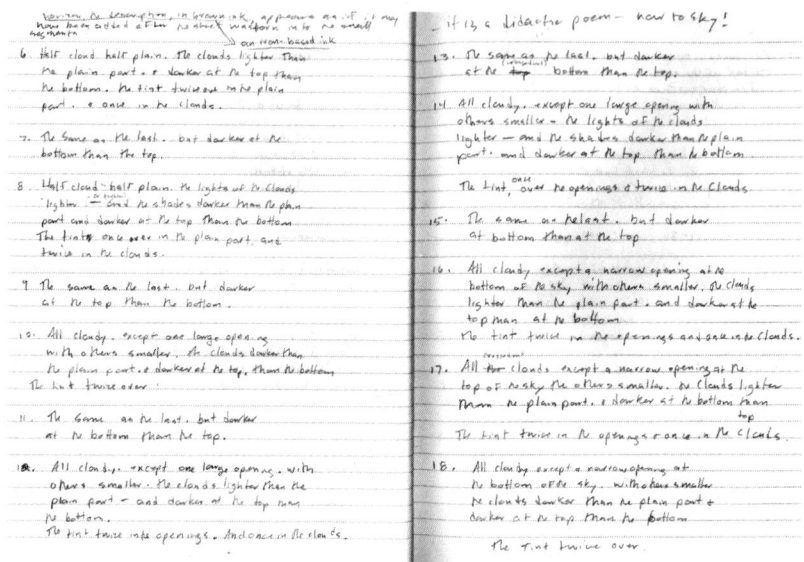

FIGURE 6.7 Lisa Robertson, transcription from Alexander Cozens's *A New Method of Assisting the Invention in Drawing Original Compositions of Landscape* in a research notebook for the composition of *The Weather*. Lisa Robertson Fonds, MsC38, Simon Fraser University Library.

notebook that follows, these descriptive statements begin to accrete into rhythmic patterns of repetition and change that resemble the descriptive texture of the poem "Tuesday." In other words, while Robertson is appropriating textual material from these still frames of the sky, as these descriptive fragments accumulate, they produce a kind of rhythmic descriptive score of the changing sky. (See figure 6.7.) The procedural methodology that becomes evident as one examines Robertson's research notebooks alongside the primary sources she was drawing on in her composition of *The Weather* reveals an affinity for documenting change, which was subsequently explicitly formulated in Robertson's collaboration with Stacy Doris, with the two of them writing as the Perfume Recordist. As I have suggested earlier, at one point in "Notes on Perfume" they specifically propose that one way of producing descriptions of change involves revealing a high resolution of detail occurring within a closed temporal frame. And this is precisely what is happening within the discrete frames that are depicted in Cozens's book, which become animated as textual material as they accrete into continuous description in Robertson's notebook.

At the same time, in elaborating on the procedures she used in the composition of *The Weather*, Robertson is careful to distinguish between these modes of textual description and descriptive practices that would rely on firsthand observation of the skies. Rather than going "skying" herself, Robertson appropriated the discourse and methodology of meteorological description:

> I looked at [the skies] a lot, but I wasn't sitting there describing them. I was approaching the idea of weather via the representation of weather. I was looking a lot at Constable, and reading a lot about Constable, who was involved in early meteorological work. And I was reading Luke Howard, who invented the nomenclature for clouds that we now use. All of these texts and visual and radio representations pertaining to the classification of weather and the representation of weather. None of it was based on my own personal observation of skies. I was researching the shift from neo-classical to romantic culture, and then the shift towards natural history, as we now understand it, as based on the sincerity of objective observation as base practice. But I myself didn't do that.[15]

In considering the question of description, I have proposed that the use of natural historical techniques by poets such as Robertson has brought them into contact with different forms of nonhuman materiality. While Robertson, as this passage suggests, conceptually circumscribes her poetics within the realm of textual research, and hence situates herself within the discursive domain,[16] in drawing on meteorological description, she nevertheless becomes attuned to the problem of describing change and the manner in which the dynamics of language can indexically register the diachronic qualities of transformation within other material dimensions. In other words, the difficulty of capturing the synchronic and diachronic effects of cloud-writing lies in conveying the activity of the changing sky in another medium, with its own and distinct capacities for dynamism. And the manner in which Robertson begins to address this problem of describing material change is in part through her examination of painters like Constable, who depict the rhythms of the changing sky in their numerous "cloud studies."

It is significant, in laying this trajectory of influence, to note that Constable too, like Robertson, was a reader of Howard's *Essay on the Modification of Clouds*, and that many of Constable's cloud studies entailed an attention to "meteorological accuracy" as elaborated in Howard's classification system.[17] In his book on Howard's contribution to meteorology and the wider cultural sphere of the early nineteenth century, *The Invention of Clouds*, Richard Hamblyn notes that Constable had in his possession an annotated and underlined copy of Thomas Forster's book *Researches About Atmospheric Phaenomena* (1813), the first chapter of which—"Of Mr. Howard's Theory of the Origin and Modifications of Clouds"—offered a laudatory explication of Howard's classification system: "These comments and underlinings reveal Constable's meteorological knowledge to have been 'considerable' [as] he was able to pick out ambiguities within the cloud classification . . . and to dispute a number of Forster's proffered conclusions."[18] Many of Constable's cloud studies are titled specifically using the Latin nomenclature for clouds that Howard developed;[19] as such, like Howard, Constable too was clearly attuned to the changing qualities of the skies. During his studies at the Royal Academy, painter Benjamin West, then president of the academy, told young Constable to "always . . . remember that light and shadow never stand still," and Constable subsequently developed the idea that the sky, with its moving configuration of clouds, forms "the *standard of scale*" through which to ascertain the flux of light and shadow in a landscape.[20]

And, as the annotations scribbled in the margins of Constable's copy of Forster's *Researches About Atmospheric Phaenomena* testify, Constable's interest in meteorology extended well beyond the visual appearance of clouds and their classification into different types. As Richard Hamblyn notes in *The Invention of Clouds*, Constable also liberally speculated on the causal dynamics of meteorological phenomena, by, for instance, disputing the accuracy of Forster's account of the generation of rain:

Constable's experiments in pursuit of meteorological understanding were conducted not by means of a recording barometer but in the brilliant crucible of paint. The scene around his folding seat was like an outdoor manufacturing laboratory. His painting box was filled with a litter of alchemical phials, whose labels, 'Red Oxide of Manganese', 'Protiodide of Mercury' and 'Sesquioxide of Chromium', recalled the basement world of Plough Court laboratory, where artists' materials were made to order amid the pharmaceutical apparatus.[21]

Hence, during his "skying" expeditions of plein-air painting, Constable was, in a sense, in the movement of his pigments across the paper, re-creating the dynamics of the moving sky. And yet Hamblyn immediately alerts us to the difficulties of paralleling the movement of water vapor in the sky in the movement of pigments on the paper by pointing out that the "results ... [were] limited by the physical properties of the paint itself," which, even when thinned down, "could not fly unimpeded across the paper."[22] The process of mediating temporality becomes evident here in the viscosity of the paint, which sets the conditions for the speed of the medium. As such, there is an incongruity between the differential dispersion of water droplets in the atmosphere and the heavier, thicker, even if finely ground, dust of the paint pigments dissolved in water. A whole strange industry comes about as a way of addressing this difficulty of mediation, this incongruity of speeds.

In "Clouds Over Europe," John Gage attempts to situate Constable's practice of "skying" in a longer history of European outdoor sky painting. What emerges is a history of quick sketches: for instance, "two sky drawings in brown wash on both sides of a single sheet of blue paper" made by Angeluccio in 1620. This economical technique of using two tones on a tinted ground allowed for speed that was of the essence in recording the fleeting phenomena of the atmosphere: the blue sky on which the moving vapors of the clouds could be overlaid would already be there, without the painter having to paint it. Nevertheless, in his treatise on painting, Rembrandt's pupil Samuel van Hoogstraten notes the incongruity between "the finiteness of the blue paper with the infinite blue of the sky."[23] And yet this technique of using blue paper as a stand-in for the sky remained popular from the seventeenth century on to the romantic period, when it came to be used by painters like Constable. What seems perhaps even more interesting in light of the speed that was required for recording the skies was that it caused writing to seep into the sketches of these painters. Vernet's pupil Valenciennes, for instance, developed a complex technique "of using annotated pencil drawings as an *aide-mémoire*" and went on to write a theoretical treatise on landscape painting—"a letter on landscape"—in which he advocated plein-air study of the same set of trees or a house at different times of day, which would allow the painter to capture their particular and changing details.[24] As I have already elaborated, this inclusion of the descriptions of the changing sky in language formed an important part of Cozens's painting manual *A New Method of Assisting the Invention in Drawing Original Compositions of Landscape*, in which the small variations in descriptive detail that populate each of the still frames produce an effect of the changing skies.

The manner in which language relates to the visual representation of the sky also plays a crucial role in *A Theory of /Cloud/*, in which Hubert Damisch offers an account of the history of painting from the Renaissance to the twentieth century, refocalized through the problem of a cloud as a meteorological phenomenon and a subject of painting, but also as a semiotic element or a sign. What interests me in particular in Damisch's account is the problem of the outline posed by clouds as "surfaceless objects": "A cloud belongs to the class of 'bodies without surfaces,' as Leonardo da Vinci was to put it, bodies that have no precise form or extremities and whose limits interpenetrate with those of other clouds." In other words, clouds, with their "luminous and aerial substance," pose a representational difficulty for an "art devoted to the apprehension of bodies considered as materially impenetrable, solid entities"[25] In my account of clouds as "soft entities," they similarly offer a limit case for considering the question of texture as a property of the surface, and yet they also allow for a rethinking of what an "edge texture" may be, not only as Robert Hooke does, in terms of the aporias of roughness that open up in a seemingly smooth surface when it is viewed at a different perceptual scale, but also in terms of dynamics, or a sense of the edge as temporally textured, at times dispersing the object into its surroundings. At the same time, for Damisch, clouds act not only as material, meteorological aspects of the atmosphere, but also on a semiotic level, as signs. He proposes that there is something about the refusal of delineation evoked by clouds that disrupts the sense of language as composed of particulate, sequentially ordered phonetic elements, a model that in my account would correspond to Lucretius's particulate analogy between atoms and the letters of the alphabet: "[A cloud] seems to call into question, thanks to its absence of limits and through the solvent effects to which it lends itself, the coherence and consistency of a syntactical ordering that is based on a clear delineation of units."[26] On one hand, this opens up the question of how the pictorial or hieroglyphic forms of writing, such as those that I locate in Howard's system of cloud annotation, may operate by different means, offering an iconic depiction of a particular cloud type as a sign, without relying on a particulate or phonetic conception of language. On the other hand, it poses the question of how poetic writing, with its capacity to exceed the representational dimension, may function rather as a set of gestural traces that index the dynamics of a changing sky through their iterative or rhythmic patterns, thus eschewing a sense of clouds as strictly delineated entities.

DEIXIS, CAUSALITY, AND PATTERNS IN TIME

In drawing on the history of painting alongside the history of meteorology, for instance, language, for Robertson, becomes akin to Constable's brilliant crucible of paint, allowing her to test out its capacities to respond to the temporal rhythms unfolding in the instantiation of another material. Formally, the poem "Sunday," which appears in *The Weather*, relies on a mixture of deixis and an enumeration of qualities that have been extracted from specific properties of materials and transposed onto other kinds of materials as a way of conveying the rhythms of changing weather patterns. The deictic quality of the sentences is created through the repetition of the adverb "here," which simultaneously produces an effect of specificity—of an unfolding situation occurring at a specific location—and also a complete indefiniteness: "And here experienced the benefits. And here again wisps. And here gained real knowledge. And here got into the wild. And here, too. Arrived here about two o'clock."[27] An aspect of the indefiniteness arises from the undecidability as to whether one is witnessing synchronic or diachronic effects. Thinking back on Howard's methodology of cloud-writing, it is possible to imagine a session of "cloud watching" in which one would delineate a specific location in the sky, deictically pointing to it as here, and then record a sequential set of events occurring at this discrete location. In that case, the appearance of "wisps" may be coterminous with the more abstract qualities of the absorption of knowledge. On the other hand, the second to last sentence suggests that "here" designates multiple locales, or that a similar event may be unfolding "here" and "here." This sense of spatial multiplicity is enhanced by the way in which the grammar of the sentences produces an effect of a figure or a number of figures moving across a ground by indirectly pointing to an absent subject or, in more posthumanist terms, an actant who is implicated in the activities of experiencing, gaining, or arriving. This synchronic effect will be emphasized later in the poem, when a deictic frame opened by the adverb "here" will carry behind it only a list of nouns pointing to different entities that make up a landscape—a "hill, dell, water, meadows, woods" (3).

In the relay of sentences just quoted, Robertson uses the conjunction "and" to produce a sequential set of relations between different sentences. This effect of sequence or a sense of an unfolding temporality is enhanced by references to time, in this case to the specific hour of "two o'clock," which was preceded a little earlier in the poem by "one o'clock" (2). The spatial and temporal effects that are produced by the grammar generate a sense of sequence or spatial relation between the different occurrences, or, at times, the poem generates a sense that the different occurrences ensue out of one another or have a causal relation to one another, but this relationship to causality always remains indefinite. In a similar manner, the form of cloud-writing proposed by Howard emphasizes the significance of the sequential "chain" of observations, so that the regularities in the patterns of modification of clouds become discernible "only in the mind before which their relations have passed, though perhaps imperceptibly, in review."[28] And yet in both cases of cloud-writing, the promise of discerning a causal pattern remains uncertain, with the data offered by making observations about a sequence of occurrences at best allowing one to observe patterns of relation and correlation. Robertson actually addresses the question of causation directly in the poem: "Here is a system. Time pours from its mouth. We design it a flickering. Here is its desolation. Here it crosses. Here it falls at last.... Quit some causes. Here, then. Here were a set. Here were two or three. So deliciously alterior. Here will be an interchange of cause and effect" (3). On one hand, this set of sentences describes a behavior of a system as it is unfolding in time, and, on the other, the indeterminate nature of paratactic relations between the discrete sentences simultaneously models the uncertainty of causal relations between different parts of a system. At the most fundamental level, this paratactic uncertainty arises because it is not clear if the appearance of "a system" as a noun in the initial syntactic element in the sequence has a definite relationship to the pronoun "it" that appears in the subsequent sentences. Nevertheless, the sequence induces the reader to track the changes that occur as though they were different shifts in a state of a complex system, such as the weather.

The questions of the uncertainty of causal relations that I have explored in my reading of "Sunday" return in "Wednesday," but this time in a different guise. Rather than working with a diffuse sense of linkage between different sentences by thinking about the uncertainties of deixis and vague pronoun reference, here Robertson uses a juxtaposition between different clauses of a sentence, dividing them with a semicolon: "A great dew; we spread ourselves sheet-like. A keen wind; we're paper blown against the fence. A little checkered at 4 PM; we dribble estrangement's sex. A long, soaking rain; we lift the description. A ripple ruffles the disk of a star; contact thinks. A sharp frost and a nightfall of snow; our mind is a skin" (28). In this way the text operates as an iterative series. Generally, the first part of a given sentence, at least in this sample of the text, presents an event, often meteorological in nature, while the second part presents an activity that appears to occur in some kind of relation to the initial event. Often, but not always, the presence of the pronoun in the second part of the sentence generates the actants, which become carriers of the action or perception in the sentence. The critical discourse on Robertson's work has extensively discussed her use of pronouns, and in particular the first-person plural pronoun "we" as a way of generating multiple personas inside of a text and thus unsettling the sense of a lyrical subjectivity. In this particular example, the pronoun "we" extends beyond the boundaries of the human and the animate and comes to indicate a coalescing of a paper being blown against the fence. The tightness of the relation between the two parts of the sentence varies, appearing to insinuate causality in the case of the "keen wind" and the "paper blown against the fence," and remaining quite abstract and elusive when it comes to the relation between "a ripple [that] ruffles the disk of a star" and a sense that "contact thinks" (28). At the same time, the phrase "contact thinks" offers a meta-descriptive quality, elaborating what is occurring between the clauses at the latch points produced by the semicolons. The clauses themselves operate at different speeds to produce temporal differentiation by setting up varying durations and speeds of activity. In this way, varying rhythms of activity are produced in the poem by mixing a specific ratio of descriptive detail and abstraction with a grammatical capacity to differentiate between instants of action and more ongoing states of activity.

The causal relations that are constructed in the varying grammatical patterns in *The Weather* can be productively compared to the manner in which Howard describes causal relations in weather systems that lead to the formation of particular types of clouds. The formation of cumulus clouds, for instance, is dependent on the upward movement of water vapor, which is "thrown into air" in an uncondensed form by the morning increase in temperature.[29] This rising water vapor, in turn, meets and "exerts its elastic force" on the cooler air in the more elevated reaches of the atmosphere, where this drop in temperature causes it to partially decompose into miniature water droplets (25). And yet, as these water droplets descend back toward the earth, they are evaporated, for the second time, at the "elevation where the temperature derived from the action of the sun's rays upon the earth, and decreasing upward, becomes just sufficient to counterbalance the pressure of the superior vapor" (25–26). At this elevation—known as the "vapor plane"—a boundary forms between the region of cloud and the region of permanent vapor. Immediately above the vapor plane the formation of clouds begins, as the vapor that is continuously being thrown up is condensed into a mixture of descending minute water drops, which, in turn, mix with the newly rising vapor. While this process is similar for the formation of both cumulus and stratus clouds, cumulus clouds arise because the small masses of water droplets that are first formed act as "so many centers, towards which all the water afterwards precipitated appears to be attracted" from the surrounding space, "and this attraction becomes more powerful as the cloud increases in magnitude, insomuch that the small clouds previously formed disappear when a large one approaches them in its increase," as the small drops composing these smaller clouds pass "in a loose manner and successively, by attraction, into the larger one" (26).

While Howard carefully explains the events that lead to the formation of a particular type of cloud, the question of strict causal relations that could produce the cloud types that he describes in his taxonomy continues to trouble him:

Are the distinct masses into which the drops form themselves, in this case, due to the attraction of aggregation alone, or is the operation of any other cause to be admitted? A rigid mathematician would perhaps answer the latter clause in the negative; and with such a conclusion we should have great reason to remain satisfied, as cutting short much of the inquiry that is to follow, were it not that it leaves us quite in the dark, both as to the cause of the variety so readily observable in clouds, and that of their long suspension, not to insist on several facts contained in the former part of this paper, which would then remain unaccounted for. The operation of one simple principle would produce an effect at all times *uniform*, and varying only in degree. We should then see no diversity in clouds but in their magnitude; and the same attraction that could bring minute drops of water together through a considerable space of atmosphere in a few minutes, ought not to end there, but to effect their perfect union into larger, [sic] and finally into rain.[30]

As these are simply descriptions of the system's changing state, it is not possible to discern any clear sense of causal relations that lead to the formation of particular cloud types, but Howard is careful to ascertain that if clouds are differentiated, then the causal patterns that lead to their formation must also be varied. In other words, if there is a single underlying principle that leads to cloud formation, then clouds would simply vary in their magnitude, rather than exhibiting the formation of specific cloud types he identifies in his cloud taxonomy. This means that in his efforts to record the diachronic and synchronic patterns of cloud formation through his methodology of cloud-writing, Howard is attempting to discern varied causal patterns, which could produce the individuated cloud types delineated by his *soft taxonomy*.

Howard's careful recording of the changing skies, with his meticulous attention to both the regularity of differentiated patterns and also continuous change, presents a conceptual and observational space in which to examine how phenomena can coalesce into distinct forms or shapes while also having the capacity for transformation. Due to their highly changeable qualities, clouds occupy the uncertain position between existing as discrete entities and operating as modes of activity. Staring at the blue horizon of the sky, one may be able to point to a discrete, fluffy cumulus cloud sailing by and exclaim "here is a cloud," but the next minute that cloud may have fused its vaporous, fuzzy edges with another cloud it encountered on the way, forming an amalgam or a mixture, which can no longer be parsed into discrete entities. In other words, Howard's cloud taxonomy offers a way for thinking about the formation of "soft entities," which are pliable and caught in a processual flow of transformation and yet are not entirely diffuse, but possess instead a capacity for variegated rhythms of coalescence and change. Howard's sense of clouds as *soft entities* can intervene in the theoretical discussions I have outlined in working to elaborate the concept of *soft matter*. In allowing for the possibility that clouds can form discrete types even as they are also always entering into relations and undergoing transformations, Howard's understanding of clouds can serve as an antidote to the trajectory of Object-Oriented Ontology (OOO), delineated at the beginning of the book. While Graham Harman's version of OOO posits a necessary relationship between the capacity for novelty and the existence of discrete objects that are on some level withdrawn from their relational contexts, Howard's thinking about the co-occurrence of these processes offers a compelling alternative. In this way, his *Essay on the Modification of Clouds* offers a specific, materially situated onto-epistemological framework in which to think through the question of how discrete entities differentiate with some regularity within the flow of time. Furthermore, Howard's unwavering attention to temporality and the notion of clouds as modifications and forms of activity softens the categories of taxonomy into shapes that are rendered more pliable through the inclusion of conjunctions, relations, and categories of activity and transformation. As such, Howard's observations of clouds and his formulation of cloud-writing can act as a conceptual laboratory in which to develop modes of description that would remain attuned to the temporal rhythms of speed and slowness of nonhuman materiality that do not collapse into sharp contrasts between fixity and change.

ON THE MOVEMENT OF QUALITIES

Robertson's own attempts to develop modes of description that can register temporal rhythms unfolding in the instantiation of various materials lead her to draw on figurative capacities of language in order to transfer a temporality or a speed of one material toward another. One of the ways that Robertson enacts this transposition of temporality involves extracting qualities from specific properties of materials—their sheen, texture, or capacity to fold and wrinkle—and then using such qualities as attributes for another kind of material or a concept: "All the soft coercions. Maybe black and shiny, wrinkled. A sky marbled with failures."[31] In this way, coercion becomes soft and, maybe, also black, shiny, and wrinkled. In the case of failure, the dynamics of this movement of qualities are more complex, with the sky acquiring the contrasting coloration encased within the veins running through a slab of marble. The concept of failure is in this way infused with material effects, or, more precisely, the material effects of something failing to take form. At the same time, the active and fluid quality of water vapor that composes clouds ricochets back and inserts a different temporality into the hardness of marble, pointing to the gradual process of metamorphism that brings marble into existence, and the manner in which the veins and swirls of colored marble are a result of this process, acting on various mineral impurities, such as clay, silt, sand, and iron oxides, which were originally present as grains or layers in the limestone.

Such attention to the changeable quality of materials is a reoccurring concern in Robertson's poetic and essayistic work. The term *soft*, which I have been returning to again and again, signals this concern with transience within materiality and efforts of language to render itself similarly malleable and reactive as a way of responding to this liveliness of matter. As I outlined in chapter 1, this use of the term comes in part from soft-matter physics and in part from Robertson's appropriation of the term *soft architecture* from architectural theory, where it signals both a plasticity of a material and its ability to respond to changing circumstances and needs. As a structure composed of soft, vaporous materials that are continuously changing in response to the meteorological environment around them, the Blur Building is an exemplary case of soft architecture. The capacity of the Blur Building to react through cybernetic feedback to meteorological changes by collecting and sensing atmospheric information and responding to the instabilities in the climatic conditions of the surrounding environment is an example of a system that possesses such responsive softness. As such, the term *soft architecture* encompasses the idea that an entity may possess the capacity for responsiveness and change, based on the tactile malleability of the material that constitutes it or as a consequence of operating as a system that is participating in ongoing feedback relations with the environment that surrounds it.

In a manner that resonates with her earlier discussions of shacks, tents, and other temporary modes of soft architecture, Robertson extends her discussion of architecture to the space of language or the text, writing about the codex as a form of shelter in her book *Nilling*. The material configuration of the codex as an object in this sense offers a spatiality that has the capacity to lead to elaboration and differentiation without the foreclosure of a determinate identity: "I open the codex; with a skirty murmur, commodiousness arrives. It figures in a sequence that addresses me as its potential. And so I like to face this device. Its structural modesty and discretion conceal a formally generous aptitude for proliferation, complexity and differentiation."[32] The description of the codex in this passage immediately produces a textured spatiality: "By *commodious* I mean: This object furnishes hospitable conditions for entering and tarrying; it shelters without fastening; it conditions without determining" (12). The word "commodious" is evocative of a comfortable, roomy, generously configured space. Given Robertson's propensity for fabrics and folds, it suggests a cavelike space lined in its interior with undulant folds. As such, the materiality of the codex assumes architectural significance, so that language, along with paper, binding, and hide, the substrates that carry it, begins to posit a habitable spatiality—a form of soft architecture that membranously enfolds the body.

At one point Robertson refers to the codex as the "soft bomb of potential" (12). On one hand, this conjunction of terms *soft* and *bomb* is paradoxical in that the threatening sharpness of a weapon is transformed into a soft, malleable texture. Within this phrase, the voluptuousness of confectionary matter, marshmallowy and dimpled with shallow concavities or something bloblike rendered in three-dimensional software, is imbued with the explosive properties of sudden change. Or, the piercing sharpness of shrapnel and the sudden force of explosion are subtracted, within this metaphoric chiasmus, from the concept of the bomb, opening out its explosive potential toward a dissipation or spreading of softness—a blurring of boundaries rather than a piercing or a cutting. But even the very concept of a bomb contains a kind of negotiation between a telos of its explosion and the potential for an uncertain outcome in that the event predicated by an unexploded bomb has not occurred yet and carries with it a degree of uncertainty. And the paradoxical effect produced by conjoining the words "soft" and "bomb" is primarily textural in that opening up the thinking about softness as a form of temporality, as my reading of the concept of soft matter has done, shifts the emphasis from the shapeliness of materiality and toward the indeterminacy of its temporal unfolding. In this discussion of the term *soft*, I have focused on the temporality of transience or, in more rudimentary terms, the undoing of the notion of fixed structure by the agitation of time. This kind of temporality is always at work, even in the most intransigent of materials, which, with this shift of attention to time, become evidently constituted through lively modes of gradual iteration and transformation.

FROM SHAPE TO TIME: LUCRETIAN SWERVE AND VIBRATORY MOLECULES

The question of potentiality and the form of temporality that the codex produces is a reoccurring concern in "Time in the Codex," as Robertson works to theorize ways of thinking about material indeterminacy: "I can't fix what materiality is. Reading, I enter a relational contract with *whatever* material, accepting its fluency and swerve."[33] Here, Robertson is referencing the Lucretian *clinamen*, in order to articulate how materiality escapes determinate patterns of causation: "Again, if all movement is always interconnected, the new arising from the old in a determinate order—if the atoms never swerve so as to originate some new movement that will snap the bonds of fate, the everlasting sequence of cause and effect—what is the source of the free will possessed by living things throughout the earth?"[34] The swerve, as I explore throughout, is Lucretius's way of accounting for the occurrence of unaccountable change in the universe or the capacity of matter to act in ways that cannot be explained through mechanistic patterns of cause and effect. Without this indeterminate, swerving change in direction "everything would fall downwards like raindrops through the abyss of space," no collisions between atoms would ensue, and "thus nature would never have created anything."[35]

One element that characterizes several of the writers that this project investigates, including Robertson and Bök, is that they have all played a part in twentieth- and twenty-first-century reception history of Lucretius. While poets such as Bök have emphasized Lucretian atomism and the parallel he draws between letters and atoms as constitutive units, which in their recombination create the universe, the role that Robertson plays in the reception of Lucretius in post-1945 poetics sidesteps the atomist logic of discrete particulate units in favor of considering the temporal dimension through which entities coalesce and dissipate. While Bök, in the course of composing *The Xenotext Experiment*, reconceptualizes his initial understanding of DNA as a code to account for the three-dimensionality of its molecular shape, Robertson complicates the very notion of shape by emphasizing that form is simply a coalescing of temporal rhythms that permeate the material world. In this way Robertson's work suffuses the arc of the cosmology I am constructing in this project, which moves from code to shape, with the malleability of time.

As a consequence, the instantiation of particulate entities in Robertson's poetics, such as atoms and molecules, is transfigured into considerations of materiality as vibration and rhythm. Robertson and Doris explicitly explore such a consideration of molecular shapes as forms of vibration in "The Perfume Recordist," when they consider how smell works as a sensation on a molecular level. Until recently, smell has been understood as a process of binding of interlocking shapes in which a scent molecule fits like a key into the inverse but matching shape of an olfactory receptor. In 1996 the biophysicist Luca Turin shifted away from this lock-and-key model, which emphasized shape, in favor of a vibrational theory of olfaction: "According to Turin's theory, the receptors in the nose respond to the different vibrations of a molecule, and vibration, rather than the shape of the molecule, produces the experience of smell."[36] Within this vibrational theory of smell, the shape of molecules blossoms into temporalities of rhythm and duration. The movement away from the concreteness of shape and toward temporality and vibration, which insert themselves into and soften the particulate grain of materiality itself, leads Robertson and Doris's analysis of smell beyond Lucretius's analysis of olfaction as an interlocking of specific atomic shapes. In *De rerum natura*, Lucretius proposes that smell is really a form of touch, whereby the "the nostrils are touched" by an emission of a widely diffused stream of smells, each of which possesses a distinct shape. Elaborating on this, Lucretius offers a nonanthropocentric, species-specific theory of why different kinds of animals are attracted to different smells, suggesting that "particular smells, owing to their distinctive shapes, are better adapted to particular species of animals."[37] "Bees," for instance, "are attracted for unlimited distances through the air by the smell of honey, vultures by carcasses," while "the scent of man," Lucretius informs us, "is detected far in advance by that lily-white guardian of the citadel of the sons of Romulus, the goose."[38]

In taking up Lucretius, Robertson persistently refigures this emphasis on shape in his work to consider the problem of vibration and time. In this sense, the orientation in Robertson's work toward nonmonumental temporalities, which in a sense permeate and hence blur and soften all material entities, places her poetics within a genealogy of recent feminist materialist thought, alongside figures such as Elizabeth Grosz and Karen Barad, who have emphasized the temporal dimension of materiality. As I have discussed, in *Becoming Undone* Grosz, for instance, shifts the emphasis away from the category of "new materialism," with its sense of matter as a substance that composes discrete, stable entities, and turns instead toward "temporal and durational entwinements" of matter and life, which guide the processes of differentiation and becoming, as a way of examining "how change occurs, that is, how difference elaborates itself."[39] Such attention to the changeable quality of materials is likewise a concern in Robertson's poetic and essayistic work. The poem "Lucite," for instance, in *Magenta Soul Whip* includes a long list of materials undergoing the process of change: "First the dull mud softened, resulting in putrefaction, lust and intelligence, pearl globs, jeweled stuff like ferrets, little theatres of mica."[40] The materials on this list are *softened* by transience, reiterating Robertson's emphasis on the temporary or, even more generally, pointing to the temporal flux at the heart of all matter. The "dull mud" softens into putrefaction, producing a sense of a substance deteriorating into a messy, sticky form of dissolution. The animate and the inanimate mix, so that ferrets, small, rodentlike animals, are understood to be "jeweled." And mica, a shiny silicate mineral with a layered structure, found as minute scales in granite and other rocks, generates a performative spatiality of a theater, in a manner that is evocative of a kind of low-level drama of recalcitrant matter unfolding within the active mixtures that comprise both organic and inorganic matter. And yet this all arises within a speck of mud, a bit of matter that is undergoing a series of *figurative-material* transformations, straddling the line between the inanimate and the animate, so that what appears inanimate is always threatening to erupt into a proliferation of animated forms in a manner that is evocative of Leibniz's sense of matter as a series of nested configurations or topographies in which each drop of matter contains within itself a garden and a fishpond, and each drop of matter within such a topography, in turn, contains, recursively, another and another, and so on ad infinitum.

As with many of the other poets that appear in *Poetics of Liveliness*, Robertson's writing spans from the microcosmologies of matter to the more astral dimensions of cosmological space. This span becomes evident in her discussion of Lucretius, and it acts as a primary frame in her chapbook-length essay *Thinking Space*, where, among other topics, she explores astronomy and in particular Johannes Kepler's discovery that the orbit of a planet around a star is in fact elliptical rather than circular. Robertson argues that Kepler's conceptualization of the orbit's shape as an ellipse involves a stepping away from the idealized shape of a circle and hence a stepping away from the whole epistemic configuration received from "the classical regularity of the Greco-Roman cosmos and Platonic and Aristotelian thought."[41] Instead, the ellipse emerges from the wobbliness and the dynamism of the planet's movement, and not the fixity of shape as an idealized pattern of its orbit:

> The point of the ellipse is not that it has two foci, although that is how it can be modeled on a two-dimensional plane; the point of the ellipse is that the movement of a body in space cannot be *formally* described, only hypothetically. The ellipse is not a path that *precedes* a planet's movement, but the trace of dynamic motion itself, as it wobbles, speeds up, swoops, in relationship to other moving bodies. The equant is the computational substitute for this dynamism. The ellipse is not a shape, but a temporality.[42]

In other words, even to say that the orbit of the planet's movement is elliptical in shape is incorrect; rather, what we may call a "shape," in this sense, is an unfolding in time and not an idealized geometrical figure. This incorporation of the irregularities of the planet's actual movement represents a "turn away from a symmetrical and stable cosmos" and a turn toward a dynamic cosmology in which irregularity and indeterminacy play a role in a singular manner in which any pattern is formed as an unfolding through time. The sentence "the ellipse is not a shape, but a temporality," when latched onto the phrase "from code to shape," indexes the full cosmological arc that is being described in *Poetics of Liveliness*. This arc starts with a hylomorphic disarticulation of the semiotic from the material, encapsulated within a sense of code as a disembodied form of information, extending toward a more entangled relation that places emphasis on the haptic—textural and sensuous—dimensions of material and linguistic surfaces. The second conceptual movement of the book's cosmology turns finally toward a softening of such shapes and surfaces through their perfusion with temporal rhythms, which render them subject to continuous processes of flux and formation.

"DESCRIPTION IS THE IMAGINATION OF MATTER"

Robertson's attentiveness to the transience of materiality is rendered explicit in a short talk published in *Nilling* titled "7.5 Minute Talk for Eva Hesse (Sans II)," in which she turns to the work of the postminimalist, feminist artist Eva Hesse. Referencing Hesse's use of sculptural materials that are subject to transience or relatively rapid temporalities of deterioration, such as latex or fiberglass, Robertson pinpoints the way that temporality enters Hesse's work: "So time enters the work in two ways: in the gestural present of making, and in the durational time of deterioration, given Hesse's choice to work with unstable materials. No— it enters the work in three ways, the third being the time of a haunting."[43] In these intersecting modes of temporality, the gestural, indexical trace of the body meets the temporal rhythms of the setting resin, which in turn, of their own accord, carry and transform these gestural traces, leading to their eventual dissipation. In addition to considering the ways in which temporality may inhabit materiality in multiple ways, in "7.5 Minute Talk for Eva Hesse (Sans II)" Robertson also explicitly begins to theorize how language, and in particular figurative language, may relate to these material transformations: "Metaphorical space can't be inhabitable without welcoming meaning's propensity to move across materials: Metaphorical meaning does not identify itself with a position; it moves in a fluctuation, serially, to indicate modes of materiality" (44). This sense of metaphor as a form of movement of qualities across materials is evident in how Aristotle defines metaphor in *On Poetics*, where he suggests that metaphor involves "the application of a word belonging to something else either from the genus [*genos*] to a species [*eidos*], or from the species to the genus."[44] In my reading of how Robertson's descriptive techniques register the temporal dynamics of nonhuman materiality, I have emphasized that she often uses figurative capacities of language to transpose temporal dynamics of one material onto another, in this way imbuing marble and cement, for instance, with a sense of softness. In other words, my analysis of how Robertson's techniques of poetic description register the temporalities unfolding within materiality continuously skirts this edge between the material and the figurative in hope that poetics can act as a kind of chiasmic site that moves across the material and the semiotic without abandoning either of these dimensions.

In bringing into view what I have been calling a *material-figurative* dimension of how language and materiality are entangled with each other, poetics can intervene in the emerging theoretical discussions about materiality in a generative way: while the recent turn toward materiality has productively unsettled the linguistic turn, I have argued throughout that it is significant not to set the two terms, *language* and *matter*, in opposition to each other, as an overcorrective strategy that will configure the turn toward materiality as a disavowal of thinking about language. As I explored in chapter 2, certain figures in science studies, including Donna Haraway and Karen Barad, have similarly insisted that the turn toward nonhuman materiality need not be a turn away from the semiotic dimension. While they have offered helpful terms, such as material-discursive and material-semiotic, little work has been done on how to think about these nondualistic conjunctions between language and materiality, particularly as they unfold in their poetic and aesthetic dimensions. In other words, while I believe that this turn toward materiality is crucial, it is currently at an impasse of figuring out foundational questions of methodology, and, in particular, the difficult question of how to actually "turn toward matter" in disciplines such as literature, which have primarily focused on language. In this context, the explorations of language and materiality that play out in the work of poet-naturalists that my project considers can offer a much more multifaceted account than has been hitherto realized in the context of unfolding conversations in science studies and critical theory.

The descriptions of the Blur Building at the opening of this chapter are an investigation of how the *figurative-material* qualities of poetic description can convey the movement of meaning across materials that Robertson refers to in "7.5 Minute Talk for Eva Hesse (Sans II)." In figuratively carrying the sheen of egg white, the texture of wool, the inner marbling of an oyster shell into the luminosity, or a tint that shifts as a thread through the assembling and reassembling clouds, these descriptions are testing the capacity of poetic language to carry isolate textures and durations across materials, in turn producing a kind of amplification of detail that indexes minute temporalities of change. This manner of tracking minute shifts or microdynamics of change and, in turn, developing a complex language of description, capable of tracking the shifting qualities of the sky in all their delineated detail, resembles the attunement to the details of the changing weather that is evident in the early weather journals of Dorothy Wordsworth and Gerard Manley Hopkins, from which these descriptions of the Blur Building draw. It is this attention to the details of the changing sky that allows Hopkins to note that the vaporous film of a cloud is peeling off as if with a texture of "tearing cloth," and then an instant later folding "like the corner of a handkerchief" and beginning to coil "as a ribbon or a carpenter's shaving may be made to do."[45] Or, for Wordsworth, to note the changing appearance of the sea in her *Alfoxden Journal* as "perfectly calm blue, streaked with deeper color by the clouds, and tongues or points of sand" on January 23, 1798, and then again as "the blue-grey sea, shaded with immense masses of cloud, not streaked" on the subsequent date of January 26.[46] These descriptions possess a level of detail and procedural diligence of repeated observations and recording of the subtle, incremental changes occurring in the same landscape over the course of days or years.

Another illustration of how the sense of movement between materialities that is enabled by figurative language can generate a rhythmic set of transformations, which can in turn register the changes occurring within nonlinguistic forms of materiality, occurs in an essay that followed the publication of *The Weather*, titled "Weather: A Report on Sincerity." In this essay, Robertson cites a passage from Thomas Ignatius Forster's treatise *Researches About Atmospheric Phaenomena* (1813), in which Forster offers the following description of a cirrus cloud:

> Comoid tufts, like bushes of hair, or sometimes like erected feathers; angular flexure; streaks; recticular intersections of them . . . which look like nets thrown over the firmament; forms of arrows; stars with long fibrous tails, cyphen shaped curves, and lines with pendulous or with erect fringes, ornament the sky; still different appearances of stars and waves again appear, as these clouds change to cirrocumulus or cirrostratus, which modifications also seem to form and subside spontaneously, in different planes, and with the varied and dissimilar appearances of flocks at rest, fleeces of wool, or myriads of small specks; of long tapering columns like the tail of the great manis, or of mackerel back skies, or of striae, like the grains of wood.[47]

This sentence reveals not only the difficulty of describing something as abstract and changing as masses of vapor moving in the sky, but also the entwined and complex relationship among metaphor, materiality, and temporality. In her reading of the sentence, Robertson suggests that Forster "proceeds by a series of phrasal modifications, miming the process of transmutation in the clouds themselves, even discernibly within the real time of those observed fluctuations" (34). In this way, Forster's complex description draws on the propensity of "metaphorical meaning" to move "in a fluctuation, serially" across "modes of materiality" in order to create a sense of the changing shape of a cirrus cloud. In doing this, it stacks and presses different kinds of material qualities against each other, and the resulting metaphoric movement from one isolate material quality to another is so rapid that it generates its own rhythm, which in turn indexes the dynamics of change occurring in the vaporous configuration of a cloud. Similarly, each of the stacked material elements acts as a lens that isolates or focalizes a particular textural element in the one beside it, moving a microgranularity of luminous detail across different textural configurations and scales.

The phrase with which this section of the chapter opens, "description is the imagination of matter," appears in one of Robertson's notebooks archived at Simon Fraser University's Special Collections and Rare Books Library. The phrase is jotted underneath a page of notes based on Robertson's reading of Grosz's work. This notebook not only acts as archival evidence that the particular philosophical tradition of feminist materialism I am exploring here is directly informing Robertson's work, but it also suggests that she is positing a sense of continuity between description and materiality, almost as though description were a substance secreted by matter, or a kind of attenuated Lucretian film that is simply sloughing off the surface of materiality. As well as using formal qualities of description to re-create the microdynamics of change through the sense of movement generated by figurative language or the grammatical variation of her sentences, Robertson also considers description as a form of elaboration and ornamentation operating within the parameters of the material cosmology itself. The description of a cirrus cloud from Forster's *Researches About Atmospheric Phaenomena*, for instance, can act as an illustration of a mode of description that possesses an ornamental relation to the object in question—in this case a cirrus cloud like the one visible in figure 6.8, an image from Forster's book—because it transposes a myriad of analogous materialities onto the vaporous shape of this cloud, through which the cloud is transformed into the textural likeness of "feathers," "nets," "fleeces of wool." In this sense, for Robertson, description does not operate representationally, as a transparent

FIGURE 6.8 *Cirrus clouds*. Thomas Forster, *Researches About Atmospheric Phaenomena*. London: Harding, Mavor, and Lepard, 1823. Courtesy of HathiTrust.

layer through which phenomena are observed; rather, it operates additively, as a mode of decoration, which elaborates the surfaces of entities. In "Soft Architecture: A Manifesto" Robertson links the work of Soft Architecture to the practices of description: "The work of the SA, simultaneously strong and weak, makes new descriptions on the warp of former events."[48]

This irresolvable quality of attachment between description and any exteriority of materiality that may reside outside of language testifies to the problematic asserted in the Manifesto of the Office for Soft Architecture that description operates in an additive manner, ornamenting "the warp of former events." One way in which this mode of descriptive ornamentation works involves a proliferation of descriptions, so that each description exceeds and deforms the warp of the former descriptive event. In an interview with Lytle Shaw, published in *Printed Project*, Robertson suggests that her interest in the proliferation of description arose out of her extensive readings in feminist literature. Reading across the disciplines, the work of feminist writers including "de Lauretis, Penley, Spivak, Haraway, Brown, Grosz, Kelly, Pollack, Butler, Min-Ha, Riley, Irigaray" led, for Robertson, to the technique of producing a proliferation of descriptions that would collectively dismantle the stability of the gendered, institutionally sanctioned perspective: "Part of the critical technique was simply proliferative: to make more and more descriptions that undid the historical and institutional assumptions and naturalized biases."[49]

Another way in which Robertson explores the decorative capacities of description arises from her consideration of the textural dimension of language. Robertson thinks of syllables and sentences as built surfaces, composed of differentiated materials, and these compositional units allow her to experiment with how specific material qualities give rise to different affective resonances. As mentioned in chapter 2, this leads her to think of herself as "a gentleman collector of sentences," evoking in the process discourses of natural history and producing a sense that linguistic forms, such as syllables or lines, can be thought of as linguistic specimens, which possess "nubby," "knobbly," "jugged," "swoony," or flat qualities.[50] As such, Robertson's writing can be categorized as a mechanism for generating sentences as built surfaces, composed of different materials, constituted by the textural qualities arising at the level of syntax, diction, and, in particular, the minute level of the syllable: "I'll describe the latinate happiness that appears to me as small tufted syllables in the half-light, greenish and quivering as grasses."[51] In this example from *XEclogue*, an early poetic text closely attuned to the writings of Virgil, the Latin of Virgil's syllables acquires textural properties as the syllables extend to become tufted surfaces. In comparing them to grasses, Robertson endows these syllables with animate properties, pushing the language into the realm of flora and suggesting that it possesses the properties of lively forms of materiality that composes plants and animals. This is extended by the more specialized definition of "tufted" in the vocabularies of anatomy and zoology, where for a structure to possess tufts may mean that it is elaborated with a bunch of small blood vessels, or that it may extend out from itself a bunch of respiratory tentacles or other small anatomical structures. These "tufted syllables" are rendered animate and responsive, possessing a quivering quality, setting out from the surface of the page as a set of sensory bristles, always operating at that threshold between having the capacity to register sensory inputs or vibrational resonances and simply offering a textual surface that may produce affective resonance in another organism. It is in such consideration of the overlap between the ornamental qualities of linguistic surfaces and the textured configurations that compose the surfaces of the material world that Robertson's work can be situated within a tradition of *haptic poetics*, in which both linguistic and material textures interweave to produce affective resonances and effects.

CODA

Toward a Haptic Poetics

OF GOLD LEAF AND GOLD CUBES: ATTENUATION OF MATTER AT THE LIMITS OF MATERIALISM

In the treatise *The History of Dense and Rare*, Francis Bacon sets out to determine "the quantity of matter, and how it is distributed in bodies (abundantly in some, sparingly in others)," so as to ascertain the density of various substances, among them copper, loadstone, touchstone, marble, flint, crystal, alabaster, powder of pearls, chalk, mutton, pressed mint juice, raw calves brains, pressed borage juice, urine, powder of white sugar, distilled rose water, fir wood, and raw winter pear. To perform this set of measurements, Bacon fashions a gold cube of exact proportions and then creates corresponding cubes of all other substances that could be fashioned into a shape of a cube, as well as a small hollow prism with an interior space matching exactly the proportions of such a cube into which liquids and powders could "be placed so exactly to fit." By comparing the weight of the gold cube to these other miniature substance cubes, he determines the difference in their weight and, as they are of the same volume, through this, their density. At one point he even makes a list of substances that "could not be included . . . first, [among them] those which will not go into the shape of a cube, as leaves, flowers, pellicles, and membranes; secondly, those which are unequally hollow and porous, as sponge, cork, and wool; and thirdly, pneumatic bodies, as air and flame, because they are not endowed with weight." At this far edge, where the most "rare," the lightest, materials are found, he also speculates that there are "no doubt . . . both in vegetables and likewise in the parts of animals . . . many bodies to be found far lighter than fir wood." Among the lightest of such light materials, Bacon lists various residues sloughed off organic bodies, as well as remainders of such bodies that persist after some form of artificial extraction has taken place: "For the down of some plants, the wings of flies, the slough of snakes, and also various artificial productions, as tender rose-leaves remaining after distillation, and the like, are (as I conceive) lighter than the lightest woods."[1]

What strikes me about these lists of the lightest of the light materials is the manner in which they represent a kind of attenuation of materiality, as if they gradually, through various flimsy, fine, and porous textures, seek to reach a kind of limit of materiality itself. A similar movement toward the attenuation of matter is evident in *De rereum natura*, where the thoroughly materialist system that Lucretius is proposing must account for phenomena such as perception, thought, and finally language and eventually even metaphor through permutations of materials, which get thinner and thinner and flimsier in the process. First, Lucretius suggests that all perception is in a sense tactile as it occurs as very thin films are cast off the surfaces of objects and strike the senses. He refers to such films as "'skins' or 'bark'" and compares them to substances such as smoke, given off by a fire, or to those that are "denser and more closely-knit," as the leavings of "cicadas, for instance, [which] in summer periodically shed their tubular jackets; calves at birth [which] cast off cauls from the surface of their bodies; or . . . the slippery green snake [which] divests itself of its clothing on thorns." Lucretius accounts even for thought through the movement of such films, arguing that films through which perception is carried into thought "are certainly of a much flimsier texture, since they penetrate through the chinks of the body" and are able to "set in motion the delicate substance of the mind." While such films originate within perception, they can even account for thoughts of imaginary things: Lucretius explains how "the image of a Centaur, for instance, [while] certainly not formed from life, since no living creature of this sort has ever existed," arises when "surface films from a horse and a man accidentally come into contact" and "easily stick together on the spot, because of the delicacy and flimsiness of their texture." "When . . . [such films] encounter one another in the air," Lucretius writes, "they easily amalgamate, like spider's web or gold-leaf."[2] As such, it is the delicate, fine texture of such films that is key for this process of amalgamation, which Lucretius associates with imagination.

In this way, by considering a kind of attenuation of materiality within a textural model that emphasizes a variety of very fine, flimsy, and filmlike textures, Lucretius is able to account for phenomena such as thought, imagination, language, and even the figurative dimension of language, through an ontology that does not resort to a dualism between language and the material world. When in *The Logic of Sense* Gilles Deleuze draws on Lucretius, and more predominantly on the Stoics and Lewis Carroll, to explain what he calls "sense," and which in some of its aspects corresponds to the semiotic dimension, he often describes forms of materiality that are also ephemeral, amorphous, and delicate in texture: "Yet, what is more intimate or essential to bodies than events such as growing, becoming smaller, or being cut? What do the Stoics mean when they contrast the thickness of bodies with these incorporeal events which would play on the surface, like a mist over the prairie (even less than a mist, since a mist is after all a body)?"[3] What Deleuze is pointing at here is a distinction that the Stoics made between bodies and their attributes, so that states of "being cut" or "growing," or, in the case of the objects in *Tender Buttons*, reddening, crackling, softening, or perhaps turning into dust, are not fully material in themselves but are instead the incorporeal effects that flicker across the surfaces of objects. Deleuze compares such incorporeal effects to the fine texture, the atmospheric qualities of mist, but he also withdraws from this comparison in that the mist is still a body no matter how attenuated and fine, while such events are incorporeals and in that sense are not material bodies.

Within this model surface is once again a site at which change occurs. This is resonant with Lisa Robertson's sense of the surface or Gertrude Stein's account of minute transformations, minute events transpiring on the surfaces of objects. Or, as Deleuze describes it quite poetically, "events are like crystals, they become and grow only out of the edges, or on the edge." In parallel with this, "a surface which reddens and becomes green" is also a site at which sense arises—sense in this model being a condition of possibility that inheres in the propositional aspect of signification. "'Green,'" for instance, "is not a being and does not qualify a being"; rather, it "designates a quality, a mixture of things, a mixture of tree and air where chlorophyll coexists with all the parts of the leaf." In this sense, to say that "*the tree greens*," through its attribute, is to consider the tree as a "tree occurrence," as "the event expressed by . . . [the] verb," so that the event, in this case, has "an essential relationship to language"—the event subsists in language, but it happens to things. In this way, in *The Logic of Sense*, Deleuze examines the manner in which "Epicureanism and Stoicism . . . attempted to locate in things that which renders language possible." He ascertains that the Stoic model privileges the relation between verbs and "incorporeal events," while the Epicurean model remains bound to nouns and adjectives, with nouns acting "like atoms or linguistic bodies."[4] This dichotomy maps in certain ways onto Stein's relationship with nouns and verbs—or the simultaneous feeling that she expresses in "Poetry and Grammar" of a distaste for nouns and their perceived stasis and a preference for the kinetic dynamism of verbs, even as she also writes about poetry as "nothing but using losing refusing and pleasing and betraying and *caressing* nouns."[5] In this sense, the problem of the event as it is articulated here by Deleuze through the work of the Stoics poses the same question about how language may convey the kinetics of *soft entities* that I am asking in the context of this book. While Deleuze moves beyond the edges of materialism in working through this problem, I have attempted to articulate here a resolutely materialist poetics, even if such a poetics relies on the ephemeral, changing, and at times very flimsy, attenuated and atmospheric forms of *soft matter*.

In the contemporary theoretical moment, the Stoic position, with its emphasis on reaching and extending beyond the limits of materiality into the incorporeal, has been taken up by Elizabeth Grosz in her book *The Incorporeal: Ontology, Ethics, and the Limits of Materialism*, where she seeks to complicate current conversations about materialism by pointing to "'the incorporeal'... [as] the subsistence of the ideal *in* the material," without resorting to either a Platonic dualism or an Aristotelian hylomorphism. Such a position suggests that ideality is immanent in materiality so as to provide the framing conditions for a nonreductive materialism. In other words, it seeks to "frame, orient, and direct material things and processes," allowing matter to become other than what it is in the present and to assume meaning.[6] In considering what I call soft matter, I would like to linger for a moment here on the thin, flimsy, or even atmospheric substances, which figures such as Lucretius, and even Deleuze at times, rely on to explain the phenomena of signification or becoming—to stay with the mists as bodies, even if very diffuse and ephemeral ones, rather than following their dissipation into a space of immaterial effects. In other words, I would like to consider the reactive, moving, agglomerating properties of texture and the encounters they allow and disallow as a way of holding on to the recalcitrance of materiality while attempting to account for processes of temporal change and the generation of meaning. In doing this, I propose a kind of haptic poetics, in which variegations of texture offer a way to consider the contact points between materiality of language and the materiality of the world.

Such contact points may operate through the grammar of touch that is there when Robertson explores the "knobbly quality, or a torsion or a jaggedness or a swoony kind of movement from syllable to syllable," or as one proprioceptively navigates the forest floor in search of mushrooms on the pages of John Cage's *Mushroom Book*.[7] What is clear is that there is an ethics of ornamentation at play here—one that seeks to proliferate the surfaces for possible encounters so that, as Spinoza would put it, bodies can affect and be affected in more expansive and differentiated ways, in much the same way that the growing corals unfold their shapes along hyperbolic geometries so as to maximize the surface area with which they can touch their surroundings.

In interweaving Bacon's sensory protocols for observation and experimentation throughout much of *Poetics of Liveliness*, I am drawn to how a text such as *The History of Dense and Rare* reveals a complex imbrication of sensory modalities involved in assessing the density of matter—ones that rely on precise measurement, but also on descriptive accounts of various thin or powdery substances as well as processes of change and decomposition. My first encounter with *The History of Dense and Rare* occurred when in 2013 I was awarded a commission from the New York–based arts magazine *Triple Canopy*, for which I proposed to re-create Bacon's experiments on the density of substances in this treatise. As a first step, I gathered as many of the substances that Bacon lists as possible (which in itself posed a lot of difficulty as many of these substances, while standard to a toolkit of a seventeenth-century natural philosopher, proved more obscure in the present moment), and while I fell short of fashioning the proper apparatus of gold cubes and receptacles for the measurement of their densities, the poetic text that I created relied extensively on close and direct observation—a kind of sensory immersion in their shapes, colors, and textural properties, which, in turn, transformed the linguistic dimension of the poem. It was this process of performing an "experiment" in description that led to many of the critical questions I am asking in this book, and in particular the manner in which the notion of the experiment, borrowed from the natural sciences, sets the conditions for poetic description, while also offering a procedural model for haptic contact with material specimens—specimens that I aggregated, sorted, rubbed, dusted, spilled, crumpled, and often watched slowly decompose, as was the case when I tried to replicate one of the observations that Bacon performs with a sliced lemon: "I remember that in summer time I once left by chance a cut lemon in a close room, and two months afterwards I found a putrefaction growing on the cut part; tufts of hair an inch high at least; and on the top of each hair a kind of head, like the head of a small snail,—plainly beginning to imitate a plant."[8] No "head of a small snail" sprouted from my lemon, but it did get covered over with green dots, which soon formed a fuzzy surface, sticky when touched, that eventually caused its three-dimensional structure to cave inward.

THE FOLDED UNIVERSE

In proposing a reach toward a haptic poetics with its attention to the textured materialities of poetic language as continuous with entities such as molecules, minerals, lemons, frogs, and clouds, I would like to suggest that the recent turn toward ontology and various kinds of materialisms in critical thought offers a new way to read the archive of twentieth- and twenty-first-century poetics. I argue that the turn toward the ontological, the material, and the nonhuman can work to disentangle a dualist loop that poetics often finds itself in—a loop structured around an oscillation between a sense of language as a material site that is often accompanied by a foreclosure of referential access to nonlinguistic forms of materiality and the chiasmic inverse of this, an emphasis on the properties of the material world that renders language into a transparent lens through which such a world is observed and represented, thus obfuscating the material recalcitrance and opacity of language itself.

Glimpses of this shift in thinking in the context of poetics are already evident among the concepts put forward by several of the critics of materialist poetics who have likewise focused on the conjunction between poetry and science, among them Daniel Tiffany, Amanda Jo Goldstein, and Nathan Brown. Arguing that poets who have drawn on scientific methodologies are perhaps uniquely positioned to attend to the sensuous details of the material world, *Poetics of Liveliness* extends this dialogue specifically into the realms of biological materiality, configuring a poetics of molecular shapes and vibrations that is attentive to the biosemiotics of protein folding, but also to the microscales of sensation, which are at times as delicate as a silkworm navigating the textured surface of a mulberry leaf. At the same time, its purview is not solely biological as it seeks out moments when poetic form amplifies the dynamics of other material processes, such as the wispy movements of vapor that constitute an edge of a cloud.

In this light, my reach toward a haptic poetics within the cosmology of this book can also be understood in the context of what Laura Marks calls "haptic criticism" in an effort to configure a critical practice that does "not master the object but brushe[s] it, *almost* touche[s] it" instead, developing a kind of sensitivity, "a form of subtle complexity, building toward its object, brushing into its pores and touching its varied textures." Following Maurice Merleau-Ponty, Marks explains that such a mode of haptic criticism involves a perceptual process that generates folds in the world and hence allows for haptic points of contact upon which surfaces touch:

> Each time we express something we have perceived of the world, we make a fold in its thickness, the way folds in the brain permit chemical communication among its surfaces. One of my favorite metaphors from quantum physics is that the universe is like a great surface that has been infinitely folded together, until points that were unfathomably distant in space-time come to touch each other. I once watched someone make a strudel, beginning with a pliant sheet of dough, so thin it was translucent, that covered the top of a large table, and then folding and folding it until those thin layers pressed close together in a dense roll (with apples and raisins). The universe is like a strudel. Each time we perceive something, we acknowledge the continuity between its many layers.[9]

Such a haptic approach of folding and refolding with its concomitant proliferation of surfaces once again seeks to "increase the surface area of experience" and hence the kinds of contact points between the materialities of perception, expression, language, and various bodies that occupy the material world.[10] But Marks also opens the macrocosm of this scene of baking a strudel to a sense of what I would call a *poetic cosmology*, predicated on a sensuous apprehension of the materials at hand, but also their manipulation through touch in a manner that seems to engender a proportion of a whole universe within its figurative-material folds.

NOTES

INTRODUCTION

1. Heather N. Cornell, John M. Marzluff, and Shannon Pecoraro, "Social Learning Spreads Knowledge About Dangerous Humans Among American Crows," *Proceedings of the Royal Society of London B: Biological Sciences* 279, no. 1728 (2012): 499–508, doi: 10.1098/rspb.2011.0957.
2. Terence P. T. Ng et al., "Snails and Their Trails: The Multiple Functions of Trail-Following in Gastropods," *Biological Reviews* 88 (2013): 683–700, doi: 10.1111/brv.12023.
3. Monika A. Gorzelak et al., "Inter-plant Communication Through Mycorrhizal Networks Mediates Complex Adaptive Behaviour in Plant Communities," *AoB Plants* 7 (2015): 1–13, doi: 10.1093/aobpla/plv050.
4. Evelyn F. Keller and Lee A. Segel, "Initiation of Slime Mold Aggregation Viewed as an Instability," *Journal of Theoretical Biology* 26, no. 3 (1970): 399–415, doi: 10.1016/0022-5193(70)90092-5.
5. Jakob von Uexküll, *A Foray Into the Worlds of Animals and Humans: With a Theory of Meaning*, trans. Joseph D. O'Neil (Minneapolis: University of Minnesota Press, 2010), 43.
6. Jakob von Uexküll, "An Introduction to Umwelt," *Semiotica* 134, no. 4 (2001): 107.
7. Uexküll, *A Foray Into the Worlds of Animals and Humans*, 50.
8. Uexküll, "An Introduction to Umwelt," 108.
9. In *Discourse on Method*, Descartes writes that "if there were such machines having the organs and the shape of a monkey or of some other animal that lacked reason, we would have no way of recognizing that they were not entirely of the same nature as these animals." René Descartes, *Discourse on Method*, trans. Donald A. Cress (Indianapolis, Ind.: Hackett, 1998), 31.
10. Robert Hooke, *Micrographia: or Some Physiological Descriptions of Minute Bodies Made by Magnifying Glasses* (London: Royal Society, 1665), n.p.

11. Lloyd Strickland, *Leibniz's Monadology: A New Translation and Guide*, trans. Lloyd Strickland (Edinburgh: Edinburgh University Press, 2014), 28.
12. Jen Bervin, "Studies in Scale," introduction to *The Gorgeous Nothings*, by Emily Dickinson, ed. Jen Bervin and Marta Werner (New York: New Directions, 2013), 8. All quotes in this paragraph are from the same page.
13. The etymology of "fabric" dates to the fifteenth century, where it was used to indicate "structure," particularly in the context of construction or building. *Merriam-Webster's Dictionary* suggests that the term is borrowed from "Middle French *fabrique* 'act of construction, something created or constructed, the created world, structure, construction and maintenance of a church,'" or from "medieval Latin *fabrica*, 'process of making something, craft, art, workshop.'" The term can also indicate an underlying structure or makeup in a more abstract sense, as in "the fabric of society," and even such detailed element of patterning as "the appearance or pattern produced by the shapes and arrangement of the crystal grains in a rock." *Merriam Webster's Dictionary*, s.v. "fabric (*n.*)," https://www.merriam-webster.com/dictionary/fabric.
14. Titus Lucretius Carus, *On the Nature of the Universe*, ed. John Godwin, trans. R. E. Latham (London: Penguin, 1994), 5:419–26. All citations of Lucretius in the text are from the Latham translation unless otherwise indicated.
15. Lucretius, 2:217–20, italics in the original. Addional pages cited in the text.
16. Charles Olson, *Collected Prose*, ed. Donald Allen and Benjamin Friedlander (Berkeley: University of California Press, 1997), 240. Additional pages cited in the text.
17. Gertrude Stein, *Look at Me Now and Here I Am: Writings and Lectures 1909–45*, ed. Patricia Meyerowitz (New York: Penguin, 1971), 100, 119.
18. bp Nichol, *The Alphabet Game: A bpNichol Reader*, ed. Lori Emerson and Darren Wershler-Henry (Toronto: Coach House, 2004), 310.
19. In *On Poetics*, Aristotle similarly turns the concept of *mimêsis* away from a sense of imitation of discrete entities or characters and instead places the emphasis on the implication of *mimêsis* for actions as they unfold within the plot of tragedy. The emphasis that Aristotle places on action here is significant, so that, in a sense, characters arise simply as a secondary effect of these actions: "[The actors] do not act in order to imitate characters, but they include characters because of actions; . . . without action, tragedy could not come to be, but without characters it could come to be." Aristotle, *On Poetics*, trans. Seth Benardete and Michael Davis (South Bend: St. Augustine's, 2002), 1450a21–26.
20. In *The Nick of Time*, for instance, Elizabeth Grosz argues that the biological dimension of bodies prefigures all social and cultural variation. Rather than seeing this biological dimension in essentialist terms as a form of fixity, Grosz suggests that the biological realm is a source of continuously evolving potentiality: "Biology does not limit social, political, and personal life: it not only makes them possible, it ensures that they endlessly transform themselves and thus stimulate biology into further self-transformation. The natural world prefigures, contains, and opens up social and cultural existence to endless becoming; in turn, cultural transformation provides further impetus for biological becoming." Elizabeth Grosz, *The Nick of Time: Politics,*

Evolution, and the Untimely (Durham, N.C.: Duke University Press, 2004), 1–2. For more in-depth examination of biology and feminist theory, see also *Gut Feminism*, in which Elizabeth Wilson poses the question of "what conceptual innovations would be possible if feminist theory wasn't so instinctively antibiological." Elizabeth A. Wilson, *Gut Feminism* (Durham, N.C.: Duke University Press, 2015), 1.

21. To develop the agential realist account of *entanglement*, Barad draws on the concept of entanglement in quantum physics, where the term indicates that two entities are connected so that acting on one of them affects the other even if they are separated by a great distance. Entanglement is significant for speculative realist thought because it informs the concept of intra-action, through which entities arise out of their relations, and also addresses the ontological effects that Barad ascribes to the act of observation through her reading of Niels Bohr: "Bohr understands entanglements in ontological terms (what is entangled are the 'components' of phenomena). For Bohr, phenomena—entanglements of objects and agencies of observation—constitute physical reality; phenomena (not independent objects) are the objective referent of measured properties." Karen Barad, *Meeting the Universe Halfway: Quantum Physics and the Entanglement of Matter and Meaning* (Durham, N.C.: Duke University Press, 2007), 309.
22. Barad, 19.
23. Barad, 151 (italics in original).
24. For a more in-depth view of the various thinkers and perspectives that make up speculative realism, see Levi Bryant, Nick Srnicek, and Graham Harman, eds., *The Speculative Turn: Continental Materialism and Realism* (Melbourne: re.press, 2011).
25. Graham Harman, "On Vicarious Causation," *Collapse* 2 (2007): 195.
26. For Harman's detailed response to Barad's philosophy, see Graham Harman, "Agential and Speculative Realism: Remarks on Barad's Ontology," *Rhizomes* 30 (2016), doi.org/10.20415/rhiz/030.e10.
27. Martin Heidegger, *Poetry, Language, Thought*, trans. Albert Hofstadter (New York: Harper Collins, 1971): 164–65. For further disambiguation between objects and things, see Bill Brown's essay "Thing Theory," where he explains that things exceed the delimitations of the subject-object relation: "But the very semantic *reducibility* of *things* to *objects*, coupled with the semantic *irreducibility* of *things* to *objects*, would seem to mark one way of recognizing how, although objects typically arrest a poet's attention, and although the object was what was asked to join the dance in philosophy, things may still lurk in the shadows of the ballroom and continue to lurk there after the subject and object have done their thing, long after the party is over." For Brown, one may "confront the thingness of objects," for instance, at moments when objects break down and stop functioning in a way that changes their story of a relation to a human subject. Bill Brown, "Thing Theory," *Critical Inquiry* 28, no. 1 (2001): 3, 4. The distinction that Brown posits between objects and things parallels the one posited by Heidegger: "An independent, self-supporting thing may become an object if we place it before us, whether in immediate perception or by bringing it to mind in a recollective re-presentation. However, the thingly character of the thing does not consist in its being a represented object, nor can it be defined in any way in terms of the

objectness, the over-againstness, of the object." Confusion may arise within this framework because the notion of the object articulated by Object-Oriented Ontology is perhaps closer to what Heidegger and Brown would call a "thing," simply because the emphasis for OOO theorists is not on the manner in which the subject of knowledge apprehends the object but on the object itself, even, and perhaps especially, as it escapes such modes of apprehension. In *Object-Oriented Ontology: A New Theory of Everything*, Harman defends his choice to use the term "object" rather than "thing" and complicates the genealogy that he is using to derive the term object: "Heidegger employs the word 'thing' to mean the hidden thing in its own right, beyond any false objectifications of it, while 'object' is its negative inverse: the thing reduced to our perception or use of it. Heidegger is free to do this, of course, though I fail to see why we should follow him in this practice. 'Object' is a perfectly clear and flexible term that ought to be retained. More importantly, my discussion of objects is motivated less by Heidegger than by the Austrian and Polish philosophers immediately preceding him, who use the term 'object' in nearly as broad a sense as OOO: Franz Brentano, Kasimierz Twardowski, Edmund Husserl, and Alexius Meinong." Graham Harman, *Object-Oriented Ontology: A New Theory of Everything* (London: Penguin, 2018), 42.

28. Jane Bennett, *Vibrant Matter: A Political Ecology of Things* (Durham, N.C.: Duke University Press, 2010), 4, 2.

29. The term *new* has also been used to distinguish this form of materialism from historical materialism. In *Vibrant Matter* (xiii), Bennett writes that "it is important to follow the trail of human power to expose social hegemonies (as historical materialists do). But my contention is that there is also public value in following the scent of a nonhuman, thingly power, the material agency of natural bodies and technological artifacts." Perhaps this need not be an either-or choice: Marx himself wrote a doctoral thesis on *The Difference Between the Democritean and Epicurean Philosophy of Nature*, addressing, in particular, the significance of the swerve as a concept that emerged with Epicurus.

30. See, for instance, Linda van Speybroeck, Dani de Waele, and Gertrudis Van de Vijver, "Theories in Early Embryology: Close Connections between Epigenesis, Preformationism, and Self-Organization," in *From Epigenesis to Epigenetics: The Genome in Context*, ed. Linda van Speybroeck, Gertrudis van de Vijver, and Dani de Waele (New York: New York Academy of Sciences, 2002), 7–49.

31. Donna Haraway, "Situated Knowledges: The Science Question in Feminism and the Privilege of Partial Perspective," *Feminist Studies* 14, no. 3 (1988): 595, 581.

32. Cecilia Åsberg, Kathrin Thiele, and Iris van der Tuin, "Speculative *Before* the Turn: Reintroducing Feminist Materialist Performativity," *Cultural Studies Review* 21, no. 2 (2015): 151.

33. Åsberg, Thiele, and van der Tuin, 149. The article they reference is Stacy Alaimo, "Thinking as the Stuff of the World," *O-Zone: A Journal of Object-Oriented Studies*, 1 (2014): 13–21; see also Stacy Alaimo, *Bodily Natures: Science, Environment, and the Material Self* (Bloomington: Indiana University Press, 2010).

34. Elizabeth Grosz, *Becoming Undone: Darwinian Reflections on Life, Politics, and Art*, (Durham, N.C.: Duke University Press, 2011), 1, 5. In her most recent book, *The Incorporeal*, Grosz reaches a kind of limit of the term "materialism," seeking an "intimate entwinement of the orders of materiality and ideality," but without reasserting a dualistic relationship between them. She argues that an articulation of a "nonreductive materialism" requires an understanding of the incorporeal conditions that "frame, orient, and direct material things and processes, . . . so that they occupy space and time, [and] have possible meanings and directions that exceed their corporeality." Elizabeth Grosz, *The Incorporeal: Ontology, Ethics and the Limits of Materialism* (New York: Columbia University Press, 2017), 5. While a shift toward the incorporeal as a concept may seem like a departure from Grosz's consistent focus on bodies and materiality, in many ways it is an extension of her long-standing considerations of time in books such as *The Nick of Time*, where temporality offers a framework for materiality to exist within a universe of possibility, which can open out to unforeseeable modes of future becomings.

35. Robertson, in fact, composes some of her work by developing a persona of the "Office for Soft Architecture." See Lisa Robertson, *Occasional Work and Seven Walks from the Office for Soft Architecture* (Astoria, Ore.: Clear Cut, 2003).

36. In considering questions of relational becoming, I am drawing in part on Barad's notion of intra-action, according to which entities are constituted or arise only as a consequence of relations. In my analysis, this is one possibility. At the same time, I would also like to hold a space for considering how entities can carry the traces of past relations and histories—something that I register with particular attention to texture—even as they enter into new encounters. This requires theorizing a range of rhythms of coalescing forms as they differentiate and transform in time and sometimes persist through multiple histories of encounter.

37. Eve Kosofsky Sedgwick, *Touching Feeling: Affect, Pedagogy, Performativity* (Durham, N.C.: Duke University Press, 2003), 13.

38. The importance of kinetics for both Olson and Stein can be attributed at least in part to their shared interest in process philosophy of Alfred North Whitehead, for whom the basic premises of metaphysics involve process and change, rather than a partitioning of reality into stable entities. In other words, for Whitehead, the universe is made up of *actual occasions*, which are processes of becoming, rather than discrete objects. While I am not directly addressing Whitehead's philosophy here, there are a number of critical works that link his thought to Olson and Stein. See especially Steven Meyer, *Irresistible Dictation: Gertrude Stein and the Correlations of Writing and Science*, (Stanford, Calif.: Stanford University Press, 2001); Shahar Bram, *Charles Olson and Alfred North Whitehead: An Essay on Poetry*, trans. Batya Stein (Lewisburg, Pa.: Bucknell University Press, 2004); and Miriam Nichols, *Radical Affections: Essays on the Poetics of Outside* (Tuscaloosa: University of Alabama Press, 2010). For an account of the significance of Whitehead in recent theoretical thought, see Steven Shaviro, *Without Criteria: Kant, Whitehead, Deleuze, and Aesthetics* (Cambridge, Mass.: MIT Press, 2009); and Isabelle Stengers, *Thinking with Whitehead: A Free and*

Wild Creation of Concepts, trans. Michael Chase (Cambridge, Mass.: Harvard University Press, 2014).

39. The question of how different temporal scales may be affected by anthropogenic impact on the planet becomes politically salient if we consider, for instance, how changing temperatures affect the way different organisms experience time and consequently how the spatio-temporal edges of their distribution may change in response. The concept of physiological time suggests that temporality in a biologically relevant sense is a compound entity of other variables, such as increasing temperature, which is speeding up the time of certain biological processes, such as egg hatching or pupation. This egg time or larval time is a factor of temperature measured in units called degree-days, so that certain developmental processes require a kind of accumulation of heat that can occur over the course of a week if the temperatures are warm or may take longer if the weather is cool. Shifts in this form of physiological time have drastic effects on biological species as a result of rising temperatures associated with climate change, with "changes in, say, larval hatching times [that] can cause cascade-like changes in entire ecosystems, when these larva act as food for other animals." Jan Zalasiewicz et al., "The New World of the Anthropocene," *Environmental Science and Technology* 44 (2010): 2229. Such modalities of temporal change can affect organisms in different ways, leading asynchronous processes to occur in overlapping systems that had evolved in sync over much longer temporalities associated with evolutionary time.

40. It is important also to acknowledge here the unequal distribution of such forms of vulnerability, which offers a stark reminder of how structural forces of oppression based on race, class, and access to resources differentially shape the forms of environmental exposure that different people face. For an account of the unequal distribution of the effects of environmental destruction, see, for instance, Kathryn Yusoff, *A Billion Black Anthropocenes or None* (Minneapolis: University of Minnesota Press, 2018); and Rob Nixon, *Slow Violence and the Environmentalism of the Poor* (Cambridge, Mass.: Harvard University Press, 2011). For a consideration of how the erosion of biodiversity may contribute to the emergence and transmission of infectious diseases, see Felicia Keesing et al., "Impacts of Biodiversity on the Emergence and Transmission of Infectious Diseases," *Nature* 468 (December 2, 2010): 647–52.

41. Christian Bök, "Two Dots Over a Vowel," *Boundary 2: An International Journal of Literature and Culture* 36, no. 3 (2009): 11–24.

42. "About." Jen Bervin website, accessed February 18, 2019, http://jenbervin.com/about.

43. For an articulation of how Stein's training in the sciences influenced her early work, see, for instance, Meyer, *Irresistible Dictation*. For a sense of how her work engages with nonreferential capacities of language, see, among others, Frederic J. Hoffman's *Gertrude Stein*. In reference to *Tender Buttons*, Hoffman writes: "The objects contained here are not named; seldom do the words used to respond to them suggest them. The passages are, instead, creations in themselves, independent existences. . . . Miss Stein's language tends to fix attention entirely upon itself, not upon her or upon what context it might allusively suggest." Frederic J. Hoffman, *Gertrude Stein* (Minneapolis: University of Minnesota Press, 1961): 38. What seems interesting here

is that such critical accounts often acknowledge that Stein's writing is engaging with the qualities of the material world even as they continue to make strong claims for the nonreferential reading of her work. Hoffman, for instance, acknowledges that Stein's writing does in fact tell us something about an entity such as celery: "'Celery,' for example, retains much of what celery is known to be and taste: 'Celery tastes tastes where in curled lashes and little bits and mostly in remains'" (38).

44. Lyn Hejinian, *The Language of Inquiry* (Berkeley: University of California Press, 2000), 235.
45. Lisa Robertson, "This Animal, the Pronoun: An Interview," interview by Ted Byrne, *Capilano Review* 3, no. 15 (2011): 16.

1. SOFT MATTER

1. Margaret Wertheim and Christine Wertheim, *Crochet Coral Reef* (Los Angeles: Institute for Figuring, 2015), 18. Subsequent citations given in text.
2. Wertheim and Wertheim, 42–43.
3. Lisa Robertson, *Occasional Work and Seven Walks from the Office for Soft Architecture* (Astoria, Ore.: Clear Cut, 2003), 143. The concept of the surface as it appears in relation to Robertson's work as the Office for Soft Architecture is indebted at least in part to the history of architecture, and especially to the rejection of ornamentation in modernist architecture that is epitomized by texts such as Adolf Loos's *Ornament and Crime*. Robertson's reclaiming of ornamentation is a feminist gesture that embraces the non-monumental, the ephemeral and the decorative. In *Second Skin: Josephine Baker & the Modern Surface*, Anne Anlin Cheng offers important contextualization, arguing for the significance of race in the construction of the concept of surface or "skin" in modernist architecture: "The problem of the modern surface—that is, the heuristic and critical problem of distinguishing decoration as surplus from what is 'proper' to the thing—will hold profound implications for both the theorization of modern buildings and of modern, raced bodies.... Denuded modern surface itself bears the incrustations of a layered history about the imaginary and material presence of 'primitive skin.'" Anne Anlin Cheng, *Second Skin: Josephine Baker & the Modern Surface* (Oxford: Oxford University Press, 2010), 32–33. In *Ornamentalism*, Cheng expands this argument by linking up new materialist thought, feminist theory, and critical race theory to examine how ornamentation plays a crucial role in the construction of "the Asian/Asian American woman in American culture," through processes of racialization that transform her into "a 'body ornament' whose perihumanity demands that we approach ontology, fleshliness, and aliveness differently." Anne Anlin Cheng, *Ornamentalism* (Oxford: Oxford University Press, 2019), 1, 2.
4. Robertson, *Soft Architecture*, 143.
5. Titus Lucretius Carus, *On the Nature of the Universe*, ed. John Godwin, trans. R. E. Latham (London: Penguin, 1994), 1:317–19.
6. Renu Bora, "Outing Texture," *Novel Gazing: Queer Readings in Fiction*, ed. Eve Kosofsky Sedgwick (Durham, N.C: Duke University Press, 1997), 104.

7. Neeraj Bhatia and Lola Sheppard, "Going Soft," *Bracket* 2 (2012): 8.
8. "Silk Pavilion," Mediated Matter Group, Massachusetts Institute of Technology School of Architecture and Planning, accessed March 6, 2020, https://www.media.mit.edu/projects/silk-pavilion/overview/; Joe Flaherty, "A Mind-Blowing Dome Made by 6,500 Computer-Guided Silkworms," *Design*, November 7, 2013, http://www.wired.com/2013/07/your-next-3-d-printer-might-be-filled-with-worms/.
9. Neri Oxman, "Templating Design for Biology, and Biology for Design," *Architectural Design* 85, no. 5 (2015): 104.
10. "Silk Pavilion."
11. Robertson, *Soft Architecture*, 127.
12. Geoff Manaugh, "Soft Serve Space," *Bracket* 2 (2012): 10.
13. P. G. De Gennes, "Soft Matter," *Science* 256, no. 5056 (April 24, 1992): 495.
14. Roberto Piazza, *Soft Matter: The Stuff That Dreams Are Made Of* (Dordrecht: Copernicus, 2010), 7, 9.
15. "The true hallmark of a *real* solid is that atoms or molecules are organized in a crystal, meaning a structure that regularly repeats in space, much as floor tiles are a recurrent motif on a plane.... It is the presence of this spatial regularity that makes a solid a totally different phase of matter compared with a liquid." Piazza, 68.
16. While bubbles behave in this way to minimize surface area, other kinds of soft matter, such as colloids or suspensions of fine particles in a liquid or a gas, have a very large surface area because the material in question is broken up into small particles: "Why so much interest in these miniature materials? The first and most important reason stems from the huge surface area that is a peculiarity of colloids, together with the observation that it is through the surface that something interacts with its surroundings." Piazza, 14.
17. Francis Ponge, *Soap*, trans. Lane Dunlop (Stanford, Calif.: Stanford University Press, 1998), 13.
18. Such a way of understanding affect as a manner of action is evocative of the relationship between affect and action posited by Spinoza in the *Ethics*.
19. Manuel DeLanda, "Matter Matters," *DOMUS Magazine* (2005): 12.
20. On matter as a passive substrate, see Plato, *Timeaeus and Critias*, trans. Desmond Lee (London: Penguin, 2008); and Aristotle, *Generation of Animals*, trans. A. L. Peck (Cambridge, Mass.: Harvard University Press, 1943). With regard to matter acting in deterministic ways, in *The World* (*Le Monde*) René Descartes describes matter as having "extension, or the property ... of occupying space" with "each particular part of matter always continu[ing] in the same state unless collision with others forces it to change"—an account that he expands in the *Treatise on Man* to suggest that "the body ... [is] just a statue or a machine made of earth," with all its parts functioning in much the same way as parts of a clockwork or another mechanism. René Descartes, *The World and Other Writings*, ed. Stephen Gaukroger (Cambridge: Cambridge University Press, 2004), 24–25, 99. For Descartes, all bodies, animals, and matter in general operate as such complex machines, and what distinguishes human beings is the presence of the immaterial soul, which allows him to account for human consciousness and thought in a manner that escapes the constraints of mechanism.

21. Such a focus on matter and the body has remained challenging because many of the political gains of feminist thought have historically come from cultivating the possibility for change within cultural or discursive spheres, rather than the materiality of the body. At the same time, turning to the project of feminist materialism has been a way to resist various kinds of essentialisms, which had often persisted within the materiality of the body as forms of intransigent fixity, despite the best efforts of the projects of social constructivism to resist them by engendering the realms of culture and discourse with a sense of malleability and open-ended political possibility.

22. As Coole and Frost point out in "Introducing the New Materialisms," many of the new materialist approaches cannot simply be characterized as oppositional modes of critique toward this long and complex history of dualism. Rather, they have sought to offer a variety of methodologies, from developing new ontologies of the material world, to reading existing philosophical traditions against the grain so as to find productive sites for feminist thought. Diana Coole and Samantha Frost, "Introducing the New Materialisms," in *New Materialisms: Ontology, Agency, and Politics*, ed. Diana Coole and Samantha Frost (Durham, N.C.: Duke University Press, 2010). A good example is Emanuela Bianchi's book *The Feminine Symptom: Aleatory Matter in the Aristotelian Cosmos*, in which she uncovers a sense of indeterminacy and a kind of mercurial changeability of material processes in Aristotelian cosmology that both disrupt and help propagate the overarching teleological impulse that structures Aristotle's account of the universe. In general, within Aristotle's biology and his account of sexual reproduction, "the complex of formal cause, the source of motion (efficient cause), and final cause—*telos*—is marked as masculine (conveyed by the male sperm)," while matter, aligned with the feminine, is thought of as "that which is moved" and passive. Through Bianchi's feminist reading of Aristotle, however, a more "subterranean understanding of matter ... emerges," one that suggests that matter is not just purely passive but instead "harbor[s] opaque and unpredictable motions that have the capacity to disrupt and derail the unfolding of teleological processes." Emanuela Bianchi, *Feminine Symptom: Aleatory Matter in the Aristotelian Cosmos* (New York: Fordham University Press, 2014), 16.

In the *Timaeus* (41–42), Plato writes about the *chora* or the receptacle as a "mass of plastic material upon which differing impressions are stamped." Such material on which an impression of form is to be stamped "will not have been properly prepared unless it is devoid of all the characters which it is to receive from elsewhere." To illustrate this, Plato draws on the example of how scent is manufactured where the "liquids which are to receive the scent" are contrived to be as "odorless as possible," the same way that "those who set about making impressions in some soft substance make its surface as smooth as possible and allow no impression at all to remain visible in it."

23. For an account of the *chora* in feminist theory, see, for instance, Julia Kristeva, *Desire in Language: A Semiotic Approach to Literature and Art* (New York: Columbia University Press, 1980).

24. Plato, *Timeaeus and Critias*, 42.

25. Aristotle writes: "Is the semen inside the offspring to start with, from the outset a part of the body which is formed, and mingling with the material provided by the female; or does the physical part of the semen have no share nor lot in the business, only the *dynamis* and movement contained in it? This, anyway, is the active and efficient ingredient; whereas the ingredient which gets set and given shape is the remnant of the residue in the female animal. The second suggestion is clearly the right one, as is shown both by reasoning and by observed fact. If we consider the matter on general grounds, we see that when some one thing is formed from the conjunction of an active partner with a passive one, the active partner is not situated within the thing which is being formed; . . . Now of course the female, *qua* female, is passive, and the male, *qua* male, is active—it is that whence the principle of movement comes." Aristotle, *Generation of Animals*, trans. A. I. Peck (Cambridge, Mass.: Harvard University Press, 1943), 113.
26. See Evelyn Fox Keller, *Refiguring Life: Metaphors of Twentieth-Century Biology* (New York: Columbia University Press, 1995).
27. Mel Y. Chen, *Animacies: Biopolitics, Racial Mattering, and Queer Affect* (Durham, N.C.: Duke University Press, 2012), 2, 5, 13, 15.
28. Karen Barad, "On Touching: The Inhuman That Therefore I Am," *differences* 25, no. 3 (2012): 214.
29. Elizabeth Grosz, *The Incorporeal: Ontology, Ethics and the Limits of Materialism* (New York: Columbia University Press, 2017), 59.
30. Hasana Sharp, *Spinoza and the Politics of Renaturalization* (Chicago: University of Chicago Press, 2011), 9.
31. Gilles Deleuze, *Expressionism in Philosophy: Spinoza* (Brooklyn: Zone, 1990), 14. Deleuze further explains the dynamics of expression in Spinozan thought: "Expression is on the one hand an explication, an unfolding of what expresses itself, the One manifesting itself in the Many (substance manifesting itself in its attributes, and these attributes manifesting themselves in their modes). Its multiple expression, on the other hand, involves Unity. The One remains involved in what expresses it, imprinted in what unfolds it, immanent in whatever manifests it: expression is in this respect an involvement. . . . Expression in general involves and implicates what it expresses, while also explicating and evolving it" (16).
32. Eve Kosofsky Sedgwick, *Touching Feeling: Affect, Pedagogy, Performativity* (Durham, N.C.: Duke University Press, 2003), 8.
33. Eve Kosofsky Sedgwick and Adam Frank, "Shame in the Cybernetic Fold: Reading Silvan Tomkins," in Sedgwick, *Touching Feeling*, 108.
34. Graham Harman, "Agential and Speculative Realism: Remarks on Barad's Ontology," *Rhizomes* 30 (2016). doi.org/10.20415/rhiz/030.e10.
35. Gilles Deleuze, *Bergsonism*, trans. Hugh Tomlinson and Barbara Habberjam (New York: Zone, 1991), 31, 32.
36. Elizabeth Grosz, *Becoming Undone: Darwinian Reflections on Life, Politics, and Art*, (Durham, N.C.: Duke University Press, 2011), 1.

1. SOFT MATTER   289

37. See, for instance, part 3, proposition 6, of the *Ethics*, where Spinoza explains that "each thing, as far as it can by its own power, strives to persevere in its being." Benedict de Spinoza, *Ethics*, ed. and trans. Edwin Curley (London: Penguin, 1996), 75.

38. Gilbert Simondon's notions of individuation, metastability, and the preindividual reality offer a useful context for considering the problem of differentiation within the Deleuzean archive: "We would like to show that the search for the principles of individuation must be reversed, by considering as primordial the operation of individuation from which the individual comes to exist. . . . The individual would then be grasped as a relative reality, a certain phase of being that supposes a preindividual reality, and that, even after individuation, does not exist on its own, because individuation does not exhaust with one stroke the potentials of preindividual reality." Gilbert Simondon, "The Position of the Problem of Ontogenesis," trans. Gregory Flanders, *Parhesia* 7 (2009): 5. Simondon's understanding of individuation not as a constitution of identity but only as a partial and relative resolution within a system enables him to keep in view the multiplicity of potentials that are available to the system, as well as the sense that such a system "encloses a certain incompatibility in relation to itself." These incompatibilities or tensions place the system into a metastable equilibrium, a precarious state that, unlike the stable equilibrium, within which all the potentials have been exhausted to reach the lowest energy state, contains a multiplicity of preindividual potentials, which go on to carry the system along new trajectories of individuation.

39. Robertson, *Soft Architecture*, 15.

40. Jakob von Uexküll, *A Foray Into the Worlds of Animals and Humans: With a Theory of Meaning*, trans. Joseph D. O'Neil (Minneapolis: University of Minnesota Press, 2010), 52, 72.

41. Eva Hayward, "Fingeryeyes: Impressions of Cup Corals," *Cultural Anthropology* 25, no. 4 (2010): 585, 580.

42. Hayward, 582, 585.

43. Robertson, *Soft Architecture*, 143.

44. Spinoza, *Ethics*, 42.

45. Spinoza, 44, brackets in original translation.

46. Spinoza, 41.

47. Gilles Deleuze, *Spinoza: Practical Philosophy*, trans. Robert Hurley (San Francisco: City Lights, 1988), 28.

48. While Spinoza's thought has most often been read as an antecedent of the current within affect theory developed by Deleuze and, in the more contemporary context, figures such as Brian Massumi, Sedgwick's work on affect has been largely shaped through her reading of the psychologist, cybernetics thinker, and affect theorist Silvan Tomkins and the psychoanalyst Melanie Klein. See, for instance, Silvan S. Tomkins, *Shame and Its Sisters: A Silvan Tomkins Reader*, ed. Eve Kosofsky Sedgwick and Adam Frank (Durham, N.C.: Duke University Press, 1995). For a

delineation between these affect theory genealogies, see Melissa Gregg and Gregory J. Seigworth, eds., *The Affect Theory Reader* (Durham, N.C.: Duke University Press, 2010).

49. Sedgwick, *Touching Feeling*, 17. Susan Stewart elaborates a similar connection between touching and feeling in *Poetry and the Fate of the Senses*: "Of all the senses, touch is most linked to emotion and feeling. To be 'touched' or 'moved' by words or things implies the process of identification and separation by which we apprehend the world aesthetically." Susan Stewart, *Poetry and the Fate of the Senses* (Chicago: University of Chicago Press, 2002), 162.
50. Robertson, *Soft Architecture*, 16–17.
51. Bora, "Outing Texture," 101, 99.
52. Bora, "Outing Texture," 99.
53. Sedgwick, *Touching Feeling*, 14.
54. Sedgwick, 15.
55. Grosz, *The Nick of Time*, 4–5.
56. Gertrude Stein, *Tender Buttons* (San Francisco: City Lights, 2014), 11.
57. Chad Bennett, "Scratching the Surface: *Tender Buttons* and the Textures of Modernism," *Arizona Quarterly* 73, no. 1 (Spring 2017): 21.
58. Bennett, "Scratching the Surface," 22. On the critics mentioned, see, for instance, Jamie Hilder, "'After All One Must Know More than One Sees and One Does Not See a Cube in Its Entirety': Gertrude Stein and Picasso and Cubism," *Critical Survey* 17, no. 3 (2005): 66–84; and Marjorie Perloff, "Poetry as Word-System: The Art of Gertrude Stein," *American Poetry Review* 8, no. 5 (1979): 33–43.
59. Harriet Scott Chessman, *The Public Is Invited to Dance: Representation, the Body, and Dialogue in Gertrude Stein* (Stanford, Calif.: Stanford University Press, 1989), 88.
60. Gertrude Stein, "A Transatlantic Interview," interview by Robert Bartlett Haas, in *A Primer for the Gradual Understanding of Gertrude Stein* (Santa Barbara, Calif.: Black Sparrow Press, 1971), 25.
61. Chessman, *The Public Is Invited to Dance*, 89.
62. Gertrude Stein, *Look at Me Now and Here I Am: Writings and Lectures 1909–45*, ed. Patricia Meyerowitz (New York: Penguin, 1971), 136 (italics mine).
63. Stein, "A Transatlantic Interview," 18.
64. Rebecca Scherr, "Tactile Erotics: Gertrude Stein and the Aesthetics of Touch," *Literature Interpretation Theory*, 18, no. 3 (2007): 193, 210.
65. Stein, *Tender Buttons*, 47.
66. Robertson, *Soft Architecture*, 143.
67. Stein, *Tender Buttons*, 24.
68. See, for instance, Catharine R. Stimpson, "The Somagrams of Gertrude Stein," *Poetics Today* 6, no. 1–2 (1985): 67–80; and Elizabeth Fifer, "Is Flesh Advisable? The Interior Theater of Gertrude Stein," *Signs: Journal of Women in Culture and Society* 4, no. 3 (1979): 472–83, among others.
69. Sianne Ngai, *Our Aesthetic Categories: Zany, Cute, Interesting* (Cambridge, Mass.: Harvard University Press, 2012), 91.

70. Ezra Pound, *Literary Essays of Ezra Pound*, ed. T. S. Eliot (New York: New Directions, 1968), 285.
71. In this case Pound is referring to the work of the French poet Albert Samain.
72. Peter Nicholls, "Hard and Soft Modernism: Politics as 'Theory,'" in *A Handbook of Modernism Studies*, ed. Jean-Michel Rabaté (West Sussex: Wiley-Blackwell, 2013), 16.
73. Bennett, "Scratching the Surface," 26.
74. Bennett, 23, 25, 26.

2. POETRY AND SCIENCE

1. The phrase "covers the page" is resonant with Robert Smithson's sense that "language 'covers' rather than 'discovers' its sites and situations," expressed in his essay "A Museum of Language in the Vicinity of Art," in *The Collected Writings*, ed. Jack Flam (Berkeley: University of California Press, 1996), 78. For a critical interpretation that places Smithson in relation to post-1945 poetry and poetics, see Lytle Shaw, *Fieldworks: From Place to Site in Postwar Poetics* (Tuscaloosa: University of Alabama Press, 2013).
2. John Cage, "Cage's Loft, New York City October 21–23, 1991," interview by Joan Retallack, in *Musicage: Cage Muses on Words, Art, Music*, ed. Joan Retallack (Hanover, N.H.: Wesleyan University Press, 1996), 89.
3. Cage, 90.
4. Charles Olson, *Collected Prose*, ed. Donald Allen and Benjamin Friedlander, (Berkeley: University of California Press, 1997), 243.
5. This sensation is resonant with the modes of indeterminacy that Anna Tsing writes about in *The Mushroom at the End of the World*: "What do you do when your world starts to fall apart? I go for a walk, and if I'm really lucky, I find mushrooms. Mushrooms pull me back into my senses, not just—like flowers—through their riotous colors and smells but because they pop up unexpectedly, reminding me of the good fortune of just happening to be there. Then I know that there are still pleasures amidst the terrors of indeterminacy." Anna Lowenhaupt Tsing, *The Mushroom at the End of the World: On the Possibility of Life in Capitalist Ruins* (Princeton, N.J.: Princeton University Press, 2015), 1. The term *chance operations* as I use it here references a compositional method Cage employed, often based on the Chinese oracle book the *I Ching*, or *Book of Changes*.
6. Bruce Andrews, "Text and Context" and "Writing Social Work & Political Practice," in *The Language Book (Poetics of the New)*, ed. Bruce Andrews and Charles Bernstein (Carbondale: Southern Illinois University Press, 1984), 32, 133–34.
7. Bruce Andrews, *Paradise and Method: Poetics and Praxis* (Evanston, Ill.: Northwestern University Press, 1996), 25.
8. For one possible place to locate the discussion of the materiality of signifying processes that characterized certain elements of the "linguistic turn," see Jacques Derrida's "Typewriter Ribbon: Limited Ink," where he articulates a sense of "materiality without matter, or material substance" through a reading of Paul de Man's work.

Jacques Derrida, *Without Alibi*, ed. and trans. Peggy Kamuf (Stanford, Calif.: Stanford University Press, 2002), 151.

9. As an example of how the turn toward nonlinguistic, and often nonhuman, forms of matter has pushed against the contours of the "linguistic turn" or sought to expand them, see Karen Barad's "Posthumanist Performativity," where she states: "Language has been granted too much power. The linguistic turn, the semiotic turn, the interpretative turn, the cultural turn: it seems that at every turn lately every 'thing'—even materiality—is turned into a matter of language or some other form of cultural representation. The ubiquitous puns on 'matter' do not, alas, mark a rethinking of the key concepts (materiality and signification) and the relationship between them.... Language matters. Discourse matters. Culture matters. There is an important sense in which the only thing that does not seem to matter anymore is matter." Karen Barad, "Posthumanist Performativity: Toward an Understanding of How Matter Comes to Matter," *Signs* 28, no. 3 (Spring 2003): 801. Conversely, Mel Y. Chen "refute[s] the recent moves to evacuate substance from language," rendering it dematerialized, and, in turn, leading to the problem that "language discussions seem to disappear in the theorizing of new materialism." Chen goes on to argue that "language is as much alive as it is dead, and it is certainly material" even if, under "the influence of poststructuralist thought," it "has in many ways steadily become bleached of its quality to be anything *but* referential, or structural, or performative." Mel Y. Chen, *Animacies: Biopolitics, Racial Mattering, and Queer Affect* (Durham, N.C.: Duke University Press, 2012), 51–53.

10. Eve Kosofsky Sedgwick, *Touching Feeling: Affect, Pedagogy, Performativity* (Durham, N.C.: Duke University Press, 2003), 6.

11. For disambiguation between objectism and objectivism, see Nathan Brown, *The Limits of Fabrication: Materials Science, Materialist Poetics* (New York: Fordham University Press, 2017).

12. William Carlos Williams, *Paterson* (New York: New Directions, 1995), 139.

13. Shaw, *Fieldworks*, 4. The term *site* as Shaw uses it draws on the notion of site specificity in art, and in particular on the work of the earthworks artist Robert Smithson. Here is a fuller context for Shaw's argument, from the same page: "*Fieldworks* argues that the turn to place, and later site, allowed postwar poets and artists not just to dive into (and remain within) a luminous world of immersive specificity; instead, when they poked their heads up, as they often did, a poetics of fieldwork also enabled them to rethink their relations to neighboring disciplines—historiography and ethnography above all—and to critique and recode those fields more luminously and immersively than was possible through the pure pursuit of deracinated particulars, by now the Monet water lily poster of the poetic vocation."

14. Brown, *Limits of Fabrication*, 11.

15. As an example of such microscopic writing, Brown cites Donald Eigler and Erhard Schweizer's use of a Scanning Tunneling Microscope (STM) in 1989 to write out "IBM" by manipulating single atoms.

16. Brown, *Limits of Fabrication*, 10.

17. Olson, *Collected Prose*, 243.

18. Brown, *Limits of Fabrication*, 26.

2. POETRY AND SCIENCE 293

19. Daniel Tiffany, *Toy Medium: Materialism and Modern Lyric* (Berkeley: University of California Press, 2000), 97.
20. Amanda Jo Goldstein, *Sweet Science: Romantic Materialism and the New Logics of Life* (Chicago: University of Chicago Press, 2017), 6–7.
21. Gertrude Stein, *The Geographical History of America or the Relation of Human Nature to the Human Mind* (Baltimore: Johns Hopkins University Press, 1995), 188.
22. Robert Hooke, *Micrographia: or Some Physiological Descriptions of Minute Bodies Made by Magnifying Glasses* (London: Royal Society, 1665), n.p.
23. On vision as a privileged mode of sensation, see, for instance, David Kleinberg-Levin, *The Philosopher's Gaze: Modernity in the Shadows of Enlightenment* (Berkeley: University of California Press, 1999); and Daniela Bleichmar, *Visible Empire: Botanical Expeditions and Visual Culture in the Hispanic Enlightenment* (Chicago: University of Chicago Press, 2012).
24. Sedgwick, *Touching Feeling*, 15.
25. Gilles Deleuze and Félix Guattari, *A Thousand Plateaus: Capitalism and Schizophrenia*, trans. Brian Massumi (Minneapolis: University of Minnesota Press, 1987), 492–93.
26. Lyn Hejinian, *The Language of Inquiry* (Berkeley: University of California Press, 2000), 235.
27. Francis Bacon, *The New Organon*, ed. Lisa Jardine and Michael Silverthorne (Cambridge: Cambridge University Press, 2000), 82.
28. Bacon, *The New Organon*, 10.
29. Bacon, 16.
30. Lisa Jardine, introduction to *The New Organon*, xv.
31. Joe Bray, Alison Gibbons, and Brian McHale, introduction to *The Routledge Companion to Experimental Literature*, ed. Bray, Gibbons, and McHale (New York: Routledge, 2012), 2.
32. Hejinian, *The Language of Inquiry*, 84.
33. "And so, what we call art exists in order to give back the sensation of life, in order to make us feel things, in order to make the stone stony. The goal of art is to create the sensation of seeing, and not merely recognizing, things; the device of art is the '*ostranenie*' of things and the complication of the form, which increases the duration and complexity of perception, as the process of perception is its own end in art and must be prolonged." Viktor Shklovsy, *Viktor Shklovsky: A Reader*, ed. and trans. Aklexandra Berlina (New York: Bloomsbury, 2016), 123–24.
34. It is important to note that Mayer herself was interested in science and its relationship to writing and cowrote *The Art of Science Writing* with Dale Worsley. This interest in science came to shape her sense of protocols she followed to generate her poetic experiments. Dale Worsley and Bernadette Mayer, *The Art of Science Writing* (New York: Teachers and Writers Collaborative, 1989).
35. Titus Lucretius Carus, *On the Nature of the Universe*, ed. John Godwin, trans. R. E. Latham (London: Penguin, 1994), 1:819–23.
36. Lucretius, 2:1014–15.
37. Alfred Jarry, *Exploits & Opinions of Dr. Faustroll, Pataphysician*, trans. Simon Watson Taylor (Boston: Exact Change, 1996), 88–89.

38. 'Pataphysics was taken up by French writers such as Raymond Queneau and François Le Lionnais, who started the Collège de 'Pataphysique in 1948 in Paris, which eventually led to the development of Oulipo (*Ouvroir de littérature potentielle*), a literary movement that championed the use of various kinds of constraints and procedural recombinatory methods as a way of creating literary texts. Queneau's *A Hundred Thousand Billion Poems* (*Cent mille milliards de poèmes*) stands as an iconic example of such linguistic recombination techniques, consisting of ten sonnets with each of their fourteen lines cut up into separate strips, so that in turning the strips of paper one can create recombinations of the lines into 10^{14} different poems.
39. Christian Bök, *Crystallography* (Toronto: Coach House, 2003), 156.
40. Christian Bök, "Two Dots Over a Vowel," *Boundary 2: An International Journal of Literature and Culture* 36, no. 3 (2009): 12–13.
41. The full quote by Huebler is: "The world is full of objects, more or less interesting; I do not wish to add any more. I prefer, simply, to state the existence of things in terms of time and/or place." Douglas Huebler, "Statement," *January 5–31, 1969*, curated by Seth Siegelaub (New York, 1969). While the disavowal of the creation of objects in the first part of this statement seems to oppose the tenets of a materialist poetics that I am developing here, the second sentence, which brings in the problem of how objects are situated in time and place, complicates this and evokes the latching of temporality and materiality that I am investigating. In some sense, the practices of documentation of "situated objects" that Huebler embarks on after making this statement, which was to become one of the signposts of conceptualist art, have uncanny resemblances to the projects of some of the writers that I discuss here. For instance, Huebler's *Variable Piece #70: Global 81* (1973) entails the aim of documenting every living person before his death—an aim that in many ways resembles Stein's goal in *The Making of Americans* to describe and classify "every kind of human being."
42. "Joseph Schillinger, a minor American Cubist, who wrote, over a twenty-five-year period, an often extraordinary book called *The Mathematical Basis of the Arts*, divided the historical evolution of art into five 'zones,' which replace each other with increasing acceleration: 1. preaesthetic, a biological stage of mimicry; 2. traditional-aesthetic, a magic, ritual-religious art; 3. emotional-aesthetic, artistic expressions of emotions, self-expression, art for art's sake; 4. rational-aesthetic, characterized by empiricism, experimental art, novel art; 5. scientific, post-aesthetic, which will make possible the manufacture, distribution and consumption of a perfect art product and will be characterized by a fusion of the art forms and materials, and, finally, a 'disintegration of art,' the 'abstraction and liberation of the idea.'" Lucy R. Lippard and John Chandler, "The Dematerialization of Art," in *Changing: Essays in Art Criticism*, by Lucy R. Lippard (New York: Dutton, 1971), 255, 258.
43. Shaw, *Fieldworks*, 5.
44. Smithson, *The Collected Writings*, 61.
45. The quotation that forms the heading of this section is from Lisa Robertson's *The Weather* (Vancouver: New Star, 2001), 24.
46. Hejinian, *The Language of Inquiry*, 137.

47. Peter Quartermain, *Disjunctive Poetics: From Gertrude Stein and Louis Zukofsky to Susan Howe* (Cambridge: Cambridge University Press, 1992), 21, 22.
48. Robert Grenier, "Tender Buttons," *L=A=N=G=U=A=G=E* 6 (1978).
49. Michael Davidson, "On Reading Stein," *L=A=N=G=U=A=G=E* 6 (1978).
50. Andrews, *Paradise and Method*, 17.
51. However, Haraway's attempt to tether semiosis to materiality is notably more at ease with the metaphoricity that is at play at the boundary between nature-culture, while Barad, like many recent materialist thinkers, is afraid that the recalcitrance of nonhuman material worlds will evaporate under the guise of such figurative linguistic play. See Donna Haraway, "The Promises of Monsters: A Regenerative Politics for Inappropriate/d Others," in *Cultural Studies*, ed. Lawrence Grossberg, Cary Nelson, and Paula Treichler (New York: Routledge, 1992), 295–337. Similar anxieties are evident in Branka Arsić's *Bird Relics: Grief and Vitalism in Thoreau*, in which she offers a powerful account of Thoreau's sense of language, which permeates the nonhuman world as different beings imprint "themselves on other beings, thus literally or materially altering them, leaving their trace in them to 'read'"—a sense of language that becomes discernible through a method of "literalization," which strips metaphor, seen as human and ideational, away from materiality. Branka Arsić, *Bird Relics: Grief and Vitalism in Thoreau* (Cambridge, Mass.: Harvard University Press, 2016), 7.
52. Karen Barad, *Meeting the Universe Halfway: Quantum Physics and the Entanglement of Matter and Meaning* (Durham, N.C.: Duke University Press, 2007), 3.
53. The literature here is too extensive to list comprehensively. For a cross-section of relevant texts, see, for instance, Steven Shapin and Simon Schaffer, *Leviathan and the Air-Pump: Hobbes, Boyle, and the Experimental Life* (Princeton, N.J.: Princeton University Press, 1985); Peter Galison, *How Experiments End* (Chicago: University of Chicago Press, 1987); Brian W. Ogilvie, *The Science of Describing: Natural History in Renaissance Europe* (Chicago: University of Chicago Press, 2008); Svetlana Alpers, *The Art of Describing: Dutch Art in the Seventeenth Century*, (Chicago: University of Chicago Press, 1984); and John B. Bender and Michael Marrinan, *Regimes of Description: In the Archive of the Eighteenth Century* (Stanford, Calif.: Stanford University Press, 2005).
54. Lorraine Daston, "On Scientific Observation," *Isis* 99, no. 1 (March 2008): 98.
55. In "On Scientific Observation" (102), Daston suggests that "even after observation was demoted to the status of handmaiden to experiment in mid-nineteenth-century philosophy of science, it continued to be a fundamental scientific practice—and arguably the one most likely to generate novelties, including new ontologies." On the resurgent interest in description, see Sharon Marcus, Heather Love, and Stephen Best, "Building a Better Description," *Representations* 135, no. 1 (Summer 2016): 1–21.
56. Hejinian, *The Language of Inquiry*, 158, 215.
57. Hejinian, 84.
58. Lisa Robertson, "This Animal, The Pronoun: An Interview," interview by Ted Byrne, *Capilano Review* 3, no. 15 (2011): 16.
59. Lisa Robertson, *Occasional Work and Seven Walks from the Office for Soft Architecture* (Astoria, Ore.: Clear Cut, 2003), 67. The introduction to *The Weather* is reprinted in this work.

60. Lisa Robertson, "Lifted: An Interview with Lisa Robertson," interview by Kai Fierle-Hedrick, *Chicago Review* 51, no. 4 (2006): 49–50. All quotes in this paragraph are from the same page.
61. Robertson, *The Weather*, 24–25.
62. Robertson, 24–25.

3. MOLECULES

1. Filippo Tommaso Marinetti, *Critical Writings* (New York: Farrar, Straus and Giroux, 2006), 126.
2. The term *Brownian* here refers to Brownian motion or the random movement of particles suspended in a gas or a liquid. While this phenomenon was described by ancient thinkers such as Lucretius, it received its name from the nineteenth-century botanist Robert Brown, who observed it by looking at plant pollen underneath the microscope.
3. Marinetti, *Critical Writings*, 112.
4. For an elaboration on the critique of humanism that is implicit in futurist writing, see Christine Poggi, *Inventing Futurism: The Art and Politics of Artificial Optimism* (Princeton, N.J.: Princeton University Press, 2009), 151.
5. Marinetti, *Critical Writings*, 125.
6. Fred Wah, *Faking It: Poetics and Hybridity, Critical Writing, 1984–1999* (Edmonton, Alberta: NeWest, 2000), 243.
7. A historical triangulation is at play here, as Jarry was also influential for Marinetti. In an essay titled "Futurism, Dada and Surrealism: Some Cross-Fertilizations Among the Historical Avant-gardes," Günter Berghaus discusses the fact that Marinetti met Jarry in 1903, when Marinetti was left with the following impression of their meeting: "'I can see myself now with Alfred Jarry in the ornate salon of Mme Perier where from three to eleven at night thirty or forty men and women spouting poetry would parade.... I toss off my ode on the speed of cars and Jarry his metamorphosis of a bus into an elephant." Günter Berghaus, "Futurism, Dada, and Surrealism: Some Cross-Fertilizations Among the Historical Avant-garde," in *International Futurism in Arts and Literature*, ed. Günter Berghaus (Berlin: Walter de Gruyter, 2000), 273. Subsequently, Jarry's plays, such as *Ubu Roi*, became an influence for Marinetti's own playwriting.
8. Note that in the Canadian context the single apostrophe that precedes the French version of 'Pataphysics becomes a double apostrophe of "Pataphysics.
9. Christian Bök, *'Pataphysics: The Poetics of an Imaginary Science* (Evanston, Ill.: Northwestern University Press, 2002), 27.
10. Steve McCaffery, *Prior to Meaning: The Protosemantic and Poetics* (Evanston, Ill.: Northwestern University Press, 2001), xix–xx, 21.
11. See Karen M. Nielsen, "The Private Parts of Animals: Aristotle on the Teleology of Sexual Difference," *Phronesis* 53, no. 4–5 (2008): 373–405; Lynda Lange, "Woman Is Not a Rational Animal: On Aristotle's Biology of Reproduction," in *Discovering Reality: Feminist Perspectives on Epistemology, Metaphysics, Methodology, and Philosophy of Science*, ed. Sandra Harding and Merrill B. Hintikka (New York: Kluwer Academic, 2003), 1–16;

and Charlotte Witt, "Form, Normativity and Gender in Aristotle: A Feminist Perspective," in *Feminist Interpretations of Aristotle*, ed. Cynthia A. Freeland (University Park: Pennsylvania State University Press, 1998).

12. Elizabeth Grosz, *The Incorporeal: Ontology, Ethics and the Limits of Materialism*, (New York: Columbia University Press, 2017), 4–5, 14, 13, 18.
13. Christian Bök, *The Xenotext: Book 1* (Toronto: Coach House, 2015), 150.
14. For interviews, see, among others, Christian Bök, "Beginners, Christian Bök and Alela Diane," *Strand*, May 31, 2011, BBC World Service, http://www.bbc.co.uk/programmes/poogvpkk; and Christian Bök, "The Xenotext Experiment: An Interview with Christian Bök," interview by Stephen Voyce, *Postmodern Culture* 17, no. 2 (January 2007). The *Nature* article is Christian Bök, "Q&A: Poetry in the Genes," interview by Krista Zala, *Nature* 458 (2009): 35, doi:10.1038/458035a.
15. Bök worked on *The Xenotext* with the biologist Dr. Stuart A. Kauffman, a MacArthur Fellow who was at the time the iCore chair for the Institute for Biocomplexity and Informatics, until he retired and Dr. Sui Huang, also of IBI, took over the scientific guidance for the project.
16. Bök, *The Xenotext*, 154, 151.
17. The investigations into the material properties of language that Bök pursues in *Crystallography* by utilizing the arrangement of the letters as particulate elements positioned in a specific way on the surface of the page can be situated within the broader contours of the concrete poetry movement. See, for instance, Mary Ellen Solt, *Concrete Poetry: A World View* (Bloomington: Indiana University Press, 1970.) Concrete poetry, alongside sound poetry, represented a countercurrent in postwar poetics, within which significant explorations of language as material substance were taking place, particularly as both explored the material, tangible, and aural qualities of sublexical fragments of words and letters, and, in the case of sound and performance poetry, their relation to sound and breath.
18. Christian Bök, "Cryptic Poetry Written in a Microbe's DNA," *CultureLab*, May 4, 2011, https://www.newscientist.com/blogs/culturelab/2011/05/christian-boks-dynamic-dna-poetry.html.
19. Staffan Müller-Wille and Hans-Jörg Rheinberger, *A Cultural History of Heredity* (Chicago: University of Chicago Press, 2012), 16.
20. Evelyn Fox Keller, *Refiguring Life: Metaphors of Twentieth Century Biology* (New York: Columbia University Press, 1995), 39–40.
21. Judith Roof, *The Poetics of DNA* (Minneapolis: University of Minnesota Press, 2007), 2, 7. My own position here is not so much to be critical of the use of figuration in the context of science, as the presence of metaphor or analogy is an integral dimension of epistemic practices, as many scholars in science studies, such as Keller and Haraway, have pointed out. It seems crucial to remain aware, however, as Roof argues, of the ways in which each of these figurative dimensions shapes and limits our understanding of a particular phenomenon. A more complex interpretation is possible here if one considers what role the figurative aspects of language, such as metaphor, play in accounts of signification that refuse the dissociation of matter and language into two separate realms.

22. Müller-Wille and Rheinberger, *A Cultural History of Heredity*, 193, 184.
23. In another bioart project, referenced by Bök, the artist Joe Davis, for instance, has sought to "encode the database of Wikipedia into the genome of *Malus sieversii* (the oldest strain of apple, which has grown wild in Kazakhstan for more than 4,000 years)." Bök, *The Xenotext*, 115. This particular apple cultivar has been selected because of its age and origin as a reference to the "Tree of Knowledge," so that, in some sense, this project seeks to literalize this Christian motif in a grove or an orchard of such apple trees, each of which contains some portion of the information stored in the fifty thousand entries that compose Wikipedia. In this form of bioart, the materiality of DNA is unproblematically transformed into information, and Bök goes so far as to suggest that planting genetically engineered organisms, such as the apple trees in Joe Davis's bioart experiment or the *Arabdiopsis thaliana* that contains the line from Virgil, is equivalent to planting "groves of information" (155).
24. Bök, *The Xenotext*, 113. *Arabidopsis thaliana* is used as a model organism in plant biology and genetics and is the first plant to have had its genome sequenced. See also Sylvestre Marillonnet, Victor Klimyuk, and Yuri Gleba, "Encoding Technical Information in GM Organisms," *Nature Biotechnology* 21 (2003): 224–26.
25. Bök, "Cryptic Poetry Written in a Microbe's DNA."
26. Marillonnet, Klimyuk, and Gleba, "Encoding Technical Information," 226.
27. Christian Bök, "'Teaching Myself Molecular Biochemistry Is Just Part of the Process,'" interview by Kaveh Akbar, *Divedapper*, October 13, 2014, https://www.divedapper.com/interview/christian-bok/.
28. See Chensheng Lu, Kenneth M. Warchol, and Richard A. Callahan, "Sub-lethal Exposure to Neonicotinoids Impaired Honey Bees Winterization Before Proceeding to Colony Collapse Disorder," *Bulletin of Insectology* 67, no. 1 (2014): 125–30. For a literary critical treatment of Colony Collapse Disorder, see also Anne-Lise François, "Flower Fisting," *Postmodern Culture* 22, no. 1 (September 2011).
29. Bök, *The Xenotext*, 151.
30. Bök, 75.
31. Bök, "'Teaching Myself Molecular Biochemistry.'"
32. As I argue in my article "Cloud Writing: Describing Soft Architectures of Change in the Anthropocene," finding ways to attend to such variegated rhythms of nonhuman time has the potential to subvert the teleological logic of an apocalyptic temporality. Such an apocalyptic conception of time threatens to collapse the dire conditions of environmental degradation that we find ourselves in at this moment of the Anthropocene into the prophetic and inevitable logic of the monumental time of catastrophe—a logic that Bök's project reiterates on multiple levels, hence his desire to create an eternal work of art within the lively folds of biological materiality. Ironically, the hubris of this anthropocentric ambition has continuously been subverted by Bök's "microscopic collaborator" as it repeatedly digests the protein poem, in its lively, nonmonumental temporality of somatic unfolding. See Ada Smailbegović, "Cloud Writing: Describing Soft Architectures of Change in the Anthropocene," in *Art in the Anthropocene:*

Encounters Among Aesthetics, Politics, Environments and Epistemologies, ed. Heather Davis and Etienne Turpin (London: Open Humanities, 2015), 93–107.

33. The bees are often described through a series of epithets, for instance, "nymphlike honeybees" and "nefarious honeybees," evoking a tradition of such invocations in epic poetry.

34. Bök, *The Xenotext*, 89.

35. As Suzanne Anker and Dorothy Nelkin point out in *The Molecular Gaze*, such modes of patterning in which formal repetitions and variations are indicative of molecular structure have been employed by composers (or, in some cases, microbiologists turned composers), such as Susan Alexjander, Aurora Sanchez-Souza, and Fernando Baquero, who have used the sequence of DNA to pattern their musical compositions. Another figure, David W. Deamer, a professor of chemistry and biochemistry at the University of California, Santa Cruz, has composed "DNA Music" by mapping different nucleotides to different musical notes with the overall feel of the composition registering the repetitions and variations in molecular structure.

36. Titus Lucretius Carus, *On the Nature of the Universe*, ed. John Godwin, trans. R. E. Latham (London: Penguin, 1994), 1:908–14.

37. The relationship between the two words varies in its nearly anagrammatic permutation in the Latin original and in the various English translations. In the Latin original, the two words that Lucretius uses are *ignes* (fire) and *lignum* (tree, wood, or woody tissue). The Latham prose translation (1994) makes a comparison between "forests" and "fires," while the Melville verse translation (1999) sets up perhaps the closest anagrammatic comparison by using "fires" and "firs." Cf. Lucretius, *On the Nature of the Universe*, trans. Latham, and Lucretius, *On the Nature of the Universe*, trans. Ronald Melville (Oxford: Oxford University Press, 1999).

38. Lucretius, *On the Nature of the Universe*, 2:1022–23.

39. Lucretius, 2:445.

40. Lucretius, 2:404–5.

41. Monya Baker, "Genomics: Genomes in Three Dimensions," *Nature* 470 (February 2011): 292.

42. Bök, *The Xenotext*, 82.

43. Accompanying this shift, Bök turns to a variety of descriptions that attempt to figure the three-dimensional nature of the protein molecules, as well as the electrochemical attractions and repulsions that both constitute this three-dimensionality and govern the possibilities for interaction between different molecules. In this context, in "The March of the Nucleotides," he describes a protein segment as "a motile ribbon, which coils and bends, like a metal chain of links, all made from magnets," describing its discrete parts as a "spine" or a "backbone" "made from alternating units of amine ($-NH_2$) and carboxylic acid (-COOH)" and the "chains that branch off from the spine" as "metal charms dangling from a bracelet" (104).

44. One of the more concrete, diagram-based poems in "The March of the Nucleotides" is in fact titled "The Ribosomal Translation of RNA," and it depicts how a sequence of nucleotides is "translated" into a sequence of amino acids. Bök's use of the

terminology of translation here evokes both the actual term that biologists use to describe the process through which information moves from DNA to protein and also its poetic parallel, the process of textual translation on which so much of *The Xenotext Book I* relies. The terminology of translation is helpful here, both in terms of Bök's actual translation of the *Georgics* and in the manner in which various constraint-based procedures he employs often draw on working with source texts and biological materials in an iterative fashion, through which one form is transformed into another.

45. Eduardo Kohn, *How Forests Think: Toward an Anthropology Beyond the Human.* (Berkeley: University of California Press, 2013), 6.
46. Jesper Hoffmeyer, *Signs of Meaning in the Universe*, trans. Barbara J. Haveland (Bloomington: Indiana University Press, 1996), 74.

4. FIBERS

1. Robert Hooke, *Micrographia: or Some Physiological Descriptions of Minute Bodies Made by Magnifying Glasses* (London: Royal Society, 1665), 5, 2, 6, 7.
2. Fiorenzo G. Omenetto and David L. Kaplan, "New Opportunities for an Ancient Material," *Science* 329, no. 5991 (July 2010): 530.
3. Jen Bervin, *Silk Poems* (New York: Nightboat, 2017), 166. It is interesting to note that Bervin's "first weaving teacher created woven designs for heart valves" (167).
4. Bervin, 171.
5. John Feltwell, *The Story of Silk* (New York: St. Martins, 1991), 51.
6. Hooke, *Micrographia*, 8.
7. Hooke, n.p.
8. Charles Olson, *Collected Prose*, ed. Donald Allen and Benjamin Friedlander (Berkeley: University of California Press, 1997), 240.
9. Bervin, *Silk Poems*, 166–69.
10. Jakob von Uexküll, "An Introduction to Umwelt," *Semiotica* 134, no. 4 (2001): 108.
11. Uexküll, "An Introduction to Umwelt," 108.
12. Uexküll, "An Introduction to Umwelt," 108.
13. Bervin, *Silk Poems*, 71.
14. Feltwell, *The Story of Silk*, 72.
15. Bervin, *Silk Poems*, 33.
16. Bervin, 107.
17. Bervin, 118.
18. Jane Bennett, *Vibrant Matter: A Political Ecology of Things* (Durham, N.C.: Duke University Press, 2010), 99.
19. Bervin, *Silk Poems*, 74.
20. Feltwell, *The Story of Silk*, 42.
21. For a more detailed history of materials that were used as surfaces of inscription in China, among them silk, see Tsuen-hsuin Tsien, *Written on Bamboo and Silk: The*

Beginnings of Chinese Books and Inscriptions (Chicago: University of Chicago Press, 1962).

22. Jacques Derrida, *The Animal That Therefore I Am*, ed. Marie-Luise Mallet (New York: Fordham University Press, 2008), 50.

23. In her famous autobiography of Elizabeth Barrett Browning's dog, *Flush*, Virginia Woolf writes about how Flush is far less drawn to the aesthetic dimension of the visual elements of the landscape that surround him than are the human characters in the novel. In response to this observation, Woolf imaginatively constructs a device that could perform intersensory translation, converting the visual sensations into olfactory ones that Flush is far more sensitive to and which consequently hold a greater interest for him: "Beauty, so it seems at least, had to be crystallized into a green or violet powder and puffed by some celestial syringe down the fringed channels that lay behind his nostrils before it touched Flush's senses; and then it issued not in words, but in silent rapture. Where Mrs. Browning saw, he smelt; where she wrote, he snuffed." Virginia Woolf, *Flush: A Biography* (New York: Harcourt, 1983), 129. At moments, in the elements of her prose, Woolf attempts to formally generate such a device, shifting the focalizing point of sensation from the visual dimension to that of the sense of smell: "Then what a variety of smells interwoven in subtlest combination thrilled his nostrils; strong smells of earth, sweet smells of flowers; nameless smells of leaf and bramble; sour smells as they crossed the road; pungent smells as they entered bean-fields. But suddenly down the wind came tearing a smell sharper, stronger, more lacerating than any—a smell that ripped across his brain stirring a thousand instincts, releasing a million memories—the smell of hare, the smell of fox" (12). To convey the complexity of olfactory sensations that Flush is capable of taking in, Woolf uses the short, staccato form of a list, creating a sense of an encounter with an entangled mass of scents. This way of encountering the environment primarily through the sense of smell generates a completely different feeling of the duration and delineation of entities than that conveyed by vision. It becomes difficult to resolve whether the scents are present all at once, at moments interwoven with one another and at times falling out of that interweaving to be identified as discrete residues of the entities that gave rise to them. Moreover, as they may linger even after the passage of any particular being or substance through the landscape, they act within a different register of duration than that offered by vision, which relies on a more binary sense of presence or absence. Woolf's imaginative device for interspecies translation, the one involving a "celestial syringe" through which the entities of the world may be powdered to enter "the fringed channels" behind the nostrils, conveys in some sense this problematic of how different entities coalesce as their scents combine and are taken in all at once even as they also become differentiated as the olfactory powers of discernment generate their own sequential temporality by which the scents come to be identified.

24. Hugh Raffles, "Beetle Wrestler (Natalie Jeremijenko and Chris Woebken)," Design and Violence, Museum of Modern Art, New York, November 12, 2014, https://www.moma.org/interactives/exhibitions/2013/designandviolence/beetle-wrestler-natalie-jeremijenko-chris-woebken/

25. Rodger Kram, "Inexpensive Load Carrying by Rhinoceros Beetles," *Journal of Experimental Biology* 199 (1996): 609, 611.
26. Raffles, "Beetle Wrestler," n.p.
27. Olson, *Collected Prose*, 181.
28. Eve Kosofsky Sedgwick, *Touching Feeling: Affect, Pedagogy, Performativity* (Durham, N.C.: Duke University Press, 2003), 15.
29. Hooke, *Micrographia*, 1.
30. Sedgwick, *Touching Feeling*, 16.
31. The term *edge textures* is also a semantic play on the term *edge tempos,* which appeared in the title of an American Comparative Literature Association panel organized by Anne-Lise François and Chris Malcolm in March 2018 in Los Angeles, where I presented an early draft of this chapter.
32. Nina Katchadourian, "Uninvited Collaborations with Nature," accessed July 13, 2018, http://www.ninakatchadourian.com/uninvitedcollaborations/spiderwebs.php.
33. Eva Hayward, "Fingeryeyes: Impressions of Cup Corals," *Cultural Anthropology* 25, no. 4 (2010): 585.
34. Uexküll, *A Foray Into the Worlds of Animals and Humans*, 60.
35. Ernst Heinrich Weber, *On the Tactile Senses*, ed. and trans. Helen E. Ross and David J. Murray (Hove, UK: Erlbaum Taylor and Francis, 1996), 25.
36. Uexküll, *A Foray Into the Worlds of Animals and Humans*, 60–61.
37. Uexküll, 62.
38. Gottfried Wilhelm Leibniz, *Leibniz's Monadology: A New Translation and Guide*, trans. Lloyd Strickland (Edinburgh: Edinburgh University Press, 2014), 75.
39. Gilles Deleuze, *The Fold: Leibniz and the Baroque*, trans. Tom Conley (London: Continuum, 2006), 99.
40. Deleuze, 99.
41. Deleuze, 101.
42. Leibniz, *Leibniz's Monadology*, 134.
43. Lloyd Strickland, "The *Monadology*: Text with Running Commentary," in *Leibniz's Monadology: A New Translation and Guide* (Edinburgh: Edinburgh University Press, 2014), 74.
44. Leibniz had the insight that more senses may exist in addition to "sight, hearing, smell, taste, and touch" possessed by humans. Strickland (79) explains in the commentary to the *Monadology* that now we are aware "that birds can perceive ultraviolet light, that bats navigate via echolocation, and that catfish and sharks have an 'electrical sense' often referred to as electroreception," and while Leibniz did not know any of this, he allowed for the possibility that there may be more senses than the five delimited to human beings. Leibniz was similarly aware that our sensory limitations may mean that some or perhaps even "most of the features of objects may be concealed from us."
45. Anni Albers, *On Weaving* (London: Studio Vista, 1965), 53.
46. Albers, 53.
47. Jen Bervin, *Nets* (Brooklyn: Ugly Duckling Presse, 2017).

48. Bervin, lines 6, 10, 12, 13, 14.
49. Bervin, lines 1, 2, 5, 6.
50. Such modes of proliferation of meaning through erasure and rearrangement are exploited by a number of poetic genealogies in the twentieth century, ranging from cut-up, invented by the Dadaist Tristan Tzara and later developed by William S. Burroughs and Brion Gysin, to Oulipo.
51. Bervin, *Silk Poems*, 16. My attention was initially drawn to the multiplicity of meanings that are present in these lines of the poem during a talk by Kathryn Crim that she gave as part of a seminar on "Edge Tempos and Anti-Monuments" at the ACLA, 2018.
52. Bervin, 16.
53. Craig Saper, "Introduction: For Words," in *Words*, ed. Craig Saper (New York: Roving Eye, 2014), vii, xi.
54. Bob Brown, *Readies* (Bad Ems: Roving Eye, 1930), 27.
55. Hooke, *Micrographia*, 3 (italics in original).

5. TISSUES

1. Gertrude Stein, *The Making of Americans* (Normal, Ill.: Dalkey Archive Press, 1995), 489–90.
2. William Wordsworth, "The Tables Turned," in *Lyrical Ballads 1798 and 1802*, by Samuel Taylor Coleridge and William Wordsworth, ed. Fiona Stafford (Oxford: Oxford University Press, 2013), 118.
3. I discovered this photograph in Gerald Weissmann's essay "The Mechanistic Conception of Life: Loeb the Teacher, Stein the Student at the MBL," in *The Biological Century: Friday Evening Talks at the Marine Biological Laboratory*, ed. Robert Barlow (Woods Hole, Mass: Laboratory, 1993), 5–20.
4. On the impact of Stein's training in psychology, see, among others, Steven Meyer, "Writing Psychology Over: Gertrude Stein and William James," *Yale Journal of Criticism* 8, no. 1 (Spring 1995): 133–63; Stephanie L. Hawkins, "The Science of Superstition: Gertrude Stein, William James, and the Formation of Belief," *Modern Fiction Studies* 51, no. 1 (2005): 60–87; Liesl M. Olson, "Gertrude Stein, William James, and Habit in the Shadow of War," *Twentieth-Century Literature* 49, no. 3 (Fall 2003): 328–59.
5. Steven Meyer, *Irresistible Dictation: Gertrude Stein and the Correlations of Writing and Science* (Stanford, Calif.: Stanford University Press, 2001), 4.
6. This departure from biology in "Gertrude Stein's Brainwork" is predicated specifically on Stein's detachment of typological "differences from the body and the brain," through which, Farland suggests, Stein ultimately comes to distance herself from her early research into brain anatomy and morphology, which she conducted at Johns Hopkins: "Stein's break with the conventional fictional frame . . . takes shape around her break with the biologism of the variability hypothesis. That break with biology, I

have argued here, is crucial to Stein's breakthrough into modernism.... In this way, she can write a narrative whose elaboration of types is deeply indebted to contemporary conceptions of sexual difference but whose representational strategies move to detach those differences from the body and the brain." As such, Farland's narration of Stein's early biography as a trading in of laboratory "brain work," involving her study of actual brain anatomy at Johns Hopkins, for the "brain work" of a literary vocation, acts as a subtext for the overall reading of *The Making of Americans* as an escape from anatomy. Maria Farland, "Gertrude Stein's Brain Work," *American Literature* 76, no. 1 (2004): 141.

7. Gerald Weissmann, "The Mechanistic Conception of Life: Loeb the Teacher, Stein the Student at the MBL," in *The Biological Century: Friday Evening Talks at the Marine Biological Laboratory*, ed. Robert Barlow (Woods Hole, Mass: Laboratory, 1993), 8.

8. Paul L. Farber, "The Transformation of Natural History in the Nineteenth Century," *Journal of the History of Biology* 15, no. 1 (1982): 148–49.

9. Farber, 151.

10. Other thinkers, such as Jean-Baptiste Lamarck, preceded Darwin's articulation of evolutionary theory. What often gets lost from cursory historical accounts of the period is that the "transmutation of species" was a hotly debated topic in the first half of the nineteenth century and that what distinguished Darwin's thought was not that he understood that organisms underwent evolutionary change, but that he theorized mechanisms through which such change could occur. Darwin's understanding of natural selection as the underlying mechanism of evolutionary change differed from other approaches to understanding transmutation of species primarily because it removed the center of agency that would guide or generate such change both from the hands of "the creator" and from the agency and actions of individual organisms. For Darwin, the process of evolutionary change was much more impersonal, occurring at the level of the population, through an interaction between the variability in a particular population and the conditions of the environment. Significantly, this also made Darwin's understanding of evolution nonteleological, because the conditions of the environment could always change, leading to a shift in what made a particular organism "well adapted" to a particular environment.

11. Stein, *The Making of Americans*, 344.

12. Michel Foucault, *The Order of Things: An Archaeology of the Human Sciences* (New York: Routledge, 2002), xvi.

13. This phrase appears in an early thirty-five-page version of *The Making of Americans*, composed by Stein in 1903, in which she explores the influence that the emergence of the science of heredity in the second half of the nineteenth century has on the conceptualization of the relationship between particular instances or types of character and generalizations that could reveal something about the relations between these individual types. I will explore how this problematic of heredity inflects Stein's project in *The Making of Americans* in the second half of this chapter and evoke her terminology from this early manuscript here as a way of latching this

conversation about heredity to the more fundamental questions about taxonomy she is exploring.
14. Foucault, *The Order of Things*, xix.
15. William Coleman, *Biology in the Nineteenth Century: Problems of Form, Function, and Transformation* (Cambridge: Cambridge University Press, 1977), 2.
16. Lorraine Daston and Peter Galison, *Objectivity* (Brooklyn: Zone, 2007), 18, 58.
17. "Epistemic virtue" is a term that Daston and Galison develop in *Objectivity* as a way of signaling how a set of practices through which knowledge is derived is guided by an implicit code of virtues that translates the overall epistemic framework of that historical period into a set of daily, regimented methods and ethical imperatives performed by a particular seeker of knowledge.
18. Daston and Galison, *Objectivity*, 67. "A Linnaean botanical description singled out those features common to the entire species (the *descriptio*), as well as those that differentiated this species from all others in the genus (the *differentia*) but at all costs avoided features peculiar to this or that individual member of the species. The Linnaean illustration aspired to generality—a generality that transcended the species or even the genus to reflect a never seen but nonetheless real plant archetype: the reasoned image" (60).
19. Daston and Galison, 59.
20. Daston and Galison, 109.
21. Darwin's understanding of evolutionary change was just one conceptual site in this historical period that was beginning to open up a space for thinking about change and variability of the natural world. Such stirrings arose also in geology in the work of Charles Lyell, who develops the theory of uniformitarianism, as a way of explaining how the Earth was shaped very gradually by the same geological forces that are still ongoing in the present, thus situating unfolding phenomena within a vast duration of geological time. It is significant to note here that while Lyell theorized that geological phenomena underwent gradual change, he rejected the idea of transmutation of species in the realm of organic beings. The sense that gradual change over time can bring into existence a proliferating variety of forms was also a preoccupying concern for many of the natural historians of the period. In 1844 Robert Chambers, for instance, published *Vestiges of the Natural History of Creation*, in which he already extends the emerging understandings of geological change to the realm of organic beings, indicating that they are under control of the same natural laws as other cosmic processes and that it is "ridiculous to . . . entertain [that] . . . the august Being who brought all these countless worlds into form by the simple establishment of a natural principle flowing from his mind, was to interfere personally and specially on every occasion when a new shell-fish or reptile was to be ushered into existence." Robert Chambers, *Vestiges of the Natural History of Creation and Other Evolutionary Writings* (Chicago: University of Chicago Press, 1994), 154. There is an emerging sense, then, midway through the nineteenth century that the variability evident in the natural world is continuously multiplying as a consequence of unfolding

processes that have set the inorganic and likewise the organic aspects of the cosmos into ongoing motion.

22. Parts of Darwin's specimen collection are now housed at various natural history museums. Among them, Oxford University Museum of Natural History has Darwin's collections of crustaceans collected during the voyage of the HMS *Beagle*, while the Museum of Zoology at University of Cambridge has more extensive specimen collections, including his fish specimens, and some of the famous finches collected on the Galapagos Islands.

23. Charles Darwin, *Journal of Researches Into the Natural History and Geology of the Countries Visited During the Voyage of H.M.S. Beagle Round the World Under the Command of Capt. Fitz Roy, R.N.* (London: John Murray, 1860), 383.

24. Omri Moses, "Gertrude Stein's Lively Habits," *Twentieth-Century Literature* 55, no. 4 (2009): 446, 452.

25. Gertrude Stein, *Wars I Have Seen* (New York: Random House, 1945), 17.

26. Foucault, *The Order of Things*, xx.

27. Lyn Hejinian, *The Language of Inquiry* (Berkeley: University of California Press, 2000), 148, 84, 85.

28. Meyer, *Irresistible Dictation*, 5, 3–4.

29. Weissmann, "The Mechanistic Conception of Life," 8–9.

30. Ulla E. Dydo, ed., *A Stein Reader* (Evanston, Ill: Northwestern University Press, 1993), 504.

31. Gertrude Stein, "An Acquaintance with Description," in *A Stein Reader*, ed. Ulla E. Dydo (Evanston, Ill.: Northwestern University Press, 1993), 505.

32. For more on autopoietic systems, see Humberto R. Maturana and Francisco J. Varela, *The Tree of Knowledge: Biological Roots of Human Understanding* (Boston: Shambhala, 1987).

33. Gertrude Stein, *Look at Me Now and Here I Am: Writings and Lectures 1909–45*, ed. Patricia Meyerowitz (New York: Penguin, 1971), 85–86.

34. Weissmann, "The Mechanistic Conception of Life," 6.

35. Jane Maienschein, *Transforming Traditions in American Biology, 1880–1915* (Baltimore: Johns Hopkins University Press, 1991), 46, 48.

36. Maienschein, 22–23.

37. In fact, historians of biology such as Maienschein have argued that the epistemic shift away from the descriptive and classificatory practices of natural history and toward the more experimentally inflected episteme characterizing biology at the beginning of the twentieth century possesses rather soft edges, resembling in practice a set of overlapping epistemic concerns, rather than a sharp demarcation. It may be helpful to turn here to a rather beautiful metaphor employed by Daston and Galison, who use the image of the night sky to illustrate the soft edges of epistemic transition—in this case the transition between the eighteenth-century "truth-to-nature" episteme and the emergence of "objectivity" in the mid-nineteenth century: "The emergence of objectivity as a new epistemic virtue in the mid-nineteenth century did not abolish truth-to-nature, any more than the turn to trained judgment in the early

twentieth century eliminated objectivity. Instead of the analogy of succession of political regimes or scientific theories, each triumphing on the ruins of its predecessor, imagine new stars winking into existence, not replacing old ones but changing the geography of the heavens." Daston and Galison, *Objectivity*, 18.

38. Maienschein, *Transforming Traditions in American Biology*, 291.

39. A well-known example of the linkage of evolutionary and developmental processes of change was already at play in the middle of the nineteenth century, when Ernst Haeckel synthesized Darwin's ideas about evolution with Romantic recapitulation theory in his book *Generelle Morphologie der Organismen* (1866). Haeckel developed his famous "biogenetic law," which stated that during development an organism passes through different stages of its evolutionary history; in other words, that ontogeny recapitulates phylogeny. While this influx of evolutionary thought into the morphological tradition was already evident by the middle of the nineteenth century, Maienschein suggests that the tradition underwent further transformations in the 1880s as a result of opening out to an exploration of the "details of early stages of embryogenesis." Maienschein, *Transforming Traditions in American Biology*, 291.

40. The only examples of Stein's scientific work that did see the light of publication were two articles she coauthored with Leon Solomons for the 1896 and 1898 issues of the *Psychological Review*, which were based on the experiments that they jointly conducted on automatic writing while studying with William James. While Stein is listed as a coauthor for both of these publications, she in fact only assisted Solomons with his experiments in the 1896 article titled "Normal Motor Automatism." In *Irresistible Dictation*, 225, Meyer explains that "the first publication that Stein composed herself . . . was 'Cultivated Motor Automatism; A Study of Character in Its Relation to Attention,' published in May 1898."

41. Lewellys F. Barker, *The Nervous System and Its Constituent Neurones* (New York: Appleton, 1901), 725–26.

42. Stein, *The Making of Americans*, 351.

43. Stein, *The Making of Americans*, 345.

44. Benedict de Spinoza, *Ethics*, ed. and trans. Edwin Curley (London: Penguin, 1996), 44 (second bracket in original translation).

45. In naming these descriptive passages "histological landscapes," I am referencing the significance of the term "landscape" in Stein's subsequent literary work, and in particular her theorization of the relationship between plays and landscapes.

46. See, for instance, Ulla Haselstein, "Gertrude Stein's Portraits of Matisse and Picasso," *New Literary History* 34, no. 4 (2004): 723–43.

47. Gertrude Stein, "The Making of Americans: First version, Manuscript notebook," Beinecke Rare Book and Manuscript Library, YCAL MSS 76, unpublished manuscript, 1903, handwriting, digitized version pages 21–22. Prior to consulting the primary manuscript materials, this passage first came to my attention in a citation in Meyer's *Irresistible Dictation*.

48. Stein, "The Making of Americans: First Version," 22.

49. Stein, *The Making of Americans*, 299.

50. Stein, *Look at Me Now and Here I Am*, 128.
51. Stein, *Look at Me Now and Here I Am*, 89.
52. Stein, *Look at Me Now and Here I Am*, 96.
53. Stein, *Look at Me Now and Here I Am*, 91.
54. Daston and Galison, *Objectivity*, 11.

6. CLOUDS

1. Elizabeth Diller, Diana Murphy, and Ricardo Scofidio, *Blur: The Making of Nothing* (New York: Abrams, 2002), 44.
2. Diller, Murphy, and Scofidio, 44.
3. Diller, Murphy, and Scofidio, 44.
4. See Elizabeth Diller and Ricardo Scofidio, *Blur Building, Yverdon-les-Bains, Switzerland*, 1998–2003, Film, MoMA Number: 556.2006.a–d.
5. The project consisted of several iterations, one of which was a performance that took place as part of the Positions Colloquium organized by the Kootenay School of Writing in Vancouver, B.C., in August 2008. The citations from the project that appear in this chapter come from the published version of the project in *C Magazine*. Lisa Roberston and Stacy Doris, "The Perfume Recordist," *C Magazine* 127 (Autumn 2015): 28–35.
6. Robertson and Doris, 34.
7. Laurel Peacock, "Lisa Robertson's Feminist Poetic Landscapes," *Open Letter* 14, no. 5 (2011): 89.
8. Lisa Robertson, *The Weather* (Vancouver: New Star Books, 2001), n.p.
9. Lisa Robertson, "This Animal, the Pronoun: An Interview," interview by Ted Byrne, *Capilano Review* 3, no. 15 (2011): 16.
10. Lisa Robertson, "The Weather: A Report on Sincerity," *Chicago Review* 51, no. 4/52, no. 1 (Spring 2006): 32.
11. Luke Howard, *Essay on the Modifications of Clouds* (London: John Churchill, 1865), 1.
12. Robertson, *The Weather*, 22.
13. Robertson opens *The Weather* with an epigraph from Walter Benjamin's *The Arcades Project*, which links, through analogy, the microcosm of feeling within the individual with the macrocosm of affect circulating within the collective: "Architecture, fashion—yes, even the weather—are, in the interior of the collective, what the sensoria of organs, the feeling of sickness or health, are in the individual" (n.p.). Hence the weather becomes an index of feeling within the amorphous bounds of the social body of the collective.
14. Alexander Cozens, *A New Method of Assisting the Invention in Drawing Original Compositions of Landscape* (London: J. Dixwell, 1785), n.p.
15. Lisa Robertson, "Lifted: An Interview with Lisa Robertson." interview by Kai Fierle-Hedrick, *Chicago Review* 51, no. 4/52, no. 1 (Spring 2006): 41.
16. In the introduction to the special issue of *Open Letter* on Robertson's work, the guest editors Angela Carr and Heather Milne comment on this alignment between reading

and writing practices in Robertson's work: "In a gesture that aligns the act of reading with that of writing, Robertson gleans (and in the process, modifies) lines of text to create a densely textured poetry of assemblage, rich in transhistorical and translingual lexicons." Angela Carr and Heather Milne, "Introduction," *Open Letter* 14, no .5 (Spring 2011): 7. Developing a more specific argument about Robertson's use of various textual materials in *Field Works: From Place to Site in Postwar Poetics*, Lytle Shaw situates her writing in relation to a shift from a place-based poetics, characteristic of Williams Carlos Williams's *Paterson* and Charles Olson's *The Maximus Poems*, to the configuration of discourse itself as a site. This shift is evident in *The Weather*, where discursive sites for Robertson's research-based poetics draw on the multiplicity of disciplinary discourses, from natural history and meteorology to art history and painting.

17. For a more detailed discussion of the links between Constable and Howard, see Richard Hamblyn, *The Invention of Clouds: How an Amateur Meteorologist Forged the Language of the Skies* (New York: Farrar, Straus and Giroux, 2001). For additional illustrations and descriptions of Constable's cloud studies, see John Gage, *Constable's Clouds: Paintings and Cloud Studies by John Constable*, ed. Edward Morris, (Edinburgh: National Galleries of Scotland, 2000).
18. Hamblyn, *The Invention of Clouds*, 228.
19. See, for instance, Constable's "Study of Cumulus Clouds," painted on August 1, 1822, or "Study of Cirrus Clouds," from the same year.
20. Gage, *Constable's Clouds*, 127.
21. Hamblyn, *The Invention of Clouds*, 225.
22. Hamblyn, 225.
23. Gage, *Constable's Clouds*, 129.
24. Gage, 130.
25. Hubert Damisch, *A Theory of /Cloud/: Toward a History of Painting*, trans. Janet Lloyd (Stanford, Calif.: Stanford University Press, 2002), 124, 11, 10.
26. Damisch, 185.
27. Robertson, *The Weather*, 2.
28. Howard, *Essay on the Modifications of Clouds*, 2.
29. Howard, 25.
30. Howard, 26–27.
31. Robertson, *The Weather*, 2.
32. Lisa Robertson, *Nilling* (Toronto: Bookthug, 2012), 11–12.
33. Robertson, *Nilling*, 15.
34. Titus Lucretius Carus, *On the Nature of the Universe*, ed. John Godwin, trans. R. E. Latham (London: Penguin, 1994), 2:252–57.
35. Lucretius, 2:221–25.
36. Robertson and Doris, "The Perfume Recordist," 32.
37. Lucretius, *On the Nature of the Universe*, 4:675–79.
38. Lucretius, 4:679–84.
39. Elizabeth Grosz, *Becoming Undone: Darwinian Reflections on Life, Politics, and Art* (Durham, N.C.: Duke University Press, 2011), 5, 1.

40. Lisa Robertson, *Magenta Soul Whip* (Toronto: Coach House, 2009), 7.
41. Lisa Robertson, *Thinking Space* (Brooklyn: Organism for Poetic Research, 2013), 17.
42. Robertson, *Thinking Space*, 35–36.
43. Robertson, *Nilling*, 44.
44. Aristotle, *On Poetics*, trans. Seth Benardete and Michael Davis (South Bend: St. Augustine's, 2002), 1457b8–11.
45. Gerard Manley Hopkins, *A Hopkins Reader*, ed. John Pick (London: Oxford University Press, 1953), 46.
46. Dorothy Wordsworth, *Journals*, vol. 1, ed. William Knight (London: Macmillan, 1897), 4, 5.
47. Robertson, "The Weather: A Report on Sincerity," 34.
48. Lisa Robertson, *Occasional Work and Seven Walks from the Office for Soft Architecture* (Astoria, Ore.: Clear Cut, 2003), 17.
49. "Lisa Robertson," interview by Lytle Shaw, *Printed Project: The Conceptual North Pole* 14 (2010): 107.
50. Robertson, "Lifted," 49–50.
51. Lisa Robertson, *XEclogue* (Vancouver: New Star Books, 2012), n.p.

CODA

1. Francis Bacon, *The Works of Francis Bacon*, vol. 5, ed. James Spedding, Robert Leslie Ellis, and Douglas Denon Heath (London: Spottiswoods, 1889), 339, 342, 343, 345–46.
2. Titus Lucretius Carus, *On the Nature of the Universe*, ed. John Godwin, trans. R. E. Latham (London: Penguin, 1994), 4:51–60, 729–31, 738–43, 727–28.
3. Gilles Deleuze, *The Logic of Sense*, trans. Mark Lester with Charles Stivale, ed. Constantin V. Boundas (New York: Columbia University Press, 1990), 5.
4. Deleuze, 9, 10, 21–22, 183.
5. Gertrude Stein, *Look at Me Now and Here I Am: Writings and Lectures 1909–45*, ed. Patricia Meyerowitz (New York: Penguin Books, 1971), 138.
6. Elizabeth Grosz, *The Incorporeal: Ontology, Ethics, and the Limits of Materialism* (New York: Columbia University Press, 2017), 5.
7. Lisa Robertson, "Lifted: An Interview with Lisa Robertson," interview by Kai Fierle-Hedrick, *Chicago Review* 51, no. 4/52, no. 1 (Spring 2006): 50.
8. Bacon, *The Works of Francis Bacon*, 359.
9. Laura Marks, *Touch: Sensuous Theory and Multisensory Media* (Minneapolis: University of Minnesota Press, 2002), ix, xv, x–xi.
10. Marks, xi.

WORKS CITED

Alaimo, Stacy. *Bodily Natures: Science, Environment, and the Material Self.* Bloomington: Indiana University Press, 2010.

———. "Thinking as the Stuff of the World." *O-Zone: A Journal of Object-Oriented Studies* 1 (2014): 13–21.

Albers, Anni. *On Weaving.* London: Studio Vista, 1965.

Alpers, Svetlana. *The Art of Describing: Dutch Art in the Seventeenth Century.* Chicago: University of Chicago Press, 1984.

Andrews, Bruce. *Paradise and Method: Poetics and Praxis.* Evanston, Ill.: Northwestern University Press, 1996.

———. "Text and Context." In *The Language Book (Poetics of the New)*, ed. Bruce Andrews and Charles Bernstein, 31–38. Carbondale: Southern Illinois University Press, 1984.

Anker, Suzanne, and Dorothy Nelkin. *The Molecular Gaze: Art in the Genetic Age.* New York: Cold Spring Harbor, 2004.

Appel, Toby A. *The Cuvier-Geoffroy Debate: French Biology in the Decades Before Darwin.* New York: Oxford University Press, 1987.

Aristotle. *Generation of Animals.* Trans. A. L. Peck. Cambridge, Mass.: Harvard University Press, 1943.

———. *On Poetics.* Trans. Seth Benardete and Michael Davis. South Bend: St. Augustine's, 2002.

Arsić, Branka. *Bird Relics: Grief and Vitalism in Thoreau.* Cambridge, Mass.: Harvard University Press, 2016.

Åsberg, Cecilia, Kathrin Thiele, and Iris van der Tuin. "Speculative *Before* the Turn: Reintroducing Feminist Materialist Performativity." *Cultural Studies Review* 21, no. 2 (2015): 145–72.

Bacon, Francis. *The New Organon.* Ed. Lisa Jardine and Michael Silverthorne. Cambridge: Cambridge University Press, 2000.

———. *The Works of Francis Bacon*. Vol. 5. Ed. James Spedding, Robert Leslie Ellis, and Douglas Denon Heath (London: Spottiswoods, 1889).

Baker, Monya. "Genomics: Genomes in Three Dimensions." *Nature* 470 (February 2011): 289–94.

Barad, Karen. *Meeting the Universe Halfway: Quantum Physics and the Entanglement of Matter and Meaning*. Durham, N.C.: Duke University Press, 2007.

———. "On Touching: The Inhuman That Therefore I Am." *differences* 25, no. 3 (2012): 206–23.

———. "Posthumanist Performativity: Toward an Understanding of How Matter Comes to Matter." *Signs* 28, no. 3 (Spring 2003): 801–31.

Barker, Lewellys F. *The Nervous System and Its Constituent Neurones*. New York: Appleton, 1899.

Bender, John B., and Michael Marrinan. *Regimes of Description: In the Archive of the Eighteenth Century*. Stanford, Calif.: Stanford University Press, 2005.

Bennett, Chad. "Scratching the Surface: *Tender Buttons* and the Textures of Modernism." *Arizona Quarterly* 73, no. 1 (Spring 2017): 21–49.

Bennett, Jane. *Vibrant Matter: A Political Ecology of Things*. Durham, N.C.: Duke University Press, 2010.

Berghaus, Günter. "Futurism, Dada, and Surrealism: Some Cross-Fertilizations Among the Historical Avant-Garde." In *International Futurism in Arts and Literature*, ed. Günter Berghaus. Berlin: Walter de Gruyter, 2000.

Bervin, Jen. "About." Jen Bervin website. Accessed February 18, 2019. http://jenbervin.com/about.

———. *Nets*. Brooklyn: Ugly Duckling Presse, 2017.

———. *Silk Poems*. New York: Nightboat, 2017.

———. "Studies in Scale." Introduction to *The Gorgeous Nothings*, by Emily Dickinson. Ed. Jen Bervin and Marta Werner. New York: New Directions, 2013.

Bervin, Jen, and Charlotte Lagarde. "Su Hui's Reversible Poem (in progress)." Jen Bervin website. Accessed July 13, 2018. http://jenbervin.com/projects/su-huis-reversible-poem.

Bhatia, Neeraj, and Lola Sheppard. "Going Soft." *Bracket* 2 (2011): 8–9.

Bianchi, Emanuela. *The Feminine Symptom: Aleatory Matter in the Aristotelian Cosmos*. New York: Fordham University Press, 2014.

Bleichmar, Daniela. *Visible Empire: Botanical Expeditions and Visual Culture in the Hispanic Enlightenment*. Chicago: University of Chicago Press, 2012.

Bök, Christian. "Beginners, Christian Bök and Alela Diane." *Strand*, May 31, 2011. BBC World Service. http://www.bbc.co.uk/programmes/p00gvpkk.

———. "Cryptic Poetry Written in a Microbe's DNA." *CultureLab*, May 4, 2011. https://www.newscientist.com/blogs/culturelab/2011/05/christian-boks-dynamic-dna-poetry.html.

———. *Crystallography*. Toronto: Coach House, 2003.

———. *Eunoia*. Toronto: Coach House, 2009.

———. *'Pataphysics: The Poetics of an Imaginary Science*. Evanston, Ill.: Northwestern University Press, 2002.

———. "Poetry in the Genes." Interview by Krista Zala. *Nature* 458, no. 7234 (March 5, 2009): 35–36.

———. "'Teaching Myself Molecular Biochemistry Is Just Part of the Process.'" Interview by Kaveh Akbar. *Divedapper*, October 13, 2014. https://www.divedapper.com/interview/christian-bok.

———. "Two Dots Over a Vowel." *Boundary 2: An International Journal of Literature and Culture* 36, no. 3 (2009): 11–24.

———. *The Xenotext: Book 1*. Toronto: Coach House, 2015.

———. "The Xenotext Experiment: An Interview with Christian Bök." Interview by Stephen Voyce. *Postmodern Culture* 17, no. 2 (January 2007).

Bora, Renu. "Outing Texture." In *Novel Gazing: Queer Readings in Fiction*, ed. Eve Kosofsky Sedgwick. Durham, N.C.: Duke University Press, 1997.

Bram, Shahar. *Charles Olson and Alfred North Whitehead*. Trans. Batya Stein. Lewisburg, Pa.: Bucknell University Press, 2004.

Bray, Joe, Alison Gibbons, and Brian McHale. "Introduction." In *Routledge Companion to Experimental Literature*, 1–18, ed. Joe Bray, Alison Gibbons, and Brian McHale. New York: Routledge, 2012.

Brown, Bill. "Thing Theory." *Critical Inquiry* 28, no. 1 (Autumn 2001): 1–22.

Brown, Bob. *Readies*. Ed. Craig Saper. Bad Ems: Roving Eye, 2014.

———. *Words*. Ed. Craig Saper. New York: Roving Eye, 2014.

Brown, Nathan. *The Limits of Fabrication: Materials Science, Materialist Poetics*. New York: Fordham University Press, 2017.

Bruner, Belinda. "A Recipe for Modernism and the Somatic Intellect in *The Alice B. Toklas Cook Book* and Gertrude Stein's *Tender Buttons*." *Papers on Language & Literature* 45, no. 4 (2009): 411–33.

Bryant, Levi, Nick Srnicek, and Graham Harman. *The Speculative Turn: Continental Materialism and Realism*. Melbourne: re.press, 2011.

Cage, John. "Cage's Loft, New York City October 21–23, 1991." Interview by Joan Retallack. In *Musicage: Cage Muses on Words Art Music*, 83–167, ed. Joan Retallack. Hanover, N.H.: Wesleyan University Press, 1996.

Cage, John, Lois Long, and Alexander H. Smith. *Mushroom Book*. New York: Hollander Workshop, 1972.

Carr, Angela and Heather Milne. "Introduction." *Open Letter* 14, no. 5 (Spring 2011).

Chambers, Robert. *Vestiges of the Natural History of Creation and Other Evolutionary Writings*. Chicago: University of Chicago Press, 1994.

Chen, Mel Y. *Animaciec: Biopolitics, Racial Mattering, and Queer Affect*. Durham, N.C.: Duke University Press, 2012.

Cheng, Anne Anlin. *Ornamentalism*. Oxford: Oxford University Press, 2019.

———. *Second Skin: Josephine Baker & the Modern Surface*. Oxford: Oxford University Press, 2010.

Chessman, Harriet Scott. *The Public Is Invited to Dance: Representation, the Body, and Dialogue in Gertrude Stein*. Stanford, Calif.: Stanford University Press, 1989.

Coleman, William. *Biology in the Nineteenth Century: Problems of Form, Function, and Transformation*. Cambridge: Cambridge University Press, 1977.

Conley, Tom. "Translator's Foreword: A Plea for Leibniz." *The Fold: Leibniz and the Baroque.* Trans. Tom Conley. London: Continuum, 2006.

Coole, Diana, and Samantha Frost. "Introducing the New Materialisms." In *New Materialisms: Ontology, Agency, and Politics*, ed. Diana Coole and Samantha Frost. Durham, N.C.: Duke University Press, 2010.

Cornell, Heather N., John M. Marzluff, and Shannon Pecoraro. "Social Learning Spreads Knowledge About Dangerous Humans Among American Crows." *Proceedings of the Royal Society of London B: Biological Sciences* 279, no. 1728 (2012): 499–508. doi: 10.1098/rspb.2011.0957.

Cozens, Alexander. *A New Method of Assisting the Invention in Drawing Original Compositions of Landscape.* London: J. Dixwell, 1785.

Damisch, Hubert. *A Theory of /Cloud/: Toward a History of Painting.* Trans. Janet Lloyd. Stanford, Calif.: Stanford University Press, 2002.

Danielson, Dennis. *The Book of the Cosmos: Imagining the Universe from Heraclitus to Hawking.* Cambridge: Perseus, 2000.

Darwin, Charles. *Journal of Researches Into the Natural History and Geology of the Countries Visited During the Voyage of H.M.S. Beagle Round the World Under the Command of Capt. Fitz Roy, R.N.* London: John Murray, 1860.

Daston, Lorraine. "On Scientific Observation." *Isis* 99, no. 1 (March 2008): 97–110.

Daston, Lorraine, and Peter Galison. *Objectivity.* Brooklyn: Zone, 2007.

Davidson, Michael. "On Reading Stein." *L=A=N=G=U=A=G=E* 6 (1978): n.p.

De Gennes, P. G. "Soft Matter." *Science* 256 (April 24, 1992): 495–97.

DeLanda, Manuel. "Matter Matters." *DOMUS Magazine* (2005): 1–15.

Deleuze, Gilles. *Bergsonism.* Trans. Hugh Tomlinson and Barbara Habberjam. New York: Zone, 1991.

——. *Expressionism in Philosophy: Spinoza.* Trans. Martin Joughin. Brooklyn: Zone, 1992.

——. *The Fold: Leibniz and the Baroque.* Trans. Tom Conley. London: Continuum, 2006.

——. *The Logic of Sense.* Trans. Mark Lester with Charles Stivale, ed. Constantin V. Boundas. New York: Columbia University Press, 1990.

——. *Spinoza: Practical Philosophy.* Trans. Robert Hurley. San Francisco: City Lights, 1988.

Deleuze, Gilles, and Félix Guattari. *A Thousand Plateaus: Capitalism and Schizophrenia.* Trans. Brian Massumi. Minneapolis: University of Minnesota Press, 1987.

Derrida, Jacques. *The Animal That Therefore I Am.* Ed. Marie-Louise Mallet. Trans. David Wills. New York: Fordham University Press, 2008.

——. *Without Alibi.* Ed. and trans. Peggy Kamuf. Stanford, Calif.: Stanford University Press, 2002.

Descartes, René. *Discourse on Method.* Trans. Donald A. Cress. Indianapolis: Hackett, 1998.

——. *The World and Other Writings.* Ed. Stephen Gaukroger. Cambridge: Cambridge University Press, 2004.

Diller, Elizabeth, Diana Murphy, and Ricardo Scofidio. *Blur: The Making of Nothing.* New York: Abrams, 2002.

——. *Blur Building, Yverdon-les-Bains, Switzerland, 1998–2003.* Film, MoMA Number: 556.2006.a–d.

"Fabric." *Meriam-Webster Dictionary.* https://www.merriam-webster.com/dictionary/fabric Accessed: 19 February 2019.

Farber, Paul L. "The Transformation of Natural History in the Nineteenth Century." *Journal of the History of Biology* 15, no. 1 (1982): 145–52.

Farland, Maria. "Gertrude Stein's Brain Work." *American Literature* 76, no. 1 (2004): 117–48.

Feltwell, John. *The Story of Silk.* New York: St. Martin's, 1991.

Fifer, Elizabeth. "Is Flesh Advisable? The Interior Theater of Gertrude Stein." *Signs: Journal of Women in Culture and Society* 4, no. 3 (1979): 472–83.

Flaherty, Joe. "A Mind-Blowing Dome Made by 6, 500 Computer-Guided Silkworms." *Design*, November 7, 2013. http://www.wired.com/2013/07/your-next-3-d-printer-might-be-filled-with-worms/.

Forster, Thomas Ignatius. *Researches About Atmospheric Phaenomena.* London: Harding, Mavor, and Lepard, 1823.

Foucault, Michel. *The Order of Things: An Archaeology of the Human Sciences.* New York: Routledge, 2002.

François, Anne-Lise. "Flower Fisting." *Postmodern Culture* 22, no. 1 (September 2011).

Galison, Peter. *How Experiments End.* Chicago: University of Chicago Press, 1987.

Gage, John. *Constable's Clouds: Paintings and Cloud Studies by John Constable.* Ed. Edward Morris. Edinburgh: National Galleries of Scotland, 2000.

Goldstein, Amanda Jo. *Sweet Science: Romantic Materialism and the New Logics of Life.* Chicago: University of Chicago Press, 2017.

Gorzelak, Monika A., Amanda K. Asay, Brian J. Pickles, and Suzanne W. Simard. "Interplant Communication Through Mycorrhizal Networks Mediates Complex Adaptive Behaviour in Plant Communities." *AoB Plants* 7 (2015): 1–13. doi: 10.1093/aobpla/plv050.

Gregg, Melissa, and Gregory J. Seigworth, eds. *The Affect Theory Reader.* Durham, N.C.: Duke University Press, 2010.

Grenier, Robert. "Tender Buttons." *L=A=N=G=U=A=G=E* 6 (1978).

Grosz, Elizabeth. *Becoming Undone: Darwinian Reflections on Life, Politics, and Art.* Durham, N.C.: Duke University Press, 2011.

———. *The Incorporeal: Ontology, Ethics and the Limits of Materialism.* New York: Columbia University Press, 2017.

———. *The Nick of Time: Politics, Evolution, and the Untimely.* Durham, N.C.: Duke University Press, 2004.

Hamblyn, Richard. *The Invention of Clouds.* New York: Farrar, Straus and Giroux, 2001.

Haraway, Donna. J. "The Promises of Monsters: A Regenerative Politics for Inappropriate/d Others." In *Cultural Studies*, 295–337, ed. Lawrence Grossberg, Cary Nelson, and Paula Treichler. New York: Routledge, 1992.

———. *Simians, Cyborgs and Women: The Reinvention of Nature.* New York: Routledge, 1991.

———. "Situated Knowledges: The Science Question in Feminism and the Privilege of Partial Perspective." *Feminist Studies* 14, no. 3 (Autumn 1988): 575–99.

———. *When Species Meet.* Minneapolis: University of Minnesota Press, 2007.

Harman, Graham. "Agential and Speculative Realism: Remarks on Barad's Ontology." *Rhizomes* 30 (2016): n.p. doi.org/10.20415/rhiz/030.e10.

———. *Object-Oriented Ontology: A New Theory of Everything.* London: Penguin, 2018.
———. "On Vicarious Causation." *Collapse* 2 (2007): 171–205.
Haselstein, Ulla. "Gertrude Stein's Portraits of Matisse and Picasso." *New Literary History* 34, no. 4 (2003): 723–43.
Hawkins, Stephanie L. "The Science of Superstition: Gertrude Stein, William James, and the Formation of Belief." *Modern Fiction Studies* 51, no. 1 (2005): 60–87.
Hayles, Katherine N. *How We Became Posthuman: Virtual Bodies in Cybernetics, Literature, and Informatics.* Chicago: University of Chicago Press, 1999.
Hayward, Eva. "Fingeryeyes: Impressions of Cup Corals." *Cultural Anthropology* 25, no. 4 (2010): 577–99.
Heidegger, Martin. *Poetry, Language, Thought.* Trans. Albert Hofstadter. New York: HarperCollins, 2001.
Hejinian, Lyn. *The Language of Inquiry.* Berkeley: University of California Press, 2000.
Hilder, Jamie. "'After All One Must Know More than One Sees and One Does Not See a Cube in Its Entirety': Gertrude Stein and Picasso and Cubism." *Critical Survey* 17, no. 3 (2005): 66–84.
Hinton, David. "Su Hui's *Star Gauge*." *Welling Out of Silence* 1 (February 2012).
Hoffman, Frederic J. *Gertrude Stein.* Minneapolis: University of Minnesota Press, 1961.
Hoffmeyer, Jesper. *Signs of Meaning in the Universe.* Trans. Barbara J. Haveland. Bloomington: Indiana University Press, 1996.
Hooke, Robert. *Micrographia: or Some Physiological Descriptions of Minute Bodies Made by Magnifying Glasses. With observations and inquiries thereupon.* London: Royal Society, Printed by Jo. Martyn and Ja. Allestry, 1665.
Hopkins, Gerard Manley. *A Hopkins Reader.* Ed. John Pick. London: Oxford University Press, 1953.
Howard, Luke. *Essay on the Modifications of Clouds.* London: John Churchill, 1865.
Huebler, Douglas. "Statement." *January 5–31, 1969.* Curated by Seth Siegelaub. New York, 1969.
James, William. *The Principles of Psychology.* New York: Henry Holt, 1890.
Jardine, Lisa. Introduction. In *The New Organon*, by Francis Bacon. Ed. Lisa Jardine and Michael Silverthorne. Cambridge: Cambridge University Press, 2000.
Jarry, Alfred. *Exploits & Opinions of Dr. Faustroll, Pataphysician.* Trans. Simon Watson Taylor. Boston: Exact Change, 1996.
Katchadourian, Nina. "Uninvited Collaborations with Nature." Accessed July 13, 2018. http://www.ninakatchadourian.com/uninvitedcollaborations/spiderwebs.php.
Keesing, Felicia, Lisa K. Belden, Peter Daszak, Andrew Dobson, C. Drew Harvell, Robert D. Holt, Peter Hudson, Anna Jolles, Kate E. Jones, Charles E. Mitchell, Samuel S. Myers, Tiffany Bogich, and Richard S. Ostfeld. "Impacts of Biodiversity on the Emergence and Transmission of Infectious Diseases." *Nature* 468 (December 2, 2010): 647–52.
Keller, Evelyn Fox. *Refiguring Life: Metaphors of Twentieth-Century Biology.* New York: Columbia University Press, 1995.
Keller, Evelyn Fox, and Lee A. Segel. "Initiation of Slime Mold Aggregation Viewed as an Instability." *Journal of Theoretical Biology* 26, no. 3 (1970): 399–415. doi: 10.1016/0022-5193(70)90092-5.

Kim, Alexander B. "The Xenotext Experiment." *Triple Helix Online: A Global Forum for Science in Society*, January 8, 2014. http://triplehelixblog.com/2014/01/the-xenotext-experiment/comment-page-1/.

Kohn, Eduardo. *How Forests Think: Toward an Anthropology Beyond the Human*. Berkeley: University of California Press, 2013.

Kram, Rodger. "Inexpensive Load Carrying by Rhinoceros Beetles." *Journal of Experimental Biology* 199 (1996): 609–12.

Kristeva, Julia. *Desire in Language: A Semiotic Approach to Literature and Art*. Ed. Leon S. Roudiez. Trans. Thomas Gora, Alice Jardine, and Leon S. Roudiez. New York: Columbia University Press, 1980.

Lange, Linda. "Woman Is Not a Rational Animal: On Aristotle's Biology of Reproduction." In *Discovering Reality: Feminist Perspectives on Epistemology, Metaphysics, Methodology, and Philosophy of Science*, ed. Sandra Harding and Merrill B. Hintikka), 1–16. New York: Kluwer Academic, 1983.

Leibniz, Gottfried Wilhelm. *Leibniz's Monadology: A New Translation and Guide*. Trans. Lloyd Strickland. Edinburgh: Edinburgh University Press, 2014.

Levin, David Michael. *The Philosopher's Gaze: Modernity in the Shadows of Enlightenment*. Berkeley: University of California Press, 1999.

Lippard, Lucy R., and John Chandler. "The Dematerialization of Art." In *Changing Essays in Art Criticism*, by Lucy R. Lippard. New York: Dutton, 1971.

Loos, Adolf. *Ornament and Crime: Selected Essays*. Trans. Michael Mitchell. Riverside, Calif.: Ariadne, 1998.

Lu, Chensheng, Kenneth M. Warchol, and Richard A. Callahan. "Sub-lethal Exposure to Neonicotinoids Impaired Honey Bees Winterization Before Proceeding to Colony Collapse Disorder." *Bulletin of Insectology* 67, no. 1 (2014): 125–30.

Lucretius, Carus. *On the Nature of the Universe*. Ed. John Godwin. Trans. R. E. Latham. London: Penguin, 1994.

———. *On the Nature of the Universe*. Trans. Ronald Melville. Oxford: Oxford University Press, 1999.

Maienschein, Jane. *Transforming Traditions in American Biology, 1880–1915*. Baltimore: Johns Hopkins University Press, 1991.

Malle, Louis. *Black Moon*. 1975.

Manaugh, Geoff. "Soft Serve Space." *Bracket* 2 (2011): 10–16.

Marcus, Sharon, Heather Love, and Stephen Best. "Building a Better Description." *Representations* 135, no. 1 (Summer 2016): 1–21.

Marillonnet, Sylvestre, Victor Klimyuk, and Yuri Gleba. "Encoding Technical Information in GM Organisms." *Nature Biotechnology* 21 (2003): 224–26.

Marinetti, Filippo Tommaso. *Critical Writings*. New York: Farrar, Straus and Giroux, 2006.

Maturana, Humberto R., and Francisco J. Varela. *The Tree of Knowledge: Biological Roots of Human Understanding*. Boston: Shambhala, 1987.

McCaffery, Steve. *Prior to Meaning: The Protosemantic and Poetics*. Evanston, Ill.: Northwestern University Press, 2001.

Meyer, Steven. *Irresistible Dictation: Gertrude Stein and the Correlations of Writing and Science*. Stanford, Calif.: Stanford University Press, 2001.

———. "Writing Psychology Over: Gertrude Stein and William James." *Yale Journal of Criticism: Interpretation in the Humanities* 8, no. 1 (Spring 1995): 133–63.
Moses, Omri. "Gertrude Stein's Lively Habits." *Twentieth Century Literature* 55, no. 4 (2009): 445–84.
Müller-Wille, Staffan, and Hans-Jörg Rheinberger. *A Cultural History of Heredity*. Chicago: University of Chicago Press, 2012.
Ng, Terence P. T., Sara H. Saltin, Mark S. Davies, Kerstin Johannesson, Richard Stafford, and Gray A. Williams. "Snails and Their Trails: The Multiple Functions of Trail-Following in Gastropods." *Biological Reviews* 88, no. 3 (2013): 683–700. doi: 10.1111/brv.12023.
Ngai, Sianne. *Our Aesthetic Categories: Zany, Cute, Interesting*. Cambridge, Mass.: Harvard University Press, 2012.
Nichol, bp. *The Alphabet Game: A bpNichol Reader*. Ed. Lori Emerson and Darren Wershler-Henry. Toronto: Coach House, 2007.
Nicholls, Peter. "Hard and Soft Modernism: Politics as 'Theory.'" In *A Handbook of Modernism Studies*, ed. Jean-Michel Rabaté. West Sussex: Wiley-Blackwell, 2013.
Nichols, Miriam. *Radical Affections: Essays on the Poetics of the Outside*. Tuscaloosa: University of Alabama Press, 2010.
Nielsen, Karen M. "The Private Parts of Animals: Aristotle on the Teleology of Sexual Difference." *Phronesis* 53, no. 4–5 (2008): 373–405.
Nixon, Rob. *Slow Violence and the Environmentalism of the Poor*. Cambridge, Mass.: Harvard University Press, 2011.
Ogilvie, Brian W. *The Science of Describing: Natural History in Renaissance Europe*. Chicago: University of Chicago Press, 2006.
Olson, Charles. *Collected Prose*. Ed. Donald Allen and Benjamin Friedlander. Berkeley: University of California Press, 1997.
———. *The Maximus Poems*. Ed. George F. Butterick. Berkeley: University of California Press, 1985.
Olson, Liesl M. "Gertrude Stein, William James, and Habit in the Shadow of War." *Twentieth-Century Literature* 49, no. 3 (Fall 2003): 328–59.
Omenetto, Fiorenzo G., and David L. Kaplan. "New Opportunities for an Ancient Material." *Science* 329, no. 5991 (July 2010): 528–31.
Oxman, Neri. "Templating Design for Biology, and Biology for Design." *Architectural Design* 85, no. 5 (2015): 100–7.
Peacock, Laurel. "Lisa Robertson's Feminist Poetic Landscapes." *Open Letter* 14, no. 5 (2011): 85–95.
Perloff, Marjorie. "The Oulipo Factor: The Procedural Poetics of Christian Bök and Caroline Bergvall." *Textual Practice* 18, no. 1 (2004): 23–45.
———. "Poetry as Word-System: The Art of Gertrude Stein." *American Poetry Review* 8, no. 5 (1979): 33–43.
Piazza, Roberto. *Soft Matter: The Stuff That Dreams Are Made Of*. Dordrecht: Copernicus, 2010.
Plato. *Timeaeus and Critias*. Trans. Desmond Lee. London: Penguin, 2008.
Poggi, Christine. *Inventing Futurism: The Art and Politics of Artificial Optimism*. Princeton, N.J.: Princeton University Press, 2009.

Ponge, Francis. *Soap*. Trans. Lane Dunlop. Stanford, Calif.: Stanford University Press, 1998.
Pound, Ezra. *Literary Essays of Ezra Pound*. Ed. T. S. Eliot. New York: New Directions, 1968.
Quartermain, Peter. *Disjunctive Poetics: From Gertrude Stein and Louis Zukofsky to Susan Howe*. Cambridge: Cambridge University Press, 1992.
Raffles, Hugh. "Beetle Wrestler (Natalie Jeremijenko and Chris Woebken)." Design and Violence, Museum of Modern Art, New York. November 12, 2014. https://www.moma.org/interactives/exhibitions/2013/designandviolence/beetle-wrestler-natalie-jeremijenko-chris-woebken/.
Robertson, Lisa. "Lifted: An Interview with Lisa Robertson." Interview by Kai Fierle-Hedrick. *Chicago Review* 51, no. 4/52, no. 1 (Spring 2006): 38–54.
——. "Lisa Robertson." Interview by Lytle Shaw. *Printed Project: The Conceptual North Pole* 14 (2010): 96–107.
——. *Magenta Soul Whip*. Toronto: Coach House, 2009.
——. *Nilling*. Toronto: Bookthug, 2012.
——. *Occasional Work and Seven Walks from the Office for Soft Architecture*. Astoria, Ore.: Clear Cut, 2003.
——. *Thinking Space*. Brooklyn, N.Y.: Organism for Poetic Research, 2013.
——. "This Animal, the Pronoun: An Interview." Interview by Ted Byrne. *Capilano Review* 3, no. 15 (2011): 13–42.
——. *The Weather*. Vancouver: New Star, 2001.
——. "The Weather: A Report on Sincerity." *Chicago Review* 51, no. 4/52, no. 1 (Spring 2006): 28–37.
——. *XEclogue*. Vancouver, B.C.: New Star Books, 2012.
Robertson, Lisa, and Stacy Doris. "The Perfume Recordist." *C Magazine* 127 (Autumn 2015): 28–35.
Roof, Judith. *The Poetics of DNA*. Minneapolis: University of Minnesota Press, 2007.
Saper, Craig. "Introduction." In *Words*, ed. Craig Saper. New York: Roving Eye, 2014.
Scherr, Rebecca. "Tactile Erotics: Gertrude Stein and the Aesthetics of Touch." *Literature Interpretation Theory* 18, no. 3 (2007): 193–212.
Sedgwick, Eve Kosofsky. *Touching Feeling: Affect, Pedagogy, Performativity*. Durham, N.C.: Duke University Press, 2003.
Sedgwick, Eve Kosofsky, and Adam Frank. "Shame in the Cybernetic Fold: Reading Silvan Tomkins." In *Touching Feeling: Affect, Pedagogy, Performativity*, 93–122. Durham, N.C.: Duke University Press, 2003.
Shapin, Steven, and Simon Schaffer. *Leviathan and the Air-Pump: Hobbes, Boyle, and the Experimental Life*. Princeton, N.J.: Princeton University Press, 1985.
Sharp, Hasana. *Spinoza and the Politics of Renaturalization*. Chicago: University of Chicago Press, 2011.
Shaviro, Steven. *Without Criteria: Kant, Whitehead, Deleuze, and Aesthetics*. Cambridge, Mass.: MIT Press, 2009.
Shaw, Lytle. *Fieldworks: From Place to Site in Postwar Poetics*. Tuscaloosa: University of Alabama Press, 2013.
Shklovsky, Viktor. *Viktor Shklovsky: A Reader*. Ed. and trans. Aklexandra Berlina. New York: Bloomsbury, 2016.

"Silk Pavilion." Mediated Matter Group, Massachusetts Institute of Technology School of Architecture and Planning. Accessed February 18, 2019. https://mediatedmattergroup.com/.

Simondon, Gilbert. "The Position of the Problem of Ontogenesis." Trans. Gregory Flanders. *Parhesia* 7 (2009): 4–16.

Smailbegović, Ada. "Cloud Writing: Describing Soft Architectures of Change in the Anthropocene." In *Art in the Anthropocene: Encounters Among Aesthetics, Politics, Environments and Epistemologies*. Ed. Heather Davis and Etienne Turpin, 93–107. London: Open Humanities, 2015.

——. "Of the Dense and Rare." *Triple Canopy*. December 20, 2013. https://www.canopycanopycanopy.com/contents/of_the_dense_and_rare/#title-page Accessed: February 19, 2019.

Smithson, Robert. *The Collected Writings*. Ed. Jack Flam. Berkeley: University of California Press, 1996.

Solt, Mary Ellen. *Concrete Poetry: A World View*. Bloomington: Indiana University Press, 1970.

Speybroeck, Linda van, Dani de Waele, and Gertrudis Van de Vijver. "Theories in Early Embryology: Close Connections between Epigenesis, Preformationism, and Self-Organization." In *From Epigenesis to Epigenetics: The Genome in Context*, ed. Linda van Speybroeck, Gertrudis van de Vijver, and Dani de Waele, 7–49. New York: New York Academy of Sciences, 2002.

Spinoza, Benedict De. *Ethics*. Ed. and trans. Edwin Curley. London: Penguin, 1996.

Stein, Gertrude. "An Acquaintance with Description." In *A Stein Reader*, 504–34, ed. Ulla E. Dydo. Evanston, Ill.: Northwestern University Press, 1993.

——. *The Geographical History of America or the Relation of Human Nature to the Human Mind*. Baltimore: Johns Hopkins University Press, 1995.

——. *How to Write*. Mineola, N.Y.: Dover, 1975.

——. *Look at Me Now and Here I Am: Writings and Lectures 1909–45*. Ed. Patricia Meyerowitz. New York: Penguin, 1971.

——. *The Making of Americans*. Normal, Ill.: Dalkey Archive Press, 1995.

——. "The Making of Americans: First version, Manuscript notebook." Beinecke Rare Book and Manuscript Library. YCAL MSS 76. Unpublished manuscript, 1903, handwriting.

——. *A Stein Reader*. Ed. Ulla E. Dydo. Evanston, Ill.: Northwestern University Press, 1993.

——. *Tender Buttons*. San Francisco: City Lights, 2014.

——. "A Transatlantic Interview." Interview by Robert Bartlett Haas. In *A Primer for the Gradual Understanding of Gertrude Stein*. Santa Barbara, Calif.: Black Sparrow Press, 1976.

——. *Wars I Have Seen*. New York: Random House, 1945.

Stengers, Isabelle. *Thinking with Whitehead: A Free and Wild Creation of Concepts*. Trans. Michael Chase. Cambridge, Mass.: Harvard University Press, 2014.

Stewart, Susan. *Poetry and the Fate of the Senses*. Chicago: University of Chicago Press, 2002.

Stimpson, Catharine R. "The Somagrams of Gertrude Stein." *Poetics Today* 6, no. 1–2 (1985): 67–80.

Strickland, Lloyd. "The *Monadology*: Text with Running Commentary." In *Leibniz's Monadology: A New Translation and Guide*. Edinburgh: Edinburgh University Press, 2014.

Tiffany, Daniel. *Toy Medium: Materialism and Modern Lyric*. Berkeley: University of California Press, 2000.

Tomkins, Silvan S. *Shame and Its Sisters: A Silvan Tomkins Reader*. Ed. Eve Kosofsky Sedgwick and Adam Frank. Durham, N.C.: Duke University Press, 1995.

Tsing, Anna Lowenhaupt. *The Mushroom at the End of the World: On the Possibility of Life in Capitalist Ruins*. Princeton, N.J.: Princeton University Press, 2015.

Tsien, Tsuen-hsuin. *Written on Bamboo and Silk: The Beginnings of Chinese Books and Inscriptions*. Chicago: University of Chicago Press, 1962.

Uexküll, Jakob von. *A Foray Into the Worlds of Animals and Humans: With a Theory of Meaning*. Trans. Joseph D. O'Neil. Minneapolis: University of Minnesota Press, 2010.

———. "An Introduction to Umwelt." *Semiotica* 134, no. 4 (2001): 107–10.

Wah, Fred. *Faking It: Poetics and Hybridity, Critical Writing, 1984–1999*. Edmonton, Alberta: NeWest, 2000.

Weber, Ernst Heinrich. *On the Tactile Senses*. Ed. and trans. Helen E. Ross and David J. Murray. Hove: Erlbaum Taylor and Francis, 1996.

Weissmann, Gerald. "The Mechanistic Conception of Life: Loeb the Teacher, Stein the Student at the MBL." In *The Biological Century: Friday Evening Talks at the Marine Biological Laboratory*, ed. Robert Barlow, 5–20. Woods Hole, Mass.: Laboratory, 1993.

Wertheim, Maragaret, and Christine Wertheim. *Crochet Coral Reef*. Los Angeles: Institute for Figuring, 2015.

Williams, William Carlos. *Paterson*. New York: New Directions, 1995.

Wilson, Elizabeth A. *Gut Feminism*. Durham, N.C.: Duke University Press, 2015.

Witt, Charlotte. "Form, Normativity and Gender in Aristotle: A Feminist Perspective." In *Feminist Interpretations of Aristotle*, ed. Cynthia A. Freeland. University Park: Pennsylvania State University Press, 1998.

Wolfe, Cary. *What Is Posthumanism?* Minneapolis: University of Minnesota Press, 2009.

Wong, Pak Chung, Kwong-kwok Wong and Harlan Foote. "Organic Data Memory: Using the DNA Approach." *Communications of the ACM* 46, no. 1 (January 2003): 95–98.

Woolf, Virginia. *Flush: A Biography*. New York: Harcourt, 1983.

Wordsworth, Dorothy. *Journals*. Vol. 1. Ed. William Knight. London: Macmillan, 1897.

Wordsworth, William, and Samuel Taylor Coleridge. *Lyrical Ballads 1798 and 1800*. Ed. Fiona Stafford. Oxford: Oxford University Press, 2013.

Worsley, Dale, and Bernadette Mayer. *The Art of Science Writing*. New York: Teachers & Writers Collaborative, 2000.

Yusoff, Kathryn. *A Billion Black Anthropocenes or None*. Minneapolis: University of Minnesota Press, 2018.

Zalasiewicz, Jan, Mark Williams, Will Steffen, and Paul Crutzen. "The New World of the Anthropocene." *Environmental Science and Technology* 44 (2010): 2228–31.

INDEX

"Acquaintance with Description, An" (Stein), 206–7, 225
action, 13, 56. *See also* intra-action; kinetics
"Adenine" (Bök), 135
affect: and action, 286*n*18; and encounter/relations, 56; and soft matter, 42, 286*n*18; and texture, 55, 56–57, 217, 289*n*48; and touch, 290*n*49; and weather, 308*n*13
Agassiz, Louis, 209
agency, 19, 20, 282*n*28
Alaimo, Stacy, 21
Albers, Anni, 181
Alexjander, Susan, 299*n*35
Alfoxden Journal (Wordsworth), 264–65
"Alpha Helix" (Bök), 145–46, 147
amplification, 25; and description, 231–32; and material change, 51; and poetic form, 7, 156, 157; and sensation, 86, 88, 150–51, 154–57, 160–61, 187–88; in *Silk Poems*, 7, 96, 154, 154, 156–57, 166, 172, 187–88; and taxonomies, 194; and texture, 170–71; and typography, 166, 232. *See also* interspecies translation; scale
Andrews, Bruce, 78, 101

Animacies: Biopolitics, Racial Mattering, and Queer Affect (Chen), 45
animacy, 45
animal studies, 145
Animal That Therefore I Am, The (Derrida), 165
Anker, Suzanne, 299*n*35
anthropogenic transformation: and scale, 24, 284*n*38; and structural oppression, 284*n*39; and temporality, 131–32, 284*n*38, 298*n*32
anthropomorphism, 6, 109, 163–64, 179
Arabidopsis thaliana experiment, 127, 128, 298*nn*23–24
Arcades Project, The (Benjamin), 308*n*13
Archigram, 36
Aristotle, 44, 116, 274, 280*n*18, 287*n*22, 288*n*25
Arsić, Branka, 295*n*51
Art of Science Writing, The (Mayer and Worsley), 293*n*34
Åsberg, Cecilia, 21
atomism: and *clinamen*, 11, 25, 258; and material-semiotic relations, 83–84, 114–15; and molecular poetics, 114–15, 118; particulate analogy of, 94, 95, 113–14,

atomism (*continued*)
    135–37, 249, 273; and recombination, 10–11, 85, 93–94, 95, 259; and scale, 8, 9, 110; and texture, 137–38
attention: and haptic poetics, 28–29; and material change, 23; and poetry-science relationship, 24, 88–89; and sensation, 92
attenuation of materiality, 29, 84, 270–75

Bacon, Francis: on attenuation of materiality, 270–71, 274; and description, 101, 102; and epistemic shifts in the natural sciences, 88, 102; and figurative-material description, 72, 90–91; and poetry-science relationship, 26; on scientific method, 101; on sensation, 89–91, 92
Baker, Monya, 138
Baquero, Fernando, 299*n*35
Barad, Karen, 20; on indeterminacy, 46; on intra-action, 16–17, 21, 48, 54, 176, 281*n*20, 283*nn*33, 35; on material-semiotic relations, 16–17, 102, 117, 263–64, 292*n*9; on temporality, 260
Barker, Lewellys, 210, 211–12
becoming. *See* material change
Becoming Undone (Grosz), 49, 260
"Beetle Wrestler," 167–68, 170
Benjamin, Walter, 308*n*13
Bennett, Chad, 62–63, 70
Bennett, Jane, 18–19, 47, 164, 282*n*28
Berghaus, Günter, 296*n*7
Bergson, Henri, 19, 48, 51
Bergsonism (Deleuze), 48–49
Bernard, Claude, 91
Bervin, Jen, 25; and biomedical uses for fibers, 152, 300*n*3; and erasure, 181–83, *183*; and microperceptions, 184–85; on scale, 9–10, 112; scientific training of, 7. *See also Silk Poems*
Bhatia, Neeraj, 36–37
Bianchi, Emanuela, 116, 287*n*22
biology. *See* natural sciences

biosemiotics, 5, 27, 145–48, 185, 186. *See also* nonhuman communication
Bird Relics: Grief and Vitalism in Thoreau (Arsić), 295*n*51
Black Moon, 3–4, 6–7
Blur Building (Diller and Scofidio), 22, 227–32, *230*, 256, 264
Bohr, Niels, 16, 281*n*20
Bök, Christian: and constraint, 25, 120–21, *121*; and Lucretius, 85, 258–59; and 'Pataphysics/"Pataphysics, 113–14; scientific training of, 7. *See also Xenotext Experiment, The*
Bora, Renu, 30, 35, 57–59, 60
bpNichol, vi, 15, 113
Brooks, William Keith, 209
Brown, Bill, 281–82*n*26
Brown, Bob, 149, 187–88
Brown, Nathan, 82–83, 276
Brown, Robert, 296*n*2
Brownian motion, 109, 110, 296*n*2
Bruner, Belinda, 64
Burroughs, William S., 303*n*50

Cage, John, 72–73, *74*, 75, 76, 92, 274
Cantos, The (Pound), 70
Carr, Angela, 308–9*n*16
Carroll, Lewis, 272
"Catching Frogs" (bpNichol), vi, 15
"Celery" (Stein), 285*n*42
"Central Dogma, The" (Bök), 139
Chambers, Robert, 305*n*21
chance operations, 76–77, 291*n*5
Chandler, John, 97
Chen, Mel Y., 45, 47, 292*n*9
Cheng, Anne Anlin, 285*n*3
Chessman, Harriet Scott, 63–64
chora, 45, 115, 287*n*22
climate change, 284*n*38
clinamen (swerve), 11, 25, 94, 258, 282*n*28
clouds: and Blur Building, 22, 227–32, *230*; and scale, 7; as soft entities, 22–23, 29, 248–49; taxonomies of, 29, 89, 104, 233,

234, 235–37, *237*, *238*; and temporality, 229–31. *See also* Howard, Luke
"Clouds Over Europe" (Gage), 247
cloud-writing, 29
codex, 256–58
color, 65–66
conative trajectory, 49
conceptualism, 25–26, 27, 96–98, 120, 294*nn*41–42
concrete poetry, 80, 133, 297*n*17
condensed-matter physics, 40–42, 286*nn*15–16
Conklin, Edwin Grant, 210
Conrad, CA, 92–93
Constable, John, 233, 246–47, 248
"Constitution / Writing, Politics, Language, The Body" (Andrews), 78
constraint: and material-semiotic relations, 25–26, 27, 93, 96, 121–22, 143–44; in molecular poetics, 120–22, *121*, 133, 135, 140, 143–44; and poetry-science relationship, 25, 92, 95–96; and recombination, 95, 294*n*38; and sensation, 92–93; and shape, 140, 143, 145–46, 153. *See also* Oulipo
Coole, Diana, 19, 287*n*22
cosmologies, 111–12; and haptic poetics, 277; and kinetics, 24; Olson on, 12–13, 24; and 'Pataphysics/"Pataphysics, 93–94; and sensation, 89, 90; and texture, 76. *See also* scale
Cozens, Alexander, 233, 240, *241*, *242*, 243, *243*, 245, 248
critical race theory, 45, 285*n*3
Crochet Coral Reef (Wertheim and Wertheim), 30–32, *32*, *33*, 54–55, 59
Crystallography (Bök), 95, 113, 120–22, 132–33, *134*, 135, 297*n*17
Cubism, 63
Cultural History of Heredity, A (Müller-Wille and Rheinberger), 124–25
cuteness, 68–69
"Cytosine" (Bök), 132–33, *134*, 135, 299*n*33

Dada, 303*n*50
Damisch, Hubert, 248–49
Darwin, Charles, 164, 199, *200*, 217, 219, 304*n*10, 305*n*21, 306*n*22, 307*n*39
Daston, Lorraine, 102, 197, 198, 214, 226, 295*n*55, 305*nn*17–18, 306–7*n*37
Davidson, Michael, 100–1
Davis, Joe, 298*n*23
Deamer, David W., 299*n*35
"Death of the Literary 'I'; Matter and Molecular Life" (Marinetti), 109–10
"Death Sets a Thing Significant" (Bök), 140, *141–42*, 143, 148
deixis, 249–50
de Laat, Wouter, 138–39
DeLanda, Manuel, 43–44
Deleuze, Gilles: on affect, 56, 289*n*48; on attenuation of materiality, 274; on expression, 46–47, 288*n*31; on material change, 48–49; and new materialism, 19; on scale, 149, 180; on sensation, 87, 180; on surfaces, 272, 273; on waiting, 51
dematerialization. *See* conceptualism
"Dematerialization of Art, The" (Lippard and Chandler), 97
Democritus, 10
Dennis, Leigha, 167
De rerum natura. See Lucretius
Derrida, Jacques, 165
Descartes, René, 6, 19, 279*n*8, 286*n*20
description, 103–6, 192; and amplification, 231–32; and clouds, 227–29; Cozens on, 233, 240, *241*, *242*, 243, *243*, 244, 245; and differentiation, 212; feminist thought on, 266, 267–68; figurative-material, 72, 90–91, 255–56, 260–61, 263–66, 295*n*51; and interspecies translation, 159–62; and landscape, 307*n*45; and material change, 205, 231–32, 234, 244–46, 248; and material-semiotic relations, 99, 105–6; and morphological tradition, 215–16; and ornamentation, 266–67, 268, 274; and poetry-science relationship, 26,

description (*continued*)
29, 101–6, 203–7, 232–34, 245; and scale, 159–60; and Stein's scientific training, 205–6, 207–8, 211–15; and taxonomies, 212–13, 216, 225–26; and temporality, 264–65; and texture, 104–5, 213–14, 268–69. *See also* epistemic shifts in the natural sciences

Despret, Vinciane, 20

De Tactu (Weber), 177–78

Dewdney, Christopher, 113

Dickinson, Emily, 9–10, 112

Difference Between the Democritean and Epicurean Philosophy of Nature, The (Marx), 282n28

differentiation: and codex, 257; and description, 212; and Heisenberg uncertainty principle, 281–82n26; and material change, 17–18, 20–21, 22, 47; and sensation, 177–81, 302n44; and soft entities, 47–48, 50, 289n38; and taxonomies, 197, 200, 305n18; and temporality, 260–61

Diller, Elizabeth, 22, 229

Discourse on Method (Descartes), 6, 279n8

discursive sites, 80, 245, 292n13, 309n16

Disjunctive Poetics (Quartermain), 100

DNA. *See* molecular poetics; *Xenotext Experiment, The*

Doris, Stacy, 231–32, 244–45, 258, 308n5

dualism/nondualism: and determism, 286n20; and differentiation, 47–48; and material-semiotic relations, 116–18, 126–27, 144, 263–64. *See also* gendered dualism; material-semiotic relations

Dydo, Ulla, 206

dyeing, 34–35

edge texture, 173, 177, 181, 302n31

eidola, 84

Eigler, Donald, 292n15

encounter/relations: and affect, 56; feminist thought on, 20–21; and interspecies translation, 176–77; and intra-action, 16–17, 21, 48, 54, 176, 281n20, 283nn33, 35; and material change, 17–18; and reading as embodied act, 162–63; and sensation, 92–93; and soft matter, 65; and surfaces, 34, 35–36, 55; and taxonomies, 28; and texture, 34, 52–53, 54–55, 58–59, 60; and typography, 76

Enlightenment, 26, 86, 102, 171, 196–97

entanglement, 16–17, 281n20

Epicureanism, 273, 282n28

Epicurus, 10, 11, 84, 282n28

epistemic shifts in the natural sciences, 102–3, 192–93; and material change, 193; and material-semiotic relations, 101–2; and morphological tradition, 210; and poetry-science relationship, 203–4; soft edges of, 306–7n37; and Stein's scientific training, 208; and taxonomies, 196–99, 305nn17–18

erasure, 181–83, *183*, 303n50

Essay on the Modifications of Clouds. See Howard, Luke

essentialism: resistance to, 16, 69, 116, 223–24, 280–81n19; and Stein's scientific training, 191–92. *See also* gendered dualism

ethics, 56

Ethics (Spinoza), 55, 56, 213

Eunoia (Bök), 95, 120

"Eurydice" (Bök), *124*, 129–30

Everybody's Autobiography (Stein), 201

evolutionary theory, 192–93, 199–200, *200*, 201, 217, 304n10, 306n22, 307n39

Experimental Novel, The (Zola), 103

experimentation, 90–92, 101–2, 103, 192, 203, 204, 226, 293n33, 306–7n37; and poetry-science relationship, 90–92, 293n33. *See also* epistemic shifts in the natural sciences

"Explode Every Day: An Inquiry Into the Phenomena of Wonder," 153

Exploits & Opinions of Dr. Faustroll, Pataphysician (Jarry), 94
Expressionism in Philosophy (Spinoza), 46–47

fabric, 9–10, 181–82, 260n12. See also fibers
fabrication, 82
Faking It (Wah), 112
Farber, Paul, 192
Farland, Maria, 191–92, 303–4n6
feeling. See affect
Feltwell, John, 161
Feminine Symptom, The: Aleatory Matter in the Aristotelian Cosmos (Bianchi), 287n22
feminist thought, 20–21, 22; on description, 266, 267–68; on material-semiotic relations, 116–17; and resistance to essentialism, 16, 69, 116, 280 81n19; and resistance to gendered dualism, 115–16, 287nn21–22; and soft architecture, 285n3; and soft entities, 48; on temporality, 260
fibers: biomedical uses, 152, 300n3; protective inscriptions on, 152–53, 186; reverse-engineered, 151–52; and scale, 149–51, 151. See also fabric; *Silk Poems*
field composition, 12, 168
Fieldworks: From Place to Site in Postwar Poetics (Shaw), 80, 97, 98
figurative-material description, 72, 90–91, 255–56, 260–61, 263–66, 295n51
"Fingeryeyes: Impressions of Cup Corals" (Hayward), 53
Flush: A Biography (Woolf), 301n23
folding, 27
Foray Into the Worlds of Animals and Humans, A (Uexküll), 5–6
form. See poetic form
Forster, Thomas Ignatius, 233, 246, 265–66, 267
Foucault, Michel, 195, 196, 202
4'33" (Cage), 92
"fragment A 636/636a" (Dickinson), 9–10, 112
Frank, Adam, 47–48
Frost, Samantha, 19, 287n22

Fuller, Buckminster, 36
futurism, 94, 109–11, 112–13, 296n7

Gage, John, 247
Galison, Peter, 197, 198, 214, 226, 305nn17–18, 306–7n37
Galton, Francis, 220
gendered dualism, 288n25; feminist resistance to, 115–16, 287nn21–22; and genetics, 45, 116, 124–26; and molecular poetics, 115–16, 124–26; and soft matter, 44–45; and softness vs. hardness, 70
Generation of Animals (Aristotle), 45, 116, 288n25
Generelle Morphologie der Organismen (Haeckel), 307n39
"Genetic Code, The" (Bök), 132
genetics: and gendered dualism, 45, 116, 124–26; and material-semiotic relations, 126–27, 297n21; origins of, 193; and shape, 138–39; and Stein's scientific training, 28. See also molecular poetics; *Xenotext Experiment, The*
"Genomics: Genomes in Three Dimensions" (Baker), 138
Geographical History of America, The (Stein), 85–86
Gertrude Stein Looking Through a Microscope, 87
Goethe, Johann Wolfgang von, 84
Goldstein, Amanda Jo, 83, 84, 276
Gorgeous Nothings, The (Bervin and Werner), 9–10
"Gradual Making of *The Making of Americans*, The" (Stein), 207–8
Grenier, Robert, 100
Grosz, Elizabeth, 20; on attenuation of materiality, 273–74; on differentiation, 21, 23; on material change, 48, 49, 193; and material-semiotic relations, 116–17, 283n33; on resistance to essentialism, 280n18; on temporality, 48, 60, 193, 260, 283n33

Guattari, Félix, 87
Gut Feminism (Wilson), 281*n*19
Gysin, Brion, 303*n*50

Haeckel, Ernst, 307*n*39
Hamblyn, Richard, 246–47
haptic poetics, 28–29, 87–88, 158, 269, 274, 275–77. *See also* texture
Haraway, Donna, 20, 102, 117, 263–64, 295*n*51, 297*n*21
"Hard and Soft in French Poetry, The" (Pound), 69–70, 291*n*71
"Hard and Soft Modernism" (Nicholls), 70
hardness vs. softness, 69–70
Harman, Graham, 17–18, 21, 48, 254–55, 282*n*26
Harrison, Ross Granville, 210
Hass, Robert Bartlett, 63, 64
Hayward, Eva, 20, 53–54, 175, 176
Heap of Language, A (Smithson), 97–98
Heidegger, Martin, 18, 19, 83
Heisenberg uncertainty principle, 13–14, 16, 281–82*n*26
Hejinian, Lyn, 26, 88–89, 91, 99, 101, 103, 203–4, 234
heredity, 218–20, 221. *See also* genetics
Hesse, Eva, 262–63
History of Dense and Rare, The (Bacon), 270–71, 274–75
Hoffman, Frederic J., 284–85*n*42
holotypes, 198
Hoogstraten, Samuel van, 247
Hooke, Robert: and epistemic shifts in the natural sciences, 88, 102; on fibers, 149–50, 151, *151*, 175, 179; on micrographia, 188; on scale, 8–9; on sensation, 86, 155–56; on texture, 51, 170, 171, 248
Hopkins, Gerard Manley, 232, 264
Hortus Cliffortianus (Linnaeus), 197
Howard, Luke: and Constable, 246; and material change, 103–4, 239; and soft taxonomies, 29, 89, 104, 233, 234, 235–37, *237*, *238*, 253–54; and temporality, 250–51, 255; and typography, 237, *237*, *238*, 249
How Forests Think: Toward an Anthropology Beyond the Human (Kohn), 145
How to Write (Stein), 206, 207
Huang, Sui, 297*n*15
Huebler, Douglas, 97, 294*n*41
"Human Universe" (Olson), 12
Hundred Thousand Billion Poems, A (Queneau), 294*n*38
hybridity, 43–44
hyperbolic geometries, 30–33, *32*, *33*, 59

idealism, 12–13
immanence, 46–47
Incorporeal, The: Ontology, Ethics and the Limits of Materialism (Grosz), 116–17, 273–74, 283*n*33
incorporeality, 283*n*33
indeterminacy: and *clinamen*, 11, 25, 94, 258, 282*n*28; and deixis, 250; new materialisms on, 19; and poetry-science relationship, 291*n*5; and resistance to gendered dualism, 287*n*22; and soft matter, 44, 45–46, 257–58; and taxonomies, 220–21; and temporality, 20
individuation, 289*n*38. *See also* differentiation
inductive reasoning, 90
"Inexpensive Load Carrying by Rhinoceros Beetles" (Kram), 167
interspecies collaboration: and dyeing, 35; failure of, 130–31, 173, *174*, 175; and material-semiotic relations, 144–45; and molecular poetics, 7–8, 27–28, 38, 128–29; and recombination, 95; and scale, 175; and soft architecture, 38–39; and temporality, 131–32, 298*n*32
interspecies translation: and anthropomorphism, 164; and description, 159–62; and poetic form, 169–70; and sensation, 154–55, 167–68, 175–76, 301*n*23; in *Silk Poems*, 158,

160–62, 163, 164, 167, 169–70, 172–73; and texture, 172–73, 175, 176–77, 302*n*31; and typography, 168, 169–70
intra-action, 16–17, 21, 48, 54, 176, 281*n*20, 283*nn*33, 35
Introduction à l'étude de la médecine expérimentale (Bernard), 91
Invention of Clouds, The (Hamblyn), 246–47
Invertebrate Course Collecting Trip at the Woods Hole Marine Biological Laboratory in 1897, 190, *191*
Irresistible Dictation: Gertrude Stein and the Correlations of Writing and Science (Meyer), 190–91, 204–5
"It's a Small World" experiment, 128

James, William, 190, 206, 207–8, 307*n*40
Jarry, Alfred, 93, 94, 113, 114, 296*n*7
Jeremijenko, Natalie, 167
Johnson, Ronald, 181
just-noticeable differences, 177–78, 179

Kant, Immanuel, 18
Kaplan, David, 151–52
Katchadourian, Nina, 173, *174*, 175
Kauffman, Stuart A., 297*n*15
Keller, Evelyn Fox, 5, 20, 45, 116, 125, 126, 127, 297*n*21
Kennion, Edward, 235
Kepler, Johannes, 261
kinetics: and idealism, 13; and indeterminacy, 11; and liveliness, 14–15; and sensation, 168–69; and shape, 157; and soft entities, 273; and temporal entwinement, 24; and typography, 15, 169; Whitehead on, 283*n*37
Klein, Melanie, 289*n*48
Kohn, Eduardo, 145
Kram, Rodger, 167
Kraus, Lee von, 167

Lamarck, Jean-Baptiste, 219, 304*n*10
Lange, Lynda, 116
Language of Inquiry, The (Hejinian), 26, 204

Leibniz, Gottfried Wilhelm, 9, 179–81, 182, 183, 261, 302*n*44
Le Lionnais, François, 293–94*n*38
Leonardo da Vinci, 248
"Letter, May 2, 1959" (Olson), 12
Leucippus, 10
Lifting Belly (Stein), 64
Limits of Fabrication, The (Brown), 82–83
linguistic turn, 78–79, 85, 101, 115, 116, 292*n*9
Linnaeus, Carolus, 197, 305*n*18
Lippard, Lucy R., 97
"Lisa Robertson's Feminist Poetic Landscapes" (Peacock), 233
liveliness, and kinetics, 14–15
Loeb, Jacques, 205
Logic of Sense, The (Deleuze), 272, 273
Long, Lois, *73*, *74*, *75*, *76*
Long Gay Book, A (Stein), 225
Loos, Adolf, 285*n*3
Loschmidt, Johann Josef, 10
"Lucite" (Robertson), 260–61
Lucretius: on attenuation of materiality, 29, 84, 271–72, 274; on Brownian motion, 296*n*2; on *clinamen*, 11, 25, 94, 258; on *eidola*, 84; on material change, 35–36; and material-semiotic relations, 84–85, 136; and molecular poetics, 114, 118; and new materialism, 19; particulate analogy of, 94, 95, 114, 136–37, 249; and 'Pataphysics/"Pataphysics, 93–94; and poetry-science relationship, 84–85; on recombination, 10–11, 27, 93–94, 136, 259, 299*n*37; on scale, 8; on smell, 259–60; on texture, 137–38
Lyell, Charles, 305*n*21
Lyrical Ballads (Wordsworth), 190

McCaffery, Steve, 100, 113, 114–15, 136
Magenta Soul Whip (Robertson), 260–61
Maienschein, Jane, 210, 306*n*37
Making of Americans, The (Stein): description in, 204–5, 206, 207–8, 212, 215–16; and experimentation, 203; on

Making of Americans, The (Stein) *(continued)* heredity, 217–18, 221; material change in, 221–23, 224–25; resistance to essentialism in, 223–24; spatial composition in, 215–16; and Stein's scientific training, 8, 26, 86, 209, 216, 304*n*6; taxonomies in, 28, 89, 189–90, 194–96, 201, 212–13, 220–23, 304–5*n*13

Mall, Franklin Pierce, 192, 209, 210, 211

Malle, Louis, 3–4

Malus sieversii experiment, 298*n*23

Manaugh, Geoff, 39–40

"March of the Nucleotides, The" (Bök), 139, 140, *141–42*, 143, 299–300*nn*43–44

Marinetti, Filippo Tommaso, 109–11, 296*n*7

Marks, Laura, 276–77

Martin, Agnes, 160

Marx, Karl, 282*n*28

Massumi, Brian, 289*n*48

material change: and amplification, 51; anthropogenic transformation, 24, 131–32, 284*nn*38–39, 298*n*32; and attention, 23; and *clinamen*, 258; and description, 205, 231–32, 234, 244–46, 248; and differentiation, 17–18, 20–21, 22, 47; and encounter/relations, 17–18; and evolutionary theory, 193, 304*n*10; and figurative-material description, 90, 255–56, 260–61, 263–65; and heredity, 220; historical understandings of, 305–6*n*21; and molecular poetics, 127–28; process mimesis, 32–33; and resistance to essentialism, 223–24; and soft architecture, 36–37, 39–40; and soft entities, 22–23, 48–51, 256; and soft taxonomies, 28; and surfaces, 33–34, 35–36, 39; and taxonomies, 28, 198–99, 201–3, 221–23, 224–25, 234; and temporality, 15, 229–31; and texture, 23–24, 50, 53–54, 64; and typography, 249. See also indeterminacy

material-semiotic relations, 77–85; and biosemiotics, 145–48; and conceptualism, 96–98; and concrete poetry, 297*n*17; and constraint, 25–26, 27, 93, 96, 121–22, 143–44; and description, 99, 105–6; and discursive sites, 80, 245, 292*n*13, 309*n*16; and dualism/nondualism, 116–18, 126–27, 263–64; and figurative-material description, 263–64, 295*n*51; futurism on, 110–11; and genetics, 126–27, 297*n*21; and incorporeality, 283*n*33; and interspecies collaboration, 144–45; and language-matter-time triangulation, 15–16; and linguistic vs. ontological turns, 78–79, 85, 101, 276, 292*n*9; and Lucretius, 84–85, 136; and molecular poetics, 114–15, 116–18, 119, 127, 129, 136–37, 143–44; and nonreferential language, 26, 99–100, 284–85*n*42; and poetry-science relationship, 77, 79, 83, 276; and reading as embodied act, 76–77, 162–63; and recombination, 136–37, 299*n*37; and scale, 82–83, 292*n*15; and *Silk Poems*, 185–87; and texture, 63–65; and typography, 80, *81*, 82, 98

Mathematical Basis of the Arts, The (Schillinger), 97, 294*n*42

"Matter Matters" (DeLanda), 43–44

Maximus Poems, The (Olson), 12, 309*n*16

Mayer, Bernadette, 92, 293*n*34

"Mechanistic Conception of Life: Loeb the Teacher, Stein the Student at the MBL, The" (Weissmann), 192

mechanomorphism, 6

Mediated Matter Lab, 37–38, *38*

Meeting the Universe Halfway (Barad), 16–17, 102

"Mended Spiderweb Series, The" (Katchadourian), 173, *174*, 175

Merleau-Ponty, Maurice, 276–77

metaphor, 90, 137, 263, 297*n*21. See also figurative-material description

Meyer, Steven, 190–91, 204–5, 206, 307*n*40

Micrographia. See Hooke, Robert

micrographia, 82, 187–88, 292*n*15

Midwinter Day (Mayer), 92
Milne, Heather, 308–9*n*16
mimesis, 15, 280*n*18
Mitchell, W. J. T., 18
modernism, 69–70, 192, 203, 285*n*3, 303–4*n*6
Molecular Gaze, The (Anker and Nelkin), 299*n*35
molecular poetics, 27, 95, 109–48; *Arabidopsis thaliana* experiment, 127, 128, 298*nn*23–24; and biosemiotics, 145–48; and Brownian motion, 109, 110, 296*n*2; constraint in, 120–22, *121*, 133, 135, 140, 143–44; encipherment in, 122–23, *124*, 132–33, *134*, 136–37, 140; and futurism, 109–10; and gendered dualism, 115–16, 124–26; and interspecies collaboration, 7–8, 27–28, 38, 128–29; "It's a Small World" experiment, 128; *Malus sieversii* experiment, 298*n*23; and material change, 127–28; and material-semiotic relations, 114–15, 116–18, 119, 127, 129, 136–37, 143–44; and music, 299*n*35; and 'Pataphysics/"Pataphysics, 112–14, 120, 136; poetic form in, 133, 135–36, 299*nn*35, 37; and repetition, 135, 299*n*35; and scale, 110, 111–12, 114; shape in, 138–40, 143, 145–46, 259, 299*n*43; and texture, 137–38; thematic content in, 129–31, 132–34, 299*n*33, 300*n*44; translation in, 299–300*n*44
Morgan, Thomas Hunt, 210
morphological tradition, 209–10, 214, 307*n*39
Moses, Omri, 201
Müller-Wille, Staffan, 12–17, 124–25
Münsterberg, Hugo, 190
Mushroom at the End of the World, The (Tsing), 291*n*5
Mushroom Book (Cage, Long, and Smith), 72–73, *74, 75, 76, 77, 79*, 274
music, 299*n*35

Nabokov, Vladimir, 162–63
nanotechnology, 82, 292*n*15

Napier, Bradley, 153
Natural Phenomena (Stein), 206
natural sciences: on heredity, 218–20; morphological tradition in, 209–10, 214, 307*n*39; phylogeny vs. ontogeny in, 210, 307*n*39. *See also* epistemic shifts in the natural sciences; evolutionary theory; poetry-science relationship; taxonomies
natural selection, 193, 199, 201, 304*n*10
Nelkin, Dorothy, 299*n*35
Nervous System and Its Constituent Neurons, The (Barker), 211–12, 214
Nets (Bervin), 181–83, *183*, 184
New Materialisms: Ontology, Agency, and Politics (Coole and Frost), 19
new materialisms, 19–21; and dualism, 117, 144; and linguistic vs. ontological turns, 292*n*9; and material-semiotic relations, 144; and resistance to gendered dualism, 287*nn*21–22; and soft architecture, 285*n*3; and soft matter, 44–46; and temporality, 260
New Method of Assisting the Invention in Drawing Original Compositions of Landscape, A (Cozens), 233, 240, *241, 242, 243, 243*, 245, 248
"New Opportunities for an Ancient Material" (Kaplan and Omenetto), 152
New Organon, The (Bacon), 89–90
Ngai, Sianne, 68–69
Nicholls, Peter, 70
Nick of Time, The (Grosz), 60, 280*n*18, 283*n*33
Nielsen, Karen, 116
Nilling (Robertson), 256–57, 262–63
nondualism. *See* dualism/nondualism
nonhuman communication, 4–7, 157–58, 165–66. *See also* interspecies translation; molecular poetics
"Note on Anthropomorphism" (Bennett), 164
Novel of Thank You, A (Stein), 206
"Nucleobases, The" (Bök), 132, 133

objectivist poetry, 80
Objectivity (Daston and Galison), 197, 305nn17–18
Object-Oriented Ontology (OOO), 17, 18, 19, 21, 23, 254–55, 282n26
observation: and evolutionary theory, 199–200, *200*, 201, 306n22; and poetry-science relationship, 72, 88, 102–3, 295n55; and sensation, 155; and taxonomies, 196. *See also* description; epistemic shifts in the natural sciences
Occasional Work and Seven Walks from the Office for Soft Architecture (Robertson), 35, 38–39, 41, 65–66
Olson, Charles: on cosmologies, 12–13; on kinetics, 11–12, 13, 24, 104, 157, 168–69; and material-semiotic relations, 80, 82, 283n37; and place-based poetics, 309n16; on reading as embodied act, 76
Omenetto, Fiorenzo, 151–52, 153
onomatopoeia, 15
On Poetics (Aristotle), 280n18
"On Scientific Observation" (Daston), 102, 295n55
On the Origin of Species (Darwin), 199, 220
ontogeny, 210, 307n39
ontological turn, 78–79, 276, 292n9
"On Touching: The Inhuman That Therefore I Am" (Barad), 46
"On Vicarious Causation" (Harman), 17–18
On Weaving (Albers), 181
"Opal" (Bök), 120–21, *121*
Oppen, George, 80
Order of Things, The (Foucault), 195, 202
organicism, 190–91
Ornamentalism (Cheng), 285n3
Ornament and Crime (Loos), 285n3
ornamentation, 266–67, 268, 274, 285n3
"Orpheus" (Bök), 123, *124*
Oulipo: and Bök, 27, 94; and *clinamen*, 25; and conceptualism, 96, 97; and material-semiotic relations, 93, 95; and molecular poetics, 113, 120; origins of, 294n38
"Outing Texture" (Bora), 35, 57–58
Oxman, Neri, 37

pangenesis, 219, 220
'Pataphysics: The Poetics of an Imaginary Science (Bök), 113
'Pataphysics/"Pataphysics: Canadian movement, 112–13, 293–94n38; and constraint, 25, 27, 95, 96; and Lucretius, 93–94, 136; and molecular poetics, 112–14, 120, 136; and scale, 114; spelling of, 296n8
Paterson (Williams), 80, *81*, 309n16
Peacock, Laurel, 233
Peirce, Charles Sanders, 145
Perec, Georges, 113
Perelman, Bob, 100
"Perfume Recordist, The" (Robertson and Doris), 231–32, 244–45, 259, 308n5
phylogeny, 210, 307n39
Plato, 12, 45, 115–16, 198, 274, 287n22
poetic form: and amplification, 7, 156, *157*; and interspecies translation, 169–70; and kinetics, 14–15; and mimesis, 15, 280n18; in molecular poetics, 133, 135–36, 299nn35, 37; in *Silk Poems*, 153, 154, 156, 164–65. *See also* constraint
Poetics of DNA, The (Roof), 126, 297n21
"Poetry and Grammar" (Stein), 223, 273
poetry-science relationship, 7–8, 16–17, 28–29, 293n34; and amplification, 25; and attention, 24, 88–89; and chance operations, 76–77, 291n5; and constraint, 25, 92, 95–96; and description, 26, 29, 101–6, 203–7, 232–34, 245; and haptic poetics, 158; and Heisenberg uncertainty principle, 13–14; and indeterminacy, 291n5; and Lucretius, 84–85; and material-semiotic relations, 77, 79, 83, 276; and nonreferential language, 99–100; and observation, 72, 88, 102–3,

295n55; and 'Pataphysics/"Pataphysics, 113; and reading as embodied act, 76–77; and recombination, 93–95; and scale, 83–84; and sensation, 85–93, 293n33; and *Silk Poems*, 158; and taxonomies, 88–89; and typography, 72–73, *74*, *75*, *76*. *See also specific poets and works*
poiesis, 12, 82, 119
Ponge, Francis, 42–43
"Porchverse" (Robertson), 238
porosity, 34
"Portraits and Repetition" (Stein), 14, 240
posthumanism, 21, 111, 145, 250
Pound, Ezra, 69–70, 291n71
Prelude, The (Wordsworth), 233
Price, Cedric, 36
Prior to Meaning: The Protosemantic and Poetics (McCaffery), 114–15
process mimesis, 32–33
"Projective Verse" (Olson), 11–13, 76, 157, 169
"Proprioception" (Olson), 168–69
protosemantics, 114–15, 136

quantum physics, 16–17, 46, 281n20
Quartermain, Peter, 100
queer thought, 16, 69, 117
Queneau, Raymond, 113, 293–94n38

RADI OS (Johnson), 181
Raffles, Hugh, 167–68
recombination, 27, 85; and constraint, 95, 294n38; and material-semiotic relations, 136–37, 299n37; and poetry-science relationship, 93–95
re-enactment, 15
relation. *See* encounter/relations
repetition: and deixis, 249–50; and description, 205, 232; and kinetics, 14; and material change, 223; and molecular poetics, 135, 299n35; and soft matter, 43; and temporality, 239–40; and texture, 171
Researches About Atmospheric Phaenomena (Forster), 233, 246, 265–66, *267*

"Residence at C__" (Robertson), 105–6, 238
Rheinberger, Hans-Jörg, 124–25, 126–27
"Ribosomal Translation of RNA, The" (Bök), 299–300n44
"River" (Bervin), 181
Robertson, Lisa: on codex, 256–59; on description, 103–4, 231–32, 244–45, 266–68, 274, 308n5; and description, 99; and discursive sites, 245, 308–9n16; and experimentation, 203; and figurative-material description, 255–56, 260–61, 265–66; on juice, 65–66; and Lucretius, 85, 258–59, 260; and natural sciences, 8, 26; on shape, 260, 261–62; and soft taxonomies, 237, *238*; on surfaces, 33–35, 55, 62, 272; on temporality, 260–62; and texture, 104–5. *See also* soft architecture; *Weather, The*
romanticism, 84–85
Roof, Judith, 126, 127, 297n21
Routledge Companion to Experimental Literature, The (Bray, Gibbons, and McHale), 91
"*Rubus Armeniacus*: A Common Architectural Motif in the Temperate Mesophytic Region" (Robertson), 38–39

Sabin, Florence R., 211
Sager, Ruth, 125
Samain, Albert, 291n71
Sánchez-Souza, Aurora, 299n35
scale: and anthropogenic transformation, 24, 284n38; and cosmologies, 8–9, 10, 111–12; and description, 159–60; and Dickinson, 8–9; and differentiation, 179; and fibers, 149–51, *151*; and interspecies collaboration, 175; and material-semiotic relations, 82–83, 292n15; and molecular poetics, 110, 111–12, 114; and poetry-science relationship, 83–84; and sensation, 86, 158–60; and temporality, 52; and texture, 51, 52, 171–72. *See also* amplification

Schillinger, Joseph, 97, 294n42
Schweizer, Erhard, 292n15
Scofidio, Ricardo, 22, 229
"Scratching the Surface: *Tender Buttons* and the Textures of Modernism" (Bennett), 62–63
Second Skin: Josephine Baker & the Modern Surface (Cheng), 285n3
Sedgwick, Eve Kosofsky, 23, 47–48, 57, 59, 60, 79, 86–87, 170–72, 289n48
Segel, Lee, 5
semiotic-material relations. *See* material-semiotic relations
sensation: and amplification, 86, 88, 150–51, 154–57, 160–61, 187–88; and attention, 92; and differentiation, 177–81, 302n44; and encounter/relations, 92–93; and experimentation, 90–92, 293n33; and interspecies translation, 154–55, 167–68, 175–76, 301n23; and kinetics, 168–69; and poetry-science relationship, 85–93, 293n33; and reading as embodied act, 162–63; and scale, 86, 158–60; and taxonomies, 89–90; and *Umwelt*, 5–7, 24, 154–55, 158–60
sensorium. *See* sensation
"Sentences" (Stein), 100
"7.5 Minute Talk for Eva Hesse (Sans II)" (Robertson), 262–63, 264
shape: and constraint, 140, 143, 145–46, 153; and kinetics, 157; in molecular poetics, 138–40, 143, 145–46, 259, 299n43; and poetic form, 153, *154*; and smell, 259–60; and temporality, 259, 260, 261–62
Sharp, Hasana, 46
Shaw, Lytle, 80, 82, 97, 98, 267, 292n13, 309n16
Shelley, Percy Bysshe, 84
Sheppard, Lola, 36–37
Shklovsky, Viktor, 92, 293n33
signifier. *See* material-semiotic relations
"Silk Pavilion" (Mediated Matter Group), 37–38, *38*

Silk Poems (Bervin): amplification in, 7, 96, 154, *154*, 156–57, 166, 172, 187–88; and anthropomorphism, 163–64; constraint in, 25, 95–96, 153; description in, 160–62; and haptic poetics, 158; interspecies collaboration in, 8, 27–28, 38; interspecies translation in, 158, 160–62, 163, 164, 167, 169–70, 172–73; and material-semiotic relations, 185–87; micrographia in, 187–88; microperceptions in, 184–85; morphological analogues in, 153, 156, 186, 193–94; nonhuman communication in, 157–58, 165–66; poetic form in, 153, *154*, 156, 164–65; and protective inscriptions, 153, 186; scale in, 112, 154, 172; and soft architecture, 37; texture in, 172, 184; typography in, 168, 169; versions of, 153–54
Simard, Suzanne, 4–5
Simondon, Gilbert, 289n38
"Situated Knowledges: The Science Question in Feminism and the Privilege of Partial Perspective" (Haraway), 20
smell, 259–60
Smith, Alexander H., 73, *74, 75,* 76
Smithson, Robert, 97–98, 292n13
Soap (Le Savon) (Ponge), 42–43
"Soft Architecture: A Manifesto" (Robertson), 267
soft architecture, 22; and codex, 257–58; and interspecies collaboration, 38–39; and material change, 36–37, 39–40; and ornamentation, 267, 285n3; "Silk Pavilion," 37–38, *38*; and soft entities, 50, 256; and soft matter, 41
soft entities: clouds as, 22–23, 29, 248–49; and cuteness, 69; and differentiation, 47–48, 50, 289n38; and kinetics, 273; and material change, 22–23, 48–51, 256; and soft taxonomies, 194; and texture, 51, 54, 55, 248–49
soft matter, 22, 40–44; and affect, 42, 286n18; and attenuation of materiality,

273, 274; condensed-matter physics on, 40–42, 286nn15–16; and encounter/relations, 65; and evolutionary theory, 193; and gendered dualism, 44–45; and hybridity, 43–44; and indeterminacy, 44, 45–46, 257–58; and substance, 46–47, 288n31; surfactants, 41–43, 286n16; and taxonomies, 201; and temporality, 59, 70–71

softness vs. hardness, 69–70

"Soft Serve Space" (Manaugh), 39–40

soft taxonomies, 23, 28, 29, 89, 194, 235–37, *237, 238*, 253–55

Solomons, Leon, 307n40

(Soma)tic Poetry Rituals (Conrad), 92–93

"Sonnet 14" (Bervin), 182–83, *183*

"Speculative *Before* the Turn" (Åsberg, Thiele, and van der Tuin), 21

speculative realism, 17, 21. *See also* Object-Oriented Ontology

Spinoza, Baruch: on affect, 34, 56, 60, 286n18, 289n48; on encounter/relations, 55; on expression, 46–47, 288n31; on material change, 48, 49–50; and material-semiotic relations, 83; and new materialism, 19; on ornamentation, 274; on texture, 55, 56–57, 213

Spinoza: Practical Philosophy (Deleuze), 56

Spinoza and the Politics of Renaturalization (Sharp), 46

Spiral Jetty (Smithson), 97

Stein, Gertrude: on clouds, 227; and Cubism, 63; and description, 23, 26, 101, 104, 204–8, 211–14, 215–16, 226; and experimentation, 226; and kinetics, 14–15, 24, 283n37; on landscape, 307n45; and material-semiotic relations, 63–64, 99–101; and molecular poetics, 112–13; and nonreferential language, 26, 99–100, 284–85n42; and repetition, 43, 223, 240; and Robertson, 234; and sensation, 85–86; on surfaces, 272–73; and taxonomies, 191–92, 194–95, 216–17, 225–26; and texture, 63. *See also* Stein's scientific training; *Tender Buttons*

Stein's scientific training, *87, 191*; and description, 205–6, 207–8, 211–15; environments of, 208–11; and epistemic shifts in the natural sciences, 208; and essentialism, 191–92; and *The Making of Americans*, 8, 26, 86, 209, 216, 304n6; manuscripts, 211, 307n40; and material-semiotic relations, 99; and modernism, 303–4n6; and organicism, 190–91; and texture, 28–29

Stengers, Isabelle, 20

Stewart, Susan, 290n49

Stoicism, 272, 273–74

Story of Silk, The (Feltwell), 161

"Strangeness" (Hejinian), 99

Strickland, Lloyd, 180–81

structural oppression, 284n39

substance, 46–47, 288n31

"Sunday" (Robertson), 249–50, 251

surfaces: and atomism, 137–38; and attenuation of materiality, 272–73; and dyeing, 34–35; and encounter/relations, 34, 35–36, 55; and hyperbolic geometries, 30–33, *32, 33*, 59; and material change, 33–34, 35–36, 39; and surfactants, 41–43, 62, 286n16

surfactants, 41–43, 62, 286n16

Sweet Science: Romantic Materialism and the New Logics of Life (Goldstein), 83, 84

syntax, 94, 110, 111, 239, 249–52. *See also* repetition

Taimina, Daina, 32–33

taxonomies: anxiety about, 189–90; and causal relations, 253–54; of clouds, 29, 89, 104, 233, 234, 235–37, *237, 238*; and description, 212–13, 216, 225–26; and differentiation, 197, 200, 305n18; and epistemic shifts in the natural sciences, 196–99, 305nn17–18; and essentialism, 191–92; and generalization, 195–96, 200,

taxonomies (*continued*)
304–5*nn*13, 18; and indeterminacy, 220–21; and material change, 28, 198–99, 201–3, 221–23, 224–25, 234; and poetry-science relationship, 88–89; and sensation, 89–90; soft, 23, 28, 29, 89, 194, 235–37, 237, 238, 253–55; and syntax, 239; and temporality, 255; and texture, 194, 216–17; and typography, 237, 237, 238. *See also* soft taxonomies

"Technical Manifesto of Futurist Literature" (Marinetti), 110

temporal entwinement, 23–24

temporality: and anthropogenic transformation, 131–32, 284*n*38, 298*n*32; and clouds, 229–31; and description, 264–65; and differentiation, 260–61; and erasure, 182–83; and incorporeality, 283*n*33; and indeterminacy, 20; and material change, 15, 229–31; and molecular poetics, 131–32, 298*n*32; and repetition, 239–40; scales of, 52; and shape, 259, 260, 261–62; and soft matter, 59, 70–71; and syntax, 250–51; and taxonomies, 255; temporal entwinement, 23–24; and texture, 57–58, 59–61. *See also* material change

Tender Buttons (Stein), 61–70; attention in, 88; attenuation of materiality in, 272; color in, 65–66, 67; cuteness in, 68–69; description in, 23, 205; material change in, 29, 50, 61–62, 64, 66–67, 205; and material-semiotic relations, 63–65, 100–1; molecular poetics in, 112; nonreferential language in, 284*n*42; softness vs. hardness in, 69, 70; surfaces in, 62–63, 67–68; taxonomies in, 201

texture: and affect, 55, 56–57, 217, 289*n*48; and amplification, 170–71; and atomism, 137–38; and attenuation of materiality, 29; and description, 104–5, 213–14, 268–69; and encounter/relations, 34, 52–53, 54–55, 58–59, 60; and interspecies translation, 172–73, 175, 176–77, 302*n*31;

and material change, 23–24, 50, 53–54, 64; and material-semiotic relations, 63–65; and molecular poetics, 137–38; and poetry-science relationship, 73, 76, 87; and repetition, 171; and scale, 51, 52, 171–72; and sensation, 86–87, 138, 170; and soft entities, 51, 54, 55, 248–49; and surfaces, 63; and taxonomies, 194, 216–17; and temporality, 57–58, 59–61

texxture, 57–59

The Fold: Leibniz and the Baroque (Deleuze), 180

Theory of /Cloud/, A (Damisch), 248–49

Thiele, Kathrin, 21

thingness, 18–19, 281–82*n*26

Thinking Space (Robertson), 261–62

Third, A (Stein), 206

Thoreau, Henry David, 295*n*51

Tiffany, Daniel, 83–84, 276

Timaeus (Plato), 45, 115, 287*n*22

"Time in the Codex" (Robertson), 256–59

tissues. *See* description; Stein, Gertrude

Tomkins, Silvan, 289*n*48

touch, 290*n*49. *See also* sensation; surfaces; texture

Touching Feeling (Sedgwick), 23, 47–48, 57, 79, 86–87, 170–71

Toy Medium: Materialism and Modern Lyric (Tiffany), 83–84

transformation. *See* material change

"Transformation of Natural History in the Nineteenth Century, The" (Farber), 192

Transforming Traditions in American Biology, 1880–1915 (Maienschein), 210

translation, 299–300*n*44. *See also* interspecies translation

Tsing, Anna, 20, 291*n*5

"Tuesday" (Robertson), 239

Turin, Luca, 259

"Two Dots Over a Vowel" (Bök), 25

typography: and amplification, 166, 232; and concrete poetry, 297*n*17; and interspecies translation, 168, 169–70; and kinetics, 15, 169; and material

change, 249; and material-semiotic relations, 80, *81*, 82, 98; and poetry-science relationship, 72–73, *74*, *75*, 76; and taxonomies, 237, *237*, *238*; and transfer of energy, 11–12
Tzara, Tristan, 303*n*50

Uexküll, Jakob von, 5–6, 13, 52, 154–55, 158–60, 171, 177, 178–79
Umwelt, 5–7, 24, 154–55, 158–60
"Uninvited Collaborations with Nature" (Katchadourian), 173, *174*, 175
"Untroubled Mind, The" (Martin), 160

Valenciennes, 248
van der Tuin, Iris, 21
Variation of Animals and Plants Under Domestication, The (Darwin), 219
Vestiges of the Natural History of Creation and Other Evolutionary Writings (Chambers), 305*n*21
Vibrant Matter (Bennett), 18–19, 164, 282*n*28
"Virelay of the Amino Acids, The" (Bök), 135
visual poetry, 133
"Vita Explicata" (Bök), 135

Wah, Fred, 112
waiting, 51
Wars I Have Seen (Stein), 201, 225
Weather, The (Robertson): and affect, 308*n*13; artistic influences on, 240, 243, *243*, *244*, 245, 246–49; causal relations in, 251–53; deixis in, 249–50; epigraph of, 308*n*13; figurative-material description in, 255–56; material change in, 234, 238–40, 244–46, 255–56; material-semiotic relations in, 105–6; natural sciences research in, 8; poetry-science relationship in, 8, 29, 103–4, 233–34, 245; repetition in, 239–40, 249–50; syntax in, 249–52; temporality in, 250–51
"Weather, The: A Report on Sincerity" (Robertson), 265–66

Weber, Ernst Heinrich, 86, 177–78, 179
"Wednesday" (Robertson), 251–52
Weissmann, Gerald, 192, 205–6, 207, 209
Werner, Marta, 9
Wertheim, Christine, 30–32
Wertheim, Margaret, 30–31, 32
West, Benjamin, 246
"What Is English Literature" (Stein), 206
Whitehead, Alfred North, 17, 191, 283*n*37
Williams, William Carlos, 80, *81*, 309*n*16
Wilson, Edmund Beecher, 210
Wilson, Elizabeth, 20, 281*n*19
Witt, Charlotte, 116
Woebken, Chris, 167
Woolf, Virginia, 301*n*23
Words (Brown), 187–88
Wordsworth, Dorothy, 232, 264–65
Wordsworth, William, 190, 233
Worsley, Dale, 293*n*34

XEclogue (Robertson), 268–69
Xenotext Experiment, The (Bök): bioart context of, 127, 298*nn*23–24; and biosemiotics, 145–48; constraint in, 95, 96, 120, 133, 135, 140, 143–44; documentation of, 119–20; encipherment in, 122–23, *124*, 132–33, 136–37, 140; and failure, 130–31, 175; gendered dualism in, 124–26; interspecies collaboration in, 7–8, 27, 38, 128–29, 144–45; and material change, 127–28; material-semiotic relations in, 119, 121–22, 136–37, 143–45; and micrographia, 188; poetic form in, 133, 135–36; recombination in, 136–37, 259; scientific collaborators in, 297*n*15; shape in, 139–40, 143, 145–46, 259, 299*n*43; and temporality, 131–32, 298*n*32; thematic content in, 123–24, 129–31, 300*n*44; translation in, 299–300*n*44

"Zarathrustran 'Pataphysics" (McCaffery), 113
Zola, Émile, 91, 103, 204
Zukofsky, Louis, 80